Business Report Writing

Business Report Writing

JOEL P. BOWMAN

BERNADINE P. BRANCHAW

Department of Business Information Systems
Western Michigan University

THE DRYDEN PRESS
CHICAGO   NEW YORK   PHILADELPHIA   SAN FRANCISCO
MONTREAL   TORONTO   LONDON   SYDNEY   TOKYO
MEXICO CITY   RIO DE JANEIRO   MADRID

Acquisitions Editor: Anne Elizabeth Smith
Developmental Editor: Susan Meyers
Project Editor: Nancy Shanahan/Julia Ehresmann
Managing Editor: Jane Perkins
Design Director: Alan Wendt
Production Manager: Mary Jarvis

Text and cover designer: Margery Dole
Compositor: The Clarinda Company
Text type: 10/12 Palatino

Library of Congress Cataloging in Publication Data

Bowman, Joel P.
  Business report writing.

  Includes index.
  1. Business report writing.   I. Branchaw, Bernadine P.
II. Title.
HF5719.B68   1983   808'.066651021   83-11711
ISBN 0-03-062793-1

Printed in the United States of America
456-039-987654321

Address orders to
383 Madison Avenue
New York, NY 10017

Address editorial correspondence to
One Salt Creek Lane
Hinsdale, IL 60521

CBS College Publishing
The Dryden Press
Holt, Rinehart and Winston
Saunders College Publishing

PREFACE

Sooner or later, everyone in business, industry, or government writes reports. Only a few jobs are left that require no report writing, and that number is shrinking daily. All the evidence suggests that the number and importance of reports will continue to grow as modern society becomes increasingly dependent on the flow of accurate information. *Business Report Writing* presents the techniques necessary for writing clear, well-organized reports designed to meet the needs of the reader.

In writing this book, we have paid particular attention to meeting the diverse needs of three groups of people: teachers, students, and practitioners. We have included materials to increase the usefulness of this book to members of each of these groups.

FOR TEACHERS

This book is the most flexible work currently available for teaching report writing. It offers the most thorough coverage of topics available, and yet it is designed so that nearly any particular chapter or chapters may be omitted without detracting from a student's understanding of the material in other chapters. Teachers will especially appreciate the extensive coverage of audience analysis, questionnaire design, use of statistical information, the drawing of conclusions, and specific report-writing applications and illustrations.

The book is organized according to the common steps in the report-writing process. Part I (Chapters 1 and 2) defines and explains the relationship between report writers and readers. Part II (Chapters 3, 4, and 5) explains and describes kinds of reports and common report-writing techniques. Part III (Chapters 6, 7, 8, 9, 10, and 11) describes the procedures for defining and researching report problems. Part IV (Chapters 12, 13, 14, and 15) covers the process of writing, editing, and presenting the information. Part V (Chapters 16, 17, and 18) presents a variety of specific applications of techniques for both written and oral reports.

Because some instructors prefer to begin the course with instruction in writing and editing techniques, Part IV is designed so that its material may be presented first.

Finally, an Instructor's Manual with Transparency Masters provides teaching suggestions, answers to review questions, and exam questions. In addition, this manual includes sample schedules for both semester and quarter courses, a graded sample report, and a variety of transparency masters.

FOR STUDENTS

Each chapter begins with a list of topics to orient readers to the material and concludes with a series of review questions to serve as a self-check for what students should remember after studying the chapter. The chapters themselves are all short enough to permit easy mastery of the material. Also to facilitate learning, we have included numerous how-to-do-it lists, which can be used as a guide or checklist in preparing reports.

We have attempted to balance explanations and illustrations so that students will be able to see the application of specific techniques and to understand those techniques well enough to apply them in different situations. With only a few exceptions, the sample reports actually were used in business, industry, or government. In general, the reports that are exceptions are based on actual reports which required changing, usually for reasons of confidentiality.

This book focuses on the kind of writing students will actually be doing soon after landing that first job. Regardless of profession or career area, students will need to know the techniques for writing successful reports. Students will also find the appendixes useful. Appendix A presents the most commonly required statistical tables. The report problems in Appendix B are realistic and afford wide latitude of choice. Appendix C contains a quick guide to English usage for those who may need a review, and Appendix D contains a brief guide to punctuation. To assist students with their preparation of job application materials, Appendix E presents the fundamentals of writing resumes and letters of application. Appendix F is a list of standard correction symbols and proofreaders' marks.

FOR PRACTITIONERS

Those who are already working in business, industry, or government will find that this book provides a handy reference tool to help solve report-writing problems. The index, the lists of chapter topics, and the numerous examples and checklists will help professionals find what they need quickly and apply it easily to their own situations.

The extended coverage of designing questionnaires, interpreting data, drawing conclusions, and developing graphic aids will be especially helpful to practitioners, as will the samples of the most common types of reports. Because report writing is not a subject that can be mastered in one reading, we have designed the book not only for readability but also for convenience as a reference. Main topics are all indexed, and nearly all topics are illustrated and outlined for easy use as well as explained for fuller understanding.

ACKNOWLEDGMENTS

Many people have helped make this book possible. We have had excellent editorial assistance and guidance from Anne Smith, Susan Meyers, Julia Ehresmann, and Nancy Shanahan of The Dryden Press, the copyeditor Mary B. Barlow, and the designer Margery Dole. The reviews by Robert D. Gieselman of the University of Illinois at Urbana-Champaign, William J. Buchholz of Bentley College, Daphne A. Jameson of Cornell University, Jolene D. Scriven of Northern Illinois University, Charles B. Smith of Arizona State University, and Charles L. Snowden of Sinclair Community College provided many useful suggestions that have resulted in a much improved book. Lowell Crow and Carol Stamm of Western Michigan University, and Fred Bryant of Loyola University provided much needed assistance with the statistical information, and Emily Gillula reviewed the materials on conducting secondary research and made valuable suggestions.

We are also grateful to our friends in business, industry, and government who supplied us with copies of their reports. Raymond Beswick, Anthony C. L. Bishop, Ken Warren, David Baseler, Robert Bobb, Denise Tropp, Kim Dieterle, and Robin Mobley all contributed to this book by providing appropriate examples of reports or related materials.

Good reading.

Joel P. Bowman
Kalamazoo, Michigan

Bernadine P. Branchaw
Kalamazoo, Michigan

September, 1983

CONTENTS

PART 1
Report Writers
and Readers

CHAPTER 1
Report Writing at Work

"Submit a proposal."

"I need your findings in report form."

"It's your turn to do the annual report."

Sooner or later you will have to write a report—a report on which your business future will probably depend. While this book will not eliminate all the stress that accompanies the task of preparing reports, it will certainly make your job easier by showing what to include and how to include it. This chapter introduces the basic concepts.

Topics   Who Reports to Whom—and Why
Functional Writing in Business, Industry, and Government
Definition of a Report
Importance of Report Writing
A Good Report

Everyone in business, industry, and government submits reports on a regular basis. Some of these reports are oral; some are written. Some are informal; some are formal. Every organization needs reports to coordinate activities, to provide a record of events, and to serve as a basis for managerial decisions. While different organizations have different reporting procedures and responsibilities, *every* job in *every* organization requires reports of one sort or another.

Reports are the principal means by which members of an organization communicate with each other about job-related matters. Oral reports are exchanged daily about a wide variety of business concerns—ranging from the number of boxes of paper clips on hand to the status of billion-dollar investments. Written reports are also prepared on a regular basis. These range from brief, informal memos dashed off by hand to formal documents thousands of pages long and bound in volumes.

WHO REPORTS TO WHOM—AND WHY

Reports usually go *up* the chain of command in an organization. Those who are working on specific tasks submit reports to those higher in the organizational hierarchy. The recipients of the reports use them to make decisions and perhaps as the source of information which becomes part of new reports to be sent on to higher management. When reports are exchanged between persons of equal rank, they are still used to provide information necessary for decision making. As a rule, reports are distributed *down* the chain of command only as a means of disseminating information.

As reports go up the chain of command, the information may receive different treatment or emphasis at each level of the decision-making process. For example, a line worker may report to his or her supervisor that a top-drive press has developed a vibration.

Worker: Listen to this, Jack. Something's wrong. It may be the main bearing.

Supervisor: You're right, Nancy. I'll get on the horn and schedule maintenance as soon as possible. Meanwhile, shut this one down and use the one-point.

At the next level, Jack would report to *his* supervisor.

Jack: We've had a breakdown on line five. It may be the main bearing on the two-point top-drive press. When can we schedule maintenance? We'll need to hustle to maintain schedule on the Berman project.

Section Supervisor: I'll schedule the crew as soon as possible. Isn't this about the third breakdown this quarter for that press?

Jack: Actually, it's the fourth. Once we were able to repair it ourselves. We had only an hour's down time. We really should be thinking about replacing it.

Depending on the circumstances, the section supervisor might need to report the problem immediately and orally to the plant manager, or she or he might wait until the end of the week, month, or quarter to send a written report. The problem could be discussed in an urgent memo, an activities report, a justification report (requesting a new press), or an equipment report.

In fact, this problem might be mentioned at this and higher levels of management. It could be included in (1) a planning report, (2) a financial report, (3) a letter to the press manufacturer, (4) a progress report on a new press, or even (5) the firm's annual report to stockholders.

As you can see, business decisions depend on a flow of information that often takes the form of oral and written reports. Most of this book will concentrate on written reports because they usually require more extensive research and preparation. Oral reports are covered in Chapter 17.

FUNCTIONAL WRITING IN BUSINESS, INDUSTRY, AND GOVERNMENT

Reports generally have their inception in a need. Somebody needs information on which to base a decision; or somebody wants management to make a decision and reports the information to the appropriate person. Whether the report is reader initiated or writer initiated, reports are written to help management make decisions.

Purposes of Reports

Although the content of reports may vary from business to business depending on the nature of products and services, all reports are *functional writing*: each report has a particular function or purpose it is to perform.

Most managers in business, industry, and government cannot directly observe materials, personnel, events, and other factors that will influence their decisions. When managers (1) are too far away from an operation to observe it directly, (2) lack the time to observe it directly, or (3) lack the technical expertise to observe it accurately, they must rely on the reports of others. Persons who are in a position to make accurate, reliable, and objective observations write reports for the benefit of a person or persons who will make decisions about the observations.

Reports and Organizational Objectives

An organization is any group of people working together to achieve a common purpose. The coordination of activity this requires is made possible by communication. Communication in general and reports in particular help organizations meet the routine and special objectives necessary to reach long-term goals. Routine and special objectives can be classed as maintenance, task, or human depending on the way in which they contribute to the overall goal. Maintenance objectives are those that help an organization maintain its existence by solving regular, recurring problems. Task objectives are made necessary by special circumstances, events, or managerial decisions. Human objectives are usually satisfied by writer-initiated reports, often proposals suggesting an improvement in the writer's area of expertise.

Maintenance Objectives   Maintenance objectives require routine reports written as a regular part of a job. Every week, for example, a sales representative will submit a report on the previous week's sales. Many maintenance reports are *periodic reports* because they are prepared according to a regular time interval (weekly, monthly, quarterly, annually, or even hourly under some circumstances). Reports written to meet maintenance objectives monitor and regulate the sustenance of the organization. Because these reports are written on a regular, recurring basis, most companies use printed forms or specific guidelines to facilitate presenting facts quickly and easily in the desired form.

Task Objectives   Organizations must also solve special problems and meet special objectives. Task reports are often necessary to meet these needs. They can be as simple as a one-line memo or as complex as a long, formal report requiring months of research. Because task reports deal with special circumstances, they are prepared on a one-time basis without the aid of printed forms or specific guidelines. Report writers have general guidelines only to help them prepare task reports.

Human Objectives   People who deal with certain operations on a regular basis are often able to foresee problems and suggest improvements. Management can encourage employees to make full use of their creativity and expertise by providing them the opportunity to submit reports anticipating problems or recommending improvements in procedures, products, processes, or services. Reports of this kind are not an assigned part of a job but may be rewarded (with a percentage of the first year's savings, perhaps).

DEFINITION OF A REPORT

The word *report* covers an extremely wide range of communication activities in modern organizations. Most authorities attempt to include as many of these activities as possible in their definitions. The following definitions are typical:

> A report is a presentation of facts and/or ideas to people who need them in decision making.[1]
>
> A report is a written or oral message used to (1) convey business information about research or status from one area of business to another to assist the decision-making function of management or to (2) present a solution to a business problem.[2]
>
> A report is any record that helps people understand the business environment of which they are a part.[3]
>
> [A] report is a piece of technical writing designed to meet a specific need.[4]
>
> A business report is an orderly and objective communication of factual information which serves some business purpose.[5]
>
> A report is a written communication conveying business information about research or a situation from one area of business to another to assist in making a decision.[6]

> An effective business report is an orderly, objective presentation of factual information, with or without analysis, interpretation, and recommendations, planned to serve some business purpose, usually that of making a decision.[7]

Of all the definitions, we favor those that include both the purpose and characteristics of reports. As we will use the term in this book, *a report is an organized presentation of information to a specific audience for the purpose of helping an organization achieve an objective.*

Reports are more than the communication of random data. Because someone in the organization will use the information to help achieve an objective, it is important that the information be organized in a way that will facilitate its use. One of the characteristics that distinguishes reports from routine oral exchanges of information and most casual, written messages is the care given to organizing the presentation of information. The presentation may be either written or oral and may include a wide variety of graphic (written reports) or visual (oral presentations) aids as well.

Reports are almost always prepared for a select reader or group of readers who will use the information as a basis for making decisions about organizational matters. In addition, reports are usually assigned to those persons who are in the best position to organize, interpret, and analyze the required information. Because those responsible for making the decisions need accurate, reliable, and impartial information, another characteristic of reports is that they should be based on objective, factual data rather than on unsupported opinions. As noted previously, reports help managers achieve a wide variety of organizational objectives, including maintenance, task, and human objectives. However they are defined, reports play a vital function in both routine and special operations in every organization.

IMPORTANCE OF REPORT WRITING

Reports have assumed their central role in modern organizational life because they have long demonstrated their ability to provide essential information in usable form. A 1980–1981 study of newly promoted executives revealed that business communication, including report writing, was the single most useful area of study for those wishing to work in general managerial positions.[8] Reports and other written communications have always been important to business.

Today, reports play an important part in almost every decision made in business, industry, and government. The history of report writing reveals steadily increasing use of written reports of all types. Because the need for information is increasing daily, the need for more—and more effective—reports can only increase in the future.

History of Reports

Written reports are as old as written history. In fact, early governmental and business reports provide much of our information about ancient civilizations. Even before recorded history, oral reports were serving their primary function of providing military and other leaders with the information they needed to make decisions. With the advent of writing, written reports began to supplement the oral reporting. The abilities of writing to transcend distance, to transcend time, and to permit the careful consideration and controlled use of language were responsible for the growing importance of written reports. With the Industrial Revolution and the development of complex, modern organizations, the need for clear, concise reports increased greatly.

Current Usage

At present, reports allow managers to

1. Make decisions about operations they are unable to supervise directly due to constraints of distance or time.
2. Understand and make decisions about technical operations being supervised by specialists.
3. Retain information in easily accessible form for future use.
4. Evaluate the technical and communication skills of those preparing the reports.

Because of their general utility, reports are often seen as an essential step in any planning process. If anything, reports are more likely to be required when not needed than they are to be needed and not required! For reports to be their most useful, they must be controlled in both number and content. Managers need to ensure that routine reports continue to provide essential information and that task reports are assigned only to meet real organizational needs.

Managers need task reports primarily to answer one or more of the following questions.

Can We? Before undertaking any project, management needs to know if it is possible for the organization to do it. Current technology, for example, might not permit the completion of a particular project. Some projects may be possible for one organization but not for another because of the new capital, resources, or technology involved.

Should We? Once the feasibility of a project has been demonstrated, the next question is whether it should be undertaken. Will the expected benefits exceed the costs involved? The benefits and costs may not always be profits and monetary expenditures. Safety, public relations, and environmental impact are but a few of the concerns managers must consider.

Which Way is Best? Once management decides that a project is possible and worthwhile, it needs to determine which means of achieving the objective will provide the greatest return for the least investment.

Future Possibilities

Whatever changes take place in communication technology over the next several years, it is certain that oral and written reports will continue to play a vital role. Technological advances will undoubtedly influence reporting policies and procedures. Computers will automatically gather, collate, and transmit important data to appropriate personnel. They will also perform many of the analytical functions report writers must now perform themselves.

As technology advances, another change report writers will face will be the increasing need to prepare technical reports for nontechnical audiences. Specialists will be writing reports for managers who have only a limited knowledge of the various areas of specialization within their areas of responsibility.

Along with preparing increasingly specialized reports for general audiences, report writers will be faced with the additional challenge of writing increasingly concise reports. Over the past several years, the average length of reports has been shrinking, and this trend is likely to continue as long as organizations put a premium on managerial time.

These changes will all put increased demands on report writers, who will continue to be responsible for the flow of information that makes organizational decision making possible.

A GOOD REPORT

Regardless of the changes that new technologies will bring about, good reports have always displayed—and will continue to display—the same characteristics. A good report is

Timely: It arrives on or before it is due and contains up-to-date information.

Well written: It is clear, concise, interesting; it is free from errors in grammar, mechanics, and content; and it is helpful.

Well organized: It is designed to be read selectively, so that a reader can pay attention only to those parts necessary.

Attractive: It is clearly labeled, assembled so that it will arrive in good condition, and designed for easy readability.

Cost effective: It is designed to solve a problem for the organization that will make the investment in the report worthwhile.

In the chapters that follow, we will show you how to produce well-written, well-organized, and attractive reports to meet the needs of business, industry, and government. We will also provide guidelines to help you gauge both the possible cost effectiveness of a report and general time requirements for each step of the report writing process.

SUMMARY

Reports—long or short, formal or informal—are an integral part of business, industry, and government. Reports are the principal means by which members of an organization communicate with each other about job-related matters.

Reports usually go *up* the chain of command in an organization, as individuals at lower levels provide information to those responsible for making decisions. A problem may be mentioned in several reports as different levels of management consider the variety of decisions that must be made as a result. Reports are necessary when managers (1) are too far away from an operation to observe it directly, (2) lack the time to observe it directly, or (3) lack the technical expertise to observe it accurately. Reports help management achieve maintenance, task, and human organizational objectives by providing the routine or special information needed for managerial decisions.

A report may be defined as an organized presentation of information to a specific audience for the purpose of helping an organization achieve an objective. Reports have assumed their central role in modern organizational life because they have demonstrated their ability to provide essential information in usable form. Reports will continue to play a vital role in organizational life as advancing technology requires specialists to prepare concise, understandable reports for general audiences.

A good report is timely, well written, well organized, attractive, and cost effective.

EXERCISES

Review Questions

1. What functions do reports serve in modern organizations?

2. Why do reports usually go *up* the chain of command?

3. When are reports disseminated down the chain of command?

4. Under what circumstances are reports necessary?

5. Why might one problem be mentioned in several reports?

6. What is the relationship between reports and organizational objectives?

7. Why do organizations usually use forms and guides for maintenance reports?

8. What three questions do task reports answer?

9. How do you define the word *report?*

10. What changes are likely to take place in report procedures in the next several years?

Problems

Present the following in written or oral form as your instructor directs.

1. Based on the information presented in this chapter, what would you say are the differences between reports and term papers?

2. Interview three or four people who work in business, industry, or government and list their oral and written reports. Describe how the reports they prepare relate to their job functions.

3. If you were a district sales manager responsible for sales representatives in 17 Midwestern cities, what reports would you expect to receive from your staff and why? What reports would you expect to prepare for your supervisor? Why?

Notes

[1]C. W. Wilkinson, Peter B. Clarke, and Dorothy Colby Menning Wilkinson, *Communicating Through Letters and Reports*, 8th ed. (Homewood, IL: Richard D. Irwin, 1982), p. 407.

[2]William C. Himstreet and Wayne Murlin Baty, *Business Communications*, 5th ed. (Belmont, CA: Wadsworth, 1977), p. 243.

[3]Phillip V. Lewis and William H. Baker, *Business Report Writing* 2d ed. (Columbus, OH: Grid, 1983), p. 6.

[4]Gordon H. Mills and John A. Walter, *Technical Writing*, 4th ed. (New York: Holt, Rinehart and Winston, 1978), p. 6.

[5]Raymond V. Lesikar, *Report Writing for Business*, 5th ed. (Homewood, IL: Richard D. Irwin, 1977), p. 1.

[6]Harry M. Brown, *Business Report Writing* (New York: D. Van Nostrand, 1980), p. 4.

[7]Malra Treece, *Effective Reports* (Boston: Allyn and Bacon, 1982), pp. 5–6.

[8]H. W. Hildebrandt et al., "An Executive Appraisal of Courses Which Best Prepare One for General Management," *The Journal of Business Communication*, 19:1 (Winter 1982), pp. 5–15.

CHAPTER 2
The Reader-Writer Relationship

What you do *before* you write will have a major influence on how successful your final report turns out to be. As a writer, your main goal will be to help the reader solve a problem or make a decision. To do that, you will need to learn your reader's needs and focus your attention on those needs.

Topics

What Is Your Purpose?
Who Is Your Reader?
What Does Your Reader Need to Know?
What Does Your Reader Already Know?
What Action Is Required?
How Will Your Reader Feel about Your Message?

Reports are written to accomplish something; and, further, reports are designed to accomplish it by working through someone else. For these reasons, the reader or readers of a report are of central importance. As a report writer, you will need to ask yourself several questions to help you present the information in a way that will facilitate any action the reader may need to take.

WHAT IS YOUR PURPOSE?

Before beginning work on any report, a writer needs to determine how the report will be used and what action should occur as a result. Each of the basic organizational objectives—maintenance, task, and human—may require written reports. In addition to these general objectives of reports, each report will also have at least one of three specific objectives:

1. To inform
2. To analyze
3. To recommend

A report writer may wish (or be required) to provide information, to interpret that information for the reader, to analyze the information and reach conclusions about what the information means, or to do all of these and make recommendations based on the analysis of information. A writer needs to know which of these purposes is appropriate for a particular report. To inform only when analysis and recommendations are required is to be incomplete. To analyze and recommend when the reader wants information only is to be presumptuous.

One purpose reports do *not* have is to persuade. Although a report writer may need to use persuasive techniques to ensure a fair reception for unpopular ideas, the purposes of such reports remain to inform, analyze, and recommend. Even when a report writer desires upper management to make a specific decision, he or she has the obligation to present all the information in an accurate, impartial, and complete manner. Managers need sound evidence on which to base their decisions, and a report writer should allow the objective evidence to constitute the entire effort to persuade.

WHO IS YOUR READER?

As a rule, specialists write reports for generalists. Field sales representatives, for example, have specific, detailed knowledge of their territories. Regional sales managers know something about each of the territories in their regions, but their knowledge is less specific and detailed than that of the representatives. The vice-president of sales would know still less about any one territory and would be more concerned with general sales figures and projections.

The situation is more complicated when the report writer needs to report on a technical process to an audience unfamiliar with the field. In many instances, the person addressed may not prove the actual audience for the report. The person addressed may forward the entire report to someone higher in the organization, and that person may not be familiar with the situation or expect the report.

WHAT DOES YOUR READER NEED TO KNOW?

As a report writer, your principal obligation will be to meet the needs of the person who will take action as a result of your report. Your supervisor, or the person to whom your report is addressed, may not be that person. He or she will act as a result of the report and thus needs accurate and complete information on which to base a decision. For many task reports, the decision maker will need to know

1. The nature of the problem
2. The causes of the problem
3. Possible solutions to the problem
   a. Costs for the solutions
   b. Advantages of the solutions
   c. Disadvantages of the solutions
   d. Possible long-term results of the solutions
4. Recommended solution and supporting reasons

One of the problems decision makers face in many organizations is that report writers often distort information as it goes up the chain of command. At each level report writers tend to minimize problems and to magnify accomplishments, because naturally, no one likes to give the boss bad news. Without accurate and complete information, however, the decision maker cannot possibly solve potential problems before they become major concerns.

A friend of ours in the packaging business told us about such a problem that occurred in one of the plants where he had worked. An operator of a critical piece of machinery told his foreman that the equipment was "on its last legs" and that it needed to be replaced. The foreman told the section supervisor that the machine would need to be replaced "soon," and the supervisor reported to the plant manager that "they needed to think about replacing" the aging equipment. The problem was presented in one sentence in the plant manager's 30-page, monthly report to the vice-president. The vice-president did not mention it at all in his report to the president. Shortly thereafter, the equipment broke down so completely that it was unrepairable, and the entire plant had to close for more than six weeks while a new piece of equipment was ordered, shipped, and installed. The company lost millions of dollars worth of business.

The reader of your report will need to know anything that will influence the success of the organization. The reader, however, will probably be more concerned with the *whats* than with the *hows*. The decision maker needs to know *what* needs to be done and by *when*. The specific *hows* are usually left to be decided by those working directly with the problem.

Because managerial decision makers have general responsibilities for a number of specific areas, they want the necessary information reported in a way that facilitates the decision-making process. Report writers should provide

1.   A quick overview of the problem, including the main point and recommendation
2.   Complete facts, including costs, advantages, disadvantages, and results of any action
3.   Clear writing presented in readable format
4.   Separation of facts, inferences based on fact, and opinion
5.   Constructive suggestions

As a rule, managers expect to find this material quickly and easily without reading the entire report. For this reason, all but the briefest reports should include a summarizing abstract that covers all the critical points, an introduction that describes the problem and its background in general terms (rather than specific or technical terms), and specific conclusions and appropriate recommendations. Most managers will *not* read the body of the report unless they have a special interest in the subject, have been directly involved in the project, the problem is especially urgent, or they are skeptical of the conclusions or recommendations.

WHAT DOES YOUR READER ALREADY KNOW?

Reports written at someone's request or as a routine part of the job fit into an existing communication context. In these cases, you will have a good idea of what your reader already knows. When you initiate a report, your reader will obviously require a more comprehensive introduction to the problem and the purpose of the report.

Whether your readers expect the report or not, what they already know will influence the content of your report. No one likes to be told things he or she already knows. For that reason, you should avoid mentioning facts your reader already knows unless they are an essential part of the report. When facts already known to the reader are essential, subordinate them to some new, important piece of information with which the reader is not yet familiar.

Change this: Our company installed the new computer system in December 1982. Since that time we have discovered. . .

To this: Since December 1982, when we installed the new computer system, we have discovered. . .

Also subordinate any necessary information your reader *should* know but may not remember.

Change this: We currently have a capital investment of $2.7 million in the Hawthorne plant alone.

To this: The $2.7 million capital investment in the Hawthorne plant may now be
     fully depreciated over the next three years.

In general, it is better to assume that your reader knows little than to
assume that he or she knows too much. Your reader will forgive you
more readily for telling more than he or she wants to know than for
omitting details required to understand the situation and make a decision.

WHAT ACTION IS REQUIRED?

The ultimate objective of every report is some kind of action. Even the
most routine informational memo contains data that will eventually
contribute to a decision. A report writer needs to see that information
from the perspective of the reader. The reader's main questions are
always going to be, "What action will I have to take as a result of this
report?" and "How will the organization benefit as a result of the action?"

   Whenever you are writing a report, you'll need to anticipate
those questions even if you have not been authorized to suggest possible courses of action. When you have the opportunity to make recommendations, state them clearly and explicitly, explaining the advantages and disadvantages of each possible alternative.

   When it is obvious that no action is possible, don't bother to complete and submit a report unless the purpose of the report is to determine whether action is possible. You can avoid unnecessary communication—and the time and effort it takes to write a report—if you will
attempt to place the action you are recommending within the larger
context of the organization. If your department has been ordered to
trim its budget by 20 percent and your company has instituted a hiring
freeze, a report suggesting the hiring of additional support personnel—no matter how well written—will not be well received. Similarly,
if your organization is facing an immediate crisis, reports that can wait,
should wait.

HOW WILL YOUR READER FEEL
ABOUT YOUR MESSAGE?

Even though your reader may need bad news to make a good decision, no one will enjoy learning that the organization has a problem.
Your reader will especially resist recommendations that will require
spending significant amounts of either time or money. A reader will
also resist conclusions and recommendations that run counter to his or
her own theories and vested interests.

   How the reader is likely to feel about your message will influence the way in which you should organize the material. When your reader will welcome your recommendation and conclusions, present your information *deductively*, with the most important point (the action recommended) first. When you suspect that your reader will resent or resist your conclusions and recommendations, present the information *inductively*, with the main evidence presented before the specific recommendation. When your message will contain information the reader will consider negative, inductive order of presentation will help ensure an objective reading of your report.

SUMMARY

The reader of a report needs clear, highly organized information on which to base decisions. To present the information in the best way, the writer needs to (1) know the purpose of the report, (2) be able to identify the reader's needs, and, when appropriate, (3) recommend specific courses of action. Reports may satisfy an organization's maintenance, task, or human objectives by providing information, analyzing information, or making recommendations. Reports are *not* written for persuasive purposes because managers must base their decisions on accurate and impartial information.

The person who will act as a result of the report is the ultimate reader, even when the report is prepared for and addressed to someone else. Readers almost always have a less specific view of the situation than the report writer and need the information presented in general, nontechnical terms. In providing the information the reader needs, a report writer should be careful to avoid minimizing negative information and exaggerating accomplishments. Managers need a quick and complete presentation of information, but necessary information with which they are already familiar should be subordinated to new, important information.

A report writer should be clear and specific about recommended actions and should provide the advantages and disadvantages for alternative actions. When no action is possible, the report may be unnecessary. Reports that the reader will welcome should use a deductive structure, and reports the reader will resent or resist require an inductive approach.

EXERCISES

Review
Questions

1. What are typical report objectives?

2. Under what circumstances should a report writer use persuasive techniques?

3. What are some examples of maintenance, task, and human reports?

4. Who is the ultimate reader of a report?

5. Under what circumstances will the ultimate reader be different from the person addressed?

6. What does a typical report reader need to know?

7. In what ways does information become distorted as it goes up the organizational chain of command?

8. Why should the writer provide the reader with a general, nontechnical overview of the situation?

9. How should the writer handle necessary information with which the reader is already familiar?

10. How do the reader's feelings about the message influence the presentation of information?

Discussion Questions

1. How can a writer determine whether the person addressed is the report's ultimate reader?

2. How can managers make intelligent decisions without having the same specific knowledge of the situation as the report writer?

3. In what way do managers have better information for making a decision than the report writer?

4. If readers rarely bother with the body of a report, why should a report writer spend the time and effort required to write it?

5. Under what circumstances would you feel that you had to document important conversations and ideas by writing summary memos?

Problems

1. Select a company discussed in a recent issue of *Forbes*, *Business Week*, or *Fortune*, and
   a. Write a brief summary of the article, making sure to include a description of any problems the company faced, the decisions made or required, and any results.
   b. List possible report subjects, writers, and readers that would have contributed to the decision-making process for company management.

2. You are the field representative for a major pharmaceutical company. Yesterday, when you called on a major hospital in your territory, you were told by the hospital's chief of internal medicine that your company's new drug developed to treat glaucoma may have pernicious side effects. Of the seven patients using the drug, five have developed liver and kidney complications. You know that the company spent nearly five years and several millions of dollars developing the drug and that the FDA approved its use only after extensive and closely monitored tests. What do you report, to whom, and how do you present the information?
   Write a short paper explaining and justifying your choices.

3. Find three articles describing what managers want in the reports they receive and prepare a brief summary of their contents. Note especially the similarities and differences in what the articles say managers want.

4. Interview a business manager responsible for preparing and receiving reports and ask him or her what is essential for a good report. Write a summary of his or her comments. If your instructor requests, compare the manager's opinions with those stated in the articles used for Question 3 above.

5. Obtain an actual business report (or, if your instructor permits, use one of the samples presented in this text) and
    a. Identify the objective or objectives.
    b. Identify the ultimate reader.
    c. Identify the information necessary to make the report effective.
    d. Specify information that would have helped the reader but was not included in the report.
    e. Evaluate the report.

PART II
Report Conventions and Techniques

CHAPTER 3
The Nature of Reports

Because the reader or readers will use the report to make a decision, report writers need to ensure that they are providing accurate, impartial, and complete information.

Topics

Communication Conventions
Levels of Formality and Complexity
Functional Writing for the Reader's Benefit
Techniques of Report Writing

Most business reports are requested by the receiver. For that reason, they are designed to meet the needs of the reader. Some of these needs have been created by communication conventions, some by the demands of functional writing, some by the demands of the specific situation, and some by the techniques developed to make reports more readable. The purpose of each of these needs is to help the reader make the best decision in the shortest time possible.

COMMUNICATION CONVENTIONS

Routine patterns or conventions help people understand the actions of others. Communication is no exception. The handshake of Western culture, the bow of oriental culture, and the "hello" of American telephone usage are all examples of communication conventions. Business letters and reports, although more complex, are also conventions.

Letters and reports, for example, are the expected communication in certain situations. Further, when readers receive letters and reports, they expect the writer to have followed some fairly specific rules in writing and presenting the information. Some of these conventions are arbitrary. They have developed over time, and readers expect writers to follow them. Standard spelling and grammar are such conventions. Your readers will expect your letters and reports to be written in standard English. The appearance of letters and reports is also governed by convention. Readers expect letters and reports to look a certain way.

Letters

Letters are the most common form of written communication between an organization and outside agencies and individuals. Letters are also used in formal situations between members of the same organization. Exhibits 3.1, 3.2, and 3.3 illustrate the most widely accepted letter formats and contain explanations of the parts of letters.

Reports

Just as with letters, readers expect reports to follow certain conventions of appearance, content, and style. One of the main functions of this book is, in fact, to help you understand and interpret those conventions. The remainder of this chapter covers the conventions governing the preparation of most written reports, including the direction of communication flow, the complexity of the information being reported, the nature of functional writing, and common specific techniques.

LEVELS OF FORMALITY AND COMPLEXITY

Reports may be prepared for audiences either within or outside the writer's organization. As a rule, reports remaining in the organization are less formal than those prepared for outside agencies. The informal memo report, for example, is the single most common report in business today. The least formal report prepared for an outside agency is the letter report. Internal reports tend to increase in formality as they increase in length and importance, ranging from the casual memo to the bound volume.

Reports tend to increase in formality as they increase in length and importance. A short report going up only one or two levels in the

EXHIBIT 3.1
Modified Block, Mixed Punctuation

letterhead

CALVIN FRAME COMPANY
1492 Columbus Avenue
Cleveland, OH 44109

date

February 23, 19xx

inside address

Mr. Michael G. Rooney, President
Rooney Overhead Door Company
1066 Hastings Drive
Akron, OH 44302

salutation (colon)

Dear Mr. Rooney:

body

Your new business should prove a tremendous success, Mr. Rooney, and the 24' frame and shelf sets you ordered will help you store and organize your inventory.

You will receive your order Tuesday or Wednesday of next week. I shipped the complete order by Red Ball Express this morning. The driver will call you before delivery.

The enclosed invoice shows your down payment of $600, the balance of $632, and shipping charges of $127.50. You have 90 days from the date of delivery to pay the $759.50.

Assembly instructions are packed with the frames and shelves, Mr. Rooney. I enclosed an extra package of nuts, lock washers, and bolts to make sure that you'll have everything you'll need to assemble the units. While it is possible for one person to complete assembly without assistance, you'll find that the work will be faster and easier if you have at least one person help.

Please call me if you have questions about assembly.

signature block
complimentary close
(comma)

Sincerely,

John Calvin

typed name
title
reference initial
enclosure notation

John Calvin
President

s

enc

organizational hierarchy would probably be written as a memo. A report of 10 or more pages designed for a reader several managerial levels above the writer would be prepared as a formal report. Chapter 5 presents more information about formal and informal report forms.

Moreover, the length and formality of reports generally increase as the information becomes more complex. Because the main function

EXHIBIT 3.2
Block Format, Mixed Punctuation

letterhead

A-1 Forms

19 Century Avenue
Victoria, MO 63123

date

23 January 19xx

inside address

Mrs. Joyce James
Assistant to the President
Issuant Computers Inc.
Siliconville, CA 94040

salutation
(no punctuation)
body

Dear Mrs. James

Here are the sample sales contract and personnel evaluation forms you
requested. As you can see, each was designed to meet the specific needs
of a particular company.

The sales contract forms we designed for CALC Company, for example,
contain more options and a more complex service agreement than you will
require. Their general appearance, however, would be suitable for Issuant
Computers. The other contract forms may give you additional ideas.

The kind of personnel evaluation form you need depends on a variety of
factors, including how often each employee is to be evaluated, the purpose
of the evaluation, and how long the form itself is to be kept. As you
suggested in your letter, you'll probably wish to have a form that lends
itself to computer entry and storage of data.

The enclosed brochure describes the general requirements of forms design
and the papers and quantities available. Use the graph paper provided to
sketch the forms, and use the key on p. 17 of the brochure to indicate
type faces and size.

As soon as I receive your sketch, I'll prepare samples and have one of our
technicians test them for readability and ease of use. Call me collect if you
have questions.

signature block
complimentary close
(no comma)

Sincerely

Samuel Perelman

name, title
department
reference initial [a]

Samuel Perelman, Chief
Forms Design

t

enclosure initial
copy notation [b]

enc

c Joseph Sidney
   Forms Technician

[a]Use the initial of the typist's last name. First and last initials are required only
when more than one typist in an office has the same last initial. One change that
has taken place in recent years is the elimination of the dictator's initials. Because
the dictator's name is already typed in full in the signature line, it is not necessary
to repeat the initials.

[b]Older letter forms used "CC" for "carbon copy," but now that most copies are
made photomechanically, only the "c" (lower case, no colon) is required to show
that a copy of the letter is being sent to someone else.

EXHIBIT 3.3
Simplified Letter Form

personal return address

date

inside address

subject line

body[a]

```
                              735 Bede Drive
                              Fairview, CO 80229
                              23 February 19xx




                              Mr. Joseph Sidney
                              Forms Technician
                              A-1 Forms
                              19 Century Avenue
                              Victoria, MO 63125

                              LETTER FORMATS

                              You're right about letter formats, Joe. Modified block and block
                              formats are both used widely.  Open punctuation (which omits the
                              colon after the salutation and the comma after the complimentary
                              close), however, has never caught on.  Almost everybody uses
                              mixed punctuation.

                              Block format is a bit more economical than modified block because
                              it begins each line on the left-hand margin, whereas modified block
                              indents both the date line and the signature block.  In block format,
                              paragraphs are blocked on the left-hand margin, but modified block
                              permits both blocked and indented format.

                              The format used for this letter, Joe, is known as the Simplified Letter
                              Form (SLF).  It is more economical than block format because it omits
                              the salutation and the complimentary close.  Most companies still use
                              modified block or block formats because they feel that the SLF violates
                              too many of the expected conventions of letter writing.  Many business
                              people feel that readers will be offended by the omission of the usual
                              salutation and complimentary close.  Companies that have switched to
                              SLF for reasons of economy report that most readers don't notice the
                              difference.
```

[a]Try to use reader's name in the first line.

of a report is to help the reader make a decision, reports containing complex statistical or technological information require extra attention to organization and clarity of presentation. The techniques of report writing presented later in this chapter and the techniques presented in Chapters 12, 13, and 14 will help you present complex information in a readable way.

EXHIBIT 3.3
Simplified Letter Form (continued)

second (and following)
page heading[c]

last line[b]

name, title

reference initial

copy notation

enclosure notation[d]

postscript[e]

Mr. Joseph Sidney   23 February 19xx   2

At the end of this letter, I've indicated the common notations, which
are used regardless of the letter format you select.

Let me know when I can help again.

Karen Stone

KAREN STONE, CPS

s

c

enc

PS

---

[b]A short last line helps retain a traditional appearance. Leave five lines for the signature.

[c]Heading is the same for all formats: modified block, simplified block, and simplified.

[d]Use the enclosure notation to indicate the presence of one or more enclosures. When enclosures are especially important, list them by document title and specify the number, for example:

3 enc
1. Invoice
2. Contract
3. Sample brochure

[e]A postscript is always the last entry in a letter, and because it comes last the notation isn't necessary to indicate that it is a PS. In general, avoid postscripts in formal correspondence. It's better to rewrite a letter than to reveal a lack of planning. The main purpose of a postscript is to add a personal note to a business letter.

FUNCTIONAL WRITING FOR THE READER'S BENEFIT

The only reason to write a report is that the reader needs the information contained in it. Even in those cases when a writer is submitting proposals or suggestions not required by management, he or she is presenting ideas assumed useful to management.

Reports perform one or more of the following functions:

Serve As a Permanent Record   Organizations require records for a variety of reasons. Reports concerning income and expenditures, for example, may be required for tax purposes. Other major reasons organizations need permanent records are to avoid duplication of effort at a later date and to profit from successes and failures in a wide variety of areas.

Provide Specialized Information   As mentioned previously, reports usually convey information from those with specialized knowledge to those with more generalized responsibilities. Because of special training, experience, or proximity to matters of organizational importance, a report writer is able to observe, describe, and interpret events or problems for those making organizational decisions.

Evaluate Problems, Possibilities, and People   The specialized information provided in reports allows decision makers to see how the particular parts of a problem fit into the larger organizational whole. Reports can present the advantages and disadvantages of various possibilities, allowing decision makers to select the best possibility from a number of alternatives.

Reports help managers evaluate people in two ways: First, supervisors use reports to provide a record of their evaluations of subordinates; and second, managers use written reports to help evaluate the performance of report writers. Written reports, in fact, are one of management's chief evaluative tools because they reveal the writer's organizational ability, judgment, clarity of thought, and ability to express her- or himself.

Help in Decision Making   The report writer needs to be certain to provide the kind of information that will assist the decision-making process. The writer should know what the reader already knows about the topic of the report to avoid emphasizing an aspect of the topic with which the reader is already familiar. The writer should discover what the reader *needs* to know: Are the reader's main concerns financial, technical, organizational, or political?

The writer also needs to anticipate questions the reader may have while reading the report. Those questions will usually take the form of one of the following:

What: action do I need to take? is the next step? are my responsibilities? caused the problem? changes will be required?

Why: should I act? should the company invest in this project? should I permit the writer to act?

How: will I benefit from this? will the company benefit from this? will the project be accomplished?
much investment will be required? soon will we need to start? long will it take to finish?

Who: will benefit from this? will be affected by this? should act on this? needs to know more about this?

A good report anticipates the reader's questions and provides answers. To help the reader make the right decision, the writer should provide reliable answers to those questions. To ensure the reliability of your reports, check all data for accuracy, impartiality, and completeness.

Accurate information conforms to the truth and is free from error.

Impartial information is fair and objective. It presents all sides of critical issues so that the reader can see how you reached your conclusions and is free and able to draw different conclusions when the information may be interpreted in more than one way.

Complete information gives the reader everything he or she needs to make the best decision.

Protect the Writer Although the main function of reports is to provide information that will help a manager make a decision, reports can often serve to provide a record that will protect the writer. Some organizational communication books go so far as to recommend that employees should document every idea, telephone call, conversation, and action with a memo or longer report. We believe that excessive written documentation is dysfunctional. The paper avalanche that results from excessive documentation helps no one and, in fact, interferes with the acceptance of significant reports.

Avoid Unnecessary Reports In report writing, as in all of life, importance and emphasis are indicated by contrast; without valleys there would be no mountains. When an employee attempts to document everything, each document loses importance. Reports written by an employee who writes only a few will be read much more carefully than those written by employees who report every telephone call.

Sometimes *not* writing is the best way a writer can help her or his supervisor. Does the reader really *need* the information? Does the reader have the resources or ability to act on the recommendation? Does the reader have the time to act on the recommendation?

Organizational life is complex. Budgets are cut, crises can occur at any time, and organizational objectives can change quickly as a result of outside influences. How well will the information you intend to present fit in with the current organizational situation? Managers are slow to accept suggestions for larger expenditures in times of decreasing budgets and for any new actions in times of crisis. The timing of reports, as well as their content, should take the reader's needs into account. Submit reports not required as part of the job when management will be predisposed to accept and act on them.

TECHNIQUES OF REPORT WRITING

Regardless of the kind of report you are writing, its purpose, or its content, the report should be written for a specific audience and be highly organized.

Specific Audience

Most reports have both primary and secondary readers. The primary reader is the person who will make a decision and take action on the basis of your report. The secondary audience consists of all others who need the information to perform their jobs well. As a report writer, your main responsibility is to your primary reader—the person who will act.

Highly Organized

Because the reader's time is valuable, reports need to be highly organized and to make the organizational pattern clear, predictable, and easy to follow. For this reason, writers often use headings, itemized lists, and a variety of graphic aids to present information in a way that will enable the reader to determine quickly which parts require close attention and which can be skimmed. Chapter 12 covers common organizational patterns, outlines, and headings in detail. Chapter 15 describes and illustrates the use of graphic aids.

SUMMARY

Most business reports are requested by the receiver and should be designed to meet the receiver's needs. Business writing, like most human activities, has developed certain conventions that help writers prepare them and provide readers with expectations about appearance and content. Letters and reports are governed by several conventions.

Modified Block, Block, and Simplified Letter Form are the three most common letter formats. Report formats vary according to the purpose and formality of the report. Short, informal reports are either written in letter or memo format, depending on whether they will leave the organization or remain inside it. Some short reports and most long reports require a formal presentation.

Reports are functional writing designed for the reader's benefit. They serve as a permanent record; they provide specialized information; they help evaluate problems, possibilities, and people; and they help in the decision-making process by answering the questions of what, why, how, and who. Documentation reports can also protect the writer by providing a record of ideas, conversations, and actions. Excessive reporting, however, can detract from the significance of those reports that are truly important.

Regardless of the kind of report, it should be written for a specific audience and highly organized, making use of headings, itemized lists, and a variety of graphic aids.

EXERCISES

Review
Questions

1. What are some common communication conventions?

2. How are letters different from reports?

3. Name the three most common letter formats and describe their differences.

4. What factors influence report format?

5. In what ways is sending a report like going for an interview?

6. What functions do reports perform for readers?

7. What kinds of questions should the writer anticipate?

8. What three report characteristics will help the reader make the right decision?

9. When should reports be used to protect the writer?

10. What are the differences between primary and secondary readers?

Discussion
Questions

1. Discuss the events that may have led to the establishment of some of the common communication conventions.

2. In this chapter we say that sending a report is a little like going to an interview. Discuss the differences and similarities between communicating in writing and in person.

3. Under what circumstances do you believe it would be necessary to write a report simply to protect yourself?

4. When managers use reports to evaluate those who wrote them, on what factors do they base their evaluation?

5. Can a report writer be accurate, impartial, and complete and be persuasive at the same time?

6. Describe steps a writer should take to discover what the primary reader already knows about a particular subject.

7. What can a writer do to help ensure that an important report is taken seriously?

8. Why is communicating with others within an organization different from communicating with those outside the organization?

9. In what way is the information in a report *specialized*?

10. How do headings, itemized lists, and graphic aids contribute to the effectiveness of a report?

Problems

1. Write a letter to Henry Ludlum, President, Arcane Games, Inc., 2020 Foresight Avenue, Bloomington, Illinois 61701. Ludlum has asked you to describe briefly the most important aspects of written reports. Send him your reply in
    a. Modified block format
    b. Block format
    c. Simplified Letter Format.

2. Write a short paper describing the differences and similarities among business reports, term papers, and essays.

3. Interview three people working in the career area for which you are preparing and discover
    a. What reports they write.
    b. What reports they receive.
    c. How each report (written and received) contributes to the managerial decision-making process.
    Write a summary of your findings.

4. Make a list of the entry-level positions for which your education will prepare you. For each possible position, list the job titles of those to whom you would be reporting and the kinds of reports for which you would be responsible.

5. Under what circumstances should a report be put in writing? Explain.

CHAPTER 4
Classification of Reports

Just like people and companies, reports come in a variety of shapes and sizes. As a report writer, you will need to know how these shapes and sizes help a report achieve a particular objective. Each of the systems of classifying reports says something about how the report should be written, what it should contain, and how it will be used.

Topics

Classification by Function
Classification by Time Intervals
Classification by Length
Classification by Importance
Classification by Subject
Classification by Reader-Writer Relationship
Classification by Presentation

Because the myriad of businesses and organizations preparing reports have widely differing needs, no one system of classification has proved satisfactory for all. Report classifications vary from organization to organization depending on the purpose of the reports and the practices of the organization.

The following are the generally accepted classifications:

1. Function
   a. Informational
   b. Interpretative
   c. Analytical
2. Time Intervals
   a. Periodic
   b. Progress
   c. Special
3. Length
   a. Short
   b. Long

4. Importance
    a. Routine
    b. Important
    c. Critical
5. Subject
    a. Accounting
    b. Engineering
    c. Financial
    d. Insurance
    e. Management
    f. Personnel
    g. Sales
    h. Tax
    i. And so forth (varies from organization to organization)
6. Reader-Writer Relationship
    a. Internal
    b. External
7. Presentation
    a. Written
    b. Oral

Wherever you work and whatever kind of reports you write, your reports will be more successful if you understand the reasons behind these systems of classification.

CLASSIFICATION BY FUNCTION

The basic classification of reports is by function—by what they do. Nearly every organization acknowledges and uses this system of classification. Reports can do three things. They can give information; they can give information and examine and interpret it; and they can give information, examine and interpret it, and draw conclusions and make recommendations. According to function, then, reports are informational, interpretive, or analytical.

Informational Reports

Informational reports simply provide the facts. They do not interpret or analyze the data, nor do they offer opinions, conclusions, or recommendations. Some common examples of informational reports are financial statements, sales reports, audit reports, and minutes of meetings. See Exhibit 4.1 for an illustration of an informational report.[a]

---

[a]The examples included here are meant for illustrations only. We do *not* intend for them to be taken as perfect examples, but rather as examples of applications of a principle to a given situation.

EXHIBIT 4.1
An Informational Report

heading[a]

"Here is/are"[b]

itemized list[c]

```
                15 August 19xx



                TO:       Sonya Silverton, Sales Manager, District I

                FROM:     Martin Overloop, Sales Representative

                SUBJECT:  SALES FOR WEEK ENDING 15 AUGUST

                Here are the figures for last week's sales.
                    Calls              Sales              Amount
                    212                 52               $18,792
                The sales breakdown is as follows:
                                                Calls   Sales   Amount
                    Jewelry stores                15      18    $ 5,400
                    Clothing stores               14      15      5,022
                    Specialty shops               13       9      4,612
                    Record stores                 70       4      1,400
                    Hardware stores               55       3      1,252
                    Miscellaneous small businesses 45      3      1,106
                        Total                    212      52    $18,792
```

[a]The heading on a memo must contain the date, a "To" line, a "From" line, and a subject line. Note the use of the "international" form for the date.
[b]The words "Here is/are" are a usual beginning for letters and memos transmitting specific items of information (sales figures in this case) or enclosures.
[c]Use an itemized list (numbered or unnumbered) to increase the readability of a series of items, especially when the list includes numbers of monetary amounts.

EXHIBIT 4.2
An Interpretive Report

15 August 19xx

TO: Sonya Silverton, Sales Manager, District I

FROM: Martin Overloop, Sales Representative

SUBJECT: SALES FOR WEEK ENDING 15 AUGUST

Here are the figures for last week's sales.

Calls 212
Sales 52
Amount $18,792

The sales breakdown is as follows:

	Calls	Sales	Amount
Jewelry stores	15	18	$ 5,400
Clothing stores	14	15	5,022
Specialty shops	13	9	4,612
Record stores	70	4	1,400
Hardware stores	55	3	1,252
Miscellaneous small businesses	45	3	1,106
Total	212	52	$18,792

As the figures illustrate, jewelry stores, clothing stores, and specialty shops account for 80 percent of the sales even though they constitute only 20 percent of the calls.

heading

"Here is/are"

itemized list

interpretation[a]

[a]This paragraph *interprets* the important facts revealed by the preceding figures.

Interpretive Reports

Interpretive reports (also called examination reports) not only provide the factual information, but also explain and interpret the information. They do not draw conclusions or make recommendations. Interpretive reports are usually written when the reader requests the interpretive information or when specialists in technical areas report to managers who are generalists. The addition of a single paragraph expands the informational report in Exhibit 4.1 into the interpretive report, Exhibit 4.2.

Analytical Reports

In addition to presenting information and interpreting it, analytical reports analyze the data, draw conclusions, and offer recommendations. Analytical reports may combine several informational reports so that conclusions and recommendations can be made for a solution to a complex problem.

All analytical reports begin as informational reports to which the writer adds interpretation and analysis. In theory *any* informational report could become an analytical report if the reader needed to have the writer interpret and analyze the data. In practice, only complex, nonroutine situations call for analytical reports. Typical examples would include attitudinal surveys, product surveys, and investigations of special problems. The author of the report in Exhibit 4.3 added expository data and personal recommendations to create an analytical report.

CLASSIFICATION BY TIME INTERVALS

Another way to classify reports is by time intervals or by frequency of issue, schedule, or occurrence. Reports classified by time intervals are periodic, progress, and special.

Periodic Reports

Periodic reports are prepared regularly—daily, weekly, monthly, quarterly, or annually. Examples of periodic reports are the daily reports prepared by bank tellers, weekly reports prepared by sales representatives, monthly reports prepared by plant managers, quarterly reports prepared by auditors, and annual reports prepared by corporations to their stockholders.

Because of the availability of computers, many report writers use computers to help in preparing periodic reports. Also, many companies use standard forms for periodic reports so that all the report writer has to do is simply supply the missing facts and figures. Exhibit 4.4 illustrates a periodic report.

Progress Reports

Progress reports explain what has happened in the past on a project during a particular period of time and what can be expected in the future. Progress reports do not report on completed projects; they provide information about the status of the project. Because progress reports are submitted according to a predetermined time schedule— daily, weekly, monthly, or some other regular interval—they can be

EXHIBIT 4.3
An Analytical Report

heading

"Here is/are"

itemized list

interpretation

conclusion[a]

recommendation[b]

---

15 August 19xx

TO: Sonya Silverton, Sales Manager, District I

FROM: Martin Overloop, Sales Representative

SUBJECT: SALES FOR WEEK ENDING 15 AUGUST

Here are the figures for last week's sales.

	Calls	Sales	Amount
Jewelry stores	15	18	$ 5,400
Clothing stores	14	15	5,022
Specialty shops	13	9	4,612
Record stores	70	4	1,400
Hardware stores	55	3	1,252
Miscellaneous small businesses	45	3	1,106
Total	212	52	$18,792

As the figures illustrate, jewelry stores, clothing stores, and specialty shops account for 80 percent of the sales even though they constitute only 20 percent of the calls.

Increased need for security in jewelry, clothing, and specialty shops because of the increased value of gold and silver and increased shoplifting make our security systems necessary.

I recommend that in the future we concentrate sales calls on jewelry stores, clothing stores, and specialty shops. Sales personnel should call on other businesses only as time permits.

---

[a]*Conclusion* based on the preceding facts.
[b]*Recommendation* that naturally results from the preceding conclusion.

classified as time interval reports. Supervisors may request progress reports on continuing activities. For example, an academic department chairperson may request progress reports from faculty members who are working on special projects; a plant supervisor may request a progress report on the construction of a new plant; or a president of an

EXHIBIT 4.4
A Periodic Report Form

```
                        WEEKLY SALES REPORT


        Week of _____

        Salesperson _____

        Store No. _____


        Day                Date                Total Sales
        Monday          _____        _____
        Tuesday         _____        _____
        Wednesday       _____        _____
        Thursday        _____        _____
        Friday          _____        _____
```

organization may request progress reports from committee chairpersons.

Progress reports usually start with an initial report that gives the background of the project. Continuing reports state what has happened and what can be expected. Finally, the terminal report summarizes what has been accomplished. Progress reports generally have three divisions: (1) an introduction that gives the background or sum-

EXHIBIT 4.5
A Progress Report

opening paragraph[a]

November 2, 1982

TO: Thomas R. Clarke, Chief of Police

FROM: Kimberly M. Dieterle

SUBJECT: Progress Report--Data Management Study

Here is a four-week progress report on the Data Management Study
I am conducting for the Louisville Police Department Records
Bureau. The information included in this progress report covers
the problem background, work accomplished, and work projection.

PROBLEM BACKGROUND

Each of the hundreds of thousands of reports that pass through
the Louisville Police Department (LPD) Records Bureau is handled
by many different people in various processing stages. A computerized system was installed two and one half years ago and is
working well. The changeover, however, has caused disorder, and
reports are being misplaced and lost. The clerks in the Records
Bureau are swamped with work because of this problem. Because
of the legal problems that could arise from the current situation,
the LPD would like to streamline the paper flow system within the
Records Bureau.

WORK ACCOMPLISHED

On September 29, 1982, I met with Lt. Steven Harmon who gave me
a tour of the Police Department and introduced me to Jill Nevens,
Supervisor Records Bureau. Lt. Harmon also supplied me with
blank copies of the various report forms and his Records Manual
on how to complete those forms. On October 11, 1982, I talked
with Mrs. Nevens about what activities were performed in the
Records Bureau and read over a few completed reports. The next
day, October 12, I met again with Lt. Harmon to discuss my conversation with Mrs. Nevens. After speaking with Lt. Harmon, I
went to City Hall and briefly spoke with Mrs. Jeanne Hayden,
Human Resources Administrator. Mrs. Hayden has just completed
a similar study and was able to give me a copy of her report.

I have also designed a 17-item questionnaire which was tested
before distribution by Ms. Beth Evink, a Criminal Justice
major at Walsh College and a volunteer assistant to the Prose-
cuting Attorney for the City of Louisville. I distributed 15
questionnaires on October 22, 1982. Ten questionnaires were
sent to the clerks in the Records Bureau, three to the secretaries in the Detective Bureau, and two to the secretaries in

---

[a]The opening paragraph tells the reader what the report is about and introduces the
topics that will be covered.

marizes previous progress reports; (2) the heart of the report that details the progress for the particular time period of the report, possibly
with tentative conclusions and recommendations; and (3) the summary
which may tell the reader what can be expected on the project or present the final conclusions and recommendations for the entire project.
Exhibit 4.5 illustrates a progress report.

EXHIBIT 4.5
A Progress Report (continued)

Thomas R. Clarke, Chief of Police   November 2, 1982   2

the Police Patrol Division. Those 15 people are the only personnel directly connected with the paper-flow system. Twelve of
those questionnaires have been returned and are in the process
of being tallied. The remaining 3 questionnaires from the
Records Bureau are due next week.

WORK PROJECTION

In the next week, I expect to receive the 3 outstanding questionnaires from the KPD Records Bureau. A total tally will then
be completed. I also plan to further review Mrs. Hayden's report
and to set up an interview with her to discuss her findings.
Interviews will also be arranged with Mrs. Nevens, Supervisor
Records Bureau, and Lt. Harmon. Upon the completion of these
interviews, I will analyze the data gathered and make my recommendations. You should have the final report on December 2,
1982.

directives[b]

[b]Progress reports (and many other reports as well) should end by telling the reader who is responsible for taking what action next. When a specific date is appropriate, state it.
Source: Courtesy of Kimberly M. Dieterle

Special Reports

Exhibit 4.6 is an example of a special report.

Special reports are generally prepared not on a regular but on a one-time basis. Special because they are not likely to be requested again, these reports are nonroutine. Most special reports help solve a specific

EXHIBIT 4.6

A Special Report

typical governmental report[a]

City of Kalamazoo
Inter-Office

MEMO

To Honorable Mayor & City Commission   Date 12-2-82

From Robert C. Bobb, City Manager *RCB*

Regarding Major and Local Street Improvements

Improvements in the City's infrastructure are critical to the long-term well-being of this community. This memorandum outlines my 1983 budget recommendation for the proposed major and local street improvements.

Project Description

The proposed project provides for the reconstruction or resurfacing of approximately 10.86 miles of streets. The streets include the worst major and local streets within the City as determined by a survey of all streets performed by the Public Works staff in 1980. Some of these streets have virtually no pavement structure other than a gravel surface or a badly deteriorated sealcoat surface. For these we are recommending a minimum 2" thick asphalt strip surface.

Other streets have no curb and gutter; their current pavement is so deteriorated that an immediate repair and resurfacing is warranted. Some streets have curbs and gutters which are still relatively good, but the pavement itself requires resurfacing. The fourth category within this proposal includes streets needing the entire pavement, curb, and gutter replaced.

Street Ratings

During late 1980 and early 1981, the Public Works staff rated all the streets within the City. The system used is one developed by the Michigan Department of Transportation (MDOT) for the statewide needs study. The two items used in our determination of "worst streets" are surface condition and, where applicable, curb condition. The proposed project includes those streets with a surface rating of 5 or 4 or a curb rating of 3.

Surface condition is rated as follows:

  1--Excellent--No visible deterioration

  2--Good   --Some surface deterioration but less than 5% of the road length being rated. Average maintenance required.

---

[a]This is a typical governmental report. In this case, a city manager is submitting a recommendation for a method of financing street repairs. Inductive order (see pp. 17–18) is used because the city commission might react negatively to the recommendation for a bond issue of more than $1 million. The details in the central portion of the report have been omitted to save space.

problem or resolve a single incident. In some cases, a problem or event may require more than one special report. If an incident will require more than one report, the special report may be based on a series of progress reports that precede the concluding special report.

EXHIBIT 4.6

A Special Report (continued)

```
Major and Local
Street Improvements
Page 2

        3--Fair      --Surface deterioration on up to 25% of length
                       being rated.  May require above-average
                       maintenance but considered reasonable when
                       weighed against cost of total resurfacing.

        4--Poor      --Deterioration on over 25% of surface. Requires
                       excessive maintenance and warrants resurfacing
                       soon.

        5--Very Poor--Excessive deterioration beyond maintenance or
                       no improvement exists.  Warrants immediate
                       resurface or reconstruction.

   Curb condition is rated as follows:

        1--Good--Curb is structurally sound and height is adequate
                 for more than one resurfacing.

        2--Fair--Curb could be spot repaired on less than 50% and
                 adequate height exists for one resurfacing.

        3--Poor--Structural condition is poor and warrants total
                 replacement and inadequate height exists for
                 resurfacing.

   Kalamazoo Streets

   The City of Kalamazoo contains approximately 250 miles of public
   streets for which we are totally responsible for maintenance.
   Of this total, 82 miles are classified as major streets and the
   remaining 168 miles as local streets.  In addition, the City
   maintains approximately 12 miles of State trunkline under con-
   tract with MDOT.

   A major street generally refers to a street carrying relatively
   high traffic volumes and serving one of the following criteria:

        1.   Streets that provide extensions to State trunklines or
             County primary roads in facilitating through traffic.

        2.   Streets that provide an integral network to serve the
             traffic definitely created by industrial, commercial,
             educational, or other traffic-generating centers.

        3.   Streets that provide for the circulation of traffic in
             and around the central business district.
```

EXHIBIT 4.6
A Special Report (continued)

```
        Major and Local
        Street Improvements
        Page 3


            4.   Streets designated as truck routes.

            5.   Streets that collect traffic from an area served by an
                 extensive network of local streets.

        The City Engineer designates major and local streets subject to
        and requiring certification by MDOT.  The number of miles of
        major and local streets, as well as population, is used by the
        State in calculating the Michigan Transportation Funds (MTF)
        revenues allocated to the City annually.  The City's MTF revenues
        have steadily decreased since 1979 when we received $2,091,495 as
        compared to $1,764,254 in 1982.

        The life expectancy of a permanently paved street on an average
        is 20 years, at which point the surface should receive some form
        of preventative maintenance or resurfacing to preserve its integ-
        rity.  Streets which have never received permanent paving require
        constant repair activity and eventually end up costing more than
        it would have cost to pave the street permanently in the first
        place.  If a permanently paved street does not receive some form
        of maintenance at the end of its 20-year life, it deteriorates
        at an increased rate.  It may then require total reconstruction
        at a much higher cost than a mere resurfacing.  If this philoso-
        phy is followed for the total system of 250 miles, we should be
        resurfacing or providing a specific level of maintenance of a
        minimum of 12 1/2 miles a year to protect the investment within
        our infrastructure.
```

```
        Local Streets Recommendations

        I respectfully recommend that the City Commission finance the
        local street improvements totalling $1,000,000 by issuing
        $500,000 in MTF bonds and $500,000 in special assessment bonds.
        Your conceptual approval of this approach is requested at this
        time.  Final approval would come with the approval of the appro-
        priate resolutions.

        That process is as follows:

        a.  Approval of a resolution authorizing the City Clerk to
            publish a notice of intent to specially assess 50% of these
            projects.  This action triggers the 45-day referendum period.

        b.  During the 45-day referendum period three standard resolu-
            tions for the special assessment rolls would be considered by
            the City Commission along with the required public hearings.
```

CLASSIFICATION BY LENGTH

Although reports are often classified by length, no precise criterion exists for what makes a long report long or a short report short.

Short Reports

Generally, reports ten pages or less are classified as short reports. Short reports can be very brief, even one or two words. Most business reports are short; they are usually informal and informational. They

EXHIBIT 4.6

A Special Report (continued)

```
Major and Local
Street Improvements
Page 4

c.  If the assessment rolls are confirmed, and if there is not
    a referendum, the City Commission then considers the bond
    sale resolution.  When that is approved, the bond sale
    process begins.

In terms of the special assessment impact on the average property
owner assuming a $500,000 special assessment bond issue or half
of the total project cost, property owners would be assessed an
average $8.50 per front foot.  This is based upon a range of
$4.46 a front foot for the two-inch strip surface to $10.40 a
front foot for total reconstruction.  For a property with front-
age of 60 feet, the cost for the improvement at $8.50 a front
foot would be $510 for over 15 years at 10%.

Regarding the MTF bond issue, the same process as that which was
followed earlier this year applies.  First, plans and specifica-
tions are submitted to MDOT and the Form 2020 is filed with the
State.  Following MDOT approval, two resolutions are presented
to the City Commission, a bond resolution and a notice of sale
resolution.  Following approval of these, the bond issue package
is presented to the Michigan Finance Commission.

In conclusion, I would like to stress that we are requesting
conceptual approval of the local street projects under the
recommended funding approach of $500,000 in MTF bonds and
$500,000 in special assessment bonds.

Furthermore, I recommend approval of the MTF bond issue for
major streets totalling $1,252,000.

I look forward to discussing these projects with you.


RCB:ra

CC:  Sheryl L. Sculley
     William Nelson
     Robert Willard
     Don Schmidt
     LuAnn Stampfler
```

[b]See footnote a, Exhibit 3.2 for current practice.
[b]See footnote b, Exhibit 3.2 for more up-to-date usage.
Source: Courtesy of Robert C. Bobb, City Manager, Kalamazoo, MI.

provide the requested information, such as the sales figures for the day, the total transactions for the week, or the traffic patterns for the month.

Long Reports

Long reports generally exceed ten pages. Some can be very lengthy. Many businesses must prepare reports several volumes long to comply with governmental regulations, for example. Long reports are for the most part formal and analytical. They provide the reader with a complete analysis of the problem which may include many tables and figures. Exhibit 4.6 is an example of a long report (though we did not present the report in its entirety).

CLASSIFICATION BY IMPORTANCE

Reports can be routine, important, or critical. The content of the reports classified by importance is determined by how the content affects the reader.

Routine Reports

Routine reports are those written on a regular basis to provide information that may become useful but is not of immediate importance. Because they are routine, these reports can be submitted on a prepared form. For example, supervisors who report the readings of various pieces of equipment in a plant may provide the information on a prepared form. Exhibit 4.7 illustrates a routine report.

Important Reports

Important reports are those that need to be considered or acted upon within a short time. Circumstances will vary from organization to organization, but important reports often call for action within one to ten days. Exhibit 4.8 illustrates an important report.

Critical Reports

Critical reports are those that need to be acted upon immediately, generally within 24 to 48 hours. Again, these numbers are arbitrary. Exhibit 4.9 illustrates a critical report.

CLASSIFICATION BY SUBJECT

One of the most common methods for classifying reports is by subject matter—accounting, engineering, financial, insurance, management, personnel, sales, tax, and so forth. Each of these major divisions can be further subdivided. For example, audit, cost, inventory, and tax reports would be subdivisions under accounting. Exhibit 4.10 illustrates an accounting report.

EXHIBIT 4.7
A Routine Report

opening[a]

---

13 March 19xx

TO: Staff

FROM: Roger Ballace, Principal

SUBJECT: Update Report on Home/School Component

Consultations and Counseling

As of this date, 12 March 19xx, the Home/School Component has
received 20 requests for service. Fourteen of the requests
were from school staff and the other 6 were directly from
parents. Six of these cases are in the evaluation state, 7
are in the implementation stage, 3 are in maintenance, and 4
are terminated. In 8 of these 20 cases, all performance
objectives established have been met. Work is in progress
on the other active cases.

Since 15 February, 10 parents have indicated a need for referral
of information about community programs. All of the referrals
have been made. Eight of the referrals have been followed up
to ensure that the parents had called the community program
office. Two referrals are in process.

Communication Systems

The daily note system has been implemented and is being used in
all classrooms in the Program. Surveys have been conducted to
determine the acceptance of the daily note system, and the
results are favorable. In November, a questionnaire was sent
to participating parents. The overall rating of home/school
communication by all parents responding (on a five-point scale,
5 being excellent) was 3.2.

Another system has been developed to increase home/school communication. That is the use of report cards. Parents and school
staff were interviewed for suggestions. It was determined that
the report cards would best fit into the system as a means of
providing parents with feedback following the regular reviews
of their children's current educational program.

---

[a]Because the subject line is considered a title or a heading, most memos include a
general introductory paragraph before introducing the first subdivision of the subject.

EXHIBIT 4.8
An Important Report

BIRMINGHAM VALLEY INTERMEDIATE SCHOOL DISTRICT

Bradley Avenue School

15 December 19xx

TO: Bradley School Staff

FROM: Brenda Owens, Principal

SUBJECT: Snow Day Procedures

The Birmingham Valley Intermediate School District's programs
for students are open and in session whenever one or all of our
constituent districts are open and transporting students to our
program.

When all nine of our constituent districts are closed, our
programs at Bradley Avenue School, Youth Opportunties Unlimited,
and Valley Center will also be closed to students. Depending on
the time that the closings occur, this announcement may or may
not be heard on WBIR radio.

In all cases, all BVISD full-time staff are expected to report,
and programs at the Juvenile Home will be in session. When
weather conditions are severe, the Intermediate office will be
closed, and the announcement will be made on WBIR radio that
"no staff member needs to report."

CLASSIFICATION BY READER-WRITER RELATIONSHIP

Still another means of classifying reports is by reader-writer relationship. Although they might be called by other names, reports may be classified as either internal or external depending on whether reader and writer work at the same company.

EXHIBIT 4.9
A Critical Report

---

14 April 19xx

TO: Mike Lowery, Control Lab

FROM: Phil Bowden, Plant Superintendent

SUBJECT: Gold Paint #5764

Gold paint #5764 is showing signs of degeneration at temperatures
below 0°C. I request immediate chemical analysis.

---

telegraphic style[a]

[a]Note the "telegram" sense of urgency conveyed by this brief request.

Internal Reports

Internal reports are those written for a reader by an individual in the
same organization. They move vertically—generally up the chain of
command from subordinate to supervisor—and horizontally between
equals. Most internal reports use memo format. Exhibit 4.11 illustrates
an internal report.

EXHIBIT 4.10
An Accounting Report

short-form
auditor's report[a]

signature block[b]

Foxley Accountants
500 Scott Street
Baltimore, MD 21204

2 February 19xx

Board of Directors and Shareholders
Bixley Corporation
411 Petersen Drive
Omaha, NE 68144

Gentlemen and Ladies:

We have examined the balance sheets of Bixley Corporation as of December 31, 19xx, and December 31, 19xx, and the related statements of income and retained earnings and changes in financial position for the years then ended. Our examinations were made in accordance with generally accepted auditing standards and, accordingly, included such tests of the accounting records and such other auditing procedures as we considered necessary in the circumstances.

In our opinion, the financial statements referred to above present fairly the financial position of Bixley Corporation at December 31, 19xx, and December 31, 19xx, and the results of its operations and the changes in its financial position for the years then ended, in conformity with generally accepted accounting principles applied on a consistent basis.

Sincerely,

FOXLEY ACCOUNTANTS

Bruce Pickard

Bruce Pickard, Accountant

---

[a]The language of this short-form auditor's report has evolved over time and is clear to most people who rely on the report for financial information.
[b]The use of the company name makes this a "legal" signature block, which indicates that the company, not the writer, has the legal responsibility for the contents of the letter. Most companies now prefer to assume that responsibility in other ways because the company name makes the letter appear too formal.

EXHIBIT 4.11
An Internal Report

---

1 March 19xx

TO: William Bohn, Director of Sales

FROM: Diane Chapman, Manager, Hartford Sales District

SUBJECT: Monthly Report for Hartford Sales District

Summary

The sales figures for February increased 15 percent. Two additional sales representatives were hired to help with sales.
Sales for next month look promising.

Office Staff

Elizabeth Denomme, the office secretary, submitted her resigna-
tion effective 15 March. Ms. Denomme is moving to St. Louis
because of her husband's recent promotion. Susan Oldford,
Ms. Denomme's assistant, will be the new office secretary.
We'll be hiring an assistant for Ms. Oldford within the next
month.

External Reports

Reports submitted to an organization by an outsider are external. When management has a problem that cannot be solved internally or when an organization does not have the expertise, equipment, or facilities to provide the required information; it seeks outside assistance. A professional consulting firm, for example, may be hired to do an extensive survey of corporate-wide records management systems. External reports are usually more formal than internal reports. When they are short, external reports often use letter format. Longer external reports usually receive formal treatment. Exhibit 4.12 illustrates an external letter report. For an example of an external formal report, see Chapter 5.

EXHIBIT 4.12
An External Letter Report

Connecticut State

Department of Highways and Transportation
Hartford, CT 06101

July 1 19xx

Mr. Craig Ackerson
City Road Commissioner
City Hall
Bridgeport, CT 06611

Dear Mr. Ackerson:

transmittal function[a]

As you requested in your letter of 10 May, we conducted a study on the technical, environmental, and economic aspects of highway deicing salts. Here is our report.

Summary

informational purpose[b]

Since the early 1960s, deicing salts have been extensively used as a method of snow and ice removal. In recent years many adverse environmental and economic impacts have been found to result from the use of deicing salts. The impacts include damage to roadside vegetation, contamination of surface water and groundwater supplies, disruption of acquatic ecosystems and the corrosion of automobiles, highway structures, and the underground utilities. It has been estimated that the cost and application of deicing salts and the resulting damage amounts to close to $3 billion annually.

Technical, Environmental, and Economic Aspects

Each year snow and ice storms in the snow belt states disrupt daily activities and create emergency conditions in both rural and urban areas. Public officials are forced to determine how much of their resources should be devoted to highway snow and ice removal and what techniques should be used.

Deicing Salts

Deicing salts began to be used extensively for highway snow and ice removal in the early 1960s. Sodium chloride (NaCl) and calcium chloride (CaCl) are the most widely used salts. When applied to snow and ice, NaCl and CaCl bore and penetrate the snow and ice surface, lower the freezing point of water, allowing the resulting brine solution to spread out over the highway and weaken the bond between the ice and the road.

---

[a]The first paragraph "transmits" the information contained in the rest of the letter. It performs essentially the same function as does the letter of transmittal in a long, formal report.
[b]This is an informational report only. It does not provide interpretation, conclusions, or recommendations.

EXHIBIT 4.12
An External Letter Report (continued)

```
            Mr. Craig Ackerson
            July 1, 19xx
            Page 2


            Environmental Impacts

            The environmental impacts of highway deicing salts include
            destruction of roadside soils and vegetation, contamination of
            surface and ground water supplies, and the disruption of aquatic
            ecosystems.

            Economic Impacts

            Adverse economic impacts of highway deicing salts include the
            cost to improve or replace contaminated water supplies, damaged
            vegetation, corroded automobiles and highway structures, and
            damaged underground utilities.

            Sincerely,

            Scott Olson

            Scott Olson
            Information Clearinghouse
```

CLASSIFICATION BY PRESENTATION

Reports may be presented either in written or oral form, or the reports may require both kinds of presentation.

Written Reports

Written reports generally require more careful preparation than oral reports. Because written reports are permanent records, report writers and readers tend to pay closer attention to them. Written reports tend to be more formal than oral reports. It is especially important that written reports be accurate, clear, complete, impartial, and objective. They should be written for a particular audience and serve a definite purpose.

Oral Reports

Most oral reports in business are impromptu and require little or no specific preparation. Others, however, are more formal and require every bit as much preparation as a written report. In fact, many situations in business call for an oral report supplemented by written information or for a written report supplemented by an oral presentation. You might, for example, be asked to present your written report orally to your colleagues, to higher management, to the board of trustees, to the community, or to a professional association. In some ways, presenting the information orally is easier than presenting it in written form because you need not be concerned with spelling, punctuation, and the mechanics of writing. On the other hand, the oral presentation requires careful attention to body language—facial expressions, body posture, hand movements, eye movements, and breathing. Oral presentations will be discussed further in Chapter 17.

SUMMARY

Every business and organization prepares a report of one kind or another. These reports will vary from organization to organization depending on the purpose of the report and the practices of the organization. Reports can be classified according to function, time intervals, length, importance, subject, reader-writer relationship, and presentation. The basic classification of reports is by function. As such, reports are informational, interpretative, or analytical. Reports classified by time intervals are periodic, progress, and special. Periodic reports are prepared regularly—daily, weekly, monthly, quarterly, or annually. Progress reports explain what has happened in the past on a project during a particular period of time and what can be expected in the future. Special reports are generally prepared on a one-time only basis. Reports can also be classified by length—long or short. Generally, reports ten pages or fewer are short.

When classified by importance, reports can be routine, important, or critical. Routine reports are those written on a regular basis to provide information that may become useful but is not of immediate importance. Important reports are those that need to be considered or acted upon within a short time. Critical reports are those that need to be acted upon immediately, generally within 24 to 48 hours.

Another common method for classifying reports is through major divisions and subdivisions of subject matter. Still another means of classifying reports is by reader-writer relationship—either internal or external. Finally, reports may be presented in written or oral form, or the reports may require both written and oral presentations.

EXERCISES

Review Questions

1. Why do report classifications vary from one operation to another?

2. Explain the differences among the reports classified according to function.

3. Which reports are classified by time intervals?

4. What is a progress report?

5. What are special reports?

6. Explain the differences between internal reports and external reports.

7. What is the difference between short reports and long reports?

8. What kinds of reports are classified by importance?

9. State the reason(s) each of the reports included as exhibits in this chapter has been classified in a particular way.

Problems

1. Visit three local businesses and request sample reports. In a memo to your instructor, classify the reports on the basis of each of the classifications presented in this chapter.

2. Prepare a daily report for one week on how you spent your time (school, work, study, recreation). Make recommendations to yourself.

3. Write a progress report on your assignments in a particular class.

CHAPTER 5
Report Forms

Just as you wear different clothes depending on the activity you're engaged in and on whom you're with, reports have different appearances—forms—depending on the job they must perform and on the relationship between the reader and writer.

Topics

Informal Reports
Formal Reports
Parts of the Formal Report

INFORMAL REPORTS

Informal reports generally convey routine information and do not contain the prefatory parts (letter of acceptance, letter of transmittal, table of contents, abstract) or supplemental parts (bibliography, appendix, and index) found in formal reports. Because these prefatory and supplemental parts are not used and the information is routine, the writing style is also informal. Informal reports can be presented in memorandum or letter form.

Memorandum Reports

A memorandum report is used to convey routine information from one employee to another in the same organization. Because businesses and industries use memorandums for messages to workers within their organization, they are called interoffice memorandums or memos, for short. Memo reports are the company's major medium for internal written communication. Although a rare memo might require several pages, memorandum reports are usually neither so formal nor so long as letter reports. They can, in fact, be only one line long.

8 October 19xx

TO: Jean Burke

FROM: Jack Plano

SUBJECT: February Sales

Great job, Jean. You earned your bonus this month.

Because memo reports remain within your own organization, they use a standardized, informal format. Instead of a letterhead, printed across the top of the memo stationery, and usually in all capital letters, are the words: OFFICE MEMORANDUM, INTEROFFICE MEMORANDUM, or INTEROFFICE CORRESPONDENCE.

    Unlike letters, which use the formal inside address, salutation, complimentary close, and typed signature; memos provide four informal, printed headings: DATE, TO, FROM, and SUBJECT. While the arrangement and design may vary among companies, these four headings appear on most forms. Printing of the heading lines is either vertical or horizontal, depending on your company's preferences.

Horizontal Placements:

TO:	DATE:
FROM:	SUBJECT:

Vertical Placement:
DATE:
TO:
FROM:
SUBJECT:

You may want to include other printed headings, such as department, branch, location, or room number. Even the words *message* or *body* may be printed on the memo form to indicate where the memo message is to begin. Optional parts of the memo are the signature, reference initials, and enclosure and copy notations.

The current date appears after the "Date" line. Even though the memo report is informal, do not use all figures for the month.

Oct 14, 19xx
October 14, 19xx
14 Oct 19xx
14 October 19xx

When no printed date line is provided, type the date (omitting the word *date*) a double space after the memo heading, INTEROFFICE MEMORANDUM, or type it several spaces above the "To" line.

The name of the addressee appears after the "To" line. You may use courtesy titles (Mr., Mrs., Miss, Ms.) or professional titles (Dr.) or omit them depending on your company's preferences. A good rule to follow is this: If you use a title when talking with that individual, use a title in the memo. If you are writing to an executive of the company or to a person of a higher rank than you, you might want to use his or her title even if you are on a first-name basis when talking informally.

When an organization is large enough to warrant further identification or clarification, use department names or job titles after the name in the "To" line. If you address the memo to several people within the organization, then "See Below" appears after the "To" line. List the names of the individuals at the end of the message in alphabetical order or in rank order—president, vice-president, and so forth.

If you want to send the memo report to a particular group of people and the group is so large that it would be impossible to list all the names, then the "To" is followed by the group's identifying classification, such as "Department Heads," "Employees," or "Faculty and Staff."

When writing the memo report, place your own name after the "From" line. Do not use a courtesy title unless you are a woman and particularly concerned about how others address you: Ms., Miss, or Mrs. If you feel, however, that the reader would not know you, use your job title or department name after your name. For example:

From: Linda Lindauer, Controller
From: Gregg Houfly, Accounting Department

Although the writer's name on the "From" line makes a typed or written signature unnecessary, you may prefer to personalize your memo report or show that you have read the typed message. You may sign memos requiring authentication. If you wish to sign your name, place your handwritten initials above, below, or to the right of your typed name on the "From" line.

The "Subject" line is a brief and concise statement telling the reader at a glance what the memo is about. For example:

Subject: A Survey of Employee Qualifications
Subject: Third-Quarter Report

Because the "Subject" line immediately tells what the memo report is about, it also aids in filing the report.

After the text of the report has been presented, the typist places the initial of her or his last name a double space below the last line of the report. If several typists in the office have the same last initial, the typist should use the initials of her or his full name.

If enclosures or attachments are included with the memo report, reference is made to them by typing the words, *Enclosure, enc,* or *att* a double space below the reference initial. When several enclosures or attachments are included with the report, provide a specific list of them.

att   List of employees who participated in the survey
      Line chart showing the salary increases over a five-year span

Names of persons receiving copies of the memo report are typed below the enclosure notation. If several persons are to receive copies of the report, place their names in alphabetical order or in rank order after the copy notation. For example:

c   Tom Bieterman
    Vic Donahue
    Carrie Henderson

c   Malcolm McLean, President
    Ray Thoma, Vice-President
    Shannon Coyle, Treasurer

When a memo report contains more than one page, the heading for the second and succeeding pages begins one inch from the top edge of the paper. The memo headings are the same as those used for business letters; namely, addressee's name, date, and page number. Use either the horizontal or vertical (block) style.

Addressee's Name   Date   2
or
Addressee's Name
Date
Page 2

EXHIBIT 5.1
A Memorandum Report

```
                        INTEROFFICE CORRESPONDENCE

        November 24, 19xx

        TO:      R. T. Bloom

        FROM:    D. J. Baseler

        SUBJECT: SLIDE FILE


        Here's the report you requested on the costs involved in putting your slides
        in the existing file.

        1.  Software Development
            The file will have to be reprogrammed to enable use of an interactive
            terminal to search for a slide number.  By knowing at least two param-
            eters (such as requestor, date, division, etc.), you can use the terminal
            to determine specific slide numbers, no matter whether they are yours or
            ours.  Estimated programming cost is $5,000, and we propose that we split
            this cost.

        2.  Terminal Lease
            If you don't have access to a terminal, lease cost would be about $125
            a month.

        3.  Slide Insertion
            The cost of keypunching, verifying and inserting slides into the file is
            about $50 for each 500 slides.

        4.  Storage and Use
            Storage costs are about $2.00 a month.  Each time you do a search in the
            file, the cost is about $2.50.

        Assuming you have about 5,000 slides, the initial cost to put them in the file
        would be about $3,000.  Then annual upkeep would be about $2,200, including
        terminal lease, storage, and one search a day.

        This does not include your labor costs to sort and catalog the slides.  I'd
        suggest you consider using temporary help to do the initial job (5,000 slides
        will probably take about two to three months), then train someone on your
        staff to maintain the file.

        We're all ready to start on the software development, so we would appreciate
        your reactions as soon as possible.
```

Triple space below the heading and continue with the memo report. Exhibits 5.1 and 5.2 illustrate memorandum reports.

Letter Reports

The letter report is an external means of conveying information between organizations. Letter reports generally are more carefully organized and longer than typical business letters; they are formal, factual,

EXHIBIT 5.2

A Memorandum Report

routine heading[a]

outline form[b]

December 21, 19xx

TO: A. Hamilton

FROM: B. Kramer

MONTHLY REPORT

Here's the monthly report that you requested.

  I. Advertising
      A. Print schedule for January 1980:

          Commercial Car Journal   Fleet Owner
          Heavy Duty Trucking   Refrigerated Transporter
          Diesel Equip. Supt.   Fleet Maintenance & Spec.
          Construction Equipment   Highway & Heavy Const.
          Construction   Dixie Contractor
          Bus & Truck Transport   Motor Truck
          Fleet Specialist   Heavy Duty Distribution

      B. Radio schedule of January 1980:
          Weeks of January 7 and 21.
      C. Specific projects:
          1. Negotiated to share all 1980 covers in Commercial Car Journal
              and Heavy Duty Distribution with Freightliner and IHC, respec-
              tively.
          2. Product, Parts, and Business ads are in copy approval or pro-
              duction stage. Construction ad is in planning stage.
 II. Direct Mail
      A. First scheduled mailing is construction brochure in March.
      B. JWT is developing direct mail brochures for Construction and Fuel
          Economy. Brochure on RT-6610/6613 is in planning stage.
III. Sales Promotion
      A. Literature
          1. Shipments included 132 paid orders and 135 miscellaneous orders.
              We are two months behind on answering ad inquiries (approximately
              1000 inquiries).
          2. Ford/China Engineering sheets and Engineering Reference Book
              sheets have been printed.
          3. Mack/Fuller dealer brochure is being revised for the third time.
          4. Revision of 1157 sales sheets is in production.
      B. Audio Visual
          1. Slide production--252 original slides produced (this includes
              storyboards, art work, photography, processing, mounting, and
              filing).
          2. Other production included parts shots for Research, prints for
              Ford PRC Program, scripts for IHC Peru presentation by TCM, and
              publicity shots of visiting disc jockeys.

---

[a]The reader of this report obviously expects it and is familiar with its contents. Either the subject line or the first normally clarifies the purpose of a report.

[b]Note that this report consists primarily of lists of things. Many business reports—especially routine, periodic reports—follow this practice.

EXHIBIT 5.2

A Memorandum Report (continued)

A. Hamilton   December 21, 19xx   2

    3. Productions in progress:
      a. In-house productions include White Motor Installation
         program, Nissan Diesel slides for L. Matsuura, GMC presen-
         tation for J. Way, and Engineering Presentations for R. Denes.
         These are scheduled for completion in January.
      b. RT-9508--Jaqua Company--rough script is completed, will be
         reviewed January 8. Completion date--March 1980.
      c. Drive Instruction programs--script revision in progress.
         Completion date--February 1980.
      d. RTO-1157--Bradshaw Advertising--initial concept and budget
         being developed--ready for review by January 10. Completion
         date--March 1980.
      e. GMC Movie--initial outline approved and scripting in progress.
         Completion date--May 1980.
      f. RT-9509--all material complete except binders. Will be
         shipped first week of January.
      g. New model slides--being revised to add latest information.
         Ready in January.
    4. NOTE: Since June 1, 1975, original slides have been produced
      in-house--an average of almost 200 a month.
IV. Trade Shows
    A. First trade show of 1980 is ConAG in Houston, January 27-31. Hugh
      Sprague plans to attend.
    B. All displays are being coordinated with TCM. Specifically, the
      Fuller Parts panel is being redone.
V. Miscellaneous
    A. Personnel--transition of Product Literature and Marketing Communi-
      cations people is progressing satisfactorily.
    B. TCM Coordination--objectives have been established for slides,
      flipcharts, and direct mail. A task force (Shedden from TCM,
      Johnson from Axle, Passage from Brake, and Baseler from Trans-
      mission) has been formed to establish specific guidelines and
      formats. First meeting is January 9 in Southfield.
    C. New Building--Serge Caillet hopes to have time in January to work
      on design of conference rooms and A-V facilities. A consultant
      has been recommended and has had an initial meeting with us.
VI. Next Month (in addition to what's listed above)
    A. Establish guidelines for specialty program and begin search for
      specific items.
    B. Work closely with JWT to improve its service.
    C. Reorganize handling of purchase orders and invoices.
    D. Catch up on all literature requests.
    E. Begin cataloging of all slides for computer entry.
    F. Review copier requirements for cost-savings, quality, and efficiency.

---

and use basic report writing techniques, such as headings, itemizations, tables, and figures.

The primary objective of letter reports is to provide reliable, objective information. Common letter reports are used for personnel references, letters of recommendation, credit evaluations, and auditor recommendations.

Although letter reports are generally longer (three or four pages) than the regular business letter, they use the same format as illustrated in Exhibits 3.1–3.3. Exhibit 5.3 illustrates a typical letter report.

EXHIBIT 5.3

A Letter Report

May 9, 19xx

Ms. Alice Mitchell
Assistant Vice-President
Business Credit Incorporated
220 South Michigan Avenue
Columbus, OH 43215

Dear Ms. Mitchell:

Thank you and Mr. Denando for meeting with me on March 24 when we discussed the programming specifications for Business Credit Incorporated (BCI) to report consumer credit information to Bass Credit Data.

While discussing some of the specifications we agreed upon with some of BCI's user banks, several problems and questions were raised. I believe that the following concerns require further discussion and must be resolved before I can provide you with definitive program specifications. I am hoping that a meeting between BCI, Bass, and representatives from the major banks on the BCI system can be arranged within the next few weeks to discuss these items.

letter report defined[a]

Account Number

Some banks have expressed concern over the type of account number that would be reported to and maintained by Bass. These banks know that a certain level of security would be provided if Bass were to display an account number of the credit report that is different from the customer's true account number. Because such "scrambled" account numbers would not present a problem to the banks or BCI when verifying account information or when making purchase authorizations, Bass's security department would allow "scrambled" account numbers in Bass's file. Our understanding is that these numbers will remain the same from month to month instead of being "rescrambled" each month. Bass's security department also conducts fraud seminars which would enable BCI's users to further curtail fraud.

One of my concerns is about the account number changes planned for BCI for some time this year. As we discussed, Bass would like to begin receiving update tapes from BCI before the fourth quarter of 1980. The account number change should be accomplished before reporting to Bass is initiated to prevent account number changes within Bass's system.

If your account number change is not accomplished before the fourth quarter of 19xx, however, the banks' accounts should still be reported to Bass with the old account numbers. Then, when the new account number is assigned, it can be reported to Bass's E1 segment, which is specifically designed to effect account number changes within Bass's file. The format and use of the E1 segment will be discussed if it becomes necessary.

Status Code

We decided to report Bass status code 97 (charge off) for all accounts with a BCI status of "O". Since then I have learned from the banks that this would be improper because an "O" account might have previously had a rating

---

[a]Any letter using headings, tables, charts, or other report writing techniques is technically a letter report.

EXHIBIT 5.3
A Letter Report (continued)

Ms. Alice Mitchell   May 9, 19xx   2

of "F" (fraud). If such accounts were reported as charge off, we in effect would be penalizing the customer who might merely be the victim of the fraud. Therefore, some consideration should be given to preventing fraud charge offs from being reported as charge offs. Perhaps this could be accomplished by using a BCI status other than "O" to denote fraud charge offs.

The automated reporting of charged off accounts should be pursued even though most banks would agree to report their charge offs manually. The reason is that Bass's central file actually consists of two independent files. One contains account balance information reported by balance contributors such as BCI. The other file contains exception information reported by exception and manually reporting subscribers. Therefore, if a bank manually reports a charged off account, the balance information previously reported by BCI for that same account could not be updated, but rather, a separate transaction would be established on the file. The account would then appear in Bass's file twice, once as a charge off and again with whatever status was last reported by BCI for that account.

Another status code I am concerned about is 03 (lost or stolen card). We thought that status code 03 should be reported for all accounts with a BCI status of "L" (lost), "S" (stolen), "C" (counterfeit), or "F" (fraud). This is unsatisfactory to the banks because a new account number is not always assigned to such an account, in which case the status 03 would simply overlay any status code previously reported for the account. This would make it possible for a delinquent customer with some knowledge of credit reporting to report a lost or stolen card and have his or her delinquent history erased from Bass's file. Keep in mind that since the customer is delinquent, the bank would usually not issue a new account number to this customer, and no further reporting of that customer would occur.

As was mentioned earlier, manually reported information will not update the automated information reported by BCI. So again, we should try to eliminate the need for the banks to report status code 03 manually.

One possibility that some banks agreed to was the automated reporting of status code 03 for all accounts with status "L," "S," "C," or "F" when the balance of the account is zero. We thought that this would be safe because the customer would probably not be trying to subterfuge the intent of the reporting system if he or she had a zero balance. Most of these accounts would then be issued a new account number which would be reported to Bass.

On the other hand, those accounts with a status of "L," "S," "C," or "F" and with a balance greater than zero could be reported with a special comment code "S" which will result in the message "Special Handling--Contact Sub- scriber If Additional Information Required" on the credit report. Of course, this special comment code could be reported along with the appropriate status code (current or delinquent). The accounts should be reported in the above manner each month until the accounts reach a zero balance, at which time they could be reported with status code 03.

EXHIBIT 5.3
A Letter Report (continued)

Ms. Alice Mitchell   May 9, 19xx   3

Transaction Type Code

The most important transaction code that will be used by the BCI credit
reporting program will be transaction type code 1. This code indicates a
new account and is required for Bass to establish a new account in our files.

We tentatively thought that transaction type code 1 would be determined for
all new accounts on each monthly update tape by the date opened. This method,
however, will not work for accounts issued new account numbers due to a lost
or stolen card because the original date opened of the account is retained.

Therefore, some consideration should be given to the ability to distinguish
these replacement accounts from new accounts so that they can be properly
reported and established by Bass.

Amount

One major bank on the BCI system has expressed reluctance to report the
credit limits of its accounts. In the interest of keeping the program specifications as straightforward as possible and to establish a meaningful information exchange between all credit grantors, this information should be
reported to Bass. Currently no Bass subscribers withhold this information.

Special Comment Code

Currently, your system is not capable of detecting disputed accounts. Again,
in the interest of avoiding manual reporting by the banks, we should establish
a disputed account indicator to enable BCI to report special comment code "X"
or "Y" to produce the "Account in Dispute--Reported by Subscriber" message on
the credit report. These special comment codes can be reported manually as a
last resort.

Originally, we thought that Bass's special comment code "L" could be reported
for all accounts with a BCI status of "B" (blocked), "W" (wild), and possibly
"H" (hold). When a special comment code "L" is reported, the message "Credit
Line Closed--Reported by Subscriber" will appear on the credit report. We
thought the use of this code would provide additional information about the
account but would still allow the appropriate status code (current or delinquent) to be reported as opposed to Bass status code 20 (credit line closed,
reason unknown or by customer request) or 90 (credit line closed, not paying
as agreed) which would not indicate whether the account is current or delinquent.

I later learned that BCI status codes "B," "W," and "H" are not used uniformly
by all BCI banks. This voids the above conclusions. I hope that we can agree
on how and when to use which codes at our next meeting.

EXHIBIT 5.3
A Letter Report (continued)

Ms. Alice Mitchell   May 9, 19xx   4

I am looking forward to meeting with you and the banks' representatives at
2:00 p.m. on May 19.

Sincerely,

Donald L. Moorman
Senior Analyst
Bass Credit Data

e

c Adam Borcher--First National Bank in Columbus
   Leslie Hall--Ohio National Bank
   Richard Reddy--First National Bank of Cincinnati
   Zeke Zelner--Mercantile Trust Company N.A.

FORMAL REPORTS

Formal reports can be either short or long. Generally, short reports (fewer than ten pages) are informal and long reports (11 pages or more) are formal, although this is not always true because short reports can be presented formally. As a rule, short reports, whether informal or formal, are single-spaced. Long reports are always double-spaced.

Short Formal Reports

A short formal report uses some—but generally not all—of the major divisions of a long report, such as prefatory parts, report proper, and supplementary parts. These divisions are explained below. Exhibit 5.4 illustrates a short formal report with a title page and letter of transmittal.

Long Formal Reports

A long formal report is similar to the short formal report except in length. Long reports usually deal with more complex problems than short reports and, therefore, require greater attention to organization and logical presentation so that the reader can assimilate the material easily.

PARTS OF THE FORMAL REPORT

Although the organization of long formal reports may vary from one company to another, the formal report parts presented in this chapter are considered acceptable and desirable by most readers and organizations.

The following report parts, listed in the order in which they normally appear, are generally found in long formal, analytical reports. Depending on the requirements, complexity, and formality of the report, some of these parts may be omitted.

When your company does not provide specific guidelines, choose those parts that will best communicate the information you want to convey.

Major Divisions

Formal reports contain three major divisions: prefatory parts, report body, and supplementary parts. Each of these divisions contains several subdivisions.

Prefatory Parts
    Cover
    Title Fly
    Title Page
    Letter of Authorization

Prefatory Parts

The prefatory parts of a report include the cover, title fly, title page, letter of authorization, letter of acceptance, letter of transmittal, table of contents, table of illustrations, and abstract.

Cover The purpose of the cover sheet is to identify and protect the report. The cover contains the title of the report and the author's name. When a title is more than one line long, it should be typed in inverted pyramid style:

The Feasibility of the Restoration of the
Water Tower on the East Campus of
Clemson University

The report title should be accurate, clear, concise, complete, and descriptive. Whenever possible, it should answer who, what, when, where, why, and how. The title should not include such words or phrases as "a study of," "a report of," or "a survey of."

Title Fly The title fly merely carries the title of the report. It is generally considered unnecessary and omitted in typewritten reports.

Title Page The title page carries (1) the name or title of the report; (2) the name, title, and address of the person, group, or organization of the intended reader of the report; (3) the name, title, and address of the person, group, or organization writing the report; and (4) the date of presentation. The words, "Prepared for" or "Submitted for," or "Prepared by" or "Submitted by" often precede the names. Although the title page may be prepared in a variety of ways, the generally accepted format has the title of the report typed in all capital letters and

EXHIBIT 5.4
A Sample Short Report

title page[a]

A PRACTICAL GUIDE FOR SELECTING VISUAL AIDS

Prepared for

Ms. Opal Klammer

Director of Corporate Communication

Fine Arts Company

2030 Wallace Street

Johnson City, TX 37601

Prepared by

Mr. Pat Lemanski

Research Director

Eaton Corporation

January 26, 19xx

[a]Title page (see pp. 73–74 for a complete description).

EXHIBIT 5.4
A Sample Short Report (continued)

letter of transmittal

EATON CORPORATION
Public Relations Department
3802 Karl Avenue
Rochester, NY 14610

January 26, 19xx

Ms. Opal Klammer
Director of Corporate Communication
Fine Arts Company
2030 Wallace Street
Johnson City, TX 37601

Dear Ms. Klammer:

opening[b]

Here's the report on the visual aids that you requested on January 15, 19xx.

The report covers 35mm carousel projects, poster boards, flipcharts, overhead projectors, display boards, chalkboards, and opaque projectors.

summary[c]

The information on these items should help you make a decision about which would be best for your needs.

Let us know when we can help again.

closing[d]

Cordially,

Pat Lemanski

Pat Lemanski
Research Director

enc

[b]The first paragraph "transmits" the report.
[c]In short reports, the letter of transmittal almost always contains a brief summary of the report contents.
[d]Letters of transmittal usually conclude with an offer to help again in the future.

EXHIBIT 5.4

A Sample Short Report (continued)

ECONOMICAL GUIDELINES FOR THE USE OF VISUAL AIDS

To use audio visuals economically and yet effectively to make presentations
to internal or external audiences, several primary factors should first be
determined:

    What is the message to be conveyed?
    What is the composition of the audience?
    What part of the message lends itself to visualization?
    What equipment lends itself best to the message and the audience?
    How can the appropriate equipment be procured and used?

Deliberately excluded in this list that follows are the more expensive techniques such as video, motion pictures, and multimedia efforts, which presently
can be justified only under circumstances that clearly call for their use.
Techniques are listed generally in order of total expense--the costliest
equipment-plus-material first.

This presentation is necessarily limited in scope, but, particularly in Eaton
locations away from World Headquarters, it can serve as a useful guide in the
absence of on-the-spot professional counsel.

To seek further information, guidance, or advice as to techniques, vendors,
and the like, feel free to call Thomas R. Tucker, manager of visual media
services. With his associates, he will be happy to provide any additional
counsel desired--by phone, letter, or personally.

---

centered two inches from the top edge of the paper. It has a two-inch
bottom margin, and all lines between the top and bottom margins are
centered and spaced equally.

Letter of Authorization   The letter or memorandum of authorization
is written by the person who requests or authorizes the report. It states
the problem, the scope, and limitations of the report. The letter of

EXHIBIT 5.4

A Sample Short Report (continued)

illustrated format[e]

2

VISUAL AIDS: DESCRIPTIONS

35mm Carousel Projectors

A 35mm carousel projector is probably the
most effective method (within these guidelines) to present material, particularly
to a large audience. It is a highly flexible technique and offers the widest range
for both graphic design and ease of projection.

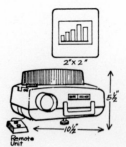

To present the most readable on-screen
image, 35mm slides should be prepared in
a 2" x 3" (horizontal) format. Vertical
slides should be avoided, if possible,
because they diminish the appearance of
uniformity and continuity. They will also
bleed off the top and bottom of the projection screen when the screen is set for
horizontal slides, thus losing considera-
ble detail.

For better readability and retention, the
less information placed on each slide the
better. If a substantial amount of information (especially financial data) is
required, it is best to separate it into
units so that the material can be shown
as a series, each part on a single slide
containing one section of the total data.

Projection is generally accomplished by throwing the image forward from the
center or rear of the room. If space permits, however, the image can be made
more effective and unobtrusive by using rear-screen projection. Using this
method, the path of projection is from behind the screen, which separates and
hides the projector from the audience.

Costs can be minimized by (1) providing sufficient time for examining data to
be used, (2) keeping the material on each slide simple and at a minimum, and
(3) allowing enough time for preparation (several days at least).

The average cost of producing a quality 35mm slide is $20, but, depending on
its complexity, it can reach $35 or $40. Duplicate slides can be produced
for about 65¢ each.

[e]Note the specialized format, which permits the parallel presentation of the text and
the accompanying illustrations.

Source: Courtesy of Eaton Corporation

EXHIBIT 5.4

A Sample Short Report (continued)

3

Poster Boards

Poster boards are almost identical in design to flipcharts. But instead of paper pads, cardboard posters are used (such as those used in COMM/PRO presentations). These can be prepared in advance, mounted on easels or even attached to walls with push pins or tape.

For more complex presentations, large acetate sheets can be hinged to the front of a board, dropped behind it, then brought forward and placed on top of the basic design as an overlay to add another step or more information to these basic data on the first sheet. China marking pencils can also be used to emphasize points--or even to make last minute changes.

Posters are available in a range of colors and textures. Standard sizes (20" x 24") cost approximately 65¢ a sheet. Simple sketches or drawings can be added for approximately $8 a sheet.

Flipcharts

A flipchart is simply a large pad of paper mounted on a movable easel.

Ideally, information or illustrations to be used should be sketched lightly with pencil on the paper prior to the presentation. Then, during the program, a felt tip marker can be used to trace the penciled lines. This technique can also serve as a personal reminder for the speaker.

If simple art sketches or drawings are required rather than freehand sketches, they can be professionally done directly on the pad for approximately $8 a page.

Overhead Projectors

An overhead projector is approximately twice the size of 35mm projectors. It uses 10" x 10" acetate transparencies projected upward from a flat glass surface above the light source. The transparencies are then reflected onto a screen from an obliquely positioned mirror held on a metal arm extending upward from the equipment.

authorization also serves as a notice that the report writer prepared and presented the report as directed. Most companies prefer to omit the letter of authorization from all but the most formal reports.

Letter of Acceptance   The letter of acceptance is the reply to the letter of authorization. It accepts the request to conduct the study and prepare the report. It restates the problem, the scope, and limitations of

EXHIBIT 5.4
A Sample Short Report (continued)

4

Key points can be discussed by using a pointer on the transparency itself without interfering with the path of projection.

The machinery is light in weight, operates quietly, and offers a bright image for easy viewing even in a fully lighted room. It also has great flexibility and can readily project line drawings, standard typewriter copy, and a variety of graphic designs, all of which can be produced on Xerox equipment.

Display Boards

Display boards, similar to blackboards, can be obtained with flannel or magnetic surfaces. Hooks, in place or added later, can also be used to hold and display materials such as three-dimensional objects.

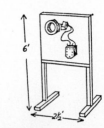

Posters of varying sizes can be sketched or drawn in advance on a variety of colored stock.

Illustration costs are similar to that of displays such as flipcharts and poster boards.

Chalkboards

Standard fixed chalkboards are generally green in tone, which aids visibility. Portable roll-around chalkboards provide additional opportunities for flexibility--and the imaginative use of multicolor chalks, stencils, chalk compasses, and the like can result in very informal and effective presentations.

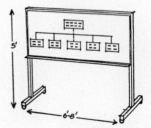

The cost for these materials is minimal.

Opaque Projectors

Opaque projectors project any opaque material (as distinct from transparencies): book pages, line drawings, blueprints, drawings, typewritten copy, and the like. This projector is much larger and more cumbersome than overhead projectors, although some newer models are slightly more compact.

This equipment's light source is bounced downward onto the flat-surface material,

the report as presented in the letter of authorization. It may confirm time limitations, fees, expenses, and other contractual agreements. The letter of acceptance is usually omitted from the report.

Letter of Transmittal   The letter of transmittal, or covering letter, accompanies the finished report to the reader and is prepared after the report is completed. The letter begins with an appropriate reference to

EXHIBIT 5.4

A Sample Short Report (continued)

5

reflected upward at an angle onto an obliquely positioned mirror, then projected onto the screen. Its image quality is not so sharp as the other
equipment. Consequently, it requires (1) the size of the audience be
relatively small, (2) the meeting room be darkened, and (3) the distance
to the screen be minimal (7-10 feet). Points to be made to the audience
can also be indicated by the built-in illuminated arrow directly on the
material as it is being projected.

the transmission of the report and to the letter of authorization. For
example:

Formal: As you requested in your letter of May 5, here is the report on . . .

Informal: Here's the report you asked me to prepare on . . .

The letter of transmittal may also include the title of the report, the
scope, the limitations, the procedure or methodology used, and ac-
knowledgments of assistance given by others. If the report does not

contain a separate abstract (or synopsis), the letter of transmittal should include major findings, conclusions, and recommendations.

The letter should end on a positive note—usually an expression of appreciation for the opportunity to do the report (an opportunity to learn or appreciation for the business, if an outside consultant), and an offer to do a similar assignment in the future.

Table of Contents   Prepare the contents page after the report has been typed and page numbers are known. The table of contents shows the organization of the report. It is the report outline and, as such, it lists the report headings exactly as they appear in the report. The table of contents serves as a guide to the reader because it lists the beginning page numbers of the major headings and subheadings of the report. It helps the reader locate information.

When typing the table of contents, center the heading, CONTENTS, (it is not necessary to type the words *table of* because it is obviously a table) in solid capital letters two inches from the top edge of the paper. The contents page may be single- or double-spaced, depending on its length.

Because the prefatory parts precede the table of contents, they should not be included. List the abstract (synopsis) first, if one is prepared separately, because it follows immediately after the contents page.

Next, type at the left margin all the major headings and subheadings of the report, preferably preceded by their outline symbols. Use leaders—a line of alternating periods and spaces—to guide the reader to the page number. Leaders are not necessary when the contents page is short. The supplemental parts of the report—appendix, bibliography, and index—are listed without outline symbols because they are not part of the report proper.

Table (or List) of Illustrations   When a report contains graphic aids (Table 1, Table 2, Figure 1, Figure 2, Exhibit 1, Exhibit 2 and so forth) a table of illustrations will help the reader locate them. When a sufficient number of each type of graphic aid is presented in the report, list each type separately (list of tables and a list of figures). When the list of illustrations is short, type it on the table of contents page provided that particular page has ample space. Otherwise, type it on a separate page immediately following the contents page.

Abstract   The abstract (or synopsis or summary) is a brief overview of the entire report; it is the report in miniature. Include one when your report is five pages or longer so that your reader won't have to read the complete report. The purpose of the abstract is to give the busy reader a quick overview of the report. Because it is a summary, the abstract is prepared after the report is completed. It should be about 10 percent of the length of the original report, but no longer than one full page. The abstract should state the problem, the scope, the limitations, the methodology used, the main ideas in the report, the conclusions drawn, and the recommendations made.

The abstract may use either the deductive (conclusions, recommendations, purpose, methodology, findings) pattern of organization or the inductive (purpose, methodology, findings, conclusions, and recommendations) pattern. When the abstract is short, it may be included in the letter of transmittal; it is, however, usually typed separately. The abstract is used frequently for oral presentations.

Two types of abstracts are descriptive (topical) and summarizing (informational). Descriptive abstracts tell only what the report is about, as does the table of contents. Summarizing abstracts are more useful than descriptive abstracts because they summarize the main ideas of the report. They briefly tell the reader what the report says.

Descriptive Language: This report contains information about oil production in Mexico.

Summarizing Language: Oil production in Mexico has increased 32 percent over the past five years.

Body of the Report

The body of the report consists of the introduction, the text, the conclusions, and the recommendations.

The Introduction   The introduction *introduces* the reader to the text of the report. Because the introduction begins the report, the title appears first on the page. Type the complete title two inches from the top edge of the paper in inverted pyramid style.

In the introduction, you should answer the questions *who, what, when, where,* and *why.* You answer these questions by giving the background of the problem, stating the problem clearly, defining the scope, and detailing the limitations of the study.

The introduction also answers the *how* question. How did you conduct the investigation? You answer this question by explaining the method of research and the sources and procedures used to gather the data for your report. When a review of the related literature will help the reader understand the problem, it should also be included in the introduction.

Presentation of data in the introduction and the report as a whole can be either deductive or inductive. The deductive—direct—plan introduces the report by presenting the conclusions and recommendations first and then presents the findings. The inductive—indirect—method of presentation gives the background information first, followed by the findings and finally the conclusions and recommendations.

The Text The text of the report follows the introduction. It is the heart and bulk of the report. It includes the findings section, the part of the report that presents, analyzes, and interprets the information the investigator has gathered. Whenever possible, the report writer discusses the important facts and findings of the report and shows their relationships with each other.

To aid the report writer in presenting the data, headings, subheadings, itemizations, and graphic aids are used.

Conclusions and Recommendations The conclusions and recommendations follow the findings section of the report when the indirect pattern of organization is used. With the direct approach, the conclusions and recommendations follow immediately after the introduction. This latter method is being used more frequently today so that the busy executive who receives many reports daily may quickly read through the conclusions and recommendations and make a decision, or decide to read the entire report for complete details.

Some report writers prefer to use separate sections for conclusions and recommendations to avoid confusion about which were the conclusions and which were the recommendations. Also, some writers prefer separate sections because conclusions are objective (factual statements) whereas recommendations are personal opinions (value judgments) based on the conclusions.

Whether they appear in one section or two, the conclusions and recommendations provide the answers to the problem statement in the introduction. While all analytical reports will have conclusions, not all will have recommendations. Conclusions are drawn and recommendations are made on the basis of the findings of the report. No new material should be presented in the conclusions and recommendations section of the report.

To help you present the conclusions and recommendations and so that you can refer to them by number, itemize and number the items in each category and follow the rules for parallel construction. Also, as an aid to the reader, provide reference page numbers after each item. Then, if your readers wish to refer to the discussion in the text, they have an immediate page reference.

Supplemental Parts

The supplemental parts of the report are the appendix, the bibliography, and the index.

The Appendix The appendix is the place for supplemental information which the reader would consider either too detailed or not important for understanding the report. The appendix supports the body of the report. It usually contains copies of the cover letter and questionnaire used in a survey, elaborate formulas, a glossary of terms, interview schedules, sample forms, statistical computations, computer printouts, and any additional information that would be of interest to the reader.

Although tables and figures should be placed in the text to aid the reader, some graphic aids may be too extensive and not necessary for understanding the report. These aids then should be placed in an appendix. The guideline to follow for deciding whether the information should be included in an appendix is that if the reader needs the material to understand the report, place it in the appropriate section, otherwise, place it in the appendix. Governmental and military reports use the term "Tab" to refer to an appendix.

The Index The index is an alphabetic listing of names, places, and subjects mentioned in the report. It provides the page reference for each item. Although most business reports do not contain an index, you may on occasion be asked to provide one. Should you need to prepare an index, underscore the main words on each page. Then prepare a 3″ × 5″ card for each underscored word, indicating the page references. Arrange all the 3″ × 5″ cards in alphabetic order. Use "See" references and "See also" references, which refer the reader to different entries, sparingly.[1]

PAGINATION

Because it is possible for pages to become separated from a report and because page numbers serve as a point of reference, pages in informal reports and formal reports should be numbered.

Informal Reports When an informal report exceeds one page, the second page and all succeeding pages should be numbered in unadorned Arabic numbers in the upper right corner one inch from the top edge of the paper.

Formal Reports Although page counting begins with the title fly page, it is not actually numbered; neither is the title page. Each of the other prefatory parts begins a new page and is numbered with lowercase Roman numerals. Center the unadorned page number one inch from the bottom of the page, and number the pages consecutively using i, ii, iii, and so forth.

Number the first page of the report proper in the center of the page one inch from the bottom edge of the paper using unadorned Arabic number 1. Number consecutively the succeeding pages of the report one inch from the top edge of the paper and even with the right margin. On each page beginning a new chapter, part, or division, type the page number in the center of the page one inch from the bottom edge of the paper.

SUMMARY

Reports can be either informal or formal depending on how the information is expressed—writing style—and presented—format. Informal reports generally convey routine information and are presented in memorandum or letter form.

A memorandum report is used to convey routine information from one employee to another in the same organization. The letter report is an external means of conveying information between organizations.

Formal reports can be either short or long. A short formal report uses some—but generally not all—of the major divisions of a long formal report, such as prefatory parts, report proper, and supplementary parts. A long formal report is similar to the short formal report except in length. Although the organization of long formal reports may vary from one organization to another, formal reports have three major divisions: prefatory parts, report body, and supplementary parts. Each of these divisions contains several subdivisions.

Because it is possible for pages to become separated from a report and because page numbers serve as a point of reference, pages in informal reports and formal reports should be numbered.

EXERCISES

Review
Questions

1. What is the difference between informal and formal reports?

2. What is a memorandum report? Letter report?

3. What are the printed headings of memorandum reports?

4. The second page heading of memorandum reports and letter reports should contain what information?

5. How does a letter report differ from a typical business letter?

6. What is the primary objective of a letter report?

7. What's the difference between short and long formal reports?

8. What are the three major divisions of formal reports?

9. What are the subdivisions of the prefatory parts? body? supplementary parts?

10. What is an abstract?

Problems

1. Obtain three reports from local businesses (or use the ones you obtained for Problem 1, Chapter 4) and analyze them. Are they informal or formal reports? Short or long? Why? Are they memo reports? Letter reports? Do the reports use headings? Are there other significant features of the report? Submit the information in a memo report to your instructor.

2. In teams of two, interview a high-ranking official of a local business. Call for an appointment and prepare a list of questions that you would like answered. Ask about the company's communication process, the importance of reports, kinds of reports written by the company employees. Are most of the reports written? oral? Who writes the reports? How often? Does the company have a special format for reports? Headings? Ask other questions that you think would be of interest to the class. Prepare a written report to your instructor.

3. Solicit memorandum forms from local businesses and prepare a bulletin board display of them. As a class, discuss the differences and similarities.

4. From your school's business library, obtain a copy of a master's thesis or doctoral dissertation on a topic of your choice. Analyze the document. Does it have the three major divisions of a report? Do these divisions have subdivisions? Bring the document to class and share your findings with the class.

Notes

---

[1]For more information about preparing an index, refer to *Concepts and Indexing Methods* by Harold Borko and Charles L. Bernier (New York: Academic Press, 1978).

PART III
Defining and Researching the Problem

CHAPTER 6
Planning

"An ounce of prevention is worth a pound of cure" applies to report writing every bit as much as it does to the practice of medicine. Planning is the "prevention" necessary to avoid serious problems as the report nears completion. The few hours it takes to plan can save countless hours of reinvestigating, restructuring, and rewriting.

Topics

Problem Identification and Definition
Preliminary Investigation
Tentative Report Plan

Military commanders are especially fond of three sayings:

1. When the going gets tough, the tough get going.
2. If you fail to plan, you are planning to fail.
3. Take the time to do it right—there's not always time to do it over.

While the relationship between the first of those sayings and report writing is accidental only, the other two are germane. Report writers frequently spend too little time planning, and, as a result, too much time writing—and rewriting.

PROBLEM IDENTIFICATION
AND DEFINITION

The amount and kind of planning necessary will naturally vary from report to report. In some cases, you may be able to carry out the entire planning process in your head before you write a brief report. In other cases, developing an acceptable plan will prove one of the more time-consuming parts of the report writing process. The discussion that follows presents all the steps necessary for planning the most complex reports. Short reports dealing with simple issues will obviously not require all the steps. We suggest that you use the planning checklist in Exhibit 6.4 (before the summary at the end of the chapter) until you are thoroughly familiar with the procedures involved.

The procedure by which investigators achieve accuracy and objectivity is known as the scientific method. Business report writers search for facts, truth, and verifiable results every bit as much as scientists working in laboratories. The scientific method consists of the following steps.

1. Define the problem and formulate it in specific terms for investigation.
2. Select an appropriate research methodology.
3. Collect data, usually through observation or experiment.
4. Organize data.
5. Interpret and evaluate data.
6. Draw conclusions based on the data.

The scientific method is the most efficient procedure for investigating and solving problems yet devised. Its chief advantage is that, when properly used, its results are accurate and verifiable. *Facts* (observable, measurable data), *inferences* (assumptions based on fact), and *value judgments* (opinions not based on fact) are explicitly identified in the interests of objectivity.

A report is a product designed to meet specific needs. Obviously the needs that may require reports are too numerous and varied for us to detail them here. Recognizing problems requires a thorough knowledge of the subject involved. As a rule, those with more experience identify the problem for the writer and assign the report, either as a regular part of the job (periodic reports) or as a special assignment (task reports). Specialists may also perceive a problem related to their specialty and submit a writer-initiated report (a proposal, for example).

When the report is a regular part of the job, the problem—or the organizational need—will remain essentially the same from report to report. In many companies, production records rarely change much from week to week or month to month. If they did, someone would insist on receiving a special report to explain the change. Task reports and writer-initiated reports require special attention to defining and limiting the problem.

**Problem
Definition**

What, exactly, have you been told to do? Or, what, exactly, have you decided needs to be done? Before you can develop an adequate plan, you need a clear and exact point from which to begin. You can begin to define the problem by clearly stating either the problem itself or the desired outcome.

In either case, begin by stating the problem or the outcome in specific, descriptive terms. Whenever possible use words that lead to acts of observing, counting, or measuring. If you are defining a problem, you may use an infinitive phrase, a question, or a declarative sentence. For example, your boss may tell you that absenteeism in your division is too high, that she wants to know why, and that she wants something done about it. Possible problem statements would include the following:

Infinitive Phrase:
  a.   To Discover the Causes of High Absenteeism in the Production Division
  b.   To Reduce the High Absenteeism in the Production Division

Question:
  a.   What Are the Causes of High Absenteeism in the Production Division?
  b.   How Can We Reduce the Rate of Absenteeism in the Production Division?

Statement:
  a.   We will examine the causes of high absenteeism in the Production Division.
  b.   The rate of absenteeism in the Production Division needs to be reduced.

As you read these possibilities, you can quickly see that some are better than others because they result in a clearer, more forceful conception of the problem. In general, we prefer the infinitive phrase because it results in a concise, goal-directed problem statement. When using this form of goal statement in any written presentation, however, you will need to remember to put it in the form of a complete sentence:

The purpose of my investigation will be <u>to discover the cause of high absenteeism in the Production Division</u>.
I propose <u>to reduce the rate of absenteeism in the Production Division</u>.

You'll also note that we have divided the problem into two main parts, one which focuses on the causes of absenteeism and one which focuses on reducing absenteeism. The same logical division would occur if you were to focus on the desired outcome of your investigation. In this case, however, you would need to determine what you wanted to result from your investigation. Results should be stated in terms of goals or specific objectives:

To ensure a rate of absenteeism of less than 4 percent in the Production Division.

Note that to accomplish this result, you would need to discover the current rate of absenteeism, the causes of the absenteeism, and the most logical methods for reducing absenteeism—*if* it really does need to be reduced.

Whether you use a problem statement or a long-range goal or short-term, specific objective as a starting point, a clear and measurable outcome *must* result from your research and reporting procedure. Consider the following:

How do you know absenteeism really is high in your division?

What is the rate of absenteeism in your division?

What is the rate of absenteeism in other divisions of the company?

How does the rate of absenteeism in your division compare with that in the production divisions of other companies in similar industries?

If the rate of absenteeism is high, is the cause something over which you will have control?

If you can control the cause, what is the best method for reducing the rate of absenteeism?

Obviously, what began as a simple directive from your boss—to find out why your division has a high rate of absenteeism and to do something about it—has turned into a complex report-writing situation. Is it worth it? That depends. How high is the absenteeism? How much is it costing your company? How much would corrective action cost?

PRELIMINARY INVESTIGATION

Your boss will naturally not want you to spend more time and money solving the problem than the problem is worth. Before conducting a full-scale investigation, answer those questions you can answer quickly and easily. In the case of high absenteeism, you could check your division's records for the past several years, the records of other divisions within your own company, and the records of production divisions in similar companies. You might also want to speak informally with several people in your division. By then you'll have a good idea of the extent of the problem, which will enable you to decide whether to pursue the issue, and—if you need to pursue—how to go about it.

Unless you are very sure of yourself and of your boss's attitudes and managerial style, you should take the results of your preliminary investigation back to your boss to make sure that she agrees with your assessment of the problem and the need for further study. Until you have that approval, you can't be sure that you and your boss are actually concerned about the same issues.

Unlike most term papers which you have written for instructors in school, reports are not usually specific assignments which you complete as best you can. Rather, reports are likely to be a step-by-step process of investigation and evaluation. The report writer, supervisor, and others concerned about the outcome work together to define the problem and determine the best method for investigating it.

With the problem of absenteeism, for example, your boss made the statement that the rate of absenteeism was "too high." Some of the possible problem statements presented for investigating this problem in effect challenged that statement. Before you would begin an investigation that might prove your boss wrong, you would obviously want to discuss the possibilities and approaches with her. See the problem from her point of view *before* you begin.

This is one of the critical differences between business research and scientific research. Business researchers use the scientific method when it is essential to achieve absolutely accurate results regardless of cost. In many cases, however, accuracy that is less than absolute will prove more cost effective. Business research should be impartial and objective, but sometimes the speed of a decision will be more important than the completeness of the research. Determine before you begin a project what kind of research will be appropriate.

Once you and your boss agree, restate the problem in writing, using specific language once again. An accurate and impartial investigation of the problem requires language that leads to measurements of one sort or another. We can't, for example, know whether absenteeism is "high" until we know what constitutes "high"—is it 5 percent, 10 percent, or 25 percent? Similarly, we cannot effectively reduce absenteeism until we set a specific objective.

Even in those cases that do not lend themselves to exact measurements, the more precise you can be in defining the problem or the desired outcome, the better off you will be. Many business decisions must, of course, ultimately rest on a manager's intuition about a course of action. Guesswork, however, is most successful when it is based on a solid foundation of knowledge established by the accumulation of facts.

Problem Scope and Limits

In addition to defining the problem, you will be responsible for defining both what the problem *is* and what it is *not*. The word *scope* refers to what will be covered in the report. The word *limits* refers to the boundary of the scope. The two are usually defined together in one or two sentences early in the report. In the case of the Production Division's absenteeism, for example, absenteeism caused by on-the-job accidents may be beyond the scope of your final report because it has no bearing on the kind of absenteeism causing the problem.

> **Because absenteeism caused by on-the-job accidents is not the result of morale problems in the Production Division, I have excluded it from my analysis. Appendix A includes material from a state study of the relationship between morale and on-the-job accidents.**

A clear statement of the problem requires a specific scope that identifies the boundaries of the problem.

Do not confuse the *limits* or *scope* with the term *limitations*. *Limitations* refer to those factors that prevented you from conducting as complete an investigation as warranted by the circumstances. Lack of time or money, small sample size, or conflicting data are typical limitations.

TENTATIVE REPORT PLAN

Once the problem is defined and limited, you are ready to develop a tentative report plan, which includes preliminary statements of (1) purpose, (2) research methodology, (3) audience, and (4) probable questions and problems.

Purpose

What do you hope to achieve as a result of your report? In Chapter 1, we pointed out that reports help an organization achieve its task, maintenance, and human objectives, and in Chapter 2 we discussed the general objectives all reports share: to inform, to analyze, or to recommend. In addition to these general recommendations, each report will have its own specific objective:

To *inform* District Manager Olive Schatz about the accident involving the company truck.

To *analyze* the causes of accidents involving company trucks.

To *recommend* that Olive Schatz change the current practice of inspecting company vehicles twice a year to a quarterly inspection system.

When the statement of purpose does not also clarify the scope of the problem, add a sentence (or paragraph) to define the limits of your investigation.

Research Methodology

How can you best solve the problem you've been assigned? The method you will use to gather information will depend on the nature of the problem, the relative costs of possible research methods, the possible benefits that will result from your solution, the time available, and the degree of accuracy required.

Many problems are best stated in the form of a hypothesis or null hypothesis. A *hypothesis* is a statement that can be proved true or false by means of research:

Poor working conditions are responsible for the high rate of absenteeism in the Production Division.

Whereas a hypothesis states that the relationship between two variables is positive, a *null hypothesis* states that the relationship is negative, that no relationship exists:

> **The high rate of absenteeism in the Production Division is not caused by the working conditions.**

In most business situations, stating the problem as a goal statement, hypothesis, or null hypothesis will be a matter of individual choice. The main objective of beginning with a provable statement is to ensure the validity of the results. Unless you have an identifiable goal or a provable (or disprovable) beginning, your activity will be directionless.

Problem Subtopics

The purpose and the scope identify the problem in its entirety. The next planning phase is to determine possible subtopics that will require investigation. You may, for example, think of your report as a pie, which you are going to divide (slice) into logical sections (see Exhibit 6.1).

Some of these subtopics may be eliminated as your investigation proceeds, and you may discover new subtopics that require investigation and inclusion. Vertical and horizontal charts are also effective

EXHIBIT 6.1
Report with Subtopics

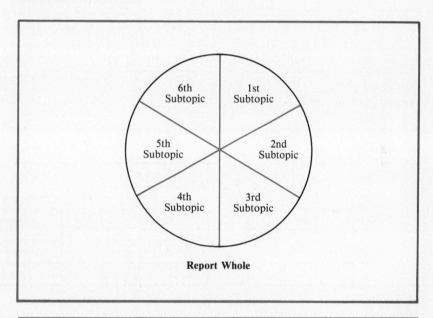

Report Whole

means of factoring a problem into its component parts. As with the pie concept, begin with the whole problem and proceed to break it down into its logical component parts (see Exhibits 6.2 and 6.3).

The advantage of factoring or charting the problem is that it allows you to anticipate many of the problems you will encounter in investigating and reporting the problem. In determining possible subtopics, be sure to consider the reporter's "serving men": who, what, when, where, why, and how.

Not all report writing situations will require a formal, scientific methodology with a hypothesis or null hypothesis for investigation. When the problem is complex, however, a formal approach is essential. And even when the problem is simple and easily solved, familiarity with the basics of the scientific method will enable you to discover the best solution more quickly.

Audience

While most of your planning time will be spent determining what you are going to investigate and how you will go about it, analyzing your audience is also important. In addition to knowing that your reader may well have a less specific knowledge of the subject area than you do and that he or she will be interested in those factors that will influence a decision, audience analysis needs to include such factors as

> *Background.* Is your reader a former specialist in the area being investigated? A former CPA or financial officer, whose main interest may be costs and other financial data? A lawyer, whose concerns may center on the legal implications of the problem?

> *Personality.* What does your primary reader like in reports? Have you seen samples of reports your reader considers good? Does your

EXHIBIT 6.2
Vertical Chart

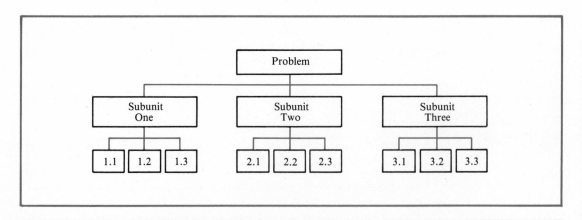

EXHIBIT 6.3
Horizontal Chart

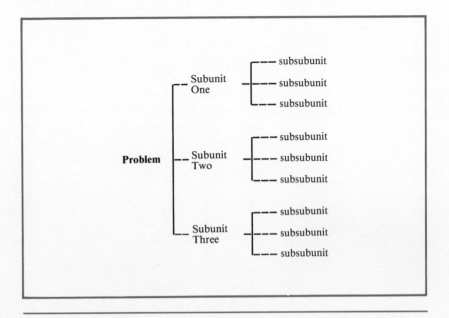

reader prefer a brief overview focusing on solutions to the problem, or does he or she prefer to be given all the details and draw his or her own conclusions?

Vested interests. Does your reader have a hidden agenda? Is he or she expecting the report to reveal something specific? Would a particular conclusion be inappropriate for political reasons?

Obviously, you won't always be able to answer all these and other related questions before you write your report. You may not learn until too late, for example, that the truck driver you have reported as incompetent and responsible for several accidents is your boss's cousin. The more you know about your audience, however, the better able you will be to write a report that will present the evidence and any appropriate conclusions in both an objective and an acceptable manner. Unless a report is acceptable, it can't possibly be effective.

Probable Problems and Questions

The final phase of planning is to list problems you think you may encounter in conducting your investigation or in analyzing the data.

Will you have sufficient time to do the job right?

Will you have enough money?

Do you have access to the appropriate resources (people, materials, facilities, etc.)?

EXHIBIT 6.4
Report Planning Checklist

```
                         Report Planning Checklist


          The following checklist shows you the steps to take in planning
          to solve typical report problems.
              1.  Define the problem or objective.
                  1.1  Use specific language.
                  1.2  Set limits.
              2.  Conduct an informal, preliminary investigation.
                  2.1  Check easily obtainable sources.
                  2.2  Reevaluate problem.
              3.  Confirm problem statement with the primary reader of
                  the proposed report.
                  3.1  Cite results of preliminary investigation.
                  3.2  Estimate the cost effectiveness of the report and
                       any changes that may occur as a result.
              4.  Develop a tentative report plan.
                  4.1  State the general purpose of the report.
                       4.1.1  To inform
                       4.1.2  To analyze
                       4.1.3  To recommend
                  4.2  State the specific purpose of the report, using
                       language that leads to quantifiable data or to
                       verifiable observations (see Chapter 9).
                  4.3  Develop a research methodology.
                       4.3.1  Use a hypothesis or null hypothesis when
                              appropriate.
                       4.3.2  Divide report whole into possible component
                              parts by factoring or charting.
                       4.3.3  Analyze the audience--How will the
                              reader's(s') background, personality,
                              and vested interests influence the
                              reception of the report?
                       4.3.4  Anticipate problems and questions.
                              4.3.4.1  How much time will your study
                                       require?
                              4.3.4.2  How much will your study cost?
                              4.3.4.3  What resources will you require
                                       to conduct your study?
                              4.3.4.4  What questions--technical or
                                       nontechnical--will readers have
                                       about the study?
```

Will your investigation require the cooperation of others?

Will your investigation require specialized knowledge which you don't have?

In the case of high absenteeism, for example, you might need to find out from those employees who are absent most often why they miss work. How will you persuade them to tell you their *real* reasons? Or perhaps you might anticipate that an accurate analysis of the problem will require the assistance of a statistician. By anticipating problems of this variety, you'll be in a better position to solve them when they occur.

Likewise, you should anticipate questions your audience may have about the problem, your research, and possible solutions. Because the reader will be using your report to make a decision, many of her or his questions will center on those aspects of the situation that lead to a possible action, including costs, options, advantages, disadvantages, benefits, and timing.

Keep in mind that technical and nontechnical audiences tend to ask different sorts of questions. Technical readers will have fewer questions about how technical processes work and more questions about costs, options, and possible benefits. Nontechnical audiences will naturally have more questions about technical processes and their advantages and disadvantages.

After you have completed your initial planning, you'll need to begin appropriate research. When the problem is complex, you'll conduct both secondary research (discussed in Chapter 7) and primary research (discussed in Chapter 8) before you begin the process of organizing and interpreting the data (Chapter 10).

SUMMARY

The amount and kind of planning will vary from report to report, but every report requires planning if it is to be effective. Because reports are expected to be accurate, impartial, and complete, most reports at least informally follow the guidelines of the scientific method.

Report writers should first define the problem in specific terms for investigation. A hypothesis or null hypothesis or other statement that can be proved or disproved is useful in many cases. Sometimes a desired objective can form the starting point for a report.

Second, the investigator should divide or factor the problem into its probable component parts. Pie charts, vertical charts, and horizontal charts help a report writer visualize the component parts of a report problem.

Finally, after conducting some preliminary research, the writer should develop a tentative report plan which includes statements of purpose, research methodology, audience needs, and probable questions and problems. When appropriate, the writer should present the tentative report plan to the person who authorized the report to ensure that the final product will meet the reader's expectations.

EXERCISES

1. What is planning?

2. What is the scientific method?

3. What is a problem statement? What three forms may a problem statement take?

4. What are the purposes of a preliminary investigation?

5. What should a tentative report plan include?

6. Explain the functions of and differences between a hypothesis and a null hypothesis.

7. Why is specific language important in report formulation?

8. How can factoring or charting help a report writer?

9. How will a reader's background, personality, and vested interests influence an investigation of a problem?

10. What categories of problems and questions should a writer anticipate?

Problems

For each of the report writing situations listed below (or for one or more of the cases in Appendix B) provide the following:

Statement of the problem(s)
    a. Using an infinitive phrase
    b. Using a question
    c. Using a declarative sentence

Possible hypotheses and null hypotheses

Possible problem subtopics

Procedures for preliminary investigation

A tentative report plan, stating logical assumptions about your purpose, research methodology, audience, and probable problems and questions.

1. As national marketing manager, you must report on the impact of caffeine-free cola sales on the sale of your Quench Cola, which contains caffeine.

2. You've been asked to prepare a report on recent management-union negotiations in anticipation of your own company's upcoming negotiations.

3. The owner/manager of a major department store in your area wants to know:
    a. What kind of service his/her sales clerks are providing.
    b. Why sales in the Toy Department have dropped by 22 percent over the past 14 months.
    c. Whether he/she should begin validating parking tickets for customers who park in the city lot adjacent to the store.
    d. Whether he/she should add a new line of microcomputers to the store's TV-Stereo department.

Treat each of these as a separate problem.

4.   The president of the savings and loan association for which you work has requested a report analyzing the effects recent changes in interest rates will have on your organization.

5.   You have been asked to report to the City of Kingsport, TN, on the costs of replacing a 75-year-old, one-lane, 28-foot bridge spanning Coopers Creek on the edge of town. The new bridge will be two lanes wide.

6.   The laboratory in which you work needs a new piece of research equipment. Be specific about the kind of laboratory and the piece of equipment, and write the report to your vice-president of Research and Development.

7.   Your local Chamber of Commerce has asked you how it can increase its membership.

8.   Your company—a manufacturer of petrochemicals—has asked you how it can improve its image in the community. Local ecological groups have been picketing your main plant because your manufacturing process does produce a noticeable odor and you do discharge effluents (filtered to meet federal and state requirements) into the river that passes close to town.

9.   The senator for whom you work has asked you to prepare a report on the relative effectiveness of free and controlled market systems.

10. The president of your company wants to know what the impact would be of replacing 200 of your organization's 1,200 hourly employees with computer-controlled robot devices.

11. A hardware store in Cedar City, UT, is using your company name, "Fair Deal." Although you do not currently have an outlet in the Cedar City area, you don't want the local store confused with your national chain of hardware stores. What action should your company take?

12. Your company recently negotiated a new, tough contract with the union, forcing the union members to make many concessions in wages and benefits because of the current economic difficulties in your industry. Now, less than two months after the new contract went into effect, the company's board of directors has awarded many managerial personnel huge bonuses, and the furious union members are talking about going on strike. As the Director of Public Relations, you've been asked to recommend the best course of action.

13. Over the past six months, you've received 15 reports from doctors that people taking your new medication "Tachinol" to control mood fluctuations in manic-depressives, have developed high fevers and convulsions, with one death attributed to the drug. As the person responsible for supervising the field tests of the drug, you are required to submit a report to the company president.

14. You have discovered that a simple change in your organization's security system could reduce by half the losses resulting from em-

ployee theft of the small computer components your firm manufactures. The losses over the last two years have amounted to nearly $800,000.

15. Should the publishing company for which you work publish a new magazine in your field? Consider the audience (size, distribution, etc.), and circulation, potential advertisers, content, and costs and problems of production.

CHAPTER 7

Conducting Secondary Research

What was the annual salary in 1980 of petro engineers in Texas? In 1970–1980, what marketing method resulted in highest sales of powdered milk in Central Africa? These questions can be answered through secondary research.

Topics

Secondary Sources
Guides to Secondary Sources
Note Taking
Documentation
Style Manuals
Bibliography and Annotated Bibliography
Form for Footnotes and Bibliographic Entries
Computerized Databases

After you have determined the purpose of your report and defined the problem, you will need to conduct research to arrive at a solution to the problem. Your preliminary investigation will have uncovered several possible sources of information. You will probably have already taken a quick look through your company records, for example, to see whether a similar problem has occurred in your company before. During the preliminary investigation, your search may have been informal and incomplete. You may have called two or three "old hands" to see if they remembered anything similar and had anything in their files. At this point, however, you'll have to be formal and thorough in your investigation of the problem, using secondary or primary sources of information or both. Although secondary data studies do not need primary data, all primary data studies need secondary data to the extent that you have shown diligent search of the literature. This chapter covers secondary sources, and Chapter 8 discusses the process of collecting primary data.

SECONDARY SOURCES

Secondary sources are just that—secondhand. They contain information that others have collected and reported. Secondary sources may be published—printed for public distribution or sale—or unpublished. Where do you begin to look for information? In many cases, your first step should be a search of company records and company libraries.

Company Records and Libraries

Company records can provide useful secondary information; in fact, they may provide information that you won't be able to obtain elsewhere. Use company records for historical, financial, or operational information. You might also find useful information for your report from other company records, such as sales reports, audit and tax reports, and annual reports. Prepared speeches given by company personnel may also help you in your investigation.

The company library may house specialized collections of reports, books, magazines, journals, newspapers, and other publications that might prove useful in your investigation.

In addition to the company library, check with key personnel of the company. They may give you information you need or else direct you to information and materials that may be stored in the company's (1) inactive files, (2) centralized files, or (3) decentralized files of executives or departments.

Research in Other Libraries

After you have thoroughly investigated your company's materials, your next step is to locate information in libraries—public, college or university, and private. Because most secondary information can be found in libraries, secondary research is frequently referred to as library research. Someone may have already researched and recorded a solution to a similar problem, so examining that material may save you hours of collecting new information. Although you may find both published materials (books, periodicals, newspapers) and unpublished materials (dissertations, manuals, brochures, booklets) in public libraries, you can also check special libraries, such as those maintained by businesses, trade, professional, and technical groups.

The first place to check whether the library has the documents you need is the card catalog, which is arranged alphabetically by author, subject, and title. The card catalog will give you the call number—the location of the document on the shelves in the library. Because the material in the card catalog is often outdated, check current periodicals (see guides to secondary sources).

Another section of the library that can provide useful information is the reference section. Later in the chapter, you will find a list of specific reference sources.

Because of the continual increase in the number of published materials and because of limited budgets, libraries cannot possibly afford to purchase as many works as they would like; they need to be selective in their acquisitions. When it happens that your library does not have a particular source that you need for your report, it may be possible to obtain a copy of that work through a system called interlibrary loan. The interlibrary loan system is a process by which a library will lend its materials to another library which does not have that particular item. After you have definitely determined that your library does not have the source you need, ask the librarian if another library has it and if it is possible to get it through interlibrary loan. You'll probably need to submit a request form with complete and accurate information about the author, title, year, and where you found the source listed. The librarian will locate the lending library, which will forward the document to your library, which will then notify you.

Selection

A word of caution about using secondary resources: be discriminating. From the abundance of information available, select only that information that relates specifically to your problem. Secondary sources that may prove useful to your investigation include the following:

Almanacs	Documents
Annual Reports	Encyclopedias
Articles	Government Publications
Books	Newspapers
Brochures	Pamphlets
Dictionaries	Periodicals (magazines, journals)
Directories	Yearbooks

Most of these secondary sources are available in typical public and college libraries. But of all sources available, your reference librarian is the one who can help you the most. Be sure to check with him or her when you need assistance. The expertise of the reference librarian can save you hours of searching and frustration.

GUIDES TO SECONDARY SOURCES

When you don't know where to begin searching for the information you need, begin with one of the many guides to secondary sources. Again, ask a librarian for help. With the information explosion that has taken place over the past 25 years, the number of sources of information has increased so greatly that no one source can be complete. You may find helpful materials in sources that you would initially dismiss as unrelated to your topic. Suppose, for example, you had to prepare a report on computer graphics for your company. The following list shows you a sample of recent sources of information about computer graphics.

Gafner, Milden K. "Computer Graphics: Looking Sharp for the Eighties." *Administrative Management,* 42, No. 5 (May 1981), pp. 29–31, 54, 65.

Jarett, Irwin M. "Computer Graphics: A Reporting Revolution?" *Journal of Accountancy,* 151, No. 5 (May 1981), pp. 46–57.

Miller, Irwin M. "Computer Graphic Applications." *Journal of Systems Management,* 31, No. 11, Issue 235 (November 1980), pp. 22–35.

Spencer, Michael. "Livening Reports with Computer-Generated Graphics." *Management World,* 8, No. 8 (August 1979), pp. 22–23.

"The Spurt in Computer Graphics." *Business Week,* No. 2641 (June 16, 1980), pp. 104–106.

Fortunately, most publications are *indexed,* which means that the record of their content is listed in separate publications so that users can find information they need. Guides to secondary sources tell you where to find material about specific topics. Although hundreds of reference sources are available, the following ones should prove helpful—especially to the beginning researcher.

Almanacs and Atlases

Almanacs are excellent tools for locating quick answers to a variety of questions on nations, states, people, education, sports statistics, and lists of colleges and universities. The *Dow Jones-Irwin Business Almanac* in particular provides data on business, finance and economics; and includes tables, graphs, rankings, and contacts for business information.

Dow Jones-Irwin Business Almanac. Homewood, IL: Dow Jones-Irwin, 1977 to date.

Information Please Almanac, Atlas and Yearbook. New York: Simon & Schuster, 1947 to date.

Reader's Digest Almanac and Yearbook. New York: N.W. Norton, 1966 to present.

The World Almanac and Book of Facts. New York: Doubleday, 1868 to present.

Bibliographies

A bibliography is a listing of publications often focusing on one particular topic. A general source for bibliographies, the *Bibliographic Index* provides a listing of books and other published sources that contain a bibliography.

Bibliographic Index: A Cumulative Bibliography of Bibliographies. New York: H. W. Wilson, 1937 to date.

Bibliographic indexes can be specialized. For example:

Walsh, Ruth M., and Stanley J. Birkin. *Business Communications: An Annotated Bibliography*. Westpoint, CT: Greenwood Press, 1973.

Falcione, Raymond L. and Howard H. Greenbaum and Associates. *Organizational Communication*. Beverly Hills, CA: Sage Publications, 1980.

Thompson, Marilyn Taylor. *Management Information: Where to Find It*. Metuchen, NJ: Scarecrow Press, 1981.

Biographical References

Biographical references contain information on well-known people, living or dead. Specialized references are available for sections of the United States—*Who's Who in the East, Midwest, South and Southwest,* and *West*. Also, many fields have specialized biographical directories. Check with your librarian for specific titles.

Biography Index. Bronx, NY: H. W. Wilson, 1946 to date.

Current Biography. Bronx, NY: H. W. Wilson, 1940 to date.

Who's Who in America. Chicago: Marquis Who's Who. Similar biographical references include *Who's Who in Finance and Industry, Who's Who in Education*, and *Who's Who in Insurance*.

Books

Not all books that have been published are in your library. The following references list books currently in print. Entries generally include author, title, subject, price, and publisher. *Books in Print* is probably the best source for quickly determining what books are currently available on a given topic.

Books in Print. New York: R. R. Bowker, 1948 to date.

Subject Guide to Books in Print. New York: R. R. Bowker, 1957 to date.

Business and Economics Books and Serials in Print. New York: R. R. Bowker, 1981 to date.

Cumulative Book Index. New York: H. W. Wilson, 1928 to date.

Business, Financial, and Credit References

The following references provide information on companies, including their subsidiaries, financial statements, properties, products, corporate histories, and the like. In addition, the *Value Line Investment Survey* offers trend analysis and gives summary information on selected industries.

Moody's Manuals. New York: Moody's Investors Service. *Bank and Finance, Industrial, International, Municipal and Governmental, OTC Industrial, Public and Utility, and Transportation Manuals*.

Standard Corporation Records. New York: Standard & Poor's, 1940 to date.

Value Line Investment Survey. New York: Arnold Bernhard & Co., 1969 to date.

Directories

Directories furnish information about businesses and organizations, their operations, products, and other facts. Many of them provide names and addresses of the companies and identify their officers or directors.

Business Organizations and Agencies Directory. Detroit: Gale Research, 1980.

Directory of Directories. Detroit, MI: Gale Research, 1980 to date.

Dun & Bradstreet, Inc. Million Dollar Directory. New York: Dun & Bradstreet, 1959 to date.

Guide to American Directories. 10th ed. New York: B. Klein Publications, 1978.

National Trade & Professional Associations of the U.S. and Canada. Washington, DC: Columbia Books, 1966 to date.

Standard & Poor's Register of Corporations, Directories and Executives. New York: Standard & Poor's, 1928 to date.

Thomas Register of American Manufacturers. New York: Thomas Publishing, 1905 to date.

Trade Directories of the World. Queens Village, NY: Croner Publications, 1952 to date.

World Guide to Trade Associations. 2d ed. Detroit, MI: Distributed by Gale Research, 1980.

Encyclopedias

Encyclopedias are best used as sources of general background information.

Encyclopedia Americana. International ed. Grolier Educational, 1829 to date.

The New Encyclopaedia Britannica. 15th ed. Chicago, IL: Encyclopaedia Britannica Education, 1981.

In addition several specialized encyclopedias are available, such as the *Accountant's Encyclopedia, Encyclopedia of Associations, Encyclopedia of Banking and Finance, Encyclopedia of Information Systems and Services,* and *International Encyclopedia of the Social Sciences.*

Guides

A wide variety of guides is available to help researchers locate business information.

Brownstone, David M. and Gorton Curruth. *Where to Find Business Information: A Worldwide Guide for Everyone Who Needs the Answers to Business Questions.* 2d ed. New York: John Wiley, 1982.

Daniells, Lorna M. *Business Information Sources.* Berkeley: University of California Press, 1976.

Fiqueroa, Oscar and Charles Winkler. *A Business Information Guidebook.* New York: AMACOM, 1980.

Grant, Mary and Norma Cote. *Directory of Business and Finance Services.* 7th ed. New York: Special Libraries Assn., 1976.

Johnson, H. Webster. *How to Use the Business Library: With Sources of Business Information.* 4th ed. Cincinnati: South-Western Publishing, 1972.

Piele, Linda J., John C. Tyson, and Michael B. Sheffey. *Materials and Methods for Business Research.* New York: Neal-Schuman, 1980.

Wasserman, Paul, Charlotte Georgi, and James Way. *Encyclopedia of Business Information Sources.* 4th ed. Detroit: Gale Research Co., 1980.

Government Publications

The U.S. government provides thousands of publications each year. The various departments, bureaus, divisions, and agencies release information that is vital to business.

American Statistics Index, Washington, DC: Congressional Information Service, 1973 to date.

Guide to U.S. Government Publications. McLean, VA: Documents Index, 1981 (microfiche only).

Federal Index. Cleveland, OH: Predicasts, 1977 to date.

Monthly Checklist of State Publications. U.S. Library of Congress, Processing Department. Washington, DC: Government Printing Office, 1910 to date.

Monthly Catalog of United States Government Publications. U.S. Superintendent of Documents. Washington, DC: Government Printing Office, 1895 to date.

Statistical Abstract of the United States. Washington, D.C.: Government Printing Office, 1878 to present.

U.S. Bureau of Census Publications: *Census of Manufacturers, Census of Retail Trade, Census of Service and Industries, Census of Wholesale Trade.*

Newspaper Indexes

Newspaper indexes summarize news by subject, person, and frequently by company. They contain a variety of information on topics covered in today's newspapers—political, technical, medical, educational, and business.

Bell & Howell Newspaper Index. Wooster, OH: Bell & Howell, 1972 to date. (Indexes for *Chicago Sun Times, Chicago Tribune, Christian Science Monitor, Denver Post, Detroit News, Houston Post, Los Angeles Times, New Orleans Times Picayune, St. Louis Post Dispatch, San Francisco Chronicle,* and *Washington Post*).

The New York Times Index. New York: The New York Times, 1913 to date.

The Wall Street Journal Index. New York: Dow Jones, 1958 to date.

Periodical Indexes

Periodical indexes give references to articles (and occasionally to books) arranged by subject or topic. They provide excellent coverage of the business, social, and political fields. Each of the indexes will tell you which periodicals are included.

Accountants Index Supplement. New York: AICOA, 1921 to date.

American Statistics Index. Washington, D.C.: Congressional Information Service, 1973 to date.

Applied Science and Technology Index. New York: H. W. Wilson, 1958 to date.

Business Periodicals Index. New York: H. W. Wilson, 1958 to date.

Education Index. New York: H. W. Wilson, 1929 to date.

Engineering Index. New York: Engineering Index, 1928 to date.

F & S Index. Cleveland, OH: Predicasts, 1960 to date.

Index to Legal Periodicals. New York. H. W. Wilson, 1908 to date.

P.A.I.S. (Public Affairs Information Service Bulletin) New York: P.A.I.S., 1915 to date.

Reader's Guide to Periodical Literature. New York: H. W. Wilson, 1900 to date.

Social Sciences Index. New York: H. W. Wilson, 1974 to date.

NOTE TAKING

When you have located information you want to include in your report, you'll need to take accurate notes. Note taking is more than just copying information along with the bibliographic data and reference page numbers. It requires a careful analysis and evaluation. Should the material be copied verbatim? paraphrased? summarized?

A well-organized plan for recording essential information obtained from secondary sources can save you time when you begin the writing process.

EXHIBIT 7.1
A 3″ × 5″ Bibliographic Note Card

5

Feinberg, Lilian O. Applied Business Communication.

Sherman Oaks, CA: Alfred Publishing, 1982.

Photocopiers

With the availability of photocopiers, your note-taking task has been simplified. Now you can simply photocopy pages of information instead of laboriously copying copious notes that you may not be able to read or may not be able to use.

Note Cards

One system of note taking that has proved both efficient and effective is the use of 3″ × 5″ note cards for bibliographic data and 5″ × 7″ note cards for content data. Use the 3″ × 5″ cards to record the bibliographic data—author, title of book or magazine, title of article, edition number, volume number, page numbers, date of publication, publisher, and location of publisher—of the reference. It is a good practice to record the library call number on the card in case you need to relocate a reference quickly. Because the cards will be used to prepare the bibliography, record the information in proper bibliographic format, and use a separate card for each reference. Also, number the cards consecutively so that they can be keyed with the 5″ × 7″ content cards.

The 5″ × 7″ content cards are used for recording information. Use a separate card for recording information on one topic from each reference source. When possible, place a subject heading (topic or subtopic) at the top of the card. Subject headings can be useful when you are ready to organize your data. Be sure to record the corresponding number of the bibliography card and the page number on which you found the data. Exhibits 7.1 and 7.2 illustrate the 3″ × 5″ bibliographic note card and the 5″ × 7″ content note card.

EXHIBIT 7.2
A 5″ × 7″ Content Note Card

MOB   5

   "Management by objective (M.B.O.) was conceived as a
technique that managers could use to make employees aware
of the organization's objectives and to motivate employees to
achieve those objectives." p. 33

After you have determined the system you will use for note taking, then you need to decide how to record the information you select from the various secondary sources. Three common ways of reporting information are to copy it verbatim, to paraphrase it, or to summarize it. To help you identify your notes, code them by (1) using quotation marks for material copied verbatim, (2) writing *p* or *par* for paraphrased material, and (3) writing *s* or *sum* for summarized material.

A passage from J. D. Reed's, "A Wedding Every 20 Minutes," (*Time*, 6 December 1982, p. 83) is used to illustrate the three kinds of note taking.

Verbatim: "An estimated 90,000 Japanese couples this year will spend their wedding nights in Hawaii, a favorite honeymoon spot. In addition, 5,000 couples elope each year to the islands or remarry there. Wesley Walker and his son Gary, ordained Church of Christ ministers in Honolulu, marry more than 3,000 Japanese couples each year for a modest $300 per ceremony."

Paraphrase: In 1982 about 90,000 Japanese couples will honeymoon in Hawaii. Each year 5,000 couples elope to the islands or remarry there. Ordained Church of Christ ministers, Wesley Walker and son Gary, marry over 3,000 Japanese couples every year for a reasonable $300 fee for each couple.

Summary: About 90,000 Japanese couples will spend their honeymoon in Hawaii this year. In addition 5,000 couples each year elope to the islands or remarry there. Every year Wesley Walker and son Gary, ordained Church of Christ ministers, marry over 3,000 Japanese couples for a $300 fee for each ceremony.

Before deciding which method of documentation to use, check to see whether the company, association, publisher, professor, or person for whom you are writing has preferences or guidelines to be followed.

The main objective with the note card system of note taking or any other recording system is to be able to relocate and use the information in writing your report. Use the system that works best for you.

DOCUMENTATION

Whenever you use secondary sources, whether directly (verbatim) or indirectly (reworded), you must document the source; that is, give credit to the originator by giving a reference number *and* quotation marks if the material is quoted verbatim. Not to do so would be to plagiarize. Documentation not only gives credit where credit is due, but also adds credibility to the report. Documentation of reference sources is essential under copyright laws and common law. Ideas, words, statements, or passages not originated by you must be acknowledged and identified. Not to give credit, which leads the reader to believe that you originated the information, is unethical and, in most cases, illegal.

Plagiarism

To present the ideas or material—condensed or abstracted—of others as your own is plagiarism and is punishable by law. In other words, if you were to use material from another source—books, periodicals, newspapers, dictionaries, television, radio, lectures, other students' papers, speeches, letters, interviews—and did not give proper credit to that source, you would be guilty of plagiarism.

Only when information is considered general knowledge and cannot be attributed to one particular source are you not obligated to cite the source. For example, if you say that two methods of collecting primary or original data are experimentation and observation, you would not need to give credit for that statement because it is general knowledge. If you quote information verbatim, however, you must give credit to that particular source even when material is considered general knowledge. The reference to a source of information is called a citation.

Copyright Laws

Copyright laws protect published materials from being copied without permission. Whenever you wish to use published or copyrighted materials, you need to obtain permission from the author or the holder of the copyright to reproduce that material. The copyright holder may legally charge you a fee. Fifty years after the death of the author or copyright holder, the material becomes public domain. You need not have permission to quote the material, but you do need to acknowledge the source.

Placement

Documentation of reference sources can be

1. In the text
2. In the bibliography
3. At the end of the chapter or report
4. At the bottom of the page

Regardless of placement—text, bibliography, endnotes, or footnotes—references to cited works are often referred to as footnotes or simply as notes.

Text Citations within the text of the report are popular because of the ease in reporting them for the writer and the ease in referring to them by the reader. When you will have only a few reference notes in your report, give the complete citation within the text itself. For example:

> According to Alan Lakein (How to Get Control of Your Time and Your Life, New York: Signet, 1973, p. 11), "To waste your time is to waste your life, but to master your time is to master your life and make the most of it."

Shortened citations may also be placed in the text of a report that contains a bibliography. The bibliography is arranged alphabetically or serially—in order of citation within the text. Because references are listed only once, the alphabetic arrangement of the bibliography is preferred. Items in the bibliography are referred to in the text by author and number or by author and year.

In the *author-and-number format*, the bibliography lists the reference serially or alphabetically, and then numbered sequentially. This number identifies the citation in the text of the report. For example, if Fisher were the second item in the bibliography, then reference in the text would be Fisher (2).

When necessary to cite a page number, then the reference would read

Fisher (2:25) or Fisher (2,25)

or

Fisher (2:25–36) or Fisher (2,25–36).

In the *author-and-year (or date) format,* the author's name and the year of publication of the work appear in the appropriate place in the text. Reference is made to the alphabetically arranged bibliography (which is not numbered) by author and year of publication rather than by the number list. Here are several examples using this method:

Fisher (1980) found that . . .
A recent study of job interviews (Fisher, 1980) showed that . . .
In 1980, Fisher noted that . . .

When necessary to refer to a particular page rather than to an entire study or work, present the citation as follows:

Fisher (1980:12–15)

If Fisher had a second or third publication in the same year, present the citation as

Fisher (1980b:12–15)

or

Fisher (1980c:4–11).

Bibliography   References to the bibliography require the reader to refer to the bibliography for a complete citation of the reference. A number is used after the citation, which directs the reader to the source in the bibliography. The bibliographic items are numbered, and each citation is given the corresponding bibliographic number. Following the material to be identified, you would enclose in parentheses the number for the reference, a comma (or colon), and the page number. For example:

"No matter how ambitious or capable you may be, you cannot become the kind of employee you want to be, or the kind of employee management wants you to be, without learning how to work effectively with people." (12,3)

Item 12 in the bibliography would identify the author, title of the work, publisher, and other bibliographic data. For example:

12. Chapman, Elwood N. <u>Your Attitude is Showing.</u> 4th ed. Chicago: Science Research Associates, 1983.

Endnotes   When references to cited sources are at the end of the chapter, manuscript, paper, or report, they are called notes or endnotes. Endnotes are numbered consecutively throughout the chapter or report, starting with number one. Use Arabic numbers and type them without punctuation a half space above the typewritten line. No bibliographic data are given in the text; they are given at the end of the chapter or report on a separate page. Here's an example of a citation that will appear as an endnote.

"The term *reprographics* refers to the reproduction and duplication of documents, written materials, drawings, and designs by photocopy, offset printing, microfilming, and office duplicating."[1]

The endnote would appear as follows at the end of the chapter or paper. The entry form for endnotes is similar to that of footnotes except that endnotes are double-spaced and footnotes are single-spaced.

[1]Arnold Rosen and Rosemary Fielden, <u>Word</u> <u>Processing</u>, 2d ed. (Englewood Cliffs, NJ: Prentice-Hall, 1982), p. 197.

Footnotes   Footnotes are placed at the "foot" or bottom of the page. They identify the source of information, provide explanations or additional comments, or refer the reader to other sections of the text.

Footnotes appear at the bottom of the page on which references are made to them. They are separated from the last line of the text by a one and one-half inch horizontal line beginning at the left margin. Use the underscore key on the typewriter to make the line. Type it a single space below the last line of the text and double-space after it. Even if the page contains only a few lines of typewritten material, place the footnote at the bottom of the page. Indent the first line of each footnote five spaces (or the same number of spaces for paragraph indentions within the text). Type the reference number a half line space above the footnote. Space once after the raised number. Single-space succeeding lines of the same footnote beginning at the left margin. The next footnote begins a double-space after the preceding one. Whenever possible, footnotes should be complete on one page. Footnotes are keyed to the text by raised Arabic numbers. These numbers are typed a half space above the typewritten line in the text immediately after the last typed character in the words cited. Number footnotes consecutively throughout the report or begin anew for each chapter.

Examples of typical footnotes will be presented at the end of the bibliographic section in this chapter so that they can be presented for comparison with bibliographic entries.

STYLE MANUALS

A style manual provides a reference on how to prepare papers, reports, manuscripts, and other scholarly research papers. Style manuals give explicit directions on the form of the paper—margins, spacing, indentions, typing, footnoting, table and figure illustrations, documentation, and pagination.

Many companies, associations, colleges and universities, journals, and publishers ask that you follow a particular style manual in the preparation of your paper. When you are not directed to follow a particular format or style manual, you have a wide choice. Some of the more widely used style manuals are

Campbell, William Giles and Stephen Vaughan Ballou. *Form and Style: Theses, Reports, Term Papers.* 5th ed. Boston: Houghton Mifflin, 1978.

The Chicago Manual of Style. 13th ed. rev. Chicago: The University of Chicago Press, 1982.

Keithley, Erwin M. and Philip J. Schreiner. *A Manual of Style for the Preparation of Papers & Reports.* 3d ed. Cincinnati: South-Western, 1980.

MLA Handbook for Writers of Research Papers, Theses, and Dissertations. New York: Modern Language Association, 1977.

Publication Manual of the American Psychological Association. rev. ed. Washington, DC: 1974.

Turabian, Kate L. *A Manual for Writers of Term Papers, Theses, and Dissertations.* 4th ed. Chicago: University of Chicago Press, 1973.

BIBLIOGRAPHY AND ANNOTATED BIBLIOGRAPHY

The bibliography is an orderly listing of source materials. The bibliographic entries refer to entire works, not just parts or pages as do the footnotes, and they come at the end of the report or paper.

Because the prefix *biblio* is the Greek word for book, some people prefer the heading *References* or *List of Works Cited.* However, bibliography is appropriate for all source materials, whether books, periodicals, interviews, letters, speeches, films, or other secondary sources.

Include in your bibliography all works referred to in the text or in the footnotes. Do not include works that you have consulted and did not use.

Arrange bibliographic entries in alphabetical order by the author's last name. When no author is given or when a work is anonymous, use the first word in the title other than a definite or indefinite article (*A Map of Maps* would be alphabetized under *M*). When you have a number of diverse sources, you may further arrange your bibliography by classifications, such as books, periodicals, government publications, and others. You may also arrange your bibliography by primary and secondary sources, by chronological order, or by subject. When you use separate categories, alphabetize the entries within them.

When the bibliography entry gives a brief description of the value and content of the source, it is called an annotated bibliography. See Chapter 10 for examples.

FORM FOR FOOTNOTES AND BIBLIOGRAPHIC ENTRIES

Bibliographic entries are similar to those of footnotes, but there are some minor differences. Compare the two entries in the following examples based on the *MLA Handbook* cited earlier in this chapter. The first entry is a footnote; the second is the bibliographical entry.

Book with one author:

1 Bernadine P. Branchaw, <u>English Made Easy</u> (New York: Gregg Division/McGraw-Hill), p. 163.

Branchaw, Bernadine P. <u>English Made Easy.</u> New York: Gregg Division/
   McGraw-Hill, 1979.

Book with two or more authors (cite authors as they appear on title page):

2 Joel P. Bowman and Bernadine P. Branchaw, <u>Effective Business Correspondence</u> (New York: Harper & Row), p. 35.

Bowman, Joel P. and Bernadine P. Branchaw. <u>Effective Business Correspondence.</u> New York: Harper & Row, 1979.

In the bibliography, when you have two or more works by the same author(s), give the name(s) of the author(s) in the first entry only. For the succeeding entries, type ten hyphens, followed by a period and two spaces and then the title of the book. For example:

----------. <u>Successful Communication in Business.</u> New York: Harper &
   Row, 1980.

Book with no author given or an anonymous book:

3 <u>MLA Handbook</u> (New York: Modern Language Association, 1977), p. 45.

<u>MLA Handbook.</u> New York: Modern Language Association, 1977.

An edited book:

4 John Stewart, ed., <u>Bridges Not Walls; A Book About Interpersonal Communication</u> 3d ed. (Reading, MA: Addison-Wesley, 1982), p. 12.

Stewart, John, ed. <u>Bridges Not Walls; A Book About Interpersonal Communication.</u> 3d ed. Reading, MA: Addison-Wesley, 1982.

An unpublished dissertation:

5 Lowell E. Crow, "An Information Processing Approach to Industrial Buying: The Search and Choice Process," Diss. Indiana University, 1974, p. 24.

Crow, Lowell E. "An Information Processing Approach to Industrial Buying: The Search and Choice Process." Diss. Indiana University, 1974.

Book without place of publication, publisher, date, or pagination:

n.p.—no place of publication given
n.p.—no publisher given
n.d.—no date of publication given
n.pag.—no pagination given

The abbreviations are given where the full information would be cited
if available. For example:

(New York: Harper & Row, 1981), p. 52.
(n.p.: n.p., n.d.), n.pag.

An article in a periodical:

6 Pamela S. Rooney, "Teaching the Job Search: Yet Another Approach," The ABCA Bulletin, 45, No. 1 (1982), pp. 34–35.

Rooney, Pamela S. "Teaching the Job Search: Yet Another Approach." The
ABCA Bulletin, 45, No. 1 (1982), pp. 34–35.

An article in a reference book:

7 "Fleet Street," Encyclopedia Americana, 1950 ed.

"Fleet Street." Encyclopedia Americana, 1950 ed.

An article from a daily newspaper:

8 Steven Arnold Seiden, "Over Taxing Short-Term Gains," The Wall
Street Journal, 12 May 1982, Sec. 1, p. 26, cols. 3–5.

Seiden, Steven Arnold. "Over Taxing Short-Term Gains." The Wall Street
Journal. 12 May 1982. Sec. 1, p. 26, cols. 3–5.

An editorial:

9 "Persuasive Case Yet to Be Made for Change to City Ward System,"
Editorial, Kalamazoo Gazette, 16 May 1982, Sec. A, p. A–6.

"Persuasive Case Yet to Be Made for Change to City Ward System." Editorial. Kalamazoo Gazette. 16 May 1982, Sec. A, p. A–6.

Government publications:

Because of the thousands of materials published by the government, it
would be impossible to give examples of footnotes to cover all situations. Briefly, when citing a government publication, give the author's
name (if known) first, then the agency, such as

U.S. Congress, Senate;
U.S. Congress, House;

Michigan Department of Transportation;

then the title of the publication (underscored), followed by the place, publisher (Government Printing Office (GPO),) date, and pages.

[10] U.S. Department of Commerce, Bureau of the Census, Population Estimates and Projections (Washington, DC: GPO, 1980), p. 3.

U.S. Department of Commerce, Bureau of the Census. Population Estimates and Projections. Washington, DC: GPO, 1980.

Personal letters:

[11] Letter received from Daniel Schultz, 15 May 1982.

Schultz, Daniel. Letter to author. 15 May 1982.

Personal or telephone interview:

[12] Personal (or Telephone) interview with Ian Johnson, 1 September 1981.

Johnson, Ian. Personal (or Telephone) interview. 1 September 1981.

COMPUTERIZED DATABASES

Because of the competitiveness of business today, timely information is essential. With the availability of computers, researchers now have the ability to acquire, worldwide, all kinds of information—business, educational, government, legal, medical, technical—on any topic of interest, within minutes. In other words, you don't need to do the searching; you can have the computer do it for you. Report writers now have a remarkable ease of access to a wealth of information because of a method called online.

Online Search

An online information search is an interactive method of requesting citations on specific topics from vast quantities of data stored in approximately 500 databases. A database is simply computer-stored information from a given source. Database producers lease or sell their databases to online vendors (or search services), who sell access to databases through their computer systems.

The online search process is not complicated. The computer operator enters into the computer key words or phrases (most data bases have their own Thesaurus or check the Library of Congress Subject Heading List), names of authors, and other specific information for the search. The computer then performs the search and provides a printout of the text citations. A printout is a permanent record of your search. You have a choice of an online print or an offline print. An online print is an immediate printout of the results of your search from the database computer to your terminal. The advantage of this method is that you have the information immediately. The disadvantage is that you have to pay the online rate for the time required to complete the printout. The offline print is the same as the online printout except that it is run after you terminate your online search. The rate is less than that charged for online printouts. Most vendors mail your printout within 24 hours.

Classifications

Databases are classified as bibliographic, factual, and numeric.

Bibliographic A bibliographic database contains the title, author, source, and summary of published information found in sources, such as articles and books.

Factual A factual database contains organization names and addresses, licenses available, transportation routes, and the like.

Numeric A numeric database contains manipulable data, such as economic and labor statistics, prices, and demographic data.

Typical Databases

The following databases are typical of those available. The producers of the databases are given in parentheses. These databases are available through the producers or through vendors. Five major vendors are listed later in this chapter.

ABI/INFORM (Data Courier, Inc.). 1971 to date; updated monthly; bibliographic. U.S. and international coverage of over 400 periodicals including a wide variety of information about business, management techniques, and personnel.

ACCOUNTANTS (American Institute of Certified Public Accountants). 1974 to date; updated quarterly; bibliographic. Covers over 300 journal titles. Includes literature of accounting, auditing, financial reporting, investments, securities, and taxation.

BI/DATA INTERNATIONAL TIME SERIES (Business International Corporation). Dates of coverage vary; updated periodically; numeric. Several thousand time series with measures of economic and marketing activities.

CIN—CHEMICAL INDUSTRY NOTES (American Chemical Society). 1974 to date; updated weekly; bibliographic. Includes information on companies operating within the chemical industry covering such items as production, pricing, sales, and products.

DOW JONES NEWS RETRIEVAL (Dow Jones & Company). Current; bibliographic, factual, and numeric. Information about companies listed on the New York, OEB, and American Stock exchanges, corporate financial information, stock quotes, acquisitions, and process. Also industry news, economic reports, and more.

PREDICAST F & S INDEX and PTS PROMT (Predicasts, Inc.). 1972 to date; updated monthly; bibliographic. Includes company and industry information on mergers, acquisitions, new products, earnings, market data, and foreign operations.

LABORDOC (International Labour Organization). 1965 to date; updated monthly; bibliographic. Information on management, employment, working conditions, labor issues, and economic conditions and policies.

MANAGEMENT CONTENTS (Management Contents). 1974 to date; updated monthly; bibliographic. Provides information on business and management topics including accounting, finance, marketing, organizational behavior, and others.

P/E NEWS—PETROLEUM/ENERGY BUSINESS NEWS INDEX (American Petroleum Institute). 1975 to date; updated weekly; bibliographic. Covers information on companies operating within the energy and petroleum industries.

PHARMACEUTICAL NEWS INDEX (Data Courier, Inc.). 1975 to date; updated monthly; bibliographic. News about pharmaceuticals, cosmetics, and related health areas. Indexes articles on drugs, government legislation, and other news items.

STANDARD AND POOR'S NEWS (Standard & Poor's). 1979 to date; updated weekly; factual and numeric. Covers information on more than 9,000 companies including management changes, contract awards, mergers, acquisitions, and corporate background.

TRADE AND INDUSTRY INDEX (Information Access Corporation). 1981 to date; updated monthly; bibliographic. Information from trade journals and newspapers on all areas of business including wholesale and retail trade, construction, transportation, banking, taxation, and others.

Database Vendors

Here is a list of the five major vendors.

1. Bibliographic Retrieval Services
    Corporation Park, Building 702
    Scotia, NY 12302
    (518) 374–5011

2. Dow Jones News Service
    Box 300
    Princeton, NJ 08540
    (609) 452–2000

3. Lockheed Information Retrieval Service (Dialog)
    Marketing Department
    3460 Hillview Avenue
    Palo Alto, CA 94304
    (800) 227–1960

4.   New York Times Information Service, Inc.
     Mt. Pleasant Office Park
     1719 A Route 10
     Parsippany, NJ 07054
     (201) 539–5850

5.   System Development Corporation (SDC)
     2500 Colorado Avenue
     Santa Monica, CA 90406
     (213) 829–7511

SUMMARY

After determining the purpose and defining the problem of your report, you will need to research all the resources available. Secondary sources contain information that others have collected and reported. Company records can provide useful secondary information; use them for historical, financial, or operational information.

After you have investigated your company's materials, then locate information in public libraries, college and university libraries, and private libraries. Card catalogs, reference books, and reference librarians can help you locate the information you need.

When you have located information you want to include in your report, you need to take accurate notes. Note taking requires a careful analysis and evaluation of the reference source. Not all information will be needed to be copied verbatim. You'll definitely need bibliographic data for documentation.

Plagiarism is presenting ideas or materials of others as your own and is punishable by law. Copyright laws protect published materials from being copied without permission.

Documentation of reference sources can be in the text, in the bibliography, at the end of the chapter or report, or at the bottom of the page.

A style manual provides a reference on how to prepare papers, reports, manuscripts, and other scholarly research papers. Style manuals give explicit directions on how to prepare the final report.

The bibliography is an orderly listing of source materials. Bibliographic entries refer to entire works, not just parts or pages as do the footnotes, and they come at the end of the report or paper. Bibliographic entries are arranged in alphabetical order; by classifications, such as books, periodicals, government publications; by subject; and by chronological order.

With the availability of computers, researchers now have the ability to acquire—worldwide—all kinds of information on any topics of interest within minutes. An online information search is an interactive method of requesting citations on specific topics from vast quantities of data stored in approximately 500 databases. A database is simply computer-stored information—bibliographic, factual, and numeric.

EXERCISES

1. What are secondary sources? Give five examples.

2. What is library research?

3. What is the interlibrary loan system?

4. What is documentation, and why is it necessary?

5. What is plagiarism?

6. Where can documentation of reference sources be placed?

7. What is the difference between endnotes and footnotes?

8. What are style manuals? Name two of them.

9. What is a bibliography? An annotated bibliography?

10. What is an online information search?

Problems

1. Write a brief memo report to a student who is interested in pursuing a career in your major. Check your local library and make a list of available resources, such as abstracts, biographical references, bibliographies, dictionaries, directories, periodical guides, indexes, and government reports. Be extra helpful by providing the call numbers.

2. Construct a classified bibliography of five books and five periodicals and newspapers on a topic of your choice.

3. Construct an annotated bibliography of five books that you are using in classes this semester.

4. Write a letter report to an English-speaking foreign student who plans to enroll in your college next term. The student plans to major in accounting and would like you to check the school library and provide him/her with a list of five accounting periodicals to which the library subscribes. Briefly tell the student why those periodicals are important and what their strengths are.

5. Prepare footnotes (assume page numbers) and the corresponding bibliographic entries using the following:
    a.   A book with one author
    b.   A book with three authors
    c.   An edited work
    d.   An article in a magazine
    e.   An article in a reference work
    f.   An unpublished dissertation
    g.   A government publication
    h.   An article from a newspaper
    i.   A lecture
    j.   A telephone interview

6. Prepare a 20-item bibliography on a topic of your choice. Include books, encyclopedias, magazine articles, newspapers, lectures, dissertations, and government publications.

7. Check your library's subject card catalog and select a topic on which you have little information. Prepare a bibliography of between five and ten sources giving call numbers after the bibliographic entry.

8.   Using your library, locate, record, and document information on the following:

    a.   The origin of the word bibliography

    b.   The names and addresses of the executive officers of IBM

    c.   Titles and sources of information of three articles on computerized databases

    d.   The *New York Times'* headline on the day you were born. Provide the information in a memo report to your instructor.

9.   In a memo to your boss, describe a problem situation and the sources you would use to solve the problem.

10.   Write a letter report to a student from a foreign country who plans to enroll in your college and wants to know more about the city.

11.   In the *Business Education Index*, locate three articles on report writing. Give the biographical data for each of the three articles.

12.   Check your library's bound periodicals and locate issues of *Time* and *Newsweek* for the day you were born. Prepare a short report on the happenings covered in that issue. What were the cover stories? What films were being reviewed? What books were being reviewed? What was reported on education? national news? medicine? Give complete bibliographical data.

13.   In any one of *Moody's Manuals* that your library possesses, locate information on a business of your choice. In a memo report, provide that information along with complete bibliographical data to your instructor.

14.   In the *Monthly Catalog of United States Government Publications*, list the names and prices of five publications that interest you.

15.   Ask a librarian at your school which computerized databases are available through your school. Prepare a memo report for your instructor.

16.   Select a passage from last week's issue of *Time* or *Newsweek* and quote it verbatim, paraphrase it, and summarize it.

CHAPTER 8

Conducting
Primary Research

Information gathered by experimenting, asking questions, or watching others is called primary research because *you* are the first to obtain it. Secondary sources may not provide the information you need to make a decision. When you cannot find the data you need in an existing source, you'll have to collect it yourself.

Topics

Observation
Experimentation
Survey

After you have thoroughly checked the secondary sources available to solve the problem you're investigating, you may need to conduct some original research. In other words, you may need to obtain the information firsthand.

Information you obtain by asking and analyzing questions, watching and interpreting the behavior of others, and testing and evaluating, is called primary research because you are the first to find and interpret that information. Because primary research is more time consuming and more expensive than secondary research, primary research is conducted only when necessary to understand a situation or solve a problem. When secondary research provides the information you need, use it. Do not duplicate someone else's research unless you need to verify the accuracy of applicability of that research. As a researcher, you need to decide what kind of information to gather, where, and how you will gather it. This will require extensive and careful planning on your part. The overall plan or strategy for investigating a problem is called a *research design*. It includes a procedure for collecting, measuring, analyzing, and interpreting data. Three main methods of collecting primary data are observation, experimentation, and surveys.

OBSERVATION

Collecting raw data by watching or seeing what is happening to people, objects, or events and noting that information is called *observation*. Observation is used when you need to obtain data through the use of the five senses—seeing, hearing, touching, tasting, or smelling. For example, you use observation when you need to (1) count the number of women wearing slacks in an office; (2) listen to sounds of music; (3) touch various samples of cloth; (4) taste food and drink; or (5) smell such items as flowers, perfumes, spices, or wines.

You examine phenomena under existing conditions. You merely observe what is taking place; no attempt is made to control or manipulate conditions. Observation requires a systematic procedure for observing the phenomena and for recording that information.

In a supermarket, you can determine brand preferences by observing shoppers as they make their selections; in an office, you can determine the number of women wearing slacks or dresses; or standing on a corner at a busy intersection, you can determine the number of people who pass by.

Observation can also include a search of a company's records for such items as production figures, advertising costs, volume of sales, and amount of sales. These figures will provide you with primary data. In Chapter 7, we discussed using company records as secondary data. The difference depends on whether you will use material or information already recorded by someone else or are searching company records to collect new data. For example, if you were to use a salesperson's call report for a customer's profile, that would be secondary research. (The salesperson recorded the description first in the call report.) On the other hand, if you were using that call report and other call reports for that same company to record the total sales for each call and then using that raw data for a report, that would be primary investigation. You would be taking raw data—sales figures—from company records to prepare an original report on total sales in a particular region. When accountants examine or observe and analyze the company's financial records to prepare their audit reports, they are conducting primary research—using raw data—to draw new conclusions.

Procedure

Before you attempt to make your observations of certain phenomena, you should have a clear understanding of the purpose of your investigation. Do you want to know the exact number of minutes that a secretary spends typing in one hour? two hours? in the morning? afternoon? When the purpose is clear, then you can design a form for recording and tabulating your observations. The form should be arranged so that it allows for quick and easy recording of observations that you make. In addition to the form, you also need to decide who, what, when, where, and how.

Who: Whom will you observe? typists? secretaries? administrative assistants? anyone who types?

What: What job classification will you use? What is to be observed? What companies should you investigate? financial institutions? medical? educational? government agencies?

Which: Which section of the city should be included? East? West? North? South? some from each? all?

When: When will you conduct the investigation? morning? afternoon? what day? week? month? year?

How: How many observations should be made? How long will you observe? How will you record the observations? stopwatch? counter? tally sheet?

Your plan of action should be specific so that when several people are doing the observing, each will be following the same procedure.

Advantages

The advantages of using observation as a research technique are the following:

1. Observation may be the only method for recording those particular phenomena that can be seen; such as physical activities, company records, processes, environment, and human behavior.

2. The accuracy of observation is high. Trained observers record only what they see—not what others tell them. They attempt to report accurately what they see in spite of any prejudices or biases they may have.

3. Observers report activities, behaviors, or phenomena rather than interpret them. They report the overt acts, not the reason for those actions.

4. Tallying the results is not complicated. The results lend themselves easily to drawing conclusions.

Disadvantages

The disadvantages tend to be the reverse of the advantages.

1. Observation is limited to those phenomena that can be seen. The observer can only record what happened but cannot explain why it happened. You can't observe a person's attitude, opinion, or reasoning. A shopper, for example, might select a particular brand of peanut butter. Observation can record that fact, but it can't tell us why the shopper selected one brand rather than another.

2. Because of the human tendency to interpret what is seen on the basis of past experiences, observation is not totally accurate. For instance, a task-oriented supervisor sent to observe in a people-oriented office will probably see and interpret human behavior differently than a people-oriented supervisor.

3. Observation can be more expensive and time consuming than surveying—interviews or questionnaires—especially when you need to observe behavior that occurs infrequently. For example, an observer may have to wait weeks for an accident to occur at a downtown intersection, whereas a survey could determine quickly that a traffic light would increase safety.

4. When a person knows that he or she is being observed, he or she may behave differently, possibly affecting the reliability of the results.

EXPERIMENTATION

The experimental method of research is also referred to as the cause and effect method or the pretest-posttest method. It is one in which controlled conditions are established for an orderly form of testing that is highly reliable and accurate.

Experimentation is a form of observation under controlled—not natural—conditions. It is a form of research which manipulates one variable while holding all others constant. In other words, the experimental method of research attempts to control a particular situation so that nothing changes, except for the introduction of an experimental factor—a variable—which may then be said to be responsible for whatever change has taken place in the experiment.

Variables can be independent or dependent. When the experimenters have control over a variable, that is, when they are able to manipulate or change it by varying the conditions or subjects, the variable is said to be *independent*. When the experimenters have no control over a variable, however, and it changes as the result of changes in the independent variable, then that variable is said to be *dependent*.

For example, suppose an experimenter wanted to study the differences in metabolism time of various alcoholic beverages. The beverages, which the experimenter would control, would be the independent variable. The dependent variable would be the blood content of alcohol as measured over time and quantity of consumption. The dependent variable would be influenced by the independent variable rather than directly by the experimenter. The purpose of experimental research is to determine whether there is a relationship between an independent variable and a dependent variable. Two common experimental designs are the one-group and the two-group methods.

One-Group
Method

In the one-group method of experimentation, the experimenter adds to or subtracts a single experimental factor from a group (or an individual) and then measures the resulting change. In other words, one group is evaluated (or tested), then subjected to the influence of a variable, and then evaluated a second time. For example, an office manager wants to increase office productivity and believes the purchase of a word processor would help. First, the office manager would select an experimental group of typists and then measure the number of pages typed before introducing a word processor. After the installation of the word processor and a reasonable length of "learning" time, the office manager would again measure production. The differences in measurements could be the result of the use of the word processor.

Step 1: Select Experimental Group (Typists)
Step 2: Measure Variable (Pages Typed)
Step 3: Add Experimental Factor (Word Processor)
Step 4: Measure Variable (Pages Typed)
The difference between the measurement of Step 2 and that of Step 4 *could* be the result of the experimental factor.

In an experiment of this kind, however, serious errors can be made. For example, the office manager would need to make certain that no other factor—the enthusiasm of the office manager or typists toward the experiment, the willingness of the typists to increase productivity, the arrival of new equipment in the office, the motivation of the typists to do well, or the kinds of material typed—affected the results of the experiment.

Two-Group Method

Often the experiment may involve two or more groups. In the two-group method of experimentation, the experimenter uses two or more groups—a *control group* and an *experimental group* (or groups). The two groups must be essentially alike (age, sex, intelligence, background, familiarity with subject matter, and the like) before a variable or experimental factor is added to (or subtracted from) the experimental group. Groups are measured before and after the added or subtracted variable; the differences between the two groups can be attributed to the effect of the added or subtracted variable.

For example, let's say that the office manager wanted to test two groups of typists—a control group and an experimental group. Both groups are selected according to predetermined criteria so that they are essentially alike. At the start of the experiment, the production of both groups is measured using electric typewriters. The subjects in the experimental group are given word processors; no change is made in the control group. The production of the two groups is measured over a set period of time to determine the differences that occurred since the first production measurement. Differences between the first and last measurement within the control group could be attributed to other influences; differences between the control group and the experimental group could be attributed to the added variable—the word processor—and other influences. The word processor may or may not have been an influence on the second group of typists. Other influences may have been at work in either of the groups. See Exhibit 8.1.

EXHIBIT 8.1
Experimental Group and Control Group

Step 1: | Select Experimental Group | | Select Control Group |

Step 2: | Measure Variable | | Measure Variable |

Step 3: | Add Variable |

Step 4: | Measure Variable | | Measure Variable |

Differences in measurement at Steps 2 and 4 in the Experimental Group could be the result of the added variable and other factors. Differences in measurement between Steps 2 and 4 for the Control Group are the result of other factors only. Comparing the differences between the Experimental Group and the Control Group shows the influence of the variable.

Procedure

As is true in observation, the experimenter must have a clear under-standing of the problem under investigation. In addition, the re-searcher needs to carefully design the experiment. Will one group be used or two? How will subjects be selected? Under what conditions? setting? Because of the uniqueness of each situation, we can't provide exact procedures for all experiments. Each experimenter must design a procedure for his/her individual study. The following guidelines will help you design your study.

When the experimenter elects to use the one-group method, he/she needs to select the subject or subjects. Then the experimenter mea-sures the variable, introduces the experimental factor, and after a rea-sonable and predetermined length of time, again measures the vari-able. Differences in measurements can be attributed to the experimental factor. See Exhibit 8.1.

Assume that a company wants to determine the effectiveness of television advertising for Product A as measured by sales. The proce-dure for the experimenter would be to

1. Select the experimental group—in this case, Product A.
2. Record sales (the variable) of Product A for one month.
3. Introduce experimental factor—television advertising.
4. Record sales of Product A during the month of television advertising.
5. Find differences between the two measurements (record of sales).
6. Analyze the results, draw conclusions, and make recommendations.

Differences in sales—before and after television advertising—could be attributed to the experimental factor—television advertising. For ex-ample, if 10,000 Product As were sold before and 100,000 after televi-sion advertising, the experimenter could assume that the increase in sales was due to television advertising. Other factors that could have influenced sales—such as time of year, holidays, or economy—should be considered as well.

When the experimenter elects to use two groups—control and experimental—he/she needs to select subjects that are essentially alike. The experimenter measures the variable, introduces the experimental factor into the experimental group only, and then again measures the variable in both groups. The differences between the two measurements in the control group may be the result of other influences; and in the experimental group, differences may be the result of the experimental factor plus other influences. See Exhibit 8.1.

Assume that a company wants to determine the effectiveness of a motivational seminar for its salespeople. The procedure for the experimenter would be

1. Select subjects—salespeople—according to predetermined criteria, such as sex, age, and number of sales so that they are essentially alike.
2. Randomly place all salespeople in either the control group or the experimental group.
3. Record the sales of both groups for one month.
4. Have the experimental group attend a five-day motivational seminar. (The control group does not attend the seminar.)
5. Record the sales of both groups for one month after the seminar.
6. Find differences between the two measurements of the control group and of the experimental group.
7. Analyze the results, draw conclusions, and make recommendations.

Differences in sales between the two groups could be attributed to the experimental factor—the motivational seminar. For example, let's say that the total sales for both groups were relatively equal—about $100,000—before the motivational seminar. If after the seminar the experimental group had total sales of $250,000 and the control group had only $150,000, the experimenter could assume that the increase in sales for the experimental group was the result of the motivational seminar. Other influences (time of year, advertising) could also have affected the differences in both groups.

Advantages

Some of the advantages of using experimentation as a research technique are

1. Experimental research yields extremely precise results when conducted in the laboratory. It is especially useful in the sciences—physics, chemistry, biology, medicine.
2. Experimentation using the one-group or the two-group method can be highly reliable and accurate outside the laboratory when all variables can be controlled or held constant.

3.   Computer research can create simulated environments so that variables can be manipulated and analyzed quickly and easily.

Disadvantages   The disadvantages are

1.   Many business problems do not lend themselves to experimental research.

2.   Experimentation using the one-group method is not as reliable as using the two-group—control and experimental.

3.   It is almost impossible to have two groups exactly alike.

4.   It is difficult to control and identify all factors, such as the enthusiasm of the experimenter or the effort of subjects to do well when they know they are part of an experiment, that may affect the experiment.

SURVEY

Because not all elements can be observed or examined experimentally, you need to obtain much information by asking questions or surveying people. The survey (also called the interview technique) is a method of research used to gather information about existing situations. It is concerned with finding out who, what, when, where, and how much. (Experimental researchers, on the other hand, are concerned with the why, the cause and effect relationship.) The survey is the main procedure for investigating attitudes, opinions, and motives. It is a highly structured interview that doesn't need to be done face-to-face. Generally, a list of questions (questionnaire) is prepared first and then the survey is conducted by personal, telephone, or mail interviews. (See Chapter 9 for a further discussion on questionnaires.) People surveyed or questioned are selected by statistical procedures called *sampling*.

Sampling   When an entire population—called the *universe*—cannot be surveyed (because the population is too large or a complete survey is not economically feasible), the researcher needs to select a representative sampling of the universe. A sample is a part of a larger group. A population may be people, but it may consist of other items, too (see Chapter 10). Coffee-bean buyers, for example, determine the quality of the beans by examining a sample of the whole. The belief is that the sample will be representative—a cross-section of the whole. Three principles of sampling are representativeness, reliability, and validity.

Representativeness   The representativeness of the sample must be determined before its size; if the sample is unrepresentative, increasing the size will not make it representative. A sample selected from a population of all students living in dorms at one university, for example, would not be representative of the entire school population regardless of sample size, because not all students live on campus. The characteristics of the sample must be the same as the characteristics of the entire population.

Suppose you wanted to investigate the attitudes of the students at a local college or university. If 35 percent of your universe were freshmen; 30 percent, sophomores; 20 percent, juniors; and 15 percent, seniors; then your sample should reflect the same proportions. The sample should also take into consideration other differences, such as sex, age, and grade point average. This process of making sure that each part of the population (universe) appears in the sample in the same percentage as in the population is called *stratification.* The population is divided into strata (subgroups) and then samples are taken proportionately from each stratum.

Reliability   Reliability refers to accuracy or dependability of results. A general law of sampling says that the larger the sample, the higher degree of reliability. In other words, when a larger number of units is taken randomly (each unit in the population has an equal chance of being in the sample) from a large population, they will have a greater chance of having the same characteristics as the larger population. If the sample is reliable, no matter how many times the survey is conducted, the results would be the same—they would be consistent.

Too large a sample, however, is a waste of time and effort, and too small a sample contains chance of errors. You would probably have unreliable results if you survey only five units from an entire population of 500. As you increase your sample size, however, your findings would tend to stabilize. In other words, as the sample size increases, less fluctuation in the findings occurs. See Chapter 11.

To determine how many survey returns will produce reliability, the researchers arbitrarily select a sample size. They randomly arrange the total number of surveys and divide them into equal groups (10, 50, 100, or whatever number is best) and then select one or more questions that require the most reliability.

The researchers tally the responses for the selected question for the first group and compute the percentage (or average). They then tally the responses for the second group, combine the number with the count for the first group, and compute the percentage (or average) for the cumulative total. After they do the same for all remaining groups, they plot the cumulative percentages (or averages) on a grid. At first the percentages (or averages) will have an erratic pattern, but as the totals are accumulated, they will tend to stabilize. When any additional group's percentage (or average) does not affect the cumulative total, the researchers can assume that they have found the correct number of returns to produce reliability.

In a survey of 1,000 students, for example, the researchers first select a significant question that they want to test for reliability—whether Class A or Class B was more beneficial to the student. Although the researchers could tally either response—Class A or Class B—they decide to tally the Class A responses. They then randomly divide the 1,000 surveys into 10 groups of 100. In the first group of 100 surveys, the researchers find 80 Class A responses, or 80 percent. They plot the 80 percent on the grid. In the second group of 100, they find 70 Class A responses. They add the 70 percent to the first group's total of 80 for a cumulative total of 150 Class A responses. The cumulative percentage of Class A responses (150 ÷ 2) is 75. They plot the 75 percent on the grid.

For the third group, the researchers find 65 Class A responses. They add the 65 to the total of group 1 and 2 (150) and a new cumulative percentage of 71 (215 ÷ 3), which is plotted on the grid. The researchers continue to plot the percentage of each new group combined with those of the preceding group's. Exhibits 8.2 and 8.3 show the erratic pattern in the Cumulative Percentage of Class A Responses column at the beginning. Later, as each new group's responses are cumulated, the findings become more stabilized. At the point where the findings are stable, it is not necessary to analyze additional surveys; you would have a reliable finding for that one question. Although researchers need not test every question in the survey, they should test several of the significant questions to ensure reliability of the entire survey. *(See Chapter 11 for statistical inferences.)*

Validity   In addition to being reliable, your survey instrument must be valid; that is, the survey instrument or technique must measure what it is supposed to measure.

EXHIBIT 8.2

Cumulative Frequency Test to Determine Reliability

Group Number	Class A Responses In Group	Cumulative Class A Responses	Cumulative Percentages of Class A Responses
1	80	80	80%
2	70	150	75
3	65	215	71
4	48	263	65
5	59	322	64
6	74	396	66
7	76	472	67
8	67	539	67
9	72	611	67
10	61	672	67

EXHIBIT 8.3

Plotted Cumulative Frequencies

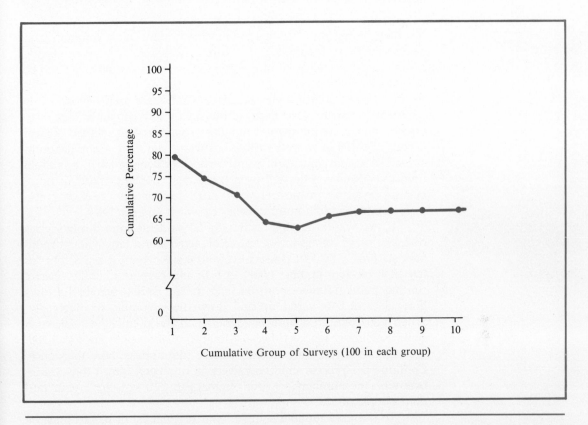

 Cumulative Group of Surveys (100 in each group)

When your survey instrument is ineffective in returning accurate and reliable data, your time and money have been wasted. As will be discussed later in the chapter, survey instruments require trial runs to reveal questionable items—items that are unclear, ambiguous, catchy, subjective, and the like.

Researchers want to develop as objective a test as possible to have a valid instrument. Although researchers should *never* seek to prove a hypothesis true, some may wish to do so by asking biased questions. This would invalidate the results of the questionnaire.

Another factor that would yield a low validity is using words unfamiliar to the reader. Consider using similar questions—questions that ask for the same information but in a different wording—to check the accuracy of the respondent.

**Sampling
Techniques**

The four major sampling techniques are random, stratified random, systematic, and quota. Other sampling techniques exist and may be described in statistical textbooks.

Random Sampling   Perhaps the most important, most common, and easiest method of sampling is random sampling. A random sample means that every element in the population has an equal chance to be selected for the sample. Let's say you wanted to draw a random sample from the seniors at the local college. First, place each senior's name on a slip of paper. Next, place all the slips into a container, mix thoroughly, and draw the desired number of names. This method is ideal if you have 100 or so in the class, but when you have a population of several thousand you might want to consider using a table of random numbers (usually generated by a computer). Books of random numbers are available in most libraries, and most statistics textbooks also carry sample random number tables to which you can refer.

If you want a random sample of 50 students from a senior class of 4,408, make an alphabetic list of all seniors and assign them numbers starting with 0001 consecutively to 4,408. Then, using a four- or five-digit random number book, turn to any page and blindly select a starting point. Numbers can be read in any order—across the rows (forward and backward), up and down the columns, or diagonally. When you come to a number higher than the population total, such as 4,506, simply ignore it because the population only goes to 4,408. Also ignore any repeat numbers—those that appear more than once. Continue the process until you select 50 numbers. Match those numbers with the numbers on your original list. You now have your random sample of 50.

To ensure a random sample, your original list of names must be complete and current. If your list of students contained names of some students who were juniors instead of seniors—or of graduates—then all items in the population would not have an equal chance of being selected. Also, if the names of some seniors had been omitted from the list, the resulting sample would not be truly random.

Stratified Random Sampling   The stratified random sampling method divides the population into subgroups (strata) and then randomly takes a sample from each subgroup (stratum). A sample size of five from each of ten subgroups would give you a sample size of 50. Each subgroup is represented in the sampling according to its proportion of the universe. If you wished, for example, to obtain information as it applies to voters, and your district contains three times as many Republicans as Democrats, your sample should include three times as many Republicans as Democrats.

Or, perhaps you want to divide a population of 2,000 people according to the sections of the United States—East, West, North, or

EXHIBIT 8.4
Stratified Random Sampling

	Total	Percent of Total	Number Selected
East	648	32	64
West	542	27	54
South	303	16	30
North	507	26	52
	2,000	100	200

South. If 32 percent (648 ÷ 2,000) of the population comes from the East, then 32 percent of the sample—64 (.32 × 200)—would also come from the East. See Exhibit 8.4.

Systematic Sampling   Systematic sampling is the method of taking selections at regular intervals from a list of the entire population. You select a starting point and then select every *nth* item. For example, if by chance you choose 12 as your first number and use 20 as the *n*, you would select the 32d (12 + 20), 52d (32 + 20), 72d, 92d, etc. item on the list.

Quota Sampling   Quota sampling is a nonrandom technique that ensures a sample with the same characteristics as the entire population. Researchers would use this technique whenever they have several factors that they believe would be important considerations in solving the problem. For example, market researchers want to survey a population of 4,000 and a sample of 100 to determine factors that influence buying a particular product. They may assume that sex, marital status, income, family size, and age are important characteristics to consider. The researchers would have quotas to fill for each factor. For example, if the total population were 1,000 and of that population 570 were female and 430 male, then the researchers would have a quota of 57 females and 43 males because 57 percent of the total are female and 43 percent are male. Exhibit 8.5 illustrates the number to be surveyed for each characteristic.

SUMMARY

Information obtained from asking and analyzing questions, watching and interpreting the behavior of others, and testing and evaluating is called primary research because you are the first to find the information and interpret it. Three main methods of primary research are observation, experimentation, and surveys.

EXHIBIT 8.5

Quota Sampling

	Population	Percent	Number to Be Sampled
Total			
	1,000	100	100
Sex			
Female	570	57	57
Male	430	43	43
Marital Status			
Single	250	25	25
Married	750	75	75
Income			
less than $10,000	50	5	5
$10,000–$19,999	250	25	25
$20,000–$29,999	320	32	32
$30,000–$39,999	260	26	26
$40,000–$49,999	40	4	4
$50,000–$59,999	30	3	3
$60,000–$69,999	30	3	3
more than $70,000	20	2	2
Family Size			
0–1	350	35	35
2–3	330	33	33
4–5	270	27	27
6–7	20	2	2
8 or more	30	3	3
Age			
0–10	10	1	1
11–20	240	24	24
21–30	360	36	36
31–40	200	20	20
41–50	110	11	11
51–60	30	3	3
61–70	40	4	4
71 and over	10	1	1

Collecting raw data by watching or seeing what is happening to people, objects, or events and recording that information is called observation.

In the experimental method of research, controlled conditions are established for an orderly form of testing that is highly reliable and accurate. Experimentation is a form of research which manipulates one variable while holding all others constant.

Because not all elements can be observed or experimentally examined, you may need to obtain your information by asking questions or surveying people. The survey is a method of research used to gather information about an existing situation. It is concerned with finding out·who, what, when, where, and how much. People surveyed or questioned are selected by a statistical procedure called sampling. The major sampling techniques are random, stratified random, systematic, and quota.

EXERCISES

Review Questions

1. Define primary research. How does it differ from secondary research?

2. What are the three main methods of primary research? Define each.

3. What are the advantages and disadvantages of the three methods of primary research?

4. Company records can be used for both primary and secondary research. Explain.

5. Describe the differences between the one-group method and the two-group method.

6. What is sampling? What is random sampling? stratified random sampling? systematic sampling? quota sampling?

7. Define reliability and validity.

Problems

1. Go to a supermarket on a Saturday afternoon between 1 and 4 p.m. and observe 25 customers as they leave the checkout lanes. Observe their appearance, purchases, sex, approximate age, and number of grocery bags purchased. Prepare an observation sheet for ease in recording the observations. Write a memo report to your instructor giving the results of your supermarket survey.

2. Conduct an experimental study on a topic of your choice for a two-week period. Use a one-group method or the two-group method. Prepare a short report.

3. Using a random number table, prepare a random sampling of a group of about 25 people. The group can be people in a particular class, people in your dorm, people at work, etc. Choose a sample size of five. Submit a memo to your instructor telling what you did and how you did it. Submit with the memo the list of the entire population, the list of selected names, and the random number table that you used.

4. Prepare a stratified random sampling of a particular population from the classified section of the telephone directory. For example, take the population for surgeons and physicians. The strata might be types of practice—allergy, cardiovascular, dermatology, etc. Write a memo report to your instructor saying how you arrived at your strat-

ified random sampling. Photocopy pages of the directory, if necessary.

5. For each of the following kinds of primary research, give five examples of the kinds of problems you could solve. Explain your choice.
    a. Experimentation
    b. Observation
    c. Survey

6. For each of the following kinds of sampling techniques, cite three examples which could use each effectively.
    a. Random sampling
    b. Stratified random sampling
    c. Systematic sampling
    d. Quota sampling (State at least four important characteristics to consider.)

CHAPTER 9
The Questionnaire

The most widely used method for asking questions to obtain primary data is the questionnaire. How do your employees feel about the flex-time policy soon to be introduced in your company? What changes could your company make in a product to increase its attractiveness to consumers? These are questions that you can answer only by asking appropriate people about their attitudes, opinions, and ideas. Surveys of this variety are best conducted with the questionnaire.

Topics

Questionnaires
Interviews
The Delphi Technique
Ethics

QUESTIONNAIRES

A questionnaire is an orderly list of questions used to obtain primary data—facts, opinions, attitudes, behavior characteristics, and preferences—from people. It provides answers to questions about what people think and why they think in a certain way. In addition, questionnaires can help answer questions about how people will react. The answers from questionnaires provide information for making decisions, improving products, recommending policies and procedures, and suggesting changes.

Advantages

Using questionnaires for obtaining information has many advantages, some of which are outlined below.

1. Mail questionnaires can be distributed at low cost.
2. They can be distributed quickly and easily.
3. They can reach large numbers of people scattered over a large geographic area.
4. Respondents can remain anonymous.
5. Prejudices and biases of the interviewer can be eliminated.
6. Respondents can complete questionnaires at a time convenient for them.
7. Time can be saved by both interviewer and interviewee.

Disadvantages

Questionnaires also have disadvantages.

1. Mail questionnaires may be sent to a representative sample of the population, but the returns may not be representative.
2. Questions may be inadequately answered, changed, overlooked, or omitted.
3. Convincing people to respond and to respond by a specific time is difficult.
4. Questionnaires can be invalid and unreliable if not prepared properly.
5. Questions that seem clear to the researcher may be ambiguous to the respondent.
6. It takes time to design, test, evaluate, and refine a questionnaire.

Guidelines

When you have a carefully prepared questionnaire, you can expect good results. The following guidelines can help you design a questionnaire that will eliminate many of the disadvantages mentioned above.

1. Identify the questionnaire by giving it a title, stating its purpose, and identifying yourself and the organization with which you are affiliated.

2. Provide clear instructions. What do you want your respondent to do? Circle? Check one? Check all that apply? Select the best answer? Rank in order of preference? Adequate instructions tend to increase reliability and validity of the questionnaire.

3. Make questions clear, easy to understand, and concerned with only one topic. Avoid ambiguous or unfamiliar words, technical jargon, vague expressions, and relative terms, such as often, regular, and the like.

    a. Do you regularly drive to work?
        (What's regular? daily? weekly? monthly?)
    b. How do you drive to work?
        (In a car? by Main Street? alone? fast?)
    c. Have you ever had amoebiasis?
        (What is it?)
    d. Why did you sell your condominium?
        (Money? neighbors? location? construction? taxes?)

4. Make questions easy to answer so that respondents can complete the questionnaire quickly and easily.

5. Design questionnaires so that respondents can mark them easily and you can tabulate them easily. Use mark sense answer sheets for machine scoring when appropriate.

6. Write questions for your particular audience. Use vocabulary appropriate for your group.

7. Avoid personal questions unless they are essential to your study. When it is necessary to know the respondent's age or income, provide ranges. Because people may be offended by personal questions, place them toward the end of the questionnaire rather than at the beginning. If the questions were at the beginning, respondents might not complete the questionnaire. If respondents encounter them at the end, they are more likely to provide the information because they have already spent the time answering the previous questions. They are also more likely to answer personal questions if you tell them how the information will be used and explain its importance to the study. Assure respondents that information will be kept confidential. Guarantee anonymity. Consider the following questions:

    a. What is your age? Check one.
        _____20 and under
        _____21–30
        _____31–40
        _____41–50
        _____51–60
        _____61–70
        _____70 and over

    b. What is your yearly income? Check one.
        _____under $10,000
        _____$10,000–19,999
        _____$20,000–29,999
        _____$30,000–39,999
        _____$40,000–49,999
        _____$50,000–59,999
        _____$60,000–69,999
        _____$70,000 and over

8. Avoid leading questions—those that strongly suggest a biased answer. Leading questions do not elicit accurate answers. Instead of asking, "Do you prefer Apple computers?" ask "What brand of computer do you prefer?" It is better to ask, "What is your favorite television program?" than "Is 'Dallas' your favorite television program?" Many respondents would answer "yes" even if they didn't watch the program.

9. Ask questions that respondents can recall easily. How many respondents, for example, would make computations for the question, "How much money do you spend each year on gas for your car?"

10. Avoid negative phrasing of questions—especially double negatives. Negative phrasing is confusing. State questions in positive terms.

Poor: Would it not be uncommon to . . . .
Did you not hear about . . . .
You subscribe to the *Wall Street Journal*, don't you?

Better: Would it be common to . . . .
What have you heard . . . .
To what daily newspaper do you subscribe?

11. Begin questions with "Who," "What," "When," "Where," "Why," or "How," and you'll probably receive specific answers.

12. Limit each question to one item. When respondents are asked a question that suggests two answers, they won't know which answer to give. Consider the question: "Would you like to receive a copy of *The Wall Street Journal* at your home? If the respondent answers "no," does it mean that he/she doesn't want *The Wall Street Journal*, or that he/she doesn't want it at home?

13. Avoid questions that make your respondents look from one question to another, such as "If you answered "a" in question 8, go to question 12; if you answered "b" go to question 15; and if you answered "c" go to . . . .

14. Use contingency questions when a question depends on a previous question. Contingency questions permit respondents to disregard questions that do not apply to them. For example

Were you ever a committee member? Yes _____No _____
If yes, how many hours a week were devoted to attending committee meetings?
_____0–4
_____5–8
_____9–12
_____13 or more

15. Include a "don't know" (or something similar) choice when you have questions that ask for a "yes" or "no" response.

16. Provide a space for "other (please specify)" answers when using a checklist. For example

What is your classification? Check one.
_____Freshman
_____Sophomore

_____Junior
_____Senior
_____Other (please specify)_____

"Other" would include any other possibility, from a graduate student to a senior citizen who has permission to attend class.

17. Arrange questions in a neat and logical order. Progress from the simple to the complex. Questions should flow smoothly from one to the other.

18. Categorize questions when possible. Grouping not only presents an organized questionnaire but also encourages respondents to complete the categories and simplifies the process of organizing the results. For example, use such categories as "Personal," "General," "Education," or "Employment."

19. Test the questionnaire with people who are similar to your intended audience. A pilot test can quickly identify weaknesses. Make corrections and improvements as necessary.

20. Keep the questionnaire short—one to two pages when possible. People don't want to take the time to answer long questionnaires. The questionnaire should not take more than 10 to 15 minutes to complete.

21. Avoid using both sides of the paper. People generally overlook the back side.

22. Be concise. Avoid adjectives, or limit them to a few. Also avoid wordy expressions (in order to) and expletives (there is, there are, it is).

23. Be precise. Such words as lovely, fantastic, evening, early, frequently, soon, often, and regularly, may have different meanings to different people.

24. Ask only those questions that you need. Phrase them so that the answers will provide the exact information you want.

25. Mail questionnaires at appropriate times. Avoid mailing, for example, at Christmas time, February 14, April 15, Mother's Day, and other heavy mail times.

26. Offer a financial reward or other incentives for completing the questionnaire by a certain date. Because many respondents would be interested in seeing your results, offer to send them a copy as an incentive.

27. Use quality paper and printing for the questionnaire. They create a good first impression. Returns are greater than for those questionnaires prepared on low-quality paper.

28. Supply space for respondents' names and addresses if you say you'll send them a copy of the report or a summary of the findings.

29. Provide a stamped, addressed envelope for returning the questionnaire, as a courtesy and to encourage the return of the questionnaire. Or, the questionnaire can be designed so that when folded and stapled, it can be returned without an envelope or stamp. See Exhibit 9.1.

EXHIBIT 9.1

Postpaid Questionnaire That Needs No Envelope

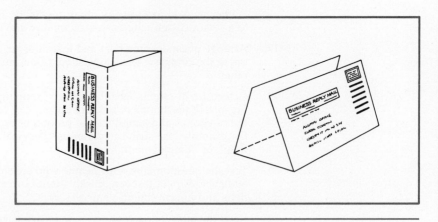

30. Provide a cover letter that clearly states the purpose and importance of the study and provides a reader benefit.

Forms of Questions

After you have compiled a list of all the conceivable items of information that you wish to obtain from the survey, you need to compose questions that will provide you with the information you desire to prepare your report.

Select the *type* of question that will best solicit the information. Also, consider the time it will take a reader to answer a question and the time it will take you to tabulate the answer. Seven types of questions most frequently used on questionnaires are as follows:

Either-Or An either-or question offers the respondent a choice between two answers, such as

yes/no	for/against
true/false	favor/oppose
agree/disagree	approve/disapprove
like/dislike	before/after

Sometimes a question needs a third choice. For example, the question, "Will you run for governor?" can be answered "Yes," "No," or "Not Sure." Other third choice selections could be "Don't know," "No opinion," or "Undecided." Either-or questions are the best questions to use because they can be answered quickly and easily by the respondents, and the replies can be accurately and easily tabulated. The disadvantage of the either-or question is that most questions cannot be answered simply by "Yes," "No," or "Don't know," as when you ask people for their opinions or motives. Consider the following either-or questions.

1. Are you currently employed? Yes _____No _____

2. Are you qualified to operate a forklift truck?
   Yes _____No _____Don't know _____

3. Manual dexterity should be a requirement for the job.
   True _____False _____Not sure _____

4. Only people with doctorates should be promoted.
   Agree _____Disagree _____No opinion _____

Checklist In a checklist, the respondent is given a statement (or question) and a list of possible answers to be checked. More than one item may be checked. A good checklist contains *all* possible options, which may include "None of the above" or "Other (please specify)." Checklists are popular with researchers because responses can be tabulated easily. They are also popular with respondents because checklists permit a quick and easy means of indicating choices. For example:

In which team sports have you participated within the last ten years? Check as many as apply.

_____Baseball   _____Rugby

_____Basketball   _____Soccer

_____Field hockey   _____Softball

_____Football   _____Volleyball

_____Hockey   _____Other (please specify) _____

Multiple Choice Multiple-choice questions are similar to the checklist (they provide several choices), but they require the respondent to choose only one answer. Again, all possible choices must be included. Include a blanket category, such as "None of the above," or "Other (please specify)" to avoid a forced answer that could reduce the reliability of the study. For example:

Which make of U.S. automobile do you prefer? Check one.

_____American Motors

_____Chrysler

_____Ford

_____General Motors

_____None of the above

_____Other (please specify)_____

Fill-in-the-Blank Fill-in-the-blank questions permit the respondent to provide a short answer. They are also used to elicit factual answers or opinions. For example:

How many years have you lived at your current address? _____

How many brothers and sisters do you have? _____

Ranking A ranking question asks the respondents to rank items in a list in order of their preferences. Lists should be kept short—not more than five items. However, if it is necessary to have longer lists, ask respondents to rank only the five most important. To avoid confusion, specify that tie rankings are not permitted. For example:

What would be your order of preference (one is high) if your company required you to travel?
_____South _____North _____East _____West

Scaling Scaling questions measure intensity of feeling. Respondents are asked to mark responses on a continuum that is closest to their feelings. A three-point scale might read
above average, average, below average.
A four-point scale might read
excellent, very good, good, fair.
A five-point scale might read
strongly approve, approve, undecided or neutral,
disagree, strongly disagree.
How would you rate your superior?

Excellent	Very Good	Good	Average	Fair	Poor	Bad
+3	+2	+1	0	−1	−2	−3

Open-Ended Open-ended questions permit respondents to express their exact feelings and opinions. They do not limit the range of possible answers as do other forms of questions. Although these questions are difficult to tabulate, they can provide valuable information.

I enjoy my time most when . . .
I would enjoy my work more if . . .
I suggest that in the future we . . .

Exhibits 9.2 and 9.3 provide good examples of questionnaires.

EXHIBIT 9.2
Questionnaire

BUSINESS LIAISON COMMITTEE
American Business Communication Association

Please return this questionnaire with your answer sheet.

1. I would be interested in subscribing to a publication that applies communication principles to solving the practical problems of business: productivity, employee cooperation, job satisfaction, issuing directives, information exchange, customer relations, public relations, goverment regulation, employee motivation, etc.

   (1) Yes

   (2) No

2. I would prefer receiving the business communication publication

   (1) Once a month

   (2) Once a quarter

   (3) Twice a year

   (4) Other (please specify) _____

Please rank items 3-20 according to the following scale:

   (1) Extremely important

   (2) Very important

   (3) Important

   (4) Relatively unimportant

   (5) Of no importance

3. Improving my writing to make it clear, concise, coherent, and courteous

4. Issuing directives

5. Improving customer relations

6. Improving public relations

7. Writing for government agencies

EXHIBIT 9.2
Questionnaire—Continued

8.   Dictation aids

9.   Good listening practices

10. Group communication techniques

11. Hints for writing evaluations

12. Letter writing hints

13. Management of training programs

14. Proposal writing tips

15. Report writing techniques

16. Speech making hints

17. Techniques for interviewing

18. Theoretical articles

19. Tips about conducting meetings

20. Other (please specify) _____

     _____

What business publications do you read? Use the following scale for marking.

     (1) Read regularly

     (2) Read sometimes

     (3) Read rarely

     (4) Never read

21. ABCA BULLETIN

22. ABCA JOURNAL

23. BUSINESS AMERICA

24. BUSINESS WEEK

25. COMPUTER WORLD

26. DATA MANAGEMENT

27. DATAMATION

28. FORBES MAGAZINE

EXHIBIT 9.2
Questionnaire—Continued

29. FORTUNE

30. INFOSYSTEMS

31. JOURNAL OF MACROMARKETING

32. JOURNAL OF MANAGEMENT STUDIES

33. JOURNAL OF MARKETING

34. JOURNAL OF MARKETING RESEARCH

35. MARKETING COMMUNICATIONS

36. MERGERS AND ACQUISITIONS

37. NEWSWEEK

38. SALES AND MARKETING MANAGEMENT

39. TIME

40. Other (please specify) _____

_____

41. I am willing to submit articles for publication.

    (1) Yes

    (2) No

42. I am interested in learning more about the American Business Communication Association.

    (1) Yes

    (2) No

    If yes, use space below to provide name and address.

43. I would like to receive the results of this questionnaire.

    (1) Yes

    (2) No

Name _____ Company _____

Address _____

City _____ State _____ Zip _____

EXHIBIT 9.3
Questionnaire

PLEASE CIRCLE THE NUMBER CORRESPONDING TO THE APPROPRIATE RESPONSE

Do you have a savings account?

1. NO ──────────▶ (IF NO) INASMUCH AS OUR SURVEY FOCUSES
2. YES   ON THE SERVICES PROVIDED BY FINANCIAL
         INSTITUTIONS AS SEEN BY PEOPLE WHO HAVE
         SAVINGS ACCOUNTS, WE DO NOT NEED YOUR
         ANSWER TO SECTIONS I, II, III, IV.
         HOWEVER, YOU MAY HELP US GAIN A BETTER
         UNDERSTANDING OF THE NON-DEPOSITOR BY
         ANSWERING THE QUESTIONS IN SECTION V.
         ABOVE ALL, PLEASE RETURN THE QUESTIONNAIRE
         IN THE SELF ADDRESSED ENVELOPE

SECTION I

Q-1. Do you have more than one savings account?

1. NO ──────────▶ (IF NO) PLEASE SKIP TO QUESTION-4.
2. YES

Q-2. Are your savings accounts in the same financial institution: bank, savings/loan, or credit union?

1. NO ──────────▶ (IF YES) PLEASE SKIP TO QUESTION-4.
2. YES

Q-3. Which of the following describes where you have your savings accounts?

1. IN BOTH A BANK AND SAVINGS AND LOAN
2. IN BOTH A SAVINGS AND LOAN AND CREDIT UNION
3. IN BOTH A CREDIT UNION AND A BANK
4. IN BANKS, CREDIT UNIONS, AND SAVINGS AND LOANS
5. OTHER COMBINATION (PLEASE SPECIFY)

Q-4. Where do you keep your largest savings account, including CD's?
(Do not consider stocks and bonds as savings accounts)

BANKS	SAVINGS/LOAN	CREDIT UNION
1. AMERICAN NATIONAL BANK	6. FIDELITY FEDERAL	10. EMPLOYEE TYPE
2. INDUSTRIAL STATE BANK	7. FIRST FEDERAL,	11. NEIGHBORHOOD TYPE
3. FIRST NATIONAL BANK	8. KALAMAZOO SAVINGS AND LOAN	12. OTHER TYPE
4. MICHIGAN NATIONAL BANK	9. OTHER SAVINGS & LOAN	
5. OTHER BANK		

13. OTHER THAN ABOVE (PLEASE SPECIFY)

Q-5. How many years have you saved at the financial institution that has your largest savings account?

1. LESS THAN 1 YEAR
2. 1 TO 5 YEARS
3. 6 TO 10 YEARS
4. OVER 10 YEARS

Q-6. When dealing with the institution that has your largest savings account, how do you handle your savings transactions a majority of the time?

1. IN PERSON AT A BRANCH OFFICE
2. IN PERSON AT THE MAIN OFFICE
3. BY MAIL
4. AUTOMATIC PAYROLL DEDUCTION
5. OTHER (PLEASE SPECIFY)

Q-7. Please try to recall the source(s) of information you used in selecting the financial institution that has your largest savings account. (You may circle more than one answer).

1. FAMILY/RELATIVES
2. FRIENDS
3. CO-WORKERS
4. NEWSPAPER ADVERTISING
5. RADIO, T.V.
6. PERSONAL VISITS TO FINANCIAL INSTITUTION
7. OTHERS (PLEASE SPECIFY)

Q-8. Before choosing a place to open your largest savings account, which of the following types of financial institutions did you consider.

1. I ONLY CONSIDER BANKS
2. I ONLY CONSIDER SAVINGS AND LOANS
3. I ONLY CONSIDER CREDIT UNIONS
4. I CONSIDERED BOTH BANKS AND SAVINGS AND LOANS
5. I CONSIDERED BOTH SAVINGS AND LOANS AND CREDIT UNIONS
6. I CONSIDERED BOTH CREDIT UNIONS AND BANKS
7. I CONSIDERED BANKS, SAVINGS AND LOANS AND CREDIT UNIONS
8. OTHER (PLEASE SPECIFY)

PLEASE CONTINUE TO SECTION II

SECTION II

When choosing a place to keep your largest savings, how important are the following factors in making your decisions? Please circle the number on the right hand page which indicates how important each factor is to you when choosing a place to keep your largest savings account. Read the examples on the top of the next page before answering.

EXAMPLES: When choosing a place to keep your largest savings account, on the first scale below, a circle around a 7 indicates that to you, "HOURS OF OPERATION" is an EXTREMELY IMPORTANT factor to consider; whereas a circle around a 1 indicates that to you, "HOURS OF OPERATION" is NOT an important factor to consider.

LIST OF FACTORS

		NOT IMPORTANT	SLIGHTLY IMPORTANT	REASONABLY IMPORTANT	MODERATELY IMPORTANT	VERY IMPORTANT	UNUSUALLY IMPORTANT	EXTREMELY IMPORTANT
1.	HOURS OF OPERATION	1	2	3	4	5	6	7
2.	LOCATION/CONVENIENCE	1	2	3	4	5	6	7
3.	REPUTATION IN COMMUNITY	1	2	3	4	5	6	7
4.	OBTAINABILITY OF MORTGAGE LOAN	1	2	3	4	5	6	7
5.	OBTAINABILITY OF OTHER LOANS (AUTO, FURNITURE, ETC.)	1	2	3	4	5	6	7
6.	PHYSICAL FACILITIES	1	2	3	4	5	6	7
7.	PERSONAL RECOGNITION BY EMPLOYEES	1	2	3	4	5	6	7
8.	FREE CHECKING WITH MINIMUM BALANCE IN SAVINGS ACCOUNT	1	2	3	4	5	6	7
9.	OVER-DRAFT PRIVILEGES	1	2	3	4	5	6	7
10.	SERVICE CHARGE ON CHECKING ACCOUNT	1	2	3	4	5	6	7
11.	RECOMMENDATION BY OTHERS (FRIENDS, RELATIVES, CO-WORKERS)	1	2	3	4	5	6	7
12.	INTEREST CHARGES & TERMS OF OTHER LOANS (AUTO, FURNITURE, ETC.)	1	2	3	4	5	6	7
13.	INTEREST CHARGES & TERMS OF MORTGAGE LOANS	1	2	3	4	5	6	7
14.	INTEREST RATES ON SAVINGS ACCOUNTS	1	2	3	4	5	6	7
15.	FULL SERVICE OFFERING (CREDIT CARDS, TRUST SERVICES, SAFETY DEPOSIT BOXES)	1	2	3	4	5	6	7
16.	EASE OF FINANCIAL TRANSACTIONS (WALK-UP & DRIVE-IN WINDOWS, MAIL DEPOSIT, PARKING, 24-HOUR AUTOMATED TELLER)	1	2	3	4	5	6	7
17.	DIRECT DEPOSITS OF CHECKS (SOCIAL SECURITY, PAYROLL)	1	2	3	4	5	6	7
18.	COMPETENT & EFFICIENT SERVICE	1	2	3	4	5	6	7

IMPORTANCE

PLEASE CONTINUE TO SECTION III

EXHIBIT 9.3
Questionnaire—Continued

SECTION III

The following list of factors is identical to those in the previous section II; however, this time the task is different. When choosing a place to keep your largest savings, you may feel that in some ways financial institutions are similar and in other ways these institutions are different. Please circle the number on the right hand page which indicates how different you feel the institutions you considered are on each factor. Once again, read the examples on the next page before answering.

EXAMPLES: When choosing a place to keep your largest savings account, on the first scale below, a circle around a 7 indicates that the institutions have EXTREMELY DIFFERENT, "HOURS OF OPERATION"; a circle around a 1 indicates that you feel there is NO DIFFERENCE between the institutions in "HOURS OF OPERATION"; a circle around an x indicates that you are NOT AWARE of any differences between the institutions in "HOURS OF OPERATION".

LIST OF FACTORS

	NOT AWARE	NO DIFFERENCES	SLIGHTLY DIFFERENT	SOMEWHAT DIFFERENT	MODERATELY DIFFERENT	VERY DIFFERENT	REMARKABLY DIFFERENT	EXTREMELY DIFFERENT
1. HOURS OF OPERATION	X	1	2	3	4	5	6	7
2. LOCATION/CONVENIENCE	X	1	2	3	4	5	6	7
3. REPUTATION IN COMMUNITY	X	1	2	3	4	5	6	7
4. OBTAINABILITY OF MORTGAGE LOAN	X	1	2	3	4	5	6	7
5. OBTAINABILITY OF OTHER LOANS (AUTO, FURNITURE, ETC.)	X	1	2	3	4	5	6	7
6. PHYSICAL FACILITIES	X	1	2	3	4	5	6	7
7. PERSONAL RECOGNITION BY EMPLOYEES	X	1	2	3	4	5	6	7
8. FREE CHECKING WITH MINIMUM BALANCE IN SAVINGS ACCOUNT	X	1	2	3	4	5	6	7
9. OVER-DRAFT PRIVILEGES	X	1	2	3	4	5	6	7
10. SERVICE CHARGE ON CHECKING ACCOUNT	X	1	2	3	4	5	6	7
11. RECOMMENDATION BY OTHERS (FRIENDS, RELATIVES, CO-WORKERS)	X	1	2	3	4	5	6	7
12. INTEREST CHARGES & TERMS OF OTHER LOANS (AUTO, FURNITURE, ETC.)	X	1	2	3	4	5	6	7
13. INTEREST CHARGES & TERMS OF MORTGAGE LOANS	X	1	2	3	4	5	6	7
14. INTEREST RATES ON SAVINGS ACCOUNTS	X	1	2	3	4	5	6	7
15. FULL SERVICE OFFERING (CREDIT CARDS, TRUST SERVICES, SAFETY DEPOSIT BOX)	X	1	2	3	4	5	6	7
16. EASE OF FINANCIAL TRANSACTIONS (WALK-UP & DRIVE-IN WINDOWS, MAIL DEPOSIT, PARKING, 24-HOUR AUTOMATED TELLER)	X	1	2	3	4	5	6	7
17. DIRECT DEPOSITS OF CHECKS (SOCIAL SECURITY, PAYROLL)	X	1	2	3	4	5	6	7
18. COMPETENT & EFFICIENT SERVICE	X	1	2	3	4	5	6	7

DIFFERENCES

PLEASE CONTINUE TO SECTION IV

Please rate the institution where you have your largest savings account on the following pairs of characteristics. Circle the number on each scale which describes how you view this place of savings (For example: on the first scale below, a circle around a "1" indicates a very progressive institution; a circle around a "7" indicates a very conservative institution; a circle around a "4" indicates an institution that is neither progressive nor conservative.

THE PLACE WHERE I HAVE MY LARGEST SAVINGS ACCOUNT IS:

1.	PROGRESSIVE	1 2 3 4 5 6 7	CONSERVATIVE
2.	IMPERSONAL	1 2 3 4 5 6 7	PERSONAL
3.	MODERN	1 2 3 4 5 6 7	OLD-FASHIONED
4.	AGGRESSIVE	1 2 3 4 5 6 7	RESERVE
5.	A LEADER	1 2 3 4 5 6 7	A FOLLOWER
6.	DYNAMIC	1 2 3 4 5 6 7	STATIC
7.	COMFORTABLE	1 2 3 4 5 6 7	UNCOMFORTABLE
8.	INTERESTED IN HELPING PEOPLE	1 2 3 4 5 6 7	INTERESTED IN MAKING MONEY
9.	CONCERNED WITH SELF	1 2 3 4 5 6 7	CONCERNED WITH COMMUNITY
10.	WELL KNOWN	1 2 3 4 5 6 7	NOT WELL KNOWN
11.	SMALL	1 2 3 4 5 6 7	LARGE
12.	FORMAL	1 2 3 4 5 6 7	INFORMAL
13.	UNRELIABLE	1 2 3 4 5 6 7	RELIABLE
14.	COMPETITIVE	1 2 3 4 5 6 7	NOT COMPETITIVE
15.	COOPERATIVE	1 2 3 4 5 6 7	UNCOOPERATIVE
16.	ORGANIZED	1 2 3 4 5 6 7	DISORGANIZED
17.	COMPLEX	1 2 3 4 5 6 7	SIMPLE

Once again, please rate the place where you have your largest savings account on the following pair of characteristics. Circle the number on each scale which describes how you view your place of savings. Follow the same method of circling response as before.

THE PLACE WHERE I HAVE MY LARGEST SAVINGS ACCOUNT HAS:

18.	STRICT PROCEDURES	1 2 3 4 5 6 7	FLEXIBLE PROCEDURES
19.	INEFFICIENT SERVICE	1 2 3 4 5 6 7	EFFICIENT SERVICE
20.	FRIENDLY EMPLOYEES	1 2 3 4 5 6 7	UNFRIENDLY EMPLOYEES
21.	LOW INTEREST ON SAVINGS	1 2 3 4 5 6 7	HIGH INTEREST ON SAVINGS
22.	FULL SERVICE	1 2 3 4 5 6 7	LIMITED SERVICE
23.	TENSE ATMOSPHERE	1 2 3 4 5 6 7	RELAXED ATMOSPHERE
24.	CLEAN FACILITIES	1 2 3 4 5 6 7	DIRTY FACILITIES

Please circle the number that reflects your overall evaluation of the financial institution that has your largest savings account.

EXTREMELY POOR	VERY POOR	POOR	AVERAGE	GOOD	VERY GOOD	EXTREMELY GOOD
1	2	3	4	5	6	7

PLEASE CONTINUE TO SECTION V

EXHIBIT 9.3
Questionnaire—Continued

SECTION V

In order to better understand your responses, we need to ask you a few final questions. Again, any information supplied in the questionnaire will not be associated with your name in any way. Please circle the correct response.

Q-1. What is your sex?

1. MALE
2. FEMALE

Q-2. Which of the following categories includes your age?

1. UNDER 18
2. 18 - 34 YEARS
3. 35 - 49 YEARS
4. 50 - 64 YEARS
5. 65 & OVER

Q-3. What is your marital status?

1. SINGLE
2. MARRIED
3. DIVORCED/SEPARATED
4. WIDOW/WIDOWER

Q-4. How many dependent children do you have?

1. NONE
2. 1 OR 2 CHILDREN
3. 3 OR 4 CHILDREN
4. OVER 4 CHILDREN

Q-5. What is the occupation of the primary income earner?

1. PROFESSIONAL
2. WHITE-COLLAR
3. BLUE-COLLAR
4. RETIRED
5. FARMING
6. SELF-EMPLOYED
7. OTHER (PLEASE SPECIFY) _____

Q-6. How long have you lived in Southwest Michigan?

1. 0 - 3 YEARS
2. 4 - 10 YEARS
3. 10 - 20 YEARS
4. OVER 20 YEARS

Q-7. Which of the following describes your housing situation?

1. I OWN MY HOME
2. I AM BUYING MY HOME
3. I AM RENTING MY HOME
4. I AM RENTING AN APARTMENT
5. OTHER (PLEASE SPECIFY) _____

Q-8. What is the level of education of the primary income earner?

1. 0 - 8 YEARS
2. 9 - 12 YEARS
3. 13 - 16 YEARS
4. OVER 16 YEARS

Q-9. Which of the following categories includes your total household income for 1979 (before taxes)?

1. UNDER $5,000
2. $5,000 to $9,999
3. $10,000 to $14,999
4. $15,000 to $19,999
5. $20,000 to $24,999
6. $25,000 to $29,999
7. $30,000 to $49,999
8. $50,000 & OVER

Q-10. Which of the following categories reflect your total savings level?

1. NONE
2. LESS THAN $3,000
3. $3,000 to $6,999
4. $7,000 to $9,999
5. OVER $10,000

THANK YOU FOR YOUR COOPERATION, PLEASE RETURN THE QUESTIONNAIRE IN THE ADDRESSED, STAMPED ENVELOPE

Source: Courtesy of Dr. Lowell E. Crow, Department of Marketing., Western Michigan University

Machine-Scored
Questionnaires

If equipment is available, you may wish to have the questionnaires scored by machine. Some organizations and many colleges have equipment that will permit the direct tabulation of data from specially prepared *sense sheets*. If you plan to have your questionnaire machine scored, ask the respondents to mark their answers on a mark sense sheet. The main advantage of using mark sense sheets is that no data transfer occurs (as with punched cards); therefore, no data transfer errors are possible. Because of these advantages, you should check with the appropriate department in your organization or with your college testing center to see what is available. Follow the instructions provided by the testing center. Exhibit 9.4 (p. 162) shows an example of a mark sense sheet.

Testing

After you have drafted, edited, and polished your questionnaire so that you believe it is an exceptionally good one, give it a trial or pilot test to debug it (eliminate errors). Testing will save you time, effort, and money in the long run. A faulty questionnaire can cause you to conduct the entire survey over again. Make several photocopies of it, and distribute to individuals who are similar to those on your selected mailing list. They can tell you if a question isn't clear. Also, their answers to the questions may reveal ambiguities that they were not aware of while completing the questionnaire. Ask these people for constructive criticism and then heed their advice. Make the necessary corrections to improve the instrument. Eliminating poorly phrased questions will result in more usable questionnaires.

Data Tally Sheet

After you have received the desired number of returns, you'll need to develop a system for tallying each question on the questionnaire. An effective system for tallying data is to prepare a data tally sheet. A data tally sheet can be a blank questionnaire with ample space for recording tallies or a sheet of paper specifically designed so that all responses can be tallied in one place for summarization. The data tally sheet displays all response options for each item. See Exhibit 9.5 on p. 163.

Because of the increasing popularity and accessibility of computers, you may be able to save yourself hours of computations. Investigate all possibilities open to you for machine scoring and computer analysis of data. In any case, prepare your data tally sheet so that it will be convenient for you to transfer figures into the computer. It may be you won't need a data tally sheet; you might be able to transfer figures directly from the questionnaire answer sheet to the computer. Again, you'll need to check with the specialists in your organization.

Here are some suggestions for tallying the results of your questionnaire.

1. Select a quiet spot where you won't be interrupted by phone or friends.

EXHIBIT 9.4
Mark Sense Sheet

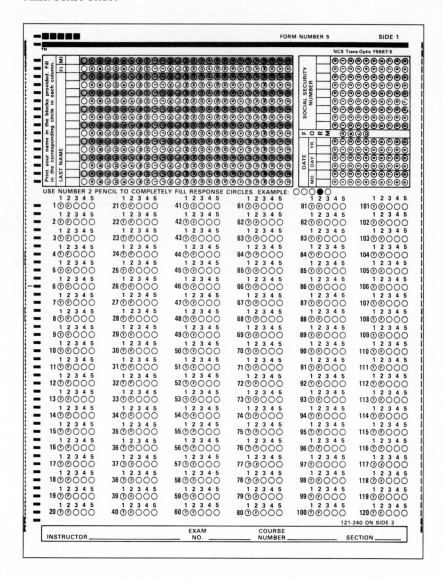

2.   Record tallies on a data tally sheet.

3.   Use stick figures in groups of four with the fifth stick crossing the fourth when you tally. It's simple and easy. For example

$$\text{卌}\quad\text{卌}\quad\text{卌}\quad\text{卌}\quad=20.$$

4.   Arrange all questionnaires in one stack and tally one complete questionnaire—item by item—before going on to the next questionnaire. To double check your work, use another data tally sheet and tally

EXHIBIT 9.5
Format for a Data Tally Sheet

1. Example: Either-Or: Would you volunteer to serve as a host/hostess?

Question #	Yes	No	Not sure
1	⊥HI ⊥HI	III	II

2. Example: Checklist: In which of the following sports have you participated?

Question #	Baseball	Basketball	Football	Volleyball
2	⊥HI ⊥HI III	III	⊥HI ⊥HI	III

3. Example: Multiple Choice: Which card game do you prefer?

Question #	Bridge	Hearts	Pinochle	Uno
3	IIII	III	⊥HI III	⊥HI III

4. Example: Fill-in-the-Blank: How many years have you attended the Indy 500?

Question #	
4	5-1-2-4-7-10-2-1-3-4

5. Example: Ranking: What is your order or preference (one is high) if you had your choice of location?

Question #	South	North	East	West
5	1-4-2-2-3	2-3-4-3-3	3-2-3-4-4	4-1-1-2-1

6. Example: Scaling: How would you rate your supervisor using the following scale?

Question #	Unsatisfactory	Poor	Satisfactory	Good	Outstanding
6	I	I	⊥HI	⊥HI	III

7. Example: Open-Ended: What is your opinion of the new vacation policy?

Question #	
7	I like it. It provides a week in summer for all, etc.

the first item for each questionnaire. Next, tally the second item for each questionnaire. After you have tallied all the questionnaires, compare the two data tally sheets. Where there is a difference in tallies, you'll need to recheck them.

Computations

After the questionnaires have been tallied, you will want to summarize the responses for the individual questions for your written report. In some cases, computations will mean only adding tallies.

When you have a ranking question, for example, you merely add the tallies. The total tally for each item ranked provides the ranking order. Consider the following:

If the office were to purchase a word processor, what is your order of preference (use "1" to indicate your first choice) of brands?

	Total Tally
_____ Apple	300
_____ IBM	100
_____ Radio Shack	400
_____ Wang	500
_____ Xerox	200

Because "1" indicates the respondents' first choice, the *lowest* total score indicates the first-ranked response.

When reporting the data in your report, you might say something like

When asked their order of preference for an office word processor, the respondents selected IBM as their first choice, Xerox as their second choice, Apple as their third, Radio Shack as their fourth, and Wang as their fifth.

Or you could refer your readers to a table by saying,

Table 15 shows the order of preference of brand names for an office word processor.

1. IBM
2. Xerox
3. Apple
4. Radio Shack
5. Wang

Another example:

Of the 50 respondents, 22 were female and 28 were male. They reported having participated in the following activities:

	Females	Males	Total
Drama	15	23	38
Music	12	7	19
Art	25	18	43
Dance	32	5	37

Sometimes you may want to convert numbers into percentages.

When asked how they learned about the Office of Management Development, the 50 respondents replied as follows:

13 Newspaper
23 Newsletter
 6 Director
 8 Colleague
50

To compute the percentage in the above example, divide the number of responses for each item by the total number of responses, and then multiply by 100. For example:

$$\frac{\text{Number of responses to item 1}}{\text{Total number of responses}} = \frac{13}{50} = 0.26 \times 100 = 26\%.$$

Newspaper	Newsletter	Director	Colleague	
13	23	6	8	= 50.
26%	46%	12%	16%	= 100%.

The total percent will always equal 100 percent even when you round off numbers. For example:

 87.5 percent rounded off = 88 percent (rounded *up* to even whole)
 12.5 percent rounded off = 12 percent (rounded *down* to even whole)
100 percent   100 percent

Example:

When asked whether they planned to get a bachelor's degree, 70 percent of the respondents said yes, and 20 percent said no. Ten percent were uncertain.

Question	Yes	No	Uncertain	
1	35	10	5	= 50.
	70%	20%	10%	= 100%.

$$\frac{\text{Number of yes responses}}{\text{Total number of responses}} = \frac{35}{50} = 0.7 \times 100 = 70\%.$$

$$\frac{\text{Number of no responses}}{\text{Total number of responses}} = \frac{10}{50} = 0.2 \times 100 = 20\%.$$

$$\frac{\text{Number of uncertain responses}}{\text{Total number of responses}} = \frac{5}{50} = 0.1 \times 100 = 10\%.$$

When respondents are asked to mark responses on a continuum, you may want to report a group average. Consider the following example:

What is your opinion about the new vacation policy?

Extremely Dislike	Dislike	OK	Like	Extremely Like
1	2	3	4	5

For computation count the number of responses for each point.

Point	Number of Responses
1	5
2	10
3	21
4	8
5	6
	Total 50

Multiply the number of responses times the value of the responses and total the results.

$$1 \times 5 = 5$$
$$2 \times 10 = 20$$
$$3 \times 21 = 63$$
$$4 \times 8 = 32$$
$$5 \times 6 = 30$$
$$150$$

Divide the value total by the total number of responses.

$$150 \div 50 = 3.$$

Three is the average (mean) response. It shows an average response. If the average were 2.3, the responses would be to the "dislike" side of the neutral point. If the average were 4.02, the responses would be to the like side of the middle.

When a group average can be misleading, avoid reporting it as the group average. It would be better for you to report the responses individually. Suppose, for example, that the responses in the preceding example fell at the two ends of the continuum making the opinions polarized—two conflicting or contrasting positions. The average would be three, but to report that result as average would mislead your readers. For example:

	Extremely Dislike	Dislike	OK	Like	Extremely Like	
Scale	1	2	3	4	5	
Responses	20	4	2	4	20	
Value × Response	20	8	6	16	100	= 150

$$150 \div 50 = 3.$$

Because 20 responded "Extremely dislike" and 20 responded "Extremely like", you could not report that the group response was average. You would need to report the bimodal—two frequency values—character of the responses.

In Chapter 11, we discuss the ways researchers can use averages and differences among data to display, summarize, and interpret results.

When reporting open-ended questions, display them in table form or in an enumerated list. Whenever possible, categorize them. For each category, list the responses reported. For example:

When asked their positive self-verbalizations, respondents' replies fell into four categories—appearance, health, accomplishments, and attitudes.

Appearance

1. I'm beautiful.
2. I like the way I look.
3. I'm happy with my physical looks.

Health

1. I feel great.
2. I like exercising.
3. I eat well.

Accomplishments

1. I can do it.
2. I enjoy working.
3. I'm glad I can type (swim, teach, supervise, manage).

Attitude

1. I like myself.
2. I feel good about my friends.
3. I'm happy.

After all the computations have been made for each question, record them on a blank questionnaire. This serves two purposes: (1) your data are summarized for you, so it should be easier for you to write the report, and (2) your readers can see an item-by-item display of the results if you place a complete copy of the questionnaire—with the typed-in results—in the appendix of the report.

Letter of Transmittal

Questionnaires sent by mail must have an accompanying letter, usually called a letter of transmittal or cover letter. The quality and tone of the transmittal letter will directly affect the rate of returns.

Generally, the rate of return for mail questionnaires is less than 15 percent. With a well-organized cover letter stressing a reader benefit, a well-prepared questionnaire, and a selected mailing list, however, the rate of return can be 50–75 percent. When returns reach 80 percent, you know your findings will be reliable and no additional returns, therefore, are required. If you receive too few responses to guarantee reliability, you can use statistical methods to determine the probability of reliability based on those returns you do receive. See Chapter 11.

Here are some recommendations for writing a good letter of transmittal:

1. Start the letter with a reader benefit. What will the reader gain by completing your questionnaire? Will a report improve the reader's environment? Is there a monetary incentive? A reward incentive (book, coupon)? Appeal to the writer's goodwill or sense of responsibility. These benefits can be classed as direct or indirect. Direct benefits are those that will contribute directly to the reader's well being. Indirect benefits are those that contribute indirectly. The same benefit might be direct for one reader and indirect for another. If you are asked to complete a report on the working conditions for secretarial personnel in your company, the improved working conditions that could result would be a direct benefit for the secretaries and an indirect benefit for management personnel.

2. Provide an explanation of the study. What is the purpose of the study, and what do you hope to accomplish? Why is the study important? Who will benefit?

3. Mention the particular person or organization who is authorizing, supporting, or directing your study. This fact not only gives credibility to your study, but will probably increase the number of responses.

4. Use you-attitude throughout the letter and make the letter personal. Use personal pronouns, such as "I," "You," and "Your." Seek the reader's contribution and cooperation in completing the questionnaire and study.

5. Assure the reader of confidentiality and anonymity. You are interested only in the answers from people who have the expertise to make the study a good one.

6. Offer to send the respondent a copy of the report, a summary of your findings, or an abstract of the report. Respondents could complete the form on the bottom of the questionnaire that solicits their names and addresses. If the respondent wishes to remain anonymous, he or she may return an enclosed postage-paid reply envelope separate from the questionnaire or may write you for a copy of the report after a certain date.

7. End date and justify the letter of transmittal. Ask the respondent to return the completed questionnaire by a specific date—usually 10 days or for those far away, about 3 weeks. Encourage a prompt return by giving a reason. For example:

EXHIBIT 9.6
Letter of Transmittal

Simulated Inside Address[a]

Opening[b]

Disclosure of Use[c]

Instructions[d]

Deadlines[e]

Offer of Response[f]

---

1 May 19xx

Are the memos and
Reports in your company
As clear and concise
As they should be?

If your company is like most, ineffective communication could be costing you
thousands of dollars a year.

Perhaps written instructions are misunderstood, or perhaps some of your
personnel have difficulty with sales presentations or media appearances.

We'd like to know whether you and your company are concerned about the
quality of communication. Will you spend a few minutes now to help the
American Business Communication Association determine whether a special
publication for business people could help solve this problem? Your answers
to the questions on the attached questionnaire will help us determine how
important you consider communication skills and how much of a problem you
have found ineffective communication to be.

Please use a No. 2 pencil to record your answers on the enclosed computer
scoring sheet. (Estimated completion time: 5 minutes.)

Because we would like to prepare your answers for the Business Liaison
Committee by 1 July, please complete and return the questionnaire to us by
15 June.

To receive a copy of the results of the questionnaire, simply mark "yes" for
item No. 43 and give us your name and address in the space provided.

Sincerely,

enc

---

[a]When you are sending a form letter to many people, using a simulated inside address will help maintain a traditional letter appearance while avoiding a general, "Dear Friend" salutation. Be sure to refer to a reader benefit or concern in the first sentence.

[b]A letter transmitting a questionnaire, unlike a letter transmitting a report or other information, should begin by showing readers that they will benefit by providing the information requested.

[c]Tell the reader how the information will be used.

[d]Provide any special instructions, and tell readers how long it should take them to complete the questionnaire.

[e]Setting and justifying an "end date" will improve your rate of return. Setting an end date without justifying it, however, would be presumptuous.

[f]When you can, offer to send a copy of your report or a summary of your findings to increase reader response.

EXHIBIT 9.7
Letter of Transmittal

Dear Student:

Are rising college costs getting you down? Attending City College gets more expensive each year and coping with these increases is often a major concern of students. Because I believe many CC students are having difficulty making ends meet, I am conducting a survey to find out how students like you are meeting their financial obligations.

The information you provide will help me to complete a research project for my report writing class. The results of this survey will also be shared with the financial aid office to improve the quality of future financial aid programs.

Your name was chosen randomly from City College's student population. It is important that each questionnaire be completed and returned to ensure statistical validity. Your answers, therefore, are critical. The survey form takes only 20 minutes to complete. Your time and assistance are much appreciated.

You are assured complete confidentiality. The questionnaire is numbered for mailing purposes only. Your name will remain anonymous. Should you have any questions about the survey, please call me after 9 p.m. at 555-7274.

Because the report is due December 1, may I please have your completed questionnaire by November 15?

Sincerely,

Robin Mobley

enc

Source: Courtesy of Robin Mobley

Because the results of the study will be presented at the Tenth Annual National Convention of Office Managers on June 1, we would appreciate your returning the completed questionnaire in the enclosed postage paid envelope by May 1.

Exhibits 9.6 and 9.7 illustrate letters of transmittal.

Follow-up Correspondence

Because mailed questionnaires often have a low rate of returns, you should plan on some follow-up procedure. After waiting three or four weeks for the return of the questionnaire or after the end date specified in your transmittal letter, you may wish to follow up on the returns so that you will have your predetermined percentage of returns or a reliable rate of return.

If the questionnaires are signed, marked, or coded so that you know which individuals did not return the questionnaire, you may telephone them and ask for a quick return. Or, you may send them a follow-up note or card asking them to do so. When you make a follow-up phone call, you might say:

> **I'm calling to ask if you have received the questionnaire that I mailed to you on (date).**

If the person says he/she did not receive the questionnaire, offer to send another. If the person says "Yes", say,

> **Because we need your input, we would appreciate your completing the questionnaire by (date).**

On the other hand, if you are unable to determine which individuals on your mailing list have not responded because of confidentiality or anonymity, send a follow-up card to everyone (providing you can handle the cost) reminding them to return the completed questionnaire by a certain date. When you follow up with a note or card, call attention to the fact that the input from the respondent is needed for reliable results and for a high rate of return. Because some of the people may have already returned the questionnaire, add a qualifying statement, such as

If you have already returned the questionnaire, please disregard this notice.

INTERVIEWS

Another source for primary data is the interview. Interviews can be done face-to-face, or they can be done over the telephone.

Personal Interviews

In the personal interview, information is obtained through face-to-face conversation with another person or a group. In addition to obtaining information through discussion, the interviewer can obtain information through observation of the interviewee or respondent. The interviewee's voice, facial expression, gestures, behavior, posture, and surroundings can sometimes reveal more than the spoken word.

Because of the expense and time involved, personal interviews are best used for a small sample size in one relatively small and compact geographic area. Personal interviews are also best for soliciting information that might not be available from mailed questionnaires, such as motives and reasons, or when the information is too complex to be gathered by any other method.

Procedure   Well-organized interviews can provide valuable information for the report and can be relaxing and rewarding as well. To ensure a carefully prepared interview, here are some suggestions for you to follow.

1.   Select interviewees carefully. Ask only those people who can provide the information you need.

2.   Call for an appointment at least one week ahead of time. Introduce yourself and explain the purpose of the interview. Let the person know that his/her responses are important for your study, and if necessary, let the person know that the information will be kept confidential.

3.   Prepare a specific list of appropriate questions for your selected audience and then organize them so that they follow a logical pattern. Don't jump from one topic to another. Ask the easy questions first, and then go on to the complex ones. Go from the general to specific questions. Ask the same questions in the same way for each interviewee.

4.   Once prepared, rehearse. Go over the questions several times so that you are familiar with them and can ask them fluently. Remember not to interrupt your speaker. Also, learn to avoid disagreeing and showing emotional responses, such as frowning, which may inhibit the respondent. *Remain neutral.*

5.   Good manners should dictate your appearance and behavior at the interview. Be well dressed, pleasant, and poised. Watch your mannerisms, posture, and other nonverbal behaviors.

6.   Arrive for the appointment on time. Although you have introduced yourself over the phone when you made the appointment, you should introduce yourself again. Explain the purpose of the interview and why you selected him or her (because of his/her knowledge of the subject, for example).

7.   Pay careful attention to what is being said in the interview. Listen not only to *what* is being said but also to *how* it is being said. When necessary, ask for a clarification or for an explanation.

8.   Choose a method of recording that makes you and the respondent comfortable. A tape recorder may make some people uncomfortable. When this is so, do not use one in the session. Although notes can be taken during the interview, take them sparingly and unobtrusively. Record key phrases and important data, such as names, dates, and figures. When necessary, though, record responses verbatim.

9.   Be sure to thank the respondent for granting you the interview. Promise him or her a copy of the report, a summary of the findings, or an abstract. Send a thank-you letter, thanking the interviewee for his/her time and information.

10.   Write or record a complete summary of the interview shortly after the interview so that you won't forget important details.

Advantages and Disadvantages   The advantages of personal interviews are

1.   They provide immediate feedback and evaluation.
2.   They provide an opportunity for the interviewer to ask for further explanations when something is not clear and to rephrase a question for the respondent when he or she doesn't understand the question.
3.   They provide an opportunity to gather complex information.

The disadvantages of personal interviews are

1.   They can be time consuming and expensive.
2.   They can be an invasion of privacy.
3.   They can report inaccurate information. Respondents may distort their answers and interviewers may incorrectly interpret responses.

Telephone Interviews

Still another source for collecting primary data is the telephone interview. It is the fastest of the survey methods. Telephone interviews are similar to personal interviews except that instead of face-to-face conversation, you have communication over the telephone. Because people can be antagonistic and reluctant to answer questions over the phone, you should keep your questions brief and limited in number.

Procedure   The procedure for conducting telephone interviews is as follows:

1.   First, determine the number of calls needed to have a reliable representation.
2.   Select your population randomly.
3.   Choose a time of day for making the telephone calls when you know your respondents will be home. It's best not to call before 8 a.m. or after 8 p.m. unless you know your audience will accept earlier or later calls.
4.   Follow the same procedure for preparing and rehearsing questions as for the personal interview.
5.   Introduce yourself after your party has answered the phone. Explain the purpose of the call and the reason the person should be a part of the survey.
6.   Listen carefully to what is being said and how it is said. When necessary, ask for a clarification or explanation. Rephrase a question when it is not clear.
7.   Be sure to have prepared an interview sheet for recording your notes after each question.
8.   Finally thank the respondent for taking the time to answer your questions.

Advantages and Disadvantages   The advantages of telephone interviews are

1.   They are fast; they can quickly reach large groups of people.
2.   They are inexpensive and can save time.
3.   They can provide a random sample when the entire population has a listed telephone.
4.   They are more economical and convenient than travel.

The disadvantages of the telephone interview are that

1.   Many people object to telephone interviews.
2.   People are reluctant to answer more than a few brief questions.
3.   Some people do not have a telephone; therefore, a random sample may not be possible.
4.   Observation is not possible.

THE DELPHI TECHNIQUE

Sometimes the use of expert judgment is necessary for developing criteria to be used in certain research studies. For example, a researcher may wish to develop a rating scale to evaluate the secretarial skills of office workers.

Getting the experts together can prove difficult and often impossible, so the Delphi Technique was developed. The Delphi Technique is a method whereby a consensus of experts is achieved—not through direct discussion—but through a series of questionnaires interspersed with comments or feedback from the other respondents. These anonymous opinions are evaluated by the other respondents. In other words, one expert's views are examined and evaluated by other experts. A respondent has an opportunity to reconsider or revise his or her original comments based on the critique of the other experts. A respondent may change his or her opinion because of an idea brought out by another participant's response. As a result of the Delphi Technique, then, the researcher is able to have the consensus of the experts for his or her research study without direct confrontation.

ETHICS

Laws protect the rights of individuals in research. When gathering data for your research project, you need to consider the ethics involved.

1.   Individuals have a right to participate or not participate in your study. Therefore they must be told the purpose of the study and how the data will be used.

2. Individuals may not be deceived or persuaded into participating.

3. Individuals need to be assured that their responses will remain anonymous.

As dictated by governmental regulations, most universities have established policies and procedures protecting human subjects.

SUMMARY

A questionnaire is a list of questions used to obtain primary data. The questions provide answers to what people think and why they think a certain way. Seven types of questions most frequently used on questionnaires are either-or, checklist, multiple choice, fill-in-the-blank, open-ended, ranking, and scaling. Questionnaires sent by mail must have an accompanying letter, called a letter of transmittal.

Another source for primary data is the interview—the personal interview and the telephone interview. In the personal interview, information is obtained through face-to-face conversation with another person or a group of persons. In the telephone interview, information is obtained, as the name implies, over the telephone.

The Delphi Technique is a method whereby a consensus of experts is achieved through a series of questionnaires interspersed with feedback from the other responding experts.

Research ethics require that individuals have the right to choose to participate in a study based on accurate knowledge of the nature and purpose of the study. Respondents also have the right to remain anonymous.

EXERCISES

Review Questions

1. What is a questionnaire?

2. State the advantages and disadvantages of questionnaires.

3. Give ten guidelines for preparing a questionnaire.

4. Define the seven types of questions used on questionnaires. Give an example of each.

5. Why is it a good idea to give your questionnaire a trial run?

6. What is a data tally sheet?

7. How do you compute an average? percentage?

8. How do you compute a scaling question?

9. What is a letter of transmittal? What should it contain?

10. Why do you write a follow-up letter? When?

11. What are personal interviews?

12. What are telephone interviews?

13. What are the advantages and disadvantages of telephone interviews?

14. What is the Delphi Technique?

15. What ethical considerations are necessary in gathering data for your research project?

Problems

1. Write three questionnaire items for each of the seven kinds of questions.

2. Prepare a 20-item mail questionnaire on a topic of your choice, using at least one example of each of the seven types of questions discussed in this chapter.

3. Give five examples of leading questions and tell why they are leading.

4. Give five examples of ambiguous questions, and tell why they are ambiguous.

5. Prepare a question for each of the following:
   a. a person's age
   b. a person's religious affiliation
   c. a person's political party
   d. a person's morals

6. Give five examples of questions that respondents cannot recall easily. Convert the questions into ones that they can easily recall.

7. Give three examples of negative questions. Restate them using positive language.

8. Give three examples of questions that have two answers. Convert the questions into two separate parts.

9. Give two examples of contingency questions.

10. Prepare a ten-item questionnaire and have ten people test it. In a memo to your instructor say what you learned from the trial run. Submit the original questionnaire, the ten tested questionnaires with the comments and corrections, and the revised questionnaire incorporating the recommendations from the ten people.

11. Design a tally sheet for an observation survey and for a questionnaire survey.

12. What are the percentages for each of the following items?

a.		b.		c.	
5	grapefruit	205	tomatoes	Yes	37
20	strawberries	168	green beans	No	63
16	melons	349	potatoes		100
25	oranges	108	corn		
10	bananas	92	peas		
24	apples	78	carrots		
100		100			

13.   How would you report the group average for **a** and **b**?
      a.

	Excellent	Very Good	Good	Fair	Poor
Value	1	2	3	4	5
Numbers	40	75	50	25	10
				Total responses	200

b.

	Excellent	Very Good	Good	Fair	Poor
Value	1	2	3	4	5
Numbers	48	52	0	54	46
				Total responses	200

14.   Prepare a cover letter and questionnaire for each of the following.
      Supply whatever additional information is necessary.
      a.   Your state representative wants to conduct a citizens' survey
               for input on such key matters as tax relief, governmental re-
               form, educational reform, health care services, and other im-
               portant proposals.
      b.   The Energy Administration of the State Department of Com-
               merce wants to conduct a survey about energy conservation in
               homes.
      c.   Your company wants to conduct a survey of all employees to
               learn which tasks are performed by each employee so that the
               company can make an evaluation of how the office is function-
               ing.

15.   Prepare five statements along with illustrations that could be mailed
      on a postcard to remind people to return their questionnaires.

16.   Interview five people on a topic of your choice. Prepare a list of
      questions that you wish to ask. Call for an appointment. Write a
      summary of your findings, and present them in a memo report to
      your instructor.

17.   Interview five people over the telephone. Prepare a list of questions
      that you intend to ask.

18.   Arrange for an interview of a person who has achieved success in
      your major. Prepare the questions and conduct the interview. Pre-
      pare a report of your findings, and submit it to your instructor.

19.   Interview 25 business people in various areas, such as banking, edu-
      cation, government, manufacturing, insurance, etc. and ask what
      professional associations they belong to and what professional maga-
      zines they subscribe to.

20.   As a class project
      a.   Brainstorm for a problem (or check with administration).
      b.   Design a questionnaire to solve that problem.
      c.   Conduct a trial run.
      d.   Select a sample technique.

e.   Prepare a cover letter.
f.   Prepare a follow-up notice.
g.   Conduct the survey.
h.   Conduct a personal survey—prepare questions, etc.
i.   Conduct a telephone survey—prepare questions, etc.
j.   Prepare the written report.

CHAPTER 10

Organizing and Interpreting Data

"Two cyclists begin to pedal toward each other at the same moment. They are thirty miles apart and their rates are equal, fifteen miles per hour. Simultaneously a fly takes off from A's handlebar to B's handlebar, and back to A's, in an ever-decreasing round trip. The fly's rate is forty miles an hour—with no allowance for stops and starts. When the cyclists meet, the hard-working fly is crushed between the handlebars. How far has the fly flown?"[1]

Topics

Initial Steps
Methods of Classifying Data
Procedures for Maintaining Objectivity

How do we determine how far the fly in Stuart Chase's story has flown? In this case, we can find the answer logically, by separating the significant details from the insignificant. It takes the cyclists one hour to cover the 30 miles, and the fly is traveling at 40 miles an hour. Thus, the fly has flown 40 miles.

INITIAL STEPS

Making sense of data[a] is one of a report writer's most important tasks. Especially today, when many are suspicious of all statistical information presented by business, report writers need to ensure that they have focused on the significant, presented data accurately, and drawn logical conclusions. The continued well-being of your organization may depend on your ability to organize and interpret information. The chances that your interpretation of data will be challenged—by your boss or someone else in your organization, by a regulatory agency, or by a consumer group—increase every day.

To be meaningful, the information you have collected needs to be organized and interpreted. These are not always easy. Our daily lives do not as a rule require the kind of logic and precision that a business or technical report must have. The same wishful thinking that is acceptable when we predict victory for our team in the absence of evidence is inexcusable if we predict success for a new product without the necessary supporting evidence.

The tasks of collecting and organizing data are obviously not as distinct as our chapter divisions imply. You begin the process of organizing with your first decision to include or exclude a particular topic in your search for information. And, as you proceed with your search, you will be forming ideas about where each item of information belongs, what significance it has, and how to use it in your report.

Nevertheless, the serious task of organizing and interpreting data begins once all the data have been collected. This task can be divided into five overlapping phases:

1. Classifying data
2. Maintaining objectivity
3. Analyzing qualitative data
4. Analyzing quantitative data
5. Drawing conclusions

Each of these steps can be complex, and we can present only general considerations here. We will present the basic rules for classification, the common logical fallacies, and the most often used techniques of qualitative and quantitative analysis. As the number of books on technical classification, logic, semantics, and statistics suggests, however, a full understanding of these subjects requires a great deal of study. We recommend the following books as supplemental reading:

Bradley, Iver E. and John B. South. *Introductory Statistics for Business and Economics*. Hinsdale, IL: Dryden Press, 1981.

---

[a]*Data* is a plural form of *datum* and usually requires a plural verb. Some writers use *data* as a collective noun with a singular verb: "The *data*, as a group, *indicates* a slight increase in product awareness." See Carter A. Daniel and Charles C. Smith, "An Argument for *Data* as a Collective Singular," *The ABCA Bulletin* (Sept. 1981), p. 31.

An excellent textbook treatment of basic statistics. The chapters on sampling and statistical quality control would be especially helpful to those working on statistical reports.

Capaldi, Nicholas. *The Art of Deception.* New York: Donald W. Brown, Inc., 1971.

Covers the use of informal logic for both presenting evidence and examining evidence presented by others. More difficult to read than Chase's *Guides,* but more thorough.

Chase, Stuart. *Guides to Straight Thinking.* New York: Harper & Brothers, 1956.

An excellent, simplified introduction to logical fallacies. Rightly considered a classic.

Cohen, Morris R. *A Preface to Logic.* New York: Dover Publications, Inc., 1972.

A thorough introduction to modern, formal logic. Coverage is more technical than many would prefer.

Engel, S. Morris. *Analyzing Informal Fallacies.* Englewood Cliffs, NJ: Prentice-Hall, Inc., 1980.

An entertaining presentation and analysis of common logical fallacies.

Hayakawa, S. I. *Language in Thought and Action.* New York: Harcourt, Brace, and World, 1939.

A classic, simplified introduction to semantics. Good coverage of the ways in which inferences and value judgments interfere with objectivity.

Huff, Darrell. *How to Lie With Statistics.* New York: W. W. Norton & Company, 1954.

The classic treatment of using statistics to manipulate an audience. Covers the common ways statistics can be used to mislead.

Johnson, Robert R. *Elementary Statistics.* 2d ed. North Scituate, MA: Duxbury Press, 1976.

A generally readable textbook introduction to statistics. Emphasizes practical applications of statistical principles.

Kahane, Howard. *Logic and Contemporary Rhetoric: The Use of Reason in Everyday Life.* 2d ed. Belmont, CA: Wadsworth Publishing Company, 1976.

A popular and thorough examination of logical fallacies, with many examples taken from business, industry, and the media. Includes both formal and informal logic.

Trueman, Richard E. *Quantitative Methods for Decision Making in Business.* Hinsdale, IL: The Dryden Press, 1981.

An advanced treatment of mathematical approaches and specialized techniques used to solve business problems. Difficult going for those not already familiar with statistics.

In this chapter we discuss methods of classifying data according to the role the data will play in the report and the procedures for maintaining objectivity. In Chapter 11 we discuss the methods of analyzing qualitative and quantitative statistical data.

CLASSIFYING DATA

In planning the report you developed a list of possible topics and subtopics, which you thought would form useful categories of information. This was the beginning of your effort to classify your materials, or arrange them according to topic or category.

Report as Whole   The information for most reports will fall into one or more of the following categories:

History   The history of the problem includes not only the discussion of the background of the problem under study, but also an examination of similar problems in your own organization and throughout the industry. If others have encountered the problem previously, what did they do about it, and with what results? The information you discover as a result of secondary research belongs in this category as a "review of literature" when you are using those sources to explain previous efforts to solve a related problem.

Criteria   Whenever you are faced with having to make a choice, carefully define the criteria on which you will base your decision. Then, classify information according to the criteria established rather than according to the items or subjects being compared. If you are trying to decide which word processing equipment to install, for example, you would organize the information by such factors as cost, ease of use, flexibility, repair record, and features rather than by brand name.

Descriptions and Explanations   What research methodology did you use and why? At some point in your report, you will need to tell your reader how you know what you know. Describing your efforts to remain objective and explaining the procedures you used to ensure valid results are your best means of convincing your reader to accept your results, conclusions, and recommendations. A description of scope, explanations for limitations, and definitions fall in this category.

Results   What did you learn as a result of your research? Results are usually presented in the form of raw data. Your reader may want to see your results to evaluate your conclusions or recommendations. For this reason, you should keep the results and your discussion and analysis of the results in separate categories.

Trends Changes over time will probably require special attention. Trends may be worthy of separate consideration, or they may influence other aspects of your report.

Discussion of Results What do your results mean? Are some aspects more significant than others? Analytical reports require you to interpret and analyze your results for your reader. Further classification may be necessary to show significant relationships among the topics examined.

Alternatives What possible courses of action are available? What are the advantages and disadvantages of each?

Conclusions and Recommendations Because conclusions and recommendations are not data but are based on data, you will need to remember that your conclusions and recommendations are separate categories of information. Be sure to note that difference for yourself as you organize your material for presentation.

Findings

In addition to placing information in general categories according to the function it will play in the report, you may need to classify the results of research to ensure a clear, systematic presentation of facts. Classification is, in fact, an important technique for demonstrating points of similarity and difference among things. In classifying data, use the following rules.

Clarify What Is Being Classified Whenever you are dividing a whole into its component parts, you need to clarify (definition, scope, limits) the whole so that the relationship among parts will be meaningful to the reader.

Select a Significant Basis for the Classification The basis for your system of classification may be suggested by your topic or purpose, reasons, factors, methods, properties, or qualities. A quality that is significant in one circumstance, however, may not be significant in another. Whether a book is hardbound or paperback may be significant in discussing cost or durability, for example, but irrelevant in discussing content.

Make Sure That the Division Is Complete Just as in geometry the whole must equal the sum of its parts, the subtopics in your division must total the entire category. When you are omitting one or more subtopics from a category in your discussion, change the title of the division to clarify what you will discuss. If you are discussing natural resources important to your industry, and you need to cover iron, zinc, and copper, your division would be "Three Key Minerals" rather than "Metals."

Complete One Basis of Classification Before Beginning the Next When possible, make your divisions mutually exclusive. Ideally, subdivisions should not overlap. Each category by its nature should exclude all other categories. It's clear that, in the previous examples, "timber" would not belong in the same category as iron, zinc, and copper. Some topics, however, can't be divided so absolutely— where do you draw the line between a short report and a long report? Because the bases for classifying reports overlap, a complete coverage of report preparation requires some overlap of categories. A memo report may also be a short analytical report. When categories do overlap, be sure to clarify the nature of the overlap and explain the difference between the categories for your reader.

Be Consistent and Logical In developing your system of classification, use parallel grammatical structure in listing the categories, and make sure that you have no single subdivisions. Arrange the categories of data in an order that will aid your reader's understanding.

MAINTAINING OBJECTIVITY

If you had the responsibility for recommending the new company cars for your organization, what brands and models would you consider and why? Would you include foreign cars in your list of those to be considered? If you automatically excluded foreign cars from your list because you believe that the domestic automobile industry needs support, you were guilty of biased thinking.

Biased—or prejudiced—thinking, however, is not always bad. It's normal and justifiable to want the local team to win. The managers of a particular organization may decide that they will consider only domestic automobiles for use in the company fleet. Biased thinking can result in problems in two ways. First, we may not be aware of our biases and overlook or distort evidence as a result. Second, if we are aware of our bias, we may still be tempted to persuade our audience to share our prejudice, and we may deliberately distort or suppress evidence.

Fairness

Objectivity in report writing (or any other facet of life, for that matter) requires that we recognize our biases and acknowledge the role they might play in the reporting process. In the case of the decision about the new automobiles for your organization, for example, you could be fair in spite of a bias in favor of domestic cars in a variety of ways.

Fair: Obtain approval for considering domestic cars only.

Fair: Establish performance criteria, obtain approval for those criteria, weigh all cars against those criteria, and recommend the car (foreign or domestic) meeting the most criteria.

Fair: Same as above, but—should a foreign car be best—recommend the domestic car meeting the most criteria and explain your reasons for selecting a domestic car in spite of a foreign car's better performance.

You could also manipulate the data in a number of ways.

Unfair: Eliminate foreign cars without providing an explanation.

Unfair: Manipulate data to ensure that a domestic car would appear superior.

Unfair: Omit data tending to show that a foreign car might be superior.

To ensure fairness, ask yourself the following questions.

1. Do you have any preconceived notions of what the results should be? Have you selected a particular hypothesis because you already believe that is what you will discover? If you have, check your results by also attempting to prove the problem's null hypothesis.

2. Do you have any vested interests? Will you profit (emotionally, or monetarily, or in some other way) if your results turn out a certain way? If you own stock in a particular automobile company, for example, you may find it difficult to avoid manipulating the facts in favor of the cars produced by that company.

In addition to a desire to be fair, to be truly objective, a report writer must have a basic working knowledge of the principles of logic and semantics.

Logic

The study of logic is traditionally divided into *formal* and *informal* branches. Formal logic deals with *syllogisms* and mathematical logic. Informal logic deals with the common logical fallacies that distort our everyday thinking. Informal logic is based on and is a natural result of the syllogism of formal logic, as is illustrated in Exhibit 10.1.

EXHIBIT 10.1
Typical Syllogism

Major Premise All men are mortal.
Minor Premise Socrates is a man.
Conclusion Socrates is mortal.

The starting point for every *proof* or *argument* is a premise. The proof consists of an orderly sequence of *propositions*, or statements which can be proved or disproved. The beginning proposition, the major premise, must have been proved already. The remaining propositions must be logical consequences or also have been proved previously. The last proposition is the conclusion. To be *valid*, the propositions used in the proof must all be true.

Valid Arguments

Most of the arguments or logical proofs we encounter on a daily basis are not, of course, set up as formal syllogisms. Even though the syllogism may not be explicit, every argument is based on a syllogism. Our usual practice is to omit propositions we assume everyone will agree to. Exhibit 10.2 illustrates the syllogism behind an informal argument.

Informal Proof: We should buy word processing equipment because it would increase office productivity.

EXHIBIT 10.2
Informal and Formal Arguments

Syllogism:
Major Premise Our office productivity needs improving.
Minor Premise Word processing equipment increases office productivity.
Conclusion   We should buy word processing equipment.

Logical Fallacies

A *logical fallacy,* or error in reasoning, can result from using premises which are not true or those which are not logical consequences of previous propositions. Most day-to-day efforts to persuade are based on fallacious reasoning, in that they attempt to convince or persuade without using the steps required by logic to establish a true conclusion. Advertisers, for example, often base their attempts to persuade on a fallacious argument.

One manufacturer of electric razors, for example, stated: "If two blades are better than one . . . try 18 of them." We can more easily examine the logic of this statement if we set it up as a syllogism:

EXHIBIT 10.3
Fallacious Argument

Implicit Premise Two safety razor blades are better than one.
Implicit Premise More blades would be better yet.
Implicit Premise What is true of safety razors must also be true of electric shavers.
Conclusion   An electric shaver with 18 blades must be better than a safety razor with two blades.

The advertiser's argument is fallacious, but the product may still do everything claimed for it. You can use fallacious reasoning and still be right. Those responsible for writing reports, however, cannot afford to use fallacious reasoning. Also, those who receive reports and make decisions based on their content need to be aware of the common logical fallacies.[b]

Fallacies of Ambiguity These are a result of confusing language. They include amphiboly, accent, hypostatization, equivocation, division, and composition.

Amphiboly Amphiboly results when a statement can mean more than one thing or when the message conveyed is obviously not what was intended.

EXAMPLE: Clothes 50 percent off.

EXAMPLE: Several good speeches will be given in the morning. Yours will be given in the afternoon.

Accent The way in which something is said or the context in which it is said may influence its meaning. The fallacy of accent occurs when a statement has more than one meaning depending on how or where it is said.

EXAMPLE: You never looked better. (But you still look awful.)

EXAMPLE: Don't speak ill of the dead. (It's all right to speak ill of the living.)

Hypostatization When we ascribe human characteristics to abstract concepts, we are guilty of the fallacy of hypostatization.

EXAMPLE: The company decided to fire Howard Lannon. (Only people can decide.)

EXAMPLE: Technology will have to work harder if it is to satisfy all our wants. (Only people can work harder.)

Equivocation The fallacy of equivocation occurs when the meaning of a key term changes so that its meaning in the conclusion is not the same as it was in the premise.

---

[b]We are using the classification system developed by S. Morris Engel (see *Analyzing Informal Fallacies*). Other writers classify logical fallacies in different ways. Engel's system is as clear and useful as any and has the additional advantage of avoiding the often-used Latin terminology, which tends to make the principles of logic seem mysterious and antiquated, even if some of his categories employ unusual vocabulary.

EXAMPLE: Your argument is sound, all sound. (*Sound* changes in meaning from *logical* to *noise*.)

EXAMPLE: He's discriminating in his choice of clothes and in his hiring practices as well. (*Discriminating* changes in meaning from *good taste* to *prejudiced*.)

Division   If we assume that what is true of the whole must also be true of the parts, we are guilty of the fallacy of division.

EXAMPLE: General Motors is a great company, and we will have no trouble if we buy their cars. (Just because GM as a whole is a great company doesn't mean that one or more GM cars won't break down.)

Composition   The fallacy of composition results from assuming that what is true of a part must also be true of the whole.

EXAMPLE: The bridge is made of first-rate steel, so it must be safe. (Even if the steel is first-rate, the design or construction may be faulty.)

Fallacies of Presumption   Fallacies of presumption are a result of misrepresentation of fact. Facts can be overlooked, evaded, or distorted. Fallacies of presumption are among the most common, and report writers should take special care to avoid them. They include sweeping generalization, hasty generalization, bifurcation, begging the question, complex question, special pleading, false analogy, false cause, and irrelevant thesis.

Sweeping Generalization   If we assume that what is true under certain conditions must be true under all conditions, we are committing the fallacy of sweeping generalizations.

EXAMPLE: More than 200 people died in that airplane crash. Flying is obviously dangerous. (Even with one bad accident, flying may be safer than other forms of travel.)

Hasty Generalization   The fallacy of hasty generalization results from examining too few specific cases before stating a general conclusion. Small sample size, short trial runs, and too little experience can all lead to erroneous, hasty generalizations.

EXAMPLE: My grandfather smoked more than a pack a day since he was 12, and he lived to be 90. Therefore, smoking doesn't cause cancer or heart disease. (One healthy smoker does not prove that smoking won't cause health problems for some people.)

Bifurcation   When we assume that two categories are mutually exclusive, we may be guilty of the fallacy of bifurcation. Confusion over contradictories (dead/alive, pregnant/not pregnant) and contraries (rich/poor, tall/short) is often responsible for bifurcation. In some cases, the either-or distinction is justified, but in most cases, a variety of possibilities is overlooked.

EXAMPLE: We must either divest ourselves of our small appliance line or sink into financial ruin. (There may be alternatives.)

Begging the Question   Begging the question is assuming, rather than proving, that the point at issue is true. Begging the question can take the form of a circular argument (in which the conclusion proves the premise that proves the conclusion) or a single word that implies a conclusion without proving the premise.

EXAMPLE: Johnson's proposal cannot possibly succeed because it is unworkable. (The proposal may not succeed, but the statement does not provide a reason. *Unworkable* merely repeats the concept of not succeeding.)

EXAMPLE: Any intelligent reader can see that Johnson's proposal can't succeed. (The word *intelligent* begs the question of why Johnson's proposal won't succeed.)

Complex Question   The fallacy of complex question results when a question cannot be answered without implying an answer to a question at issue. This fallacy is also referred to as loaded question.

EXAMPLE: Have you stopped beating your wife? (A person confesses to wife beating with either *yes* or *no*.)

EXAMPLE: Has Hamblin finally written a report worth reading? (A *yes* implies all previous reports were bad.)

EXAMPLE: Would you prefer the carpeting in tan or beige? (Implies that the customer has decided to buy the carpet and is now concerned with color only.)

Special Pleading   We are guilty of the fallacy of special pleading if we apply different standards to ourselves than we do to others.

EXAMPLE: I am clever. You are manipulative. He's sneaky.

EXAMPLE: You really can't trust the employees who work for this company. When I was checking to see how much I could get away with putting on my expense account, I discovered that some people are really padding their accounts.

False Analogy   An analogy, which compares two things, is said to be false when the things being compared are similar in insignificant ways only. To be useful, an analogy must be based on a comparison of things similar in key ways.

EXAMPLE: You've come a long way, baby. (A popular advertisement implies that the right to smoke is as important as the rights to vote and to equal pay for equal work.)

EXAMPLE: Our marketing plan for the calculators was successful using TV personalities and their kids; we should use the same plan to sell our new business computers. (The analogy falsely implies that calculators and business computers are sufficiently alike that the same marketing strategy would work with both.)

False Cause   The fallacy of false cause results when we assume that one event has caused another when a causal relationship has not been established. Both events may have been caused by a third, unidentified, event, or the two events may simply be coincidental.

EXAMPLE: Breaking a mirror means seven years' bad luck. (Breaking a mirror does not *cause* bad luck, even if some bad luck follows the breaking.)

EXAMPLE: Our new advertising campaign has resulted in a 43 percent increase in sales. (The campaign may be the cause of the sales increase, but other factors—changes in product, seasonal fluctuations, etc.—would also need to be considered.)

Irrelevant Thesis   We are guilty of the fallacy of irrelevant thesis when we attempt to prove a premise or conclusion other than the one at issue.

EXAMPLE: We should acquire Tanaka Radio because its main offices are in Tokyo, and we would be able to hold our annual meetings there. (Tokyo's good location for company meetings is an irrelevant issue.)

EXAMPLE: That job requires a lot of technical skill and the ability to make quick decisions. I don't think that we should hire a woman. (A person's sex is irrelevant. How well an applicant meets the job requirements is the key issue.)

Fallacies of Relevance   These are confusing because they substitute emotion for reason. Fallacies of relevance appeal to prejudice, envy, sympathy, vanity, pride, or fear rather than offer a logical argument. The common fallacies in this category are personal attack, mob appeal, pity, authority, ignorance, and fear.

Personal Attack   The fallacy of personal attack results from an attempt to discredit the source of an idea. The source is often, but not always, a person.

EXAMPLE: Ronald Reagan (or Edward Kennedy) couldn't possibly design a program to help the poor because he is rich. (The program, not the person, should be evaluated.)

EXAMPLE: Businesses naturally want reduced worker compensation because they stand to profit from the reduction. (While business may profit from reduced worker compensation, the reasons for the reduction may be logical and not the result of vested interest.)

Mob Appeal   The mob appeal fallacy is based on our natural tendencies to group identification and to going along with the crowd. This fallacy appeals to our emotional need to fit in rather than to our ability to decide logically.

EXAMPLE: Every other major corporation is acquiring a high-tech business, and we should, too. (Perhaps the company should acquire a high-tech business, but the fact that others are doing so is not necessarily a good reason for doing so.)

Appeal to Pity   The fallacy of appeal to pity is based on our natural desire to help those in need regardless of the logic of the situation.

EXAMPLE: If I don't get a B in this class, I'll flunk out of school. (Sad as flunking out might be, it has nothing to do with the grade earned.)

EXAMPLE: If we close the Flint plant, hundreds will be thrown out of work. (Unlike the first example, this appeal to pity is worth consideration. The Flint plant may have to be closed anyway, but the legitimate needs of others should receive consideration.)

Appeal to Authority   The fallacy of appeal to authority is the result of ascribing expertise to a source that has not earned or demonstrated expertise in the area at issue.

EXAMPLE: My doctor invested in Capriotti vineyards, so it must be a good investment. (What does the doctor know about the stockmarket, and how does he/she know it?)

Appeal to Ignorance   When we attempt to prove that our conclusion must be true because others can't disprove it, we are guilty of the fallacy of appeal to ignorance.

EXAMPLE: Smoking must not cause cancer because they haven't proved it yet. (The cause-effect relationship may be proved in the future.)

EXAMPLE: Don't object to my proposal until you have a better alternative. (Just because no one has come up with a better alternate doesn't mean that the plan under discussion is without flaw.

Appeal to Fear   We are guilty of the fallacy of appeal to fear if we use the threat of harm to persuade someone to accept a conclusion.

EXAMPLE: We have to hire a woman for this position, or we'll be in trouble with EEO. (Whether a woman is hired should depend on the qualification of the candidates, not on the possible reaction of a regulatory agency.)

EXAMPLE: You can't afford not to have insurance. What would your family do if you were to die? (This is an attempt to scare somebody into buying insurance.)

The presence of logical fallacy doesn't necessarily prove that the conclusion is incorrect. A logical fallacy shows an invalid argument rather than a false conclusion. Because an invalid argument may lead to a false conclusion, however, report writers and readers need to examine their arguments for the presence of fallacies.

Semantics

Semantics is the study of meaning as expressed in words. *General semantics* is the attempt to improve communication and understanding by analyzing the use of language. Alfred Korzybski, author of *Science and Sanity* (first published in 1933), developed the principles of general semantics to help people use words in a way that more accurately reflects the reality they represent.

Many of the principles of general semantics are related to the common logical fallacies. Both logic and general semantics are attempts to develop a systematic process of observing reality accurately in spite of the metaphorical nature of language. In a standard metaphor, one thing symbolizes—or stands for—something else:

The ship of state requires a strong hand at the helm.

This metaphor establishes analogy comparing the captain of a ship with the leader of a government. Both logicians and semanticists are concerned with the accuracy of analogies contained in metaphors, whether the metaphor is explicit (as in the "ship of state" example) or implicit (as in much daily language).

"The map is not the territory" is the phrase general semanticists use to remind us that language is a symbol system that stands for reality but is not reality itself. Just as a map—if it is accurate—gives us a picture of the territory; language—when properly used—gives us a description of reality. Inaccurate maps and faulty language can both get us into trouble, especially when we forget that both maps and language can contain errors.

The following six principles are the most important:

No Statement Tells the Whole Story   Because we cannot perceive totally or with complete accuracy, we need to recognize that we cannot make absolutely complete or accurate statements.

Each of us abstracts from reality those things seen as most important. No two people will select the same aspect of reality as the most important. When we think we know or have said everything, we are guilty of the *Allness Fallacy*. General semanticists try to avoid the allness fallacy by mentally adding *etc.* to the ends of sentences as a reminder that more remains to be said.

No Two Things Are Identical   The human mind works by a process of generalization and differentiation. When things are similar, we tend to class them together and treat them alike. Some things that seem similar, however, have significant differences. When we overlook these differences, we are guilty of the semantic fallacy, *failure to discriminate*. Because we are used to looking for similarities so that we can classify things and make generalizations about them, we need to remind ourselves to look for and evaluate differences as well.

Facts, Inferences, and Value Judgments Are Not the Same   A *fact* is something that has been verified by direct observation. We know, for example, that it is 2054 miles between Chicago, IL, and Los Angeles, CA. That distance has been measured several times by independent observers. Because both Chicago and Los Angeles are large cities, we could *infer* that several airlines would offer direct flights between them. An inference is an assumption, which—like a hypothesis—needs to be tested before we can be sure whether it is correct or incorrect. You might prefer Los Angeles to Chicago (or vice-versa), and that preference would be a *value judgment*. A value judgment is simply an opinion, which may be based on facts and inferences but is not itself a fact. You might hold the opinion that large cities are "unfit for human habitation," but that value judgment, contradicted as it is by the numbers of people who choose to live and work in large cities, says more about you than it does large cities.

Few Things Are Either-Or (See the logical fallacy, *bifurcation.*)   Like the logicians, general semanticists are concerned about our failure to recognize the middle ground between extremes. We tend to think in terms of *abstract absolutes:* best, worst; tallest, shortest; most expensive, cheapest; fastest, slowest; and so on. We need to remind ourselves that a middle ground almost always exists, and that the abstract terms are relative to something specific. Something can be "best" only in relation to other things and only in specific ways.

Time Changes All Things   More than 2,000 years ago, a Greek named Heraclitus observed that a person can't step in the same river twice.[2] Heraclitus recognized that, between steps, the river changed. The water that was there is gone. "New" water had arrived by the time of the second step. When we fail to recognize that things and people change over time, we are guilty of the fallacy, *frozen evaluation.* Semanticists recommend that we *date* observations to remind ourselves that things change and need periodic reevaluation. Judith Holcombe (1980) refused a promotion because she didn't want to relocate. Judith Holcombe (1983) may desire the promotion and be ready to relocate.

Time Sequence Alone Does Not Establish a Cause and Effect Relationship   (See the logical fallacy, *false cause.*) When one event closely follows another, we tend to assume that the first caused the second. We need to remind ourselves that the events may be unrelated, coincidental, or effects of a third event not yet identified. Because we also have the tendency to think of causes of events as immediately preceding the event in question, we tend to ignore causes that may be remote in time. It may take years, for example, to know the long-term health effects of certain modern chemicals, especially insecticides, herbicides, and even medicines. For this reason, we need to be aware that the cause of an event may be fairly far removed in time or place from the event itself.

SUMMARY

To be meaningful, data must be organized and interpreted. While the task of organizing and interpreting data begins at the inception of the report writing process, most organizing and interpreting occurs once all the data have been collected. The five overlapping phases of organizing and interpreting data include (1) classifying data, (2) maintaining objectivity, (3) analyzing qualitative data, (4) analyzing quantitative data, and (5) drawing conclusions.

Data can be classified according to how each item or category fits into the report as a whole. Possible categories for this method of classification are history of the problem, criteria leading to a choice, descriptions and explanations, trends, results, discussion of results, alternatives, conclusions, and recommendations.

Data can also be classified to ensure a clear, systematic presentation of facts. To ensure an adequate demonstration of facts, use the following rules: (1) clarify what is being classified; (2) select a significant basis for the classification; (3) make sure that the division is complete; (4) complete one basis of classification before beginning the next, and make divisions mutually exclusive; and (5) be consistent and logical in developing your system of classification.

Maintaining objectivity requires a sense of fairness, which allows the researcher to be objective in spite of preconceived notions and vested interest. In addition to a willingness to be fair, objectivity requires an understanding of logic and semantics.

Formal logic is based on the concept of the syllogism, in which a series of true propositions lead to a valid conclusion. Informal logic consists of implicit applications of a syllogism, in which some propositions may be assumed.

Logical fallacies, or errors in reasoning, can result from using premises which are not true or those which are not logical consequences of previous propositions. Fallacies of ambiguity result from the use of confusing language. Fallacies of presumption result from misrepresentation of facts, by overlooking, evading, or distorting them. Fallacies of relevance result from the substitution of emotion for reason.

Semantics is the study of meaning as expressed in words. General semantics is the attempt to improve understanding by analyzing the use of language and attempting to use it accurately. The following are the most important semantic principles: (1) no statement tells the whole story; (2) no two things are identical; (3) facts, inferences, and value judgments are not the same; (4) few things are either-or; (5) time changes all things, and (6) time sequence alone does not establish a cause and effect relationship.

EXERCISES

Review Questions

1. What materials should be included in each of the following categories?
   a. History of the problem?
   b. Criteria?
   c. Description and explanations?
   d. Results?
   e. Trends?
   f. Discussion of results?
   g. Alternatives?
   h. Conclusions?
   i. Recommendations?

2. Name and explain the five rules for classifying data.

3. How does the concept of *fairness* contribute to objectivity in report writing?

4. What is a syllogism, and what is required for a syllogism to be valid?

5. What is a logical fallacy?

6. Name and explain the fallacies of ambiguity.

7. Name and explain the fallacies of presumption.

8. Name and explain the fallacies of relevance.

9. How would a writer's study of general semantics contribute to the accuracy of his or her reports?

10. Name and explain six principles of general semantics.

Problems

1. What evidence is there that language is metaphorical? Using at least three sources, explain the metaphorical nature of language in a paper of no more than five pages. Include a brief discussion of the ways in which your findings should influence report writers.

2. Select between five and ten advertisements from a recent magazine and analyze them for logical fallacies. If your instructor directs, organize your results and draw appropriate conclusions.

3. Select a recent editorial from your local newspaper. Analyze the editorial, looking for implied syllogisms and logical fallacies. Submit your findings in whatever form your instructor directs.

4. Under what circumstances should professional athletes be allowed to bet on games in their own sport? Should referees be allowed to bet on contests even when they are not refereeing? Explain your reasoning in a paper three to five pages long.

5.   What constitutes a *vested interest?* What is the difference between vested interests and conflicts of interest? Why does the Securities Exchange Commission (SEC) prohibit those with inside knowledge of business transactions that will influence stock values from taking advantage of that knowledge? Describe and discuss a recent example of unfair behavior reported in a recent business publication. Why was the activity involved unfair? What should the people involved have done? Submit a photocopy of the article you've used as a source along with a paper of no more than five pages.

Notes

[1]Stuart Chase, *Guide to Straight Thinking* (New York: Harper & Brothers, 1956), p. 8.
[2]Wendell Johnson, *People in Quandaries: The Semantics of Personal Adjustment* (New York: Harper & Row, 1946), pp. 23–34.

CHAPTER 11
Analyzing Statistical Information

Statistics are inescapable. Very few decisions in business, industry, or government are made without some consideration of statistical data. Financial data, population demographics, attitudes of important publics, and a wide variety of other factors are best understood in terms of quantities. Wherever you work, whatever your job, you will need to use statistics to solve many of the problems you will encounter.

Topics

Qualitative Data
Quantitative Data
Descriptive Statistics
Inferential Statistics
Methods of Drawing Conclusions

Chapters 7 and 8 discussed the methods by which report writers collect data. Once the data have been collected, they will require analysis and interpretation to be meaningful.

Depending on the kind of research with which you are involved, you may be examining either *qualitative data* or *quantitative data*. In many cases, you will need to consider both.

QUALITATIVE DATA

The term qualitative data refers to the qualities or *attributes* of the items being investigated: colors, sizes, shapes, or behavioral characteristics. Stereo tape recorders, for example, come in a variety of formats: reel-to-reel, cassette, and eight-track cartridge. They are available with and without Dolby noise reduction circuits, with and without automatic reverse features, and so on. These are all qualities which would be significant in decisions about stereo tape recorders.

Qualitative data are especially important when you are trying to solve "human" problems. Attitudes, opinions, and belief systems are not always easy to measure quantitatively. Nevertheless, to be meaningful, qualitative data usually must be converted to numerical values before they can be analyzed. First, attributes can be assigned to categories. By counting the number of items in each category, we establish *nominal data*. Second, by assigning relative values to each attribute and ranking them by order of preference, we establish *ranked order*.

Suppose you have been authorized to evaluate the restaurants in your area to determine the best place for your company to entertain clients at business lunches and dinners. You could establish a variety of categories:

Location
Kind of food (French, Mexican, American, Chinese, etc.)
Quality of food
Quality of service
Atmosphere

The number of restaurants in a given area and the number of restaurants of a particular kind would be nominal data. The quality of food and the quality of service would be ranked data. Atmosphere could be either nominal (number of restaurants with a particular kind of atmosphere) or ranked (the quality of atmosphere).

Much qualitative data tend to be subjective. What constitutes a French restaurant? In some cases it's obvious that a restaurant is French: it has a French name, French service personnel, and nothing but French cuisine and wines. But what about the restaurant that has a French name and only one or two authentically French meals? Placing such a restaurant in a category calls for a subjective decision. Ranking, too, calls for a subjective evaluation. How good must food and service be before you would call them "excellent"?

QUANTITATIVE DATA

Suppose that you are working for a manufacturer of personal computers and you are assigned the task of forecasting the number of units your company should sell next year. A number of the questions you would need to answer to solve this problem call for an understanding of statistics:

How many people are likely to buy personal computers next year?
What is your market share likely to be?
How will the general economic situation affect sales of personal computers?

In Chapter 8 you learned that because it's impractical to interview everybody throughout the area where you market your computers, you will need statistics to help determine the kind of sample that will result in accurate data. Sampling is one of the most important statistical concepts for report writers. Some occupations rely heavily on statistical information as a tool for decision making. Others may not require knowledge of statistics on a regular basis, but regardless of your occupational specialty, statistics will play a sufficiently important role to justify your spending some time becoming familiar with the most common techniques of qualitative and quantitative data analysis.

Our discussion here is intended primarily for those who have a limited background in statistics, and our primary focus is on basic sampling techniques and the accurate presentation of statistical information. Those of you who will be working in market research, financial forecasting, any of the technical fields, or other occupations requiring regular use of statistics, should invest in a course in statistics.

We will begin here with definitions of basic terms.

Population The collection, or set, of individuals or objects whose properties will be analyzed (see Chapter 8.) In the example cited above, the population would probably be defined according to age, income level, and education based on what was already known about buyers of personal computers. The population must be well defined to obtain useful information. In statistics, a population can be a collection of animals, measurements, or inanimate objects.

Sample A subset of a population. Because the total population is usually too large to be examined person by person (or item by item), researchers examine a portion of the population and use statistical analysis to predict the characteristics of the whole. As we pointed out in Chapter 8, samples can be *random, stratified random,* or *systematic.*

Variable A characteristic about each individual or item of a population. Variables are those factors that may influence your results. You might discover, for example, that people who live in urban areas purchase more personal computers than do people who live in rural areas. In an experiment, a researcher may alter one factor (the *independent variable*) to observe its influence on other factors (*dependent variables*).

Parameter   A characteristic of the population as a whole. The average income of buyers of personal computers and their average level of education would be parameters of that population. A parameter is an aspect of an entire population, and the word should not be used as a substitute for the word *limit*, nor should it be used as a substitute for *characteristic* unless the reference is to the population as a whole.

Wrong: What are the *parameters* of the problem?

Right: The age *parameter* selected for the target audience was 18–30 years.

Discrete Data   Variables counted item by item, usually resulting in a whole number. Discrete (meaning separate) variables are those that can be counted. The *number* of people who purchased personal computers each year for the past several years would be discrete data. Any objects or occurrences that can be *counted* will result in discrete data.

Continuous Data   Variables that can assume virtually any value over a continuous interval. Height, weight, temperature, speed, and other variables that do not change by specific integers provide continuous data. For many business purposes, continuous data are made discrete by establishing ranges and then counting the responses in each category. Incomes of those purchasing personal computers, for example, might be tabulated according to the following scale: below $10,000 a year, $11,000–$14,999, $15,000–$19,999, $20,000–$24,999, and so on. The research in this case would not be aided by having absolutely precise, continuous data.

Probability   The chance that a given event or variable will occur when you know all possible outcomes. Probability theory and statistics are concerned with a set of variables from opposite ends: probability is concerned with the *chance* that a particular event will occur when you know all possible outcomes. Statistics are concerned with inferring probabilities based on the results of a sample.

If you know, for example, that in one community 4 people out of 4,000 had purchased personal computers in a given year, you could determine the probability of your meeting one of those 4 people by randomly knocking on a door in that community. Assuming that the person were home at the time of your visit, the probability would be 4 in 4,000. With statistics, you would sample the population, and based on the results, make predictions about the entire population. If four in 4,000 purchased personal computers in a given community, you might predict that a similar number made a similar purchase in each of several similar communities.

DESCRIPTIVE STATISTICS

Descriptive statistics are the methods used to describe aspects of a collection of numbers. The most useful methods of describing a set of numbers are measures of central tendency and measures of dispersion. These measures tell researchers where the center of a set of numbers is and how the other numbers are grouped in relation to the center.

Measures of Central Tendency

One of the most significant uses of statistics is to provide researchers with an idea of the center of a set of data. Measures of central tendency include the following.

Mean   The arithmetic average, or mean, is obtained by adding the values of the variable and dividing by the total number of cases.
    The formula for obtaining the mean is

$$\overline{X} = \frac{\Sigma X}{n}$$

in which $\overline{X}$ (X-bar) is the mean, Σ is the sum of the values of variable X, and n is the number of cases. If you were to take a course with four exams, each weighted equally, you would determine your final grade by adding your scores on each of the exams and dividing by 4.

$$
\begin{array}{ll}
\text{Exam 1:} & 78 \\
\text{Exam 2:} & 94 \\
\text{Exam 3:} & 87 \\
\text{Exam 4:} & \underline{94} \\
& 353 \div 4 = 88.25.
\end{array}
$$

Weighted Mean   The weighted mean is the arithmetic average when all variables are not weighted equally. The formula for obtaining the weighted mean is

$$\text{Weighted mean} = \frac{\Sigma w_i x_i}{\Sigma w_i}$$

in which the sum (Σ) of the variables multiplied by their weighted values is divided by the sum of the weighted values. If you were to take a course with two papers, each worth 20 percent of your final grade, a midterm worth 25 percent, and a final worth 35 percent, you could determine your final grade using the formula.

Grades		(Weight)
Paper 1:	87	(20%)
Paper 2:	96	(20%)
Midterm:	85	(25%)
Final:	94	(35%)

$$\text{Weighted mean} = \frac{.20(87) + .20(96) + .25(85) + .35(94)}{+ .20 + .20 + .25 + .35}$$

$$= \frac{17.4 + 19.2 + 21.25 + 32.9}{1}$$

$$= 90.75.$$

Median The median divides an ordered set of variables into two equal groups, with half having values less than the median and half having values greater. The median is obtained by counting the pieces of data, adding 1, and dividing by 2.

$$\text{Median} = i = \frac{n + 1}{2}.$$

You might wish, for example, to know the median income of people who have purchased one of your company's products. To do so, you would count the number of responses arranged according to ranked categories, add 1, and divide by 2.

Category	Responses
1. Below $15,000	0
2. $15,000–$19,999	15
3. $20,000–$24,999	25
4. $25,000–$29,999	32
5. $30,000–$34,999	41
6. $35,000–$39,999	26
7. Above $40,000	12
Total responses:	151

$$n = \frac{151 + 1}{2} = 76.$$

Beginning at either end, count 76 responses. The *median* occurs in the $30,000–$35,000 category, with 72 responses below that category, and 79 responses in that category and above. The *mean*, however, would fall in category 4, at about $27,450, which shows that the mean and the median are not interchangeable. The mean is influenced by extreme scores much more than the median is.

The difference between these two measures of centrality is even clearer when comparing a smaller number of specific numbers. If you examined the salaries of employees working at a small company, you might find something like those in Exhibit 11.1.

EXHIBIT 11.1
Hypothetical Company Salaries

President	$600,000 a year
2 vice-presidents	$100,000 a year, each
5 sales managers	$50,000 a year, each
1 production manager	$35,000 a year, each
50 hourly employees	$18,000 a year, each
50 hourly employees	$11,000 a year, each

The *mean* salary would be determined as follows:

$$\frac{\$2,535,000 \text{ (total salary)}}{109 \text{ (number of employees)}} = \$23,256.88.$$

The *median* would be determined as follows:

$$\frac{109 + 1}{2} = 55.$$

Or, the 55th response, counting from either end is the median salary, or $18,000.

Which "average" would a company be more likely to report?

Mode   The mode is the value that occurs most frequently. In the case of the company salaries, two figures—$18,000 and $11,000—appear with equal frequency, so there is no single mode in this case, which has *bimodal* distribution.

Midrange   The midrange is the number occurring midway between the lowest score and the highest. It is determined by adding the low score *(L)* and the high score *(H)* and dividing by two. Again, let's look at the salaries:

$$\frac{\$11,000 \text{ (L)} + 600,000 \text{ (H)}}{2} = \$305,500.$$

The differences among these figures show how important it is for the report writers to use the most significant measure of centrality for a given situation and to indicate clearly which measure is being used. When more than one measure is useful, provide both and label each clearly.

Measures of Dispersion

In addition to finding out the nature of the middle of a set of data, researchers also need to know the amount of *dispersion*, or *spread*. Measures of dispersion reveal whether the numbers being examined are close together or widely spread out. Values that are relatively close together are said to have *low dispersion,* whereas widely spaced values are said to have *high dispersion.*

The most often used measures for dispersion include range, average deviation, variance, and standard deviation. For each of these measurements, the lower the number, the lower the amount of dispersion.

Range   The *range* is simply the difference between the largest *(H)* and smallest *(L)* values in the data collected.

$$\text{Range} = H - L.$$

For the company salaries in Exhibit 11.1, for example, the range would be computed as follows:

$$600,000 - 11,000 = 589,000.$$

The range shows the total amount of spread in a set of numbers. The other measurements are used to show the amount of dispersion using the mean as a reference point. The range is easy to compute and understand. It cannot, however, provide information about values other than the extremes. If we want to understand the relationships among all the values in a given set, we will need to use one of the other measurements.

Average Deviation   The average deviation, also known as the *mean absolute deviation* (MAD), measures the average deviation around the mean. With this measure, we are concerned with the difference between individual values and the mean, as expressed by the formula $X_i - \overline{X}$, in which X_i represents the values, and $\overline{X}$ *(X-bar)* represents the mean.

Suppose we poll the members of an organization to discover how far they commute to work. We would compute the average deviation according to the steps outlined in Exhibit 11.2. (We will use all whole numbers to simplify the illustration).

The number 3.61 in Exhibit 11.2 shows how far the values are—on the average—from the mean.

Variance   Although a bit more difficult to compute, the *variance* is generally a more useful measure of dispersion. The variance is computed in essentially the same way as the average deviation, except that the deviations are squared before summing, and the average is found using *n*-1. Exhibit 11.3 illustrates the method for obtaining the variance using the data from Exhibit 11.2.

EXHIBIT 11.2
Sample Average Deviation

1.   Gather Raw Data

Miles to Work	Responses	Total Miles
1	4	4
2	6	12
3	3	9
4	8	32
5	10	50
6	2	12
7	1	7
10	3	30
22	1	22
Totals	38	178

2.   Compute the mean $\left(\text{mean} = \overline{X} = \dfrac{\Sigma X}{n} \right)$.

$$\overline{X} = \frac{178}{38} = 4.6842105.$$

For most business purposes, you will not need to figure beyond two decimal places, so round off answers to the nearest hundredth. (When rounding off a five, round to the *even* value: 7.45 to 7.4, but 7.55 to 7.6.)

The *mean* number of miles commuted would be 4.68.

3.   Subtract the mean from each of the values $(X - \overline{X})$:
Values X − mean

$$1 \times 4 \ = \ 4 - 4.68 = \ -0.68$$

$$2 \times 6 \ = 12 - 4.68 = \ \ \ 7.32$$

$$3 \times 3 \ = \ 9 - 4.68 = \ \ \ 4.32$$

$$4 \times 8 \ = 32 - 4.68 = \ 27.32$$

$$5 \times 10 = 50 - 4.68 = \ 45.32$$

$$6 \times 2 \ = 12 - 4.68 = \ \ \ 7.32$$

$$7 \times 1 \ = \ 7 - 4.68 = \ \ \ 2.32$$

$$10 \times 3 \ = 30 - 4.68 = \ 25.32$$

$$22 \times 1 \ = 22 - 4.68 = \ \underline{\ 17.32}$$

Total   137.24   (absolute value)

4.   Ignore the negative signs, and compute the average deviation using the formula

$$\text{Average deviation} = \frac{\Sigma \ X - \overline{X}}{n}$$

or

$$\frac{137.24}{38} = 3.61.$$

EXHIBIT 11.3
Sample Variance

Formula for variance:

$$\text{Variance} = S^2 = \frac{\Sigma (X - \overline{X})^2}{n-1}.$$

Values X − Mean	=	Deviation	Deviation^2
1×4 = 4 − 4.68		−0.68	0.46
2×6 = 12 − 4.68		7.32	53.58
3×3 = 9 − 4.68		4.32	18.66
4×8 = 32 − 4.68		27.32	746.38
5×10 = 50 − 4.68		45.32	2053.90
6×2 = 12 − 4.68		7.32	53.58
7×1 = 7 − 4.68		2.32	5.38
10×3 = 30 − 4.68		25.32	641.10
22×1 = 22 − 4.68		17.32	299.98
			3873.02

$$S^2 = \frac{\Sigma (X - \overline{X})^2}{n-1} = \frac{3873.02}{38-1} = 104.68.$$

The variance of a sample is a measure of the dispersion of the data about the mean. To obtain the variance for a population as a whole (rather than for the sample), simply substitute n for $n-1$ in the formula.

Standard Deviation The standard deviation is the positive square root of the variance. Exhibit 11.4 illustrates the formula for standard deviation as applied to the variance computed in Exhibit 11.3.

The standard deviation is one of the most commonly used measures of distribution because the resulting figure is in the same units as those in the mean. The standard deviation of 10.23 in Exhibit 11.4, for example, is in miles, the same units as the mean established in Exhibit 11.2. (The variance is in units *squared*.)

EXHIBIT 11.4
Sample Standard Deviation

$$S = \sqrt{\frac{\Sigma(X - \overline{X})^2}{n-1}} \text{ or } \sqrt{\frac{3873.02}{38-1}} = \sqrt{104.68}$$

$$S = 10.23.$$

Note: As was true in computing the variance, substituting n for $n-1$ will show the standard deviation for the population rather than for the sample.

EXHIBIT 11.5
Symmetrical Distribution

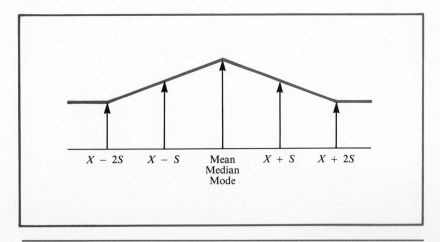

A relationship exists between measures of centrality (the mean = X and standard deviation *(S)*.

**Understanding
Centrality and
Dispersions**

Centrality is easier to visualize and understand than dispersion. The measures for centrality—especially the mean—tell us how to find the center point in a set of data. The measures of dispersion tell us how the data are grouped around that center point.

Exhibits 11.5, 11.6, and 11.7 illustrate possible distributions of data in reference to a mean.

EXHIBIT 11.6
Skewed Distributions

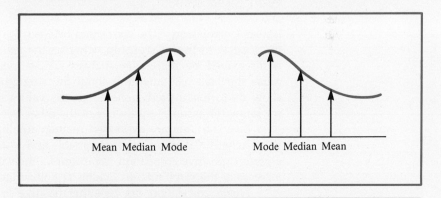

With unequal distribution, the mean and median are pulled toward the extremes.

EXHIBIT 11.7
Bimodal Distribution

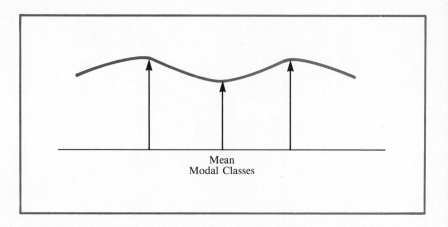

Mean
Modal Classes

Bivariate Data

Measures of centrality and dispersion describe single units of information about a population or a sample. Frequently in business, however, information about single units of information is not enough. We may need to study two pieces of data to see if a relationship exists between them.

Is there a relationship between education and income?

Is there a relationship between consumption of vitamins and health?

Is there a relationship between grades earned in college and occupational success?

Bivariate—or two variables—data are measured in two principal ways. We can examine the data for *linear correlations*, or we can study the data for *linear regression*.

Linear Correlation   The correlation between variables is a measure of the *strength* of the relationship, whereas the *nature* of the relationship is discovered by regression analysis. These measures are useful because they tell us something about the strength of relationships and allow us to make predictions about the values of one variable when we know (or assume) the values of the other.

Bivariate data are expressed mathematically in terms of ordered pairs, where X denotes the first variable and Y denotes the second. In a perfect, positive correlation, for example, the value of X and Y would increase at the same rate, as Exhibit 11.8 illustrates.

Linear correlation can be either positive or negative. A positive relationship is one in which the value of Y increases as the value of X increases. In a negative relationship, the value of Y would decrease as

EXHIBIT 11.8
Perfect Linear Correlation

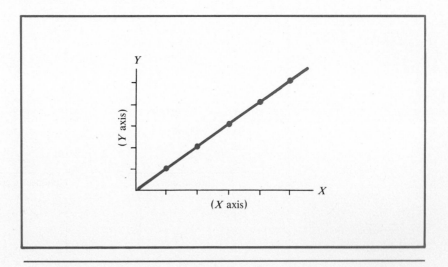

the value of X increases. The *scattergrams* in Exhibit 11.9 illustrate the possibilities.

Each of the dots in the scattergrams in Exhibit 11.9 represents the combined values of X and Y. Suppose that you wanted to compare annual incomes and the amount of money spent on home purchases. You would collect data as follows:

Buyer	Income	House Value
1	$10,000	$27,000
2	$15,000	$36,000
3	$20,000	$47,000
4	$25,000	$68,000
5	$30,000	$59,000

You would then designate one variable X and the other Y. These would be plotted on a scattergram as shown in Exhibit 11.10.

The mathematical formula for determining the *coefficient of linear correlation*, r, is complex:

$$r = \frac{n(\Sigma XY) - (\Sigma X)(\Sigma Y)}{\sqrt{n(\Sigma X^2) - (\Sigma X)^2} \times \sqrt{n(\Sigma Y^2) - (\Sigma Y)^2}}.$$

Applied to our extremely small sample of house buyers in Exhibit 11.10, the formula works like this.

EXHIBIT 11.9
Possible Correlation

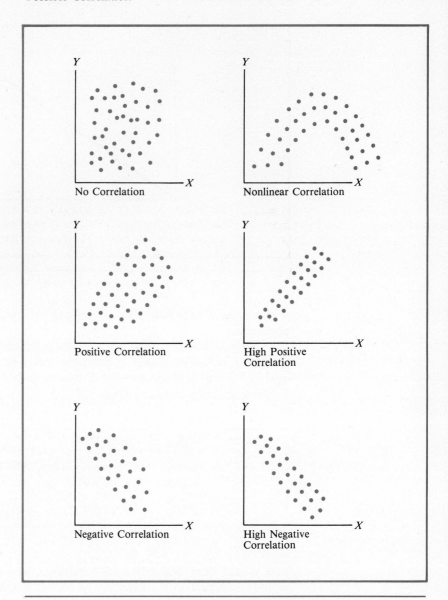

EXHIBIT 11.10
Scattergram Illustrating X and Y

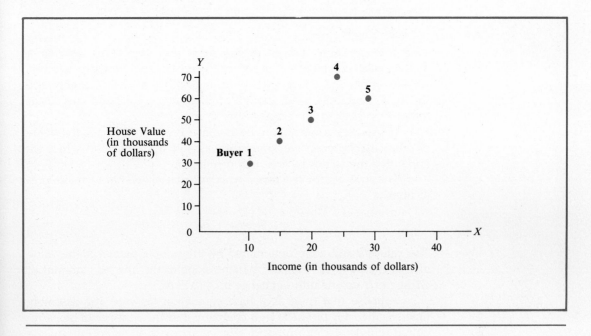

$$r = \frac{5(5220) - (100)(237)}{\sqrt{5(2250) - (10,000)} \times \sqrt{5(12,339) - (56,169)}}$$

$$r = \frac{26,100 - 23,700}{\sqrt{1,250} \times \sqrt{5,526}}$$

$$r = \frac{2,400}{(35.36)(74.34)}$$

$$r = \frac{2,400}{2628.66}$$

$$r = +.91.$$

A perfect positive correlation would be $+1$, and a perfect negative correlation would be -1. The $+.91$ indicates that, for our small sample, there is a high positive correlation between income and the amount of money spent on a house. To obtain a percentage, simply square the r. In this case $r^2 = 83$ percent. The 83 percent tells us that income accounts for 83 percent of the variance in the amount of money spent for houses among the cases examined, or that some factor other than income accounts for 17 percent of the variance in the amount of money spent for a house.

Because the complexity of the mathematics increases the possibility of error, researchers often use computer programs to determine linear correlations. You can imagine how difficult it would be to compute figures for thousands of home buyers instead of five.

Linear Regression Linear regression is the attempt to develop a mathematical equation that describes the relationship between two variables. Simple linear regressions, dealing with two variables only, are the most commonly used, though multiple regressions and curvilinear (other than straight line) regressions are possible.

Linear regressions allow us to make predictions about the value of one variable when we know the value of the other and when we know that the values have a high correlation.

The formula for the linear equation that allows us to make predictions is

$$Y = a + bX.$$

The values a and b are determined by the sample data: a is the value of Y at the point $X = 0$, and b is the slope of the line (the amount of change in Y or one unit of change in X ($\Delta Y / \Delta X$).

Suppose that there is a high correlation between the assembly time required for products in a company and the number of steps required to assemble the product. The company is about to introduce a new product and would like to predict how long the assembly of the product will take (which will help determine the cost of manufacturing the product). Exhibit 11.11 illustrates the application of the linear equation.

If the new product is going to have nine steps in the production process, we would then calculate the time required to manufacture the product as follows:

$$Y = 1.5 + (2 \times 9)$$

$$Y = 1.5 + 18$$

$$Y = 19.5 \text{ (hours required for production)}.$$

Linear correlations and linear regressions both show relationships. Neither can demonstrate a cause and effect relationship. Over the last 25 years, for example, you would find that the number of people attending college has increased. You would also find that the number of movies made each year has increased. Sampling would result in a high positive correlation, but neither increase could be said to be the cause of the other. Both are probably the result of some third factor, such as an expanding economy.

EXHIBIT 11.11
Linear Equation

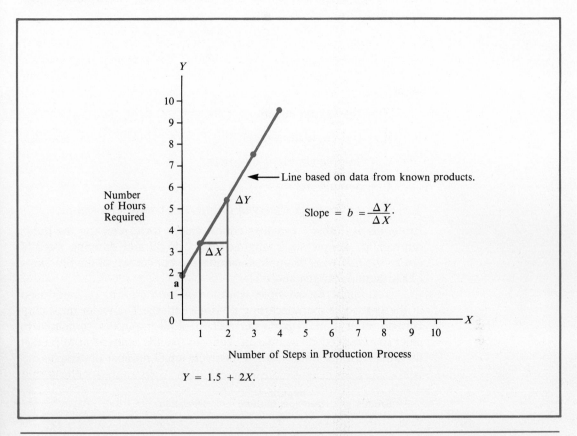

Number of Steps in Production Process

$Y = 1.5 + 2X.$

Inferential Statistics

Descriptive statistics describe the characteristics of a single set of data. In many cases, however, it is necessary to make decisions about differences among sets of data. Inferential statistics provide the means for making those decisions by testing hypotheses.

In any testing situation, it is useful to know the possibility of error. In testing our hypothesis, we will need to make inferences about the population mean, about the population proportions, and about the standard deviation.

Inferring the Population Mean   When the sample size is larger than 30, the mean of the population will be a close enough approximation of the mean of the sample for most purposes. When the sample is smaller than 30, we can increase the accuracy of our estimate of the population mean by using the *Student's t Distribution* (so called because it was originally published by W.S. Gosset under the pseudonym *student*). The formula is as follows:

$$t = \frac{X - \mu}{\frac{S}{\sqrt{n}}}$$

where

X = the sample mean

μ = the population mean

S = sample standard deviation

n = sample size

t = an index of observed differences based on a sample.

Appendix A, Table 1 provides critical values for t, showing the index number for sample sizes ranging from 2 to 30 and differing rates of error. The following example illustrates the application of the Student's t Distribution formula and table.

You might, for example, want to test for the purity of water used in the process of manufacturing pharmaceuticals. The water must contain no more than 14 parts per million of all impurities combined to meet required federal standards. You can use the Student's t to predict the quality of the water using a relatively small number of samples.

Sample	Impurities (parts per million)	Deviation
1	8	−4.1
2	14	+1.9
3	10	−2.1
4	11	−1.1
5	12	−0.1
6	16	+3.9
7	14	+1.9
8	12	−0.1
9	15	+2.9
10	9	−3.1

Sample mean = $\overline{X}$ = 12.1.

Sample standard deviation = $\sqrt{\dfrac{\Sigma(X_1 - \overline{X})^2}{n-1}}$

$$S = \sqrt{\frac{62.9}{9}}$$

$$= 2.64.$$

Now that we know that the sample mean is 12.1 and the sample standard deviation is 2.64, we can use the Student's t test to determine the probability that the water purity of the population (all the water) is the same as that in the sample. We do this in the following way:

1. State our goal as a hypothesis or null hypothesis.
    $\mu \leq 14$ppm—The water quality is acceptable.
    (Recall that μ is the population mean)
    $\mu \geq 14$ ppm—The water contains too many impurities.

2. Determine the amount of error acceptable. In this case, we will set the amount of error acceptable at 0.025, which results in 97.5 percent confidence that our hypothesis is correct.
    $\alpha = 0.025.$

3. Using Table 1, find the critical t-value for a sample size of 10 and α of 0.025.

EXHIBIT 11.12
Sample Entries for Student's t Distribution

$$T = 2.262.$$

df	Amount of α in one tail (half the total error).				
	—	—	—	—	.025
—	—	—	—	—	—
—	—	—	—	—	—
—	—	—	—	—	—
9	—	—	—	—	2.262

Note: The *df* number (degree of freedom) is always $n-1$, or 1 less than the sample size.

---

4. Use the formula to compute the observed t-value

    $$t = \frac{12.1 - 14}{2.64/10}$$

    $$t = \frac{-1.9}{.84}$$

    $$t = -2.26$$

5. Compare the critical and observed t-values. $-2.262 \leq -2.26$

6. Because the observed t-value is greater than or equal to the critical t-value, you have confirmed the hypothesis ($\mu = 14$ ppm), with 97.5 percent confidence, that the impurities in the water are less than 14ppm. While there is still a 2.5 percent chance that the impurities are equal to 14 ppm, you had already determined that this degree of risk would be acceptable. If μ had been larger than 14, you would have needed to take corrective action.

Inferring Proportions   Just as we sometimes need to make estimates of the population mean based on a relatively small sample, we sometimes need to infer proportions—or percentages—based on a small sample.

Suppose that you wanted to select one of two ads for testing in a sample geographical area, and you wanted to test the ad that had the better chance of succeeding. You could infer the proportion of the population that would prefer the one ad to the other by using a small sample and the following procedure:

1. Select a random sample. Show sample members both ads and ask which they prefer. Assume that 18 out of 25 people prefer Ad 1.

2. Determine the proportion (p) according to the formula:

$$p = \frac{X}{n} \text{ where } X \text{ is the number of persons preferring Ad 1.}$$

(Note: The conclusions would be the same if we used $X = 7$, the number preferring Ad 2, but the percentages would differ.)

$$p = \frac{18}{25} = 0.72 \text{ or } 72\%.$$

3. State the hypothesis: At least 60 percent of the population will prefer Ad 1 to Ad 2.

4. Determine a range of acceptance using Table 2 in Appendix A.

EXHIBIT 11.13
Sample Standard Normal Distribution

Second Decimal Place in Z

Z	.00	.01	.02	.03	.04	.05
.0	—	—	—	—	—	—
.1	—	—	—	—	—	—
.2	—	—	—	—	—	—
.3	—	—	—	—	—	—
.4	—	—	—	—	—	—
.5	—	—	—	—	—	—
.6	—	—	—	—	—	—
.7	—	—	—	—	—	—
.8	—	—	—	—	—	.3023
.9	—	—	—	—	—	—
1.0	—	—	—	—	—	—

The figures in this table, as is true of the Student's t Distribution, represent figures for half of the distribution. The figure for both halves is simply twice that for one. On the chart, we look for 30 percent. At a Z of 0.85, we find 0.3023, the figure closest to 30 percent.

EXHIBIT 11.14
Symmetry of the Standard Normal Distribution

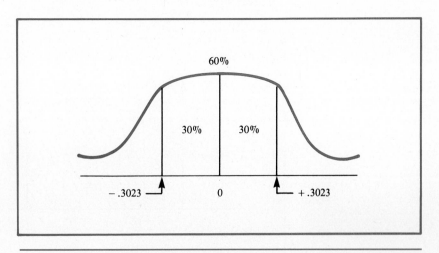

(Note that for the purposes of this test, any error should be in the direction of a larger percentage to ensure greater accuracy.) Exhibit 11.13 shows how to use the table, and Exhibit 11.14 illustrates the relationship of the numbers in the table to the standard normal distribution.

By using the table, we see that if Z is 0.85 or greater, we will have confirmed our hypothesis.

5. Use the formula

$$Z = \frac{p^1 - p}{\sqrt{pq/n}}$$

where $p^1 = X/n$,

p = hypothesized percentage,

and $q = 1 - p$.

$$Z = \frac{.72 - .60}{\sqrt{(.60)(.40)/25}}$$

$$Z = \frac{.12}{\sqrt{.24/25}}$$

$$Z = \frac{.12}{.098}$$

$$.85 \leq 1.22.$$

Because the observed Z-value is greater than or equal to the critical Z-value, we can predict that at least 60 percent of the total population would also prefer Ad 1. Exhibit 11.15 illustrates why this is true.

EXHIBIT 11.15

Standard Normal Distribution Showing Proportions in Reference to Z
Numbers

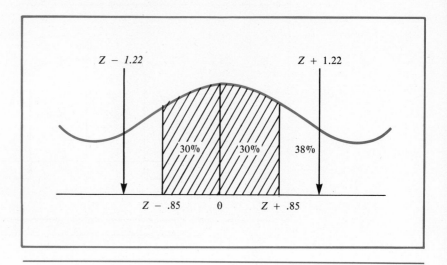

Because Z 1.22 falls outside the hypothesized figure of Z 0.85 (60 percent—or more accurately, ±30 percent), we can infer from our sample that at least 60 percent of the population will prefer Ad 1 to Ad 2. You should note that this test does not *prove* that 60 percent of the population will prefer Ad 1 to Ad 2. It is rather a measure of probability and a predictor of risk. If we wanted to be even more certain that a majority of the population would prefer one ad to the other, we would use a higher percentage in the formula, which would result in a higher critical Z-value. In this case, if we had decided on a lower degree of risk, we might not have been able to make the same positive inference the higher degree of risk permitted.

Inferring Variance and Standard Deviation   Another frequently used test is the Chi square (χ^2) test for variance. The χ^2 test is useful for determining whether a variance is within acceptable limits.

If you worked for a microchip company, for example, you would want to ensure that each microchip was exactly the correct thickness. Let's assume that a variance of 0.005 is acceptable.

Our hypothesis is that the variance is no larger than the specified 0.005. Again, we are going to compare the results of a sample with what we know to be probable. As is true of Student's *t* and proportions, the Chi-square test requires a table. Table 3, Appendix A shows the critical values for Chi-square.

EXHIBIT 11.16
Chi-Square Illustration

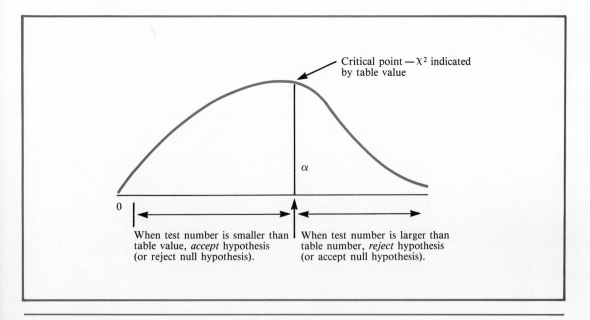

We would test the hypothesis using the following formula:

$$\chi^2 = \frac{(n-1)S^2}{\sigma^2}$$

Where S^2 = sample variance

n = sample size

σ^2 = the value specified in the hypothesis

Exhibit 11.16 illustrates the application of the formula.

To test our hypothesis, we select 14 chips at random. We discover that the variance is 0.0043.

Using Table 3, we determine the critical point of a sample of 14 with a tolerance of 0.005.

$$df = (n-1) = 13$$

$$\alpha = .005$$

$$\chi^2 = 29.8$$

Exhibit 11.17 illustrates the critical point for accepting the hypothesis.

EXHIBIT 11.17

Critical Point for Accepting the Hypothesis

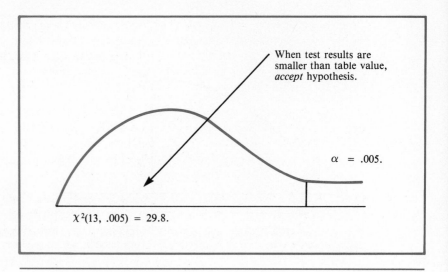

When test results are smaller than table value, *accept* hypothesis.

$\alpha = .005.$

$X^2(13, .005) = 29.8.$

Does a sample size of 14 with a variance of 0.0043 allow us to conclude that our machinery is working correctly?

$$\chi^2 = \frac{(n-1)S^2}{\sigma 2}$$

$$\chi^2 = \frac{(13) \ .0043^2}{.005^2}$$

$$\chi^2 = \frac{(13) \ .0000185}{.000025}$$

$$\chi^2 = \frac{.00024}{.000025}$$

$$\chi^2 = 9.6.$$

Because 9.6 is smaller than the table value of 29.8, we accept our hypothesis that the thickness of the microchips falls within acceptable tolerances.

METHODS OF DRAWING CONCLUSIONS

In Chapter 10 and in the preceding sections of this chapter, we have presented many of the standard rules for testing the truth of propositions and the validity of arguments. These include both tests for logic and statistical tests for acceptance of hypotheses.

Tests for Fairness   Do you have any preconceptions about the results, or do you have any biases that will influence the results?

Tests for Logical Development   Check to ensure that the explicit and implicit propositions in your argument (or that of others) are true. Is each new proposition a logical consequence of the preceding proposition? Is the proof valid?

Tests for Use of Logical Fallacies   Because reports should be objective and rely on logic to convince, you should check your report materials for the unintentional use of the common logical fallacies. Substitute propositions and logical proof for any fallacies you discover.

Tests for Statistical Accuracy   Ensure that the data you've collected justify your conclusions. If in doubt, increase your sample size, attempt to replicate your results with another population, or increase your number of observations.

While many business and technical decisions can be made on the basis of clear-cut, "hard" evidence, many cannot. Often, the decision must be made on somebody's intuitive feeling about the right course of action. All the evidence—including extensive market surveys—indicated that Ford Motor Company's Edsel would be a huge success. It flopped. Yet products like the Hula Hoop and the Pet Rock have proved successful in the absence of evidence to predict success.

The same is true in areas other than market research. What the evidence says *should* work does not always prove successful, and what the evidence says will not work, often does. It hasn't been that long since aeronautical engineers "proved" that, on the basis of body weight and wing area, it was impossible for a bumble bee to fly.

Because you can't draw the correct conclusions every time, you need to be especially careful to be explicit about what you are concluding and why. No one will expect more of you than an honest experiment or other collection of data and an objective presentation of the evidence. Use hard—quantitative—evidence when possible, but avoid using statistical analysis unless the data are truly amenable. Heavy use of statistics can intimidate and manipulate some readers, so include any explanations and interpretations of quantitative data your reader may require or appreciate.

SUMMARY

Most decisions in business, industry, and government are based at least in part on consideration of statistical data. Data are classed as qualitative or quantitative. Qualitative data include the qualities or attributes of the items being investigated. Quantitative data include the numerical factors that influence the items being investigated. Qualitative data can be quantified for analysis by counting, which results in nominal data, or by ranking, which results in ranked order.

In obtaining quantitative data, a population (of people or objects) or a sample of the population is examined with respect to one or more variables. A variable that applies to the whole population is known as a parameter of the population. Quantitative data are discrete when the variables are counted item by item and continuous when the variables can assume virtually any value.

Probability theory is concerned with the chance that an event will occur when all possibilities are known, and statistics is concerned with inferring the possibilities based on the results of a sample.

One of the most significant uses of statistics is to provide measures of central tendency. The mean, the median, and the mode all provide indications of where the center of a set of data is located, but they can give different impressions of where the center is located. Measures of dispersion are useful because they provide information about how the data are grouped about the center. Closely grouped data are said to have low dispersion, whereas widely spaced data have high dispersion. Measures of dispersion include average deviation, variance, and standard deviation.

Measures of centrality and dispersion describe single variables. It is often useful to study the relationship between two variables. Measures of bivariate data include linear correlations and regressions. Correlations show the extent to which two variables relate to each other. Linear regression is a technique for predicting future values for one variable when the value of a related variable is known or can be assumed.

Statistics also provide techniques for testing the accuracy of data. The Student's *t* Distribution test allows researchers to make inferences about the population mean. We can also infer proportions within the population based on the proportion of a sample and the standard normal distribution of populations. The Chi-square test allows predictions about variance and standard deviation.

Even following all the rules of logic and principles of semantics presented in Chapter 10 as well as accurately employing statistical analysis will not guarantee error-free conclusions. As long as researchers are careful to specify what data are significant and to explain the bases for their inferences, the report will meet the test for objectivity.

EXERCISES

Review Questions

1. Is *data* singular or plural?

2. Define and explain the concepts of qualitative data and quantitative data.

3. What are the differences between discrete and continuous data?

4. Define the following terms: population, sample, variable, parameter, and probability.

5. Define and explain the mean, median, and mode.

6. Define and explain the terms range, average deviation, variance, and standard deviation.

7. In what way does the standard deviation depend on the mean and the average deviation?

8. What is the relationship among the mean, median, and mode in a skewed distribution?

9. In what ways are linear correlations and regressions useful?

10. Define and explain the uses of the Student's *t* Test, the standard normal distribution test, and the Chi-square test.

Problems

1. For one of the problems in Chapter 6, Chapter 8, or in Appendix B, make the following calculations for all significant variables:
    a. Mean
    b. Median
    c. Mode
    d. Range
    e. Average deviation
    f. Variance
    g. Standard deviation
    h. Linear correlations between at least two related data
    i. Linear regression predicting the value of one variable when the value of another variable is known or assumed
    j. Student's *t* Test
    k. Test for proportion
    l. Chi-square test
    Be sure to label each item and to show all the steps in your work.

2. Perform the computations listed in the preceding problem on the data you have collected for your own report.

3. Perform the computations listed in Problem 1 above for the following data:

Respondent	Age	Highest Level of Education	Annual Income
1	47	H.S.	$115,000
2	52	B.A.	42,000
3	29	B.A.	37,000
4	31	M.A.	41,000
5	23	H.S.	12,000
6	62	B.A.	47,000
7	59	Ph.D.	32,000
8	47	Ph.D.	250,000
9	42	M.A.	26,000
10	46	H.S.	23,000
11	32	B.A.	33,000
12	31	Ph.D.	31,000

(continued)

Respondent	Age	Highest Level of Education	Annual Income
13	40	H.S.	17,000
14	52	H.S.	21,000
15	29	M.A.	41,000
16	47	B.A.	48,000
17	38	H.S.	30,000
18	55	B.A.	52,000
19	60	B.A.	46,000
20	60	B.A.	29,000
21	58	Ph.D.	75,000
22	49	B.A.	92,000
23	24	H.S.	13,000
24	65	M.A.	88,000
25	60	B.A.	81,000
26	47	B.A.	52,000
27	44	Ph.D.	73,000
28	30	B.A.	18,000
29	38	M.A.	48,000
30	42	H.S.	28,000

PART IV
Writing and Editing

CHAPTER 12

Organizing the Report

Organization is an aid to clarity and understanding. A logical, well-balanced presentation of information helps readers grasp and remember important points. How you organize the material in your report will be one of the critical factors in determining how well your report is received.

Topics

Basic Considerations
Common Structural Patterns
Methods of Outlining
Headings

Some of your report structure will be determined by the material itself. You might, for example, need to explain a new procedure according to the steps required for completion, or you might need to explain a problem before you can propose a solution. Regardless of the particulars, however, report organization is based on three overriding principles.

1. Every report (and every other piece of communication) must have a beginning, middle, and end.

2. Your reader will tend to be predisposed either to accept or to reject your conclusions and recommendations.

3. Central—or most important—ideas should receive emphasis.

BASIC CONSIDERATIONS

You have to start somewhere; the question is how to begin in a way that will both orient your reader to the topic of the report and be interesting as well. In general, your opening will accomplish both purposes if you begin with a statement telling what the report is about (your *purpose* or *thesis*) and explaining the need for the report. Both should be expressed in terms of the benefit the reader will gain as a result of the report.

The middle of the report is used to present and interpret data or the application of criteria. The concluding section may contain conclusions and recommendations and, when the report is long, a summary of important points. The ending should also be decision and action oriented (when the writer has been authorized to propose specific courses of action).

Organize for Reader Acceptance

Even though a report *must* be an objective presentation of facts, report writers are not always preparing those presentations for objective people. In most cases, the recipient of a report will be either inclined to accept the writer's conclusions and recommendations, or neutral—willing to examine the data with an open mind. Every now and then, however, a reader will be predisposed to reject a particular solution to problems, which the writer may have determined is the best possible solution.

When the reader is willing to accept the writer's conclusions, or when the reader has a neutral, unbiased attitude, some form of direct or immediate beginning is best. A major conclusion, a major recommendation, or a major benefit should be first. The rest of the report provides the support and explanation the opening requires. This is known as *deductive* order.

When the writer has reason to suspect that the reader will resent or resist the conclusions and recommendations in a report, a slower, more methodical approach will increase the chances that the report will receive a fair hearing. With this approach, the supporting details are presented first, and the conclusions and recommendations are withheld until all the evidence has been explained. This is known as *inductive* order. We will discuss deductive and inductive order at greater length below.

Organize for Emphasis

What do you want your reader to remember? Those ideas should receive emphasis. Obviously, not all ideas in a report will be of equal importance. You will need to select those things most important for your reader to remember and present those ideas in ways that will increase the reader's ability to retain them.

Because people tend to remember best that which they read first or last, important points belong at the beginning or end of the report as a whole, of units within the report, or of paragraphs. Readers are also more inclined to remember generalizations than they are to remember specific facts. Your reader's ability to remember your key points will depend as well on how many points you present, how well those points are related to material the reader already knows, and how well the points are related to each other. Readers remember up to about seven items of new information fairly well, but remembering more than seven items is difficult for most people. Your readers will also tend to remember those items associated with other items with which the reader is already familiar. For this reason, analogies can be an aid to memory as well as a means of explaining or illustrating.

Finally, the way in which you write about something can help your reader focus on those items you consider most important. Stylistic means of controlling emphasis include placement, proportion, language, and mechanics.

Placement   Put key points first or last in the report. Major subtopics should receive similar emphasis within report divisions. As a rule, the first sentence in a paragraph should introduce the topic or main idea of the paragraph. The rest of the paragraph usually contains supporting or explanatory details.

Proportion   How much time you spend on one topic in relation to other topics is an indication of its importance. In general, when an idea is important, you should allocate it a greater amount of space and explain it more thoroughly. When this is not possible, use one (or more) of the other means of providing emphasis to draw extra attention to the idea.

Language   Readers pay closer attention to sentences about people doing things than to sentences about ideas. Make sentences specific and people oriented:

Strong: Closing line 3 will put 57 people out of work and save the company only $1,350 a year.

Weak: The minimal savings that would result from closing line 3 will not justify the poor morale that would result from the concomitant layoffs.

Also, you can use language to emphasize an idea simply by telling your reader that it is important:

The most significant result was . . .
The important factor for our company is . . .

Mechanics You can also emphasize ideas through mechanical means. Underscoring, color, solid capital letters, main points in a numbered list, and graphic aids to help the reader visualize important ideas are all ways to stress those things you want your reader to remember.

COMMON STRUCTURAL PATTERNS

While the basic considerations just described apply in nearly every report writing situation, specialized patterns have developed because they are effective for presenting certain kinds of data. The structured patterns used most often include deductive, inductive, order or importance, chronological, step-by-step, spatial, topical, problem to solution, criteria to application, and cause and effect. In addition, some situations require the use of more than one pattern.

Reports as a whole are usually arranged either deductively or inductively, with various components employing the structural patterns most appropriate for their purposes. Entire reports, however, may make use of any of the structural patterns.

Deductive Order

The basic organizational pattern for most business reports is deductive. In deductive order, the main point, general conclusion, or most important recommendation is presented *first*. Supporting details and explanations are presented second. Exhibit 12.1 illustrates deductive order.

EXHIBIT 12.1
Deductive Order

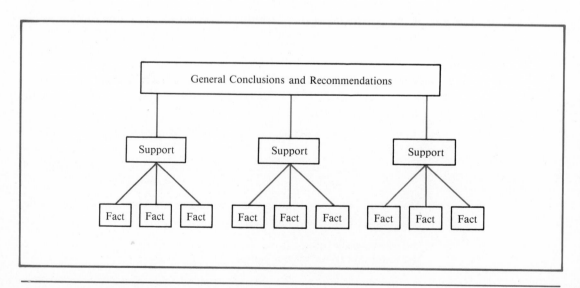

The advantage of deductive order is that it tells the reader instantly everything he or she needs to know to make a decision. Unless the reader is particularly interested in the subject or in how you reached your decision, she or he may not need to read the entire report.

The disadvantage of this organizational pattern is that it enables a biased reader to develop arguments against your conclusions before she or he has reviewed the facts that lead to the conclusion. As we mentioned previously, if your reader has a preconception or a bias which you may need to overcome, deductive order may not prove successful. You should also consider your reader's time. A reader may be more biased against the slower inductive order of presentation than he or she is biased against your idea; thus you would gain nothing by using inductive order. For most business reports, deductive order is the better organizational pattern.

Inductive Order

Inductive order is the reverse of deductive order. It presents the facts first and uses the facts to lead to a general conclusion. Exhibit 12.2 illustrates inductive order.

Inductive order is a slower order of presentation. The reader must consider a series of facts before learning the writer's point. As a result, reports presented inductively may be a little frustrating for the reader, who naturally wants to know what the facts mean.

EXHIBIT 12.2
Inductive Order

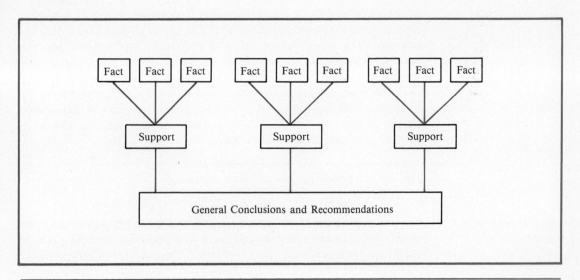

The inductive approach is best when the reader will need to be persuaded to give your ideas a fair hearing. If you know the reader has a preconception or a bias that is contrary to your findings, you may still be able to convince your reader by showing how the facts lead to only one conclusion.

Order of Importance

When you organize according to order of importance, you can use either the most important item or the least important item as a starting point. Suppose you were submitting a report on the actions your company could take to save money. You might organize these steps in decreasing order of importance, from greatest savings to least savings, because that order would probably be an order of priority as well. The advantage of this order of presentation is, as with deductive order, that it begins with the item of greatest interest to the reader. The disadvantage is that, once the main point has been stated, the remainder of the report is less interesting.

The organizational pattern leading from the least important item to the most important is also known as the *climax* order of presentation. As with inductive order, its chief use is to gain acceptance for a controversial idea. In the money-saving report, for example, if the idea that would result in the greatest savings were also something controversial, you might begin with the change that would result in the least savings. You would then work up to the more controversial idea that would result in the greatest savings.

This order of presentation is also useful in oral presentations because it places the most important point last, so the reader will be likely to remember it until he or she has an opportunity to act on it.

Chronological Order

In reporting events or procedures that happen according to a specific time sequence, chronological order is the logical choice. Police and fire reports, work schedules, minutes of meetings, trip and call reports, and accident reports are among those that call for a chronological presentation at some point within the report.

In chronological order, the items or events are arranged in the order in which they occurred or should occur. They may be designated simply as *first, second, third,* and so forth, or they may be identified as having occurred at a specific time:

The meeting was called to order at 8:05 . . .
The meeting was adjourned at 9:20.

Step-by-Step Order

Step-by-step order is an adaptation of chronological order for those events or procedures that should occur in a particular sequence but for which the time is not an important factor. Descriptions of mechanisms, explanations of processes, and instructions are usually written in step-by-step order. Exhibit 12.3 illustrates a step-by-step sequence:

EXHIBIT 12.3
Step-by-Step Sequence

Step 1:   Insert key in ignition switch on steering column.

Step 2:   Check to make sure that the transmission is in Park (P) or Neutral (N). If the transmission is in N, make sure that the hand brake is in the "set" position (see p. 7).

Step 3:   Set the automatic choke by depressing the accelerator pedal to the floor *once*. Depressing the pedal more than once may flood the engine and prevent starting.

Step 4:   Take your foot off the accelerator pedal and turn the key to "start" position.

Step 5:   Release key when engine starts or after 10 seconds.

Step 6:   If engine does not catch, wait 5 seconds and repeat steps 4 and 5.

Step 7:   If engine does not catch after three repetitions of Step 6, repeat procedure beginning at Step 3.

The biggest difficulty with step-by-step sequence is that the writer is almost always more familiar with the process or procedure than the reader, and it is easy to omit some of the steps required.

Spatial Order

When the spatial arrangement of physical features is an important factor in a report, the arrangement should be described in spatial order. Dimensions (height, width, length, depth), directions (north, south, up, down), shape (circular, rectangular, square), relationships (higher, lower, above, below), and proportions (larger, smaller, one-half, two-thirds) are the key elements in spatial ordering.

Spatial order may be used alone in describing the physical features of a construction site, a laboratory, or an office layout. It may be combined with a chronological or step-by-step pattern to show movement or progress of an item through space and time, as would be the case of components moving along an assembly line.

Spatial order is also useful for discussing factors that vary according to geographical divisions. A company might divide its marketing responsibilities according to geographical areas: Northwest Region, Southwest Region, Midwest Region, and so on. The results of market research or sales would probably be presented using that same spatial organization.

Topical Order

A topical organizational pattern presents information according to categories or topics. A company annual report, for example, might be arranged according to topic:

Letter to Shareholders
Operations Review
Sales and Income
Products and Services
Social Responsibilities
Financial Data

Topical order is most useful when the categories to be discussed are separate and distinct. The writer can cover one topic before beginning to discuss the next.

Problem-to-Solution Order

Problem-to-solution order is an application of the inductive order of presentation. The problem can be any unsatisfactory condition, and the solution would be the recommended method of correcting the difficulty. Proposals are a common use of this organization pattern. The writer perceives and defines a problem, explores possible solutions, and selects and recommends the solution with the most advantages and/or the fewest disadvantages.

Suppose, for example, you were working for a manufacturer of packaging materials that had begun as a small, midwestern company serving essentially a local clientele. Company sales reps have always traveled by car, and they still do, even though many of the company's clients are now located hundreds of miles from the plant. One day while driving nearly 800 miles between calls, you did some calculating and determined that the automobile travel—considering cost of cars, gas, hotels, and sales time lost—exceeded that of travel by air. In proposing a change to management, you would use a problem-to-solution order. You could do this in one of two ways. You could present your solution and the resultant benefit first, and then review the problem and the alternatives you considered. Or you could begin (more convincingly) with the problem and the costs associated with it, explain the alternatives, and offer the solution last.

The *basic* order in either case is inductive. The first case, which presents the solution first, appears at first glance to be deductive. The basic structural pattern, however, is inductive because it retains the inductive method of beginning with specific facts and working to a general conclusion (with the exception of letting the reader know the solution in advance). Straight deductive order would present the solution and offer those facts in support of the solution rather than provide an examination of the problem.

Criteria-to-
Application
Order

Criteria (plural of *criterion*) are the standards by which something is measured or evaluated. Criteria-to-application structure is primarily used to compare products or ideas in relation to their use. A company purchasing new equipment, for example, would want to know which brand or model would best serve its needs. By using the criteria-to-application order, the writer could evaluate costs, useful life, flexibility, and other criteria deemed significant. This pattern is also useful for evaluating the proposed solutions in the problem-to-solution organizational pattern.

When using this system, use the criteria as the major divisions and the items being evaluated as the minor divisions:

I.   First Criterion
     A.   Product 1
     B.   Product 2
     C.   Product 3
II. Second Criterion
     A.   Product 1
     B.   Product 2
     C.   Product 3

Organizing by criteria helps the reader focus on and emphasizes the points that will determine the conclusions and recommendations, rather than on the features of individual products or ideas. Of course, the criteria might need to be subordinated for complete analysis, or the applications may need further subdivision for complete coverage.

Cause-and-Effect
Order

The cause-and-effect order is useful for analyzing the possible consequences of a particular action. Its opposite, the effect-to-cause order, is useful for tracing an effect back to its cause. Either of these schemes is likely to include elements of chronological or spatial order. Cause-and-effect order moves from a known factor or event to a probable result. It is a form of forecasting: What will happen to profits if we increase prices by 12 percent?

Effect-to-cause order attempts to discover the cause of a particular event or situation. Because causes must precede effects, using a reverse chronological order is basic. This pattern may prove complex because an effect may have more than one cause, and the factor that seems to be the cause may be only a related effect.

The effect-to-cause pattern is often used to investigate problems:

What is causing the low morale in the Tennessee plant?
Why has production declined over the past 90 days?

Mixed Patterns

As the previous discussion implied, these patterns may be combined. In fact, the longer the report, the more likely it will contain more than one of these organizational patterns. Each of these patterns will help you achieve a specific objective, and when you have more than one objective, you'll naturally use more than one system of organization. In criteria-to-application order, for example, you might wish to list your criteria in decreasing order of importance so that your reader could see at a glance how the criteria were weighted.

While you don't need to be specific in telling your reader what organizational pattern you are using, the pattern itself needs to be sufficiently clear that the reader will know what you are doing at each step of the way. If you are combining chronological and spatial orders, for example, be explicit about references to time and place so that your reader will be able to tell which is which.

Also, do not confuse systems of classification—which *must* be the same throughout—with patterns of organization. A discussion of office layout, for example, would have to stick to those factors that influence layout: furniture, equipment, traffic patterns, and so forth. The discussion could include elements of spatial order, chronological order, cause-and-effect order, effect-to-cause order, criteria-to-application order, and others. The overall structure for the discussion could be either deductive or inductive.

METHODS OF OUTLINING

An outline is the skeleton of your report. It reveals the structure on which the substance will hang. Outlines will prove useful three times in the writing process. First, a tentative outline developed in the planning stage (see Chapter 6) will enable you to explore the possible sequencing of and relationships among the areas to be covered. Second, a working outline, prepared after the data have been collected and analyzed, provides the structure for the final report. The working outline is the guide you intend to follow. It is not, however, immutable. The writing process may reveal weaknesses in the outline which should be corrected. Third, once the report is complete, a final outline can serve as a table of contents and as a guide to headings within the report.

Systems of Outlining

Whatever the purpose of the outline, it will use one of three symbol systems to indicate the divisions and sequence of ideas. The most common symbol system remains the Roman numeral system, which uses Roman numerals to designate the main topics (Exhibit 12.4). The other two systems use numbers and decimals to indicate main topics and subtopics, with one system indenting to show subordination (Exhibit 12.5) and the other beginning all entries on the left margin (Exhibit 12.6). The decimal systems have been gaining popularity in recent years.

EXHIBIT 12.4
Roman Numeral System of Outlining

```
                        Title of Report
                    (superior to all divisions)

          I.    First Main Topic
                A.  Major subtopic
                      1.  Minor subtopic
                      2.  Minor subtopic
                          a.  Subsubtopic
                          b.  Subsubtopic
                                (1)  Subsubsubtopic
                                (2)  Subsubsubtopic
                                      (a)  Subsubsubsubtopic
                                      (b)  Subsubsubsubtopic
                B.  Major subtopic
          II.   Second Main Topic
                A.  Major subtopic
                B.  Major subtopic
                      1.  Minor subtopic
                      2.  Minor subtopic
          III.  Third Main Division
          IV.   (Entries follow the same pattern throughout the report.)
```

Whichever of these systems you use, the same five basic rules apply.

The Whole Must Equal the Sum of Its Parts The main divisions must add up to or equal the whole expressed by the title. That is, the title should neither state nor imply more or less than the report will actually cover. The same rule applies to each of the topics and its subtopics.

EXHIBIT 12.5
Decimal System with Indentation

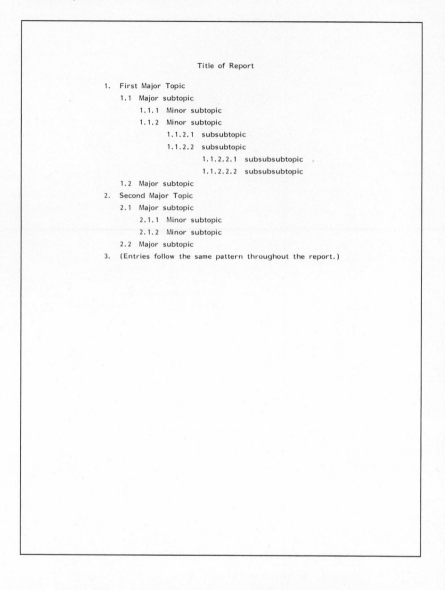

```
                           Title of Report

        1.  First Major Topic
            1.1  Major subtopic
                 1.1.1  Minor subtopic
                 1.1.2  Minor subtopic
                        1.1.2.1  subsubtopic
                        1.1.2.2  subsubtopic
                                 1.1.2.2.1  subsubsubtopic
                                 1.1.2.2.2  subsubsubtopic
            1.2  Major subtopic
        2.  Second Major Topic
            2.1  Major subtopic
                 2.1.1  Minor subtopic
                 2.1.2  Minor subtopic
            2.2  Major subtopic
        3.  (Entries follow the same pattern throughout the report.)
```

Divisions Should Be Organized for Relative Balance No one division should be very much larger or smaller than the other divisions.

Single Subdivisions Should Not Occur Because a whole cannot be divided unless at least two parts result, no topic can be divided unless at least two subtopics result.

EXHIBIT 12.6
Decimal System without Indentation

Title of Report

1.   First Main Topic
1.1   Major subtopic
1.1.1   Minor subtopic
1.1.1.1   subsubtopic
1.1.1.2   subsubtopic
1.1.2   Minor subtopic
1.2   Major subtopic
2.   (Entries follow the same form throughout the report.)

Main Divisions Should Be Expressed in Parallel Grammatical Form   Subdivisions within each division must also use parallel grammatical structure, but subdivisions of one topic need not be parallel with subdivisions of a separate topic.

Divisions and Subdivisions Should Be Selected to Help the Reader Focus Quickly on the Significant Ideas   When possible, the number of parts within any division should not be fewer than three nor more than seven.

Informal Outlines

Tentative outlines and sometimes working outlines as well are usually *informal* or *topical* outlines. Such outlines use one or two words to indicate the topic covered in each division and subdivision. Exhibit 12.7 illustrates an informal outline.

EXHIBIT 12.7
Informal Outline

Truck Accidents

I. The Accident on 23 May
    A. Police Report
    B. Driver's Report
    C. Mechanic's Investigation
II. Vehicle Repair Records
    A. Every Six Months
    B. Accidents
III. Safety Record
    A. Vehicle Breakdowns
    B. Accidents
IV. Inspections Required
    A. Procedure
    B. Costs
    C. Savings

The main use of informal or topical outlines is to help the writer organize the material in the planning or writing stage. While it allows the writer to work quickly in deciding what element belongs in which position, a topical outline does not provide enough information to be useful to a reader. Any outline that will be seen by a reader should be a formal outline.

Formal Outlines

Formal outlines are designed to communicate some essential information to the reader. To do so, they use phrases or complete sentences to describe the divisions more fully than the one or two words used in topic outlines. Exhibit 12.8 illustrates a formal outline using phrases.

The formal outline may use complete sentences in the place of phrases. In place of the phrase in I. in Figure 12.8, for example, the writer could use a complete sentence:

Phrase: The Cause of the Accident on 23 May

Sentence: Brake failure caused the accident on 23 May.

The use of full sentence outlines is limited because they supply more information than readers expect or want in an outline. A sentence outline, however, may help a writer develop *topic sentences* for the paragraphs of the report, and without the outline designations (I. A. B., 1. 1.1, 1.1.2, etc.) a sentence outline may serve as an abstract or summary of the entire report.

HEADINGS

Just as the writer uses the title of the entire report to tell a reader what the report is about, he or she can help the reader follow the report by using titles for each section of the report. Titles for the divisions and subdivisions are called *headings* or *heads* because they are placed at the "head" of sections.

A Good Heading

A good heading is both brief and specific, letting the reader see what topic the following material will cover and providing some information about that topic. A good heading also lets the reader know the relative importance of the material that follows. Is the material a main division, a subdivision, or a subsubdivision? What is its relationship to the material preceding and following it?

As a rule, the phrases developed for the formal outline may be used as the headings in the report, and the same rules apply to the use of headings as to outlining. In addition, the physical form of headings must make their relative importance clear at a glance. This requires that the system used be consistent throughout the report and that the form used for major headings appear superior to that used for minor headings.

EXHIBIT 12.8
Formal Outline Using Phrases

Reducing the Number of Truck Accidents

I. The Cause of the Accident of 23 May
   A. The Police Report Cites Brake Failure
   B. The Driver's Report Blames the Brakes
   C. The Mechanic's Investigation Confirms Brake Failure
II. Problems Revealed by Vehicle Repair Records
   A. Vehicles Examined Only Twice a Year
   B. Potential Hazard on Most Vehicles
III. Improved Safety Records Desirable
   A. The Costs of Vehicle Breakdowns
   B. The Costs of Accidents
IV. Increased Inspection in Schedule Would Help
   A. Quarterly Schedule for Inspections
   B. Some Increase in Costs
      1. Three Additional Trucks Required
      2. One Additional Mechanic Required
   C. Savings to Exceed Costs
      1. Reduced Vehicle Down Time
      2. Fewer Breakdowns on Road
      3. Fewer Accidents Caused by Mechanical Failures
      4. Reduced Risk of Potentially Serious Accidents
         in Future

In general, the relative importance of a heading is indicated by the size of type used in the heading (printed reports), its position on the page, and the amount of space allowed for it. Take a look through the pages of this book, for example, and note the type size, position, and space allocation for chapter titles and for major and minor divisions within the chapters. Note that you can easily determine which sections are main divisions and which are subdivisions by the physical appearance of the heading.

Basic Rules

The same differentiation should occur in typewritten material. While different organizations may require different systems of headings in their reports, the following rules apply in most typewritten systems.

1. Headings in solid capital letters are superior to headings that include lowercase letters.

2. Centered headings are superior to headings on the margin.

3. Headings separated from the text are superior to those that are not separated.

4. Headings in solid "caps" are not underscored, but headings using caps and lowercase letters are underscored to increase their visibility.

5. No two headings should appear without intervening text. Because no subdivision can be the equal of the main division of which it is a part, the main division must include information about all the subdivisions included within the division.

6. The report title must be in a form clearly superior to all the headings used in the report.

7. The text of the report must be coherent with all headings removed. The headings should not be used as antecedents for pronouns nor should the paragraph that follows assume that the heading has communicated specific facts.

8. Whatever forms are used, the same system must be used consistently throughout the report.

Typewritten Forms

As mentioned previously, heading use corresponds with that of outlining:

```
                        Title
I.      (or 1.) First-degree or First-level heading
        A.      (or 1.1) Second-degree or second-level heading
                1.      (or 1.1.1) Third-degree (level) heading
                        a.      (or 1.1.1.1) Fourth-degree (level heading)
                                (1)     (or 1.1.1.1.1) Fifth-degree (level) heading
```

The term *degree* or *level* is used to indicate the division designation, beginning with first-degree to indicate the main divisions, and second- through fifth-degree to indicate major and minor subdivisions. Only the longest, most formal reports are sufficiently complex to require five levels of headings. Exhibit 12.9 illustrates typewritten forms for five levels of headings with double-spaced text.

EXHIBIT 12.9
Heading Forms

```
                         R E P O R T    T I T L E


                         FIRST-DEGREE HEADING


          When the report is long enough to contain "sections" or
     "chapters" of ten or more pages each, section titles can be
     designated by first-level headings in solid capital letters.
     The heading should be centered on the page but not underscored.
     Because headings of this sort are used to introduce sections,
     they begin on a new page, two inches from the top.  Begin typing
     three or four spaces below the heading.


                         Second-degree Headings
          Major subdivisions are indicated by second-degree headings.
     In long reports, second-level heads are centered, use caps and
     lowercase, and are underscored.  Separate second-degree headings
     from the text by leaving three or four spaces above the heading
     and a double space below.


     Third-degree Headings
          Minor subdivisions are indicated by third-degree headings,
     which use caps and lowercase and appear on the margin.  They are
     underscored and have two or three spaces above and a double
     space below.

          Fourth-degree headings.  Subsubdivisions require fourth-
     degree headings.  Fourth-degree headings may be an integral part
     of the paragraph, separated from the first sentence by a period
     or a period and a dash.  They may use capitals and lowercase or
     capitalize the initial of the first word only.  Double space
     before the heading as you would before the beginning of any new
     paragraph.  This form of heading is sometimes called a run-in
     head.

          Fifth-degree headings are indicated simply by underscoring
     the first few words in the first sentence of the paragraph.  The
     initial letter of the first word is the only capital, unless
     other words are proper nouns or adjectives.  Because the heading
     should contain significant information, the sentence needs to be
     written so that the first few words contain the main idea of the
     following paragraph.  This form of heading is also called a run-
     in head.
```

Exhibit 12.9 illustrates the sequence of heading forms for reports long enough to require five levels of divisions and subdivisions. Most reports are not that long. Many reports require one level of heading only, and most reports require three or fewer levels of heads.

When one level only is required, the form shown in Exhibit 12.9 as a third-degree heading is most common. When two levels of headings are required, the forms for second and third degrees are most common. When three levels are required, main divisions can be indicated by centered heads, using caps and lowercase letters. Major subdivisions can be indicated by marginal heads, using caps and lowercase letters. Minor subdivisions in this system can be indicated by a run-in head, separated from the text by a period or a period and a dash.

Report examples throughout this text illustrate many of the possibilities. (See especially Exhibits in Chapter 16.)

SUMMARY

Report structure is influenced by the material itself, the fact that the report must begin and end somewhere, the reader's predisposition to accept or reject the report, and the need to emphasize central ideas. The opening—or introduction—should orient the reader to the problem and be interesting from the reader's point of view. The middle—or body—of the report presents and interprets data. The ending of the report may contain conclusions and recommendations or a summary.

When a reader is predisposed to accept the contents of a report, deductive structure, which places the important conclusions first, is best. Inductive structure, which begins with facts and ends with the conclusions, is best for readers who are biased against the conclusions in the report. Whichever structure is used, the writer needs to use placement, proportion, language, and mechanics to emphasize the most important ideas.

Common structural patterns include deductive, inductive, order of importance (most to least and least to most), chronological, step-by-step, spatial, topical, problem to solution, criteria to application, and cause and effect. Each of these patterns has specific uses and may also be used in combination with one or more of the other patterns to express ideas.

Outlines may employ the Roman numeral system or the decimal system. They may be informal or formal. An informal outline expresses the topic in one or two words. A formal outline uses phrases or sentences to express the topics. Headings correspond with outline entries and serve as a guide to the reader by saying something significant about the following material and by indicating the relative importance of each topic.

EXERCISES

Review Questions

1. What three basic considerations influence the organization of a report?

2. What are the differences between deductive and inductive order, and when should you use each?

3. How can organization contribute to a reader's ability to remember important information?

4. List and explain the four factors that control the emphasis of ideas.

5. When should a report be organized according to order of importance?

6. What are the differences among chronological order, step-by-step order, and topical order?

7. What are typical uses of problem-to-solution order, criteria-to-application order, and cause-and-effect order?

8. List and explain the five basic rules for outlining.

9. What are the differences between informal and formal outlines?

10. In what ways are headings similar to outline entries?

11. List and explain the eight basic rules of heading use.

12. How do headings help the reader, and when should they be used?

Problems

1. Select five reports—from those you collected previously, from those presented as examples in this text, or from another source—and identify the organizational pattern or patterns used. In a memo three to five pages long, describe the reasons the organizational patterns employed are or are not effective. Illustrate your ideas by using specific examples.

2. For each of the five reports, reconstruct the appropriate formal outline and compare the outline with the headings used. Evaluate the reports based on that comparison.

3. For each of the common structural patterns, list three possible applications. Explain why the structural patterns are appropriate for the applications.

4. For one of the problems listed in Chapter 6, in Appendix A, or for a report problem of your own choosing, prepare complete informal and formal outlines.

5. The hospital for which you work has asked you to investigate the feasibility of establishing a special burn unit. One of the things you've been asked to investigate is the efficacy of water beds in burn-care units. Prepare a formal outline showing your basic structural pattern. Along with your outline, submit an explanation of other structural patterns that might be appropriate for use within sections. If the hospital should install a burn-care unit, for example, what step-by-step procedure should be followed in establishing it? Where should the unit be located? Use as many common structural patterns as possible.

CHAPTER 13
Developing a Functional Writing Style

Although all writing—and all communication—is "functional" in that it serves a purpose, reports are functional in a special sense. Poetry, literature, and magazine articles, for example, are all written for a purpose: they communicate ideas that a writer considers important. Reports, however, are functional not only because they communicate ideas, but also because the reader will act based on the information communicated in the report. Readers of poetry or a magazine article *may* act as a result of reading, but a report is designed to help the reader decide on a course of action. Other writing may serve as a means of self-expression. Reports, however, are always written with the reader's needs in mind.

Topics

Readability
Clarity
Courtesy
Conciseness
Confidence
Correctness
Conversational Tone
Style

What does your reader want from a report? The chances are that your reader is an extremely busy person who will appreciate everything you can do to save his or her time. Certainly your reader will not expect or desire to be "entertained" by your report in the same way she or he would wish to be entertained by a novel. Report writing is *functional* writing, designed to communicate ideas quickly and easily to a reader who does not want to invest a great deal of time and effort understanding or interpreting your point. Functional writing has a businesslike style that puts the emphasis on the content—the ideas—rather than on the use of language itself.

    The characteristics of functional writing are readability, clarity, courtesy, conciseness, confidence, correctness, and conversational tone. The style of functional writing may be either formal or informal, impersonal or personal, as long as it contains these characteristics. 249

READABILITY

Before the twentieth century, most writers were not concerned with readability. Few people could read and write, and those who could had more time to spend polishing their writing and more time to read carefully the writing they received from others. Following the Industrial Revolution in the late nineteenth and early twentieth centuries, the faster pace of business life required increased information flow.

Readability
Formulas

By the 1940s, researchers were attempting to provide business writers with formulas to predict whether their letters and reports would communicate quickly and clearly to a given audience. Rudolf Flesch and Robert Gunning developed the best known of the readability formulas.[1]

The formulas they developed are based primarily on sentence length and the number of words containing three or more syllables. Because the resulting figure corresponds with the educational level required to read a given writing sample, the Gunning Fog Index has become the most widely used formula.[2] Exhibit 13.1 shows the procedure for using the Fog Index.

Take, for example, the passage following the heading "Readability" excluding the heading "Readability Formulas" and concluding at the sentence beginning "Exhibit 13.1."

$$\text{Total words} = 172$$
$$\text{Total sentences} = 7$$
$$\text{Polysyllabic words} = 20$$
$$\text{Average sentence length} = 24.6$$
$$\text{Percentage hard words} = 12$$
$$(\text{Average length} + \text{percentage}) \times 0.4 = \text{Readability level (years of education)}$$
$$(24.6 + 12) \times 0.4 = 14.64$$
$$\text{Reading level} = 14.6 \text{ (College sophomore)}.$$

While the Fog Index and other readability formulas promise mathematical precision in gauging readability, they can at best provide a rough guideline. The formulas all require arbitrary mathematical manipulation to result in a usable figure. The Flesch formula uses constants; the Fog Index adds percentages and whole numbers and multiplies by a constant. There are other problems as well. The formulas do not, for example, take into account the need for polysyllabic technical terms that may be well known to the reader or the fact that some longer words are more familiar than their shorter equivalents. A long, well-constructed sentence is also easier to read than a short sentence with a modifier out of place.

Despite the shortcomings of the formulas, the Gunning Fog Index can help you write at a level suitable for your audience. A Fog Index of 10–12 is appropriate for most business reports, although read-

EXHIBIT 13.1
Application of the Gunning Fog Index

```
                    How to Use Gunning's Fog Index

    1.  Using a sample of at least 100 words, determine the average
        number of words in a sentence by dividing the total number
        of words by the total number of sentences.  Count each
        independent clause as a separate sentence.  Example:  "We
        should expand our current operations, and we should diver-
        sify as well."  Count as two sentences.

    2.  Count the number of polysyllabic words (three syllables or
        more).  Omit from this count proper nouns (primarily names
        of people and places), verbs containing three syllables as
        a result of the addition of "es" or "ed," and combinations
        of short, easy words ("insofar," "however," "undertake").

    3.  Determine the percentage of "hard" words by dividing the
        number of polysyllabic words by the total number of words
        in the passage.

    4.  Add the average number of words in a sentence to the per-
        centage of polysyllabic words.  Multiply the total by 0.4.

    5.  The resulting figure shows the readability of the passage
        in terms of the level of education (grade) required to read
        the passage.

    EXAMPLE:  A passage contains
              152 words
               11 sentences
               21 polysyllabic words

    Average sentence length = (152/11) = 13.8.
    Percentage of hard words = (21/152) = 14%.
    Average length + percentage x 0.4
         (13.8 + 14 x 0.4) = 11.12.
    Reading level = 11.12 (11th grade).
```

ers trained in the subject matter of the report would be comfortable with material written at a higher level. The Index also provides three important clues to readability.

1. Readability is as much a function of the reader as it is of the material. Material suitable for one reader may be either too easy or too difficult for another.

2. Writing can be made easier to read by shortening the sentences and reducing the number of "hard" words.

3. Writing can be made more suitable for a well-educated audience by lengthening the sentences and using a larger number of polysyllabic words.

In applying these formulas, remember that people reading for business purposes do not want to "work" at reading. They expect reading to be easy so that they can concentrate on the work of making decisions. At the same time, however, no reader appreciates being patronized. A report with a Fog Index of 6 would be insulting to a college educated manager.

Both Flesch and Gunning recognized that factors other than sentence length and word difficulty influence readability. Those factors are not so easy to evaluate using a formula. Diction, sentence structure and variety, paragraphing, specificity, voice, tense, figures of speech, and control of emphasis influence readability as much as sentence length and word difficulty.

Diction

Your choice of words will obviously affect the readability of your writing. To be readable, the word must be used correctly, be familiar to the reader, and denote and connote appropriate meanings in the context of your report.

The words we select to express an idea have a limited range of meanings. This range of meaning is what people have agreed a word should mean. The word itself has meaning only because the people who use it agree that it does. A dictionary, then, does not show you what a word *means* as much as it shows you how people *use* the word. The way in which people use words is known as diction. The dictionary is the report writer's best tool for using words in the way others expect them to be used. Exhibit 13.2 illustrates a sample dictionary entry.

In addition, the other information provided, including the etymology (derivation and history) and the list of synonyms with abbreviated definitions and distinctions, helps writers select the exact word necessary to convey a particular meaning.

Regional, occupational, and educational differences, however, all contribute to different expectations about how a word should be used. The less familiar you are with a word, the greater your chances are of using the word incorrectly. Writers use words incorrectly for two reasons. First, they simply don't know what a word means (though they think they do). Second, they confuse one word with another similar word that has a different meaning.

The only way to prevent your own incorrect use of words is to build a large enough vocabulary so that you can express yourself with confidence. If you aren't absolutely certain how a word should be used, look it up. The larger your vocabulary, the easier you will find the process of writing. A large vocabulary not only gives you more

EXHIBIT 13.2
Dictionary Entry

Pronunciation
Parts of Speech
Spelling, Word Division
Definition

Idiomatic Usage

Etymology
Synonyms
Usage Note

ef·fect (ĭ-fĕkt') *n.* **1.** Something brought about by a cause or agent; result. **2.** The way in which something acts upon or influences an object: *the effect of a drug on the nervous system.* **3.** The power or capacity to achieve the desired result; influence. **4.** The condition of being in full force or execution: *goes into effect tomorrow.* **5. a.** Something that produces a specific impression or supports a general design or intention: *sound effects.* **b.** A particular impression: *an effect of spaciousness.* **c.** The production of a particular impression: *She cries just for effect.* **6. a.** The basic meaning. **b.** Intention; purport. **7. effects.** Movable goods; property. —*tr.v.* **-fect·ed, -fect·ing, -fects. 1.** To produce as a result; bring into existence. **2.** To bring about. —**idioms. in effect. 1.** In fact; actually. **2.** In essence; virtually. **3.** In active force; in operation. **take effect.** To become operative. —See Usage note at **affect¹**. [ME < OFr. < Lat. *effectus,* p.part. of *efficere,* to accomplish : *ex-,* out + *facere,* to make.] —**ef·fect'i·ble** *adj.*

—**Synonyms:** *effect, consequence, result, outcome, upshot, sequel, consummation.* These nouns denote occurrences, situations, or conditions that are traceable to something antecedent. An *effect* is that which is produced by the action of an agent or cause and follows it in time, either immediately or shortly. A *consequence* also follows the action of an agent and is traceable to it, but the relationship between them is less sharply definable and less immediate than that between a cause and its effect. A *result* is an effect, or the last in a series of effects, that follows a cause and that is viewed as the end product of the operation of the cause. An *outcome* is a result that has clear definition; the term is even stronger than *result* in implying finality, and may suggest operation of a cause over a relatively long period. An *upshot* is a decisive result, often arrived at abruptly or in the nature of a climax. A *sequel* is a logical but relatively long-range consequence of an antecedent action. *Consummation* refers to the final, decisive stage of an action directed toward achievement of a specific end.

© 1980 by Houghton Mifflin Company. Reprinted by permission from the American Heritage Dictionary of the English Language.

words from which to select, but also increases your confidence in your speaking and writing. Any of the paperback books on vocabulary building would be a good place to start. You should also build your own list of words based on your reading. Your vocabulary and command of the language are two undisguisable indicators of your level of knowledge. Every time you speak, every time you write something, your audience will be evaluating you based on your use of language.

You may, for example, have picked up an erroneous idea of how a word should be used because you've heard others use it incorrectly. *Unique* is an example. *Unique* is properly used to mean "one of a kind, without equal." For that reason, a solution to a problem (or anything else) cannot be "very unique," "really unique," or "most unique." Something can, however, be "truly unique" or "almost unique," although *truly* is redundant and *unusual* or *exceptional* conveys the meaning expressed in "almost unique" more clearly and with greater economy.

One area of difficulty is confusion caused by similar words with different meanings. Are you familiar with the different meanings of the following often confused words?

Affect/Effect

Affect: (verb)—to influence or change

Effect: (verb)—to bring about
(noun)—a result or consequence

Appraise/Apprise

Appraise: to estimate

Apprise: to inform

Aggravate/Irritate

Aggravate: to make worse

Irritate: to provoke

As/Like

As: (conjunction, used to introduce a clause)—*as* I said

Like: (preposition)—a manager *like* you

Assure/Ensure/Insure

Assure: to promise (to a person)

Ensure: to guarantee or make certain

Insure: to protect against loss

Continual/Continuous

Continual: on a regular basis (but interrupted)

Continuous: without interruption

Disinterested/Uninterested

Disinterested: free of bias, impartial

Uninterested: indifferent, not interested

Imply/Infer

Imply: to suggest

Infer: to draw a conclusion

Occasionally, the confusion between similar words with different meanings results in a humorous (though not to the report writer) *mala-propism*.

Your speech was *superfluous!* (for *superb*)

Your report contained many *meretricious* ideas. (for *meritorious*)

In addition to making sure that you are using words in the way they are usually used, you need to ensure that you and your reader share a common vocabulary. In Chapter 10 we pointed out that words do not provide an exact "map" of the territory they represent. While a dictionary provides a guide to the way words are used, no two people have identical conceptions of what a word means. When words are familiar—used often by most people—you can assume that your reader will attach similar meanings to the words.

Another main cause of difficulty is *jargon*. Jargon is the specialized, working vocabulary of a discipline. Computer specialists, for example, speak of *ROM, RAM, bits, bytes, bauds,* and *modems.* All these terms are legitimate and carry a specific meaning—to those familiar with computers. They constitute a functional shorthand that speeds communication with those who understand the terms. They do not, however, communicate meaning to those not familiar with computers.

Don't confuse jargon with slang. Slang is excessively informal writing and is inappropriate in professional reports.

Slang: I didn't get it.

Better: I didn't understand it.
I didn't receive it.

Slang: Is the report done?

Better: Is the report complete?
Have you finished the report?

Every discipline has its own jargon, and only a few outside the field ever are truly comfortable with it. This is one of the reasons that audience analysis is so important. Is your reader a specialist in your discipline? If so, you are safe in using technical terms, though you may wish to add some explanation for newer or less-used terminology. If not, you'll need to avoid jargon when possible and explain all technical terms essential to the meaning of your report.

Also, as suggested by the readability formulas, short, familiar words usually communicate more clearly than long, less familiar words:

Difficult Word	Easy Word
ameliorate	improve
ascertain	find out
cognizant	aware
consummate	complete
effusive	enthusiastic

(Continued)

Difficult Word	Easy Word
endeavor	try
exacerbate	make worse
excursion	trip
institute	start
interrogate	ask
jaundiced	hostile
lobscouse	stew
mandible	jaw
mordacious	biting, sarcastic
outré	improper
paraphrase	restate
sinecure	an office or charge that requires no work
transient	temporary

Naturally, well-educated readers will have a well-developed vocabulary and will expect the writer to select the exact words to carry the precise meaning intended. Likewise, a technical audience will expect to encounter a technical vocabulary. Rather than the familiar but too general *done,* for example, most readers would prefer the more specific *completed* or *finished.* Even well-educated readers, however, will appreciate your reports more if they can read them quickly and easily. The short word, however, is not always more familiar, as the table below illustrates.

Short, Unfamiliar Words	Longer But Easier Words
berm	shoulder (of road)
cahier	notebook
fend	provide or turn aside
jibe	swing (verb)
quod	prison
thewy	muscular
vie	compete

To help ensure that your reports will be clear to your readers, select words that have not only the proper denotative (dictionary) meaning but also appropriate connotative (personal) meanings. The words, *as soon as possible,* for example, may be interpreted either as "immediately" or as "when you can find the time." Just as beauty is in the eye of the beholder, the meaning of words is in the mind of the user. A *smell* may be an *aroma* to one and a *stench* to another, as the table below illustrates. The words *cheap* and *inexpensive,* for example, both denote low in cost. *Cheap* also implies low in quality, whereas *inexpensive* does not.

Note the connotations of the following words:

automobile	antique
car	hot rod
compact	wheels
station wagon	taxi
heap	limousine
clunker	import

Each of the words denotes a means of transportation, yet each carries a different set of associated meanings. To communicate effectively, a writer needs to select the word with the most appropriate connotations for the situation.

In some cases, words have connotations that many people would agree on. In other cases, the associated meanings of a word will vary greatly from person to person. How much would you have to pay for an *inexpensive* car? How much is a *significant* increase? We can eliminate confusion that might result from using words with too many possible interpretations by being specific. Words used to signify time and space are often subject to wide interpretation. How often, for example, is *often?* The meaning would vary both according to context and according to the user. *Occasionally, frequently, seldom, soon, long, short, far, near,* and many of the other words (like *many*) that we use *(regularly)* in conversation, should be defined in more specific terms in written reports.

Specificity

When you are specific, your reader automatically interprets your words in the same way you do. Specific words do not allow varied interpretations. Study the examples below.

General (Vague)	Specific
soon	January 23
significant increase	12% increase
high profits	A 57% mark up
our product	The Clark CRT
improved morale	A 43% decrease in absenteeism
a majority	51% (or 93%)

Your writing will be more readable if you substitute concrete language for abstract words and expressions. Just as specific words provide exact facts, figures, details, and amounts; concrete language focuses on people doing things:

Abstract	Concrete
It was decided	I decided
Consideration was given	I considered
My analysis is that	I think
Avoid contact with potentially lethal residue.	Don't touch. Contact may cause death.
Attitudinal improvement required before promotion.	Jim has a bad attitude and shouldn't be promoted at this time.
The data are significant.	The data indicate a 14 percent increase.
We performed a number of experiments to test the hypothesis.	Forty-two experiments support the hypothesis.

While specific language is usually easier to read and understand than general language, excessive use of specific details can be annoying. Don't say *Budweiser* when any beer will do; don't say *11:27* when *about 11:30* is close enough. When specific details are unimportant or obvious to the reader, you are better off using general language or omitting the detail completely.

Too specific: Grab your London Fog, and let's walk over to Persing's Place and have a pitcher of Budweiser.

Better: Let's go have a beer.

How specific you will need to be depends on your subject and on your audience's familiarity with it. Technical subjects usually require greater specificity than nontechnical subjects, and audiences familiar with a subject usually require fewer details. You will need to make your decisions about the appropriate level of specificity based on the needs of your subject and your analysis of the audience.

Sentence Structure

Sentence structure is another component of readability. In general, long sentences with a great deal of internal punctuation are more difficult to read than short sentences with fewer components. Simple sentences and compound sentences are the easiest to read. Complex sentences, which contain at least one subordinate clause, and compound-complex sentences are more difficult. See Appendix C for a review.

As we mentioned in the section on readability formulas, simply using all short sentences will not result in readable writing. Variety in sentence length and type is necessary to maintain reader interest. Most ideas can be expressed in different types of sentences, so recast when necessary to achieve variety *and* to keep the *average* sentence length to about 17 words.

Too simple: I inspected the building sites. I found site *A* too hilly for our purpose. Site *B* is not zoned commercial at this time. Site *C* is zoned commercial. Site *C* is level, hard-packed ground suitable for our purposes. I recommend site *C*.

Too complex: As a result of my inspection of the building sites, which revealed that site *A* is too hilly for our purposes, that site *B* is not zoned commercial at this time, and that site *C* is level, hard-packed ground and is zoned commercial, I recommend site *C*.

Good variety: I recommend site *C*. My inspection of the sites revealed that *A* is too hilly, and *B* is not zoned commercial. Site *C* is level, hard-packed ground and is already zoned commercial.

Paragraphing

Paragraphing is another factor that influences readability. As is true for sentences, long, involved paragraphs are more difficult to read than short paragraphs containing only a few ideas. Paragraph length is especially important in single-spaced material, where long paragraphs appear especially heavy and uninviting.

Variety is again the key. A series of short paragraphs, although easy to read, would seem choppy and simplistic. Report writers should strive for a mixture of paragraph length. The following rules will help:

1.   Short paragraphs are more emphatic and receive more attention than long paragraphs.

2.   Keep introductory paragraphs short (about 4 or 5 lines). Introductory paragraphs should put the material in an appropriate context (so the reader knows what you are doing) and introduce the material that follows.

3.   Developmental paragraphs—which explain, analyze, and give examples—need to contain more information and can be longer. No paragraph, however, should run much longer than 15 lines.

4.   Concluding paragraphs—which draw conclusions, make recommendations, or summarize—should also be short.

5.   As a rule, the first sentence in a paragraph should introduce the main idea or *topic* of the paragraph. Other sentences in the paragraph limit, clarify (by explaining or illustrating), or support the idea introduced in the first sentence. (See Deductive Structure.)

6.   When the first sentence does not contain the main idea of the paragraph, it should provide transition from the previous paragraph or give the reader a clear idea of where the paragraph will lead. When the first sentence does not contain the main idea of the paragraph, the last sentence should be the topic sentence. (See Inductive Structure.)

Voice

It is easier to read about people doing things than it is to read about ideas. For this reason, most sentences in business and technical reports should be in the active voice. The term *voice* refers to the relationship between the subject of the sentence and the action expressed in the verb. A sentence is in the active voice when the subject of the sentence performs the action. When the subject receives the action of the verb, the sentence is in the *passive voice*.

Passive: A final decision must be made by the selection committee no later than
June 7.
(The subject, *decision*, receives the action of the verb *made*.)

Active: The selection committee must make a final decision by June 7.
(The subject, *committee*, performs the action of the verb, *make*.)

Active voice is more readable for two reasons. First, it gives the reader
a clear picture of who is doing what. Second, the action moves forward, from the beginning of the sentence to the end. Sentences in the
passive voice do not reveal the doer of the action until the end of the
sentence. Sometimes, in fact, the doer of the action is omitted entirely
from the sentence:

It was decided to purchase new equipment.

Who made the decision? The reader's opinion may be influenced by
that missing piece of information. Neither technical subject matter nor
a formal writing style require passive voice. In fact, passive voice is
one of the main distractors from clarity in many technical and formal
business reports. To form a clear idea of what the report is about, the
reader needs to be able to identify *who* is doing (or has done) *what* to
whom and for what reason. Active voice is the best way to make these
relationships clear.

While most of your sentences should be in active voice, you can
make good use of passive voice on two occasions: (1) when the performer of the action is immaterial or unknown, and (2) when your
reader or other important person (though *not* yourself) has made a
mistake.

Doer immaterial: This machine was overhauled just last month.

(It doesn't matter who did the overhauling, so the emphasis is rightly
placed on what happened rather than on who did it.)

Doer unknown: The typewriter was stolen.

("Someone stole the typewriter" puts the emphasis on the *someone*
rather than on the typewriter.)

Doer at fault: The engineering specifications should have been
followed more closely.

(The active voice version, "The builder—or YOU—should have followed the engineering specifications more closely," is too accusatory.)

Tense

Verb tense is another factor that influences readability. The simple tenses are easier to read than the compound tenses. Likewise, the pro-
gression of tenses must be logical, giving the reader an accurate perception of when events took place. For a review of tense formation
and use, see Appendix C.

Figures of Speech

We tend to think in terms of generalization and differentation; that is, we think in terms of similarities and differences. One of the easiest ways to learn something new, in fact, is to compare the new thing with something similar already known. A figure of speech is a word or words used in an imaginative way to compare two things that are not similar in a literal sense. The statement, "Because dogs and cats are both mammals, they have a number of physiological similarities," is a literal rather than an imaginative comparison, so the statement is not a figure of speech.

Figures of speech are often useful to help explain and to illustrate, but as pointed out in Chapter 10, the items being compared must be similar in significant ways if the comparison is to be helpful. The principal figures of speech are simile, metaphor, analogy, hyperbole, metonymy, and personification.

Simile A simile makes a comparison by simple assertion. It uses "like," "as," or "so" to equate two similar items:

To be an effective sales representative, you must be *like* a tiger— aggressive.

To be an effective sales representative, you must stalk your prospect *as* a tiger stalks its prey.

As it is with tigers, *so* it is with sales representatives. To be effective, you must be aggressive.

The comparison in a simile must be figurative rather than literal. "Television is like radio in that both convert electronic transmissions into intelligible messages," is not a simile because what is said is exactly true for both items being compared. The statement, "Radio is like TV without a picture," however, *is* a simile because the resemblance described is figurative rather than literal.

Many clichés are based on overused similes: *red as a rose, go like a shot, nervous as a cat in a room full of rocking chairs.* The stronger the resemblance between the two items, the clearer the image the simile will give a reader. Expressions like *red as a rose* have become clichés because they originally provided effective illustrations of the ways in which two things were alike.

A good simile can be useful because it labels the comparison for the reader (who can see exactly what you are comparing), and it uses a known quantity to describe an unknown.

Metaphor A metaphor is more compact than a simile because it omits the labeling word, *like, as,* or *so.* A metaphor simply states that one thing *is* another:

Simile: An effective sales representative is *like* a tiger.

Metaphor: An effective sales representative *is* a tiger.

Simile: Radio is like TV without the picture.

Metaphor: Radio *is* TV without the picture.

Simile: Pollution spreads like cancer throughout the body of the lake.

Metaphor: The malignancy of pollution is evident throughout the lake.

Simile: Clear writing is like an arrow—it penetrates because it moves with force—straight and to the point.

Metaphor: Clear writing is an arrow moving with force—straight and to the point.

Mixed metaphors can be a source of unintentional humor:

Mixed: His report ruffled the waters.

Better: His report muddied the waters.

Better: His report ruffled the boss's feathers.

While metaphors may be used occasionally in business and technical writing for dramatic impact, they are more likely to mislead a reader because the comparisons are implied rather than stated explicitly. A reader must not only be able to perceive the implied comparison, but also to determine the extent of the resemblance. For example, the following metaphor could be either figuratively or literally true:

The two-point press on line 4 is a real killer.

For this reason, metaphors in reports often require explanation.

Analogy   An analogy is simply an extended simile or metaphor, comparing the two items in several respects instead of just one. Like metaphors, analogies need to be used carefully. A bad analogy may lead the reader to a false conclusion:

> **Good sales representatives are like tigers. First, they stalk their prospects, pursuing them relentlessly. Then, they frighten them into submission. Finally, they pounce with the contract and secure a signature before the prospects know what's hit them.**

Analogies, then, can be either true or false (see Chapter 10). A true analogy is one in which the resemblance is sufficiently complete and exact to provide a good illustration. A false analogy either misleads the reader into accepting a resemblance when there is none or uses the analogy to prove instead of to illustrate or explain.

Analogies are especially useful for explaining new concepts to a reader. You could, for example, easily explain television by using its similarities to radio. From a technical standpoint, the similarities would be significant. If you were writing to an advertiser making a decision about which medium to use to reach a particular audience, however, the differences would be more significant than the similarities.

The following examples illustrate the basic form of analogies, which usually state that *A* is to *B* as *C* is to *D*.

> A vocal cord (A) produces sound (B) in much the same way a guitar string (C) produces sound (D)—by vibrating.

> A transistor is like a gate. When it is open, electrons can pass through. When it is closed, they can't. By controlling the gate, we can control the flow of electrons from one side of the gate to the other.

Analogies are effective when used to define terms, explain processes, or illustrate. Analogies, however, are sometimes offered as proof. The "Domino Theory," offered in support of America's military presence in Vietnam, compared the countries of Southeast Asia to a row of dominoes, implying that if the first fell to communism, all the others would follow. Such an analogy is useful as an illustration, but analogies do not prove that what is true in one case is necessarily true in another.

Hyperbole   Hyperbole is exaggeration, using a stronger word than accuracy requires for the purpose of emphasis: "I could sleep for a week," "I'm starving" (instead of hungry) and "Your suggestion is perfect" (instead of good or excellent), are examples of hyperbole. Hyperbole is often used with humorous intent:

> A camel is a horse designed by a committee.

> Our company is in such bad financial condition that three guys went broke just reading our annual report.

While the intent of hyperbole is to intensify an impression rather than to deceive, it is more appropriate in conversation and in informal writing than in report writing.

Metonymy   When you substitute one word for another closely associated with it, you are using the figure of speech known as metonymy. If you say that your plant employs "4,000 *hands*" or that "two *heads* are better than one," you are using parts of the body to represent the whole. You might also say, "Our *plant* won the softball tournament," meaning that the plant's team won, which is using the whole to represent a part. Substituting *crown* for *king*, *bread* for *money*, *book* for *study*, or *pen* for *write* illustrates metonymy in which words frequently associated with particular ideas have come to stand for those ideas.

As with hyperbole, metonymy is not used often in formal business and technical writing, though it does have informal applications. The danger of using metonymy is that the reader might misinterpret your use of words. If your plant employs "4,000 hands," for example, does it employ 4,000 people or 2,000 people?

Personification   When the figure of speech assigns human qualities to nonhuman entities, it is known as personification. The logical fallacy *hypostatization* (see Chapter 10) is a form of personification. Pet projects or pieces of equipment may, for example, be referred to as *she*: "She's not acting quite right today." Personification is usually inappropriate in formal business and technical writing.

The generator prefers to warm up slowly.
(Obviously, a generator does not really have a preference. It should be warmed up slowly because it will last longer.)

Allow the generator to warm up at 1500 rpm for five minutes to allow complete oil circulation.

The company feels that the new computer is a good investment. (The company cannot feel—or think or decide. Only people can feel.)

Management feels (believes, thinks) that the new computer is a good investment.

Emphasis and Subordination

Not all ideas in a report will be of equal importance. For this reason, writers need to select the most important ideas for emphasis, while subordinating less important information. The basic rule of emphasis is that it is impossible to emphasize everything equally. Underlining every work in a book, for example, has the same effect as not underlining at all. You may wish to review the rules for emphasis cited in Chapter 12.

Remember that emphasis is a matter of contrast. Something can only be emphasized in relation to something else. Also, some things should be subordinated. When your reader will find part of your message negative or accusatory, for example, subordinate that part by placing it in the middle of a paragraph, putting the most negative concept in a subordinate clause (see Appendix C), and—especially when the reader has made a mistake—using passive voice.

Variety

As we implied previously, your report will be more readable if you provide variety in word usage, sentence structure, and physical appearance. The following list is a summary of techniques for achieving variety in your writing:

1. Use synonyms, pronouns, or alternate phrasing to avoid repeating the same word frequently.

2. While short, simple sentences are the easiest to read, if all of your sentences are short, your writing will seem choppy and simplistic. Use a variety of sentence lengths. Try for an average sentence length of about 17 words, with no sentence exceeding about 40 words.

3. Use a mixture of sentence types (simple, compound, complex, compound-complex—see Appendix C).

4.   Make your report *look* easy to read by keeping most paragraphs short. In single-spaced material, first and last paragraphs should be about four lines long (*lines,* not sentences). Middle paragraphs should be about eight lines. The length of the paragraphs, however, should vary. An entire report of four-line paragraphs would appear choppy. A report consisting entirely of long paragraphs would appear heavy and uninviting. Paragraph length is less critical in double-spaced material, but following the same guidelines as for single-spaced material will help ensure visual variety.

CLARITY

Clarity is obviously an important factor in readability. Clarity is the transfer of thoughts from writer to reader without misunderstanding. A report writer's first obligation to the reader is to be clear. Grammatical correctness, logical structure, and specific transitional devices provide the basis for clear writing. These topics are covered in Appendix C. In addition to the general tests for readability, clarity requires explicit use of language and complete coverage of ideas.

Explicit Statements

Because explicit statements provide the *who, what, when, why,* and *how,* they are easier to understand than implicit statements which omit one or more of those factors.

Implicit: You might find that wire too hot to handle.

Explicit: Don't touch that wire! It's carrying 10,000 volts.

Use implicit language only when an explicit statement would be too obvious or too accusatory.

Explicit (too obvious):   Currently, all of our frozen dinners are packaged in aluminum trays. Aluminum is not compatible with microwave ovens. (Reader would already know these things.)

Implicit: Because the aluminum trays our frozen dinners are packaged in are not compatible with microwave cooking, we should consider alternate methods of packaging.

Completeness

To be clear, a message also needs to be complete. After reading your report, the reader should have a clear understanding of each of the following:

1.   Your purpose. Why did you write the report?

2.   Your methodology. What procedures did you follow in gathering information?

3.   The significant fact. What have you found out about the problem under investigation?

4. Your conclusions and recommendations. Who is to do what next, and when should it be done?

While different report writing situations will place different emphasis on these four factors, any report should answer all of the reader's appropriate questions. A brief report of explanation, for example, might not contain a methodology, and a simple informational report would not contain conclusions and recommendations. A complete report contains everything necessary to answer questions that might occur to readers as they read.

COURTESY

A courteous message is written with the reader's point of view in mind. A courteous report, like a courteous person, is polite and cooperative. A courteous report explains even difficult situations in a way designed to help the reader act in the most reasonable way possible. Courtesy is achieved by using the you-attitude and through cooperation as equals.

You-Attitude

A simple definition of the you-attitude is putting your readers and their problems first. Think—and write—in terms of what a particular fact means to your reader rather than in terms of what it means to you.

Writer viewpoint: My department really needs the additional secretarial help because we are so far behind.

Reader viewpoint: With an additional secretary, my department could expedite work orders influencing the entire company.

When you and your readers have conflicting interests, acknowledge your differences in an honest way. Your readers will expect you to have legitimate interests, and they will appreciate your recognizing their interests as well.

Cooperation as Equals

Although reports usually go up the chain of command—from the person making observations to the persons making decisions—reports should be free of both undue humility and condescension. The writer should present him- or herself as knowledgeable in the area under discussion without either amplifying or diminishing the reader's expertise.

Undue humility: I know you can't be bothered by all my department's problems, but. . . .

Condescension: Here's another problem that would probably escape your attention unless I reported it.

Cooperative: I've discovered a problem you should know about.

CONCISENESS

Because no one has extra time to read wordy reports, conciseness is an important contributor to both clarity and courtesy. A concise message is usually clear, and it is courteous because it saves the reader's time.

Conciseness and brevity, however, are not synonymous. A concise message is as brief as possible without sacrificing clarity or courtesy. A brief message, on the other hand, may omit some of the details necessary for the reader to have a full understanding of the situation.

Focus on the Problem

The first step in achieving conciseness is to focus on the main problem by answering the following questions:

What Does My Reader Most Want to Know?   Answer this question as quickly as possible unless the reader will react negatively to the answer.

What Details Does My Reader Need to Understand the Situation?   Provide these details in a logical order.

What Action Should My Reader Take?   When appropriate, suggest any action your reader should take to solve the problem.

What Details Are Necessary for an Accurate Record of the Event or Situation?   Provide these details as unobtrusively as possible. Consider including them in a section specifically designed to review the history of the situation.

What Does My Reader Know Already?   Omit details your reader already knows unless repetition of those details is necessary. To include details already known to your reader, deemphasize them by allocating them as little space as possible and by subordinating them to something of greater importance.

Not this: Line 3 has never been able to match the production rate of our other 6 lines.

But this: Because line 3 has never been able to match the production rate of our other lines, we should. . .

Or this: Although line 3. . .

What Details Are Extraneous to the Core of the Problem?   Avoid discussing details that will not influence the decision the reader needs to make.

Avoid Wordy Expressions

Many messages are too wordy simply because they contain tautologies (phrases containing needless repetition), redundancies, or simple repetition.

Wordy	Concise
first of all	first
needless to say	(omit)
square in shape	square
the color red	red
true facts	facts
basic fundamentals	fundamentals
the most unique	unique
assembled together	assembled
join together	join
at all times	always
at the present time	now
in the nature of	like
until such time as	until
due to the fact that	because
in the event that	if
in the final analysis	finally
in order to	to
by means of	by
for the reason that	because
entirely complete	complete
new innovation	innovation
in the neighborhood of	about

In addition to avoiding these and similar expressions, you should also avoid repeating ideas. Make sure, for example, that your summaries actually summarize—state in abbreviated form—rather than merely repeat what you have already said.

CONFIDENCE

An effective report displays confidence. As a writer, you need to express confidence in your abilities to observe accurately, present information well, and—when appropriate—decide on the best method of solving problems.

Your reader will react more favorably to what you are saying when you use positive language. Most ideas can be expressed in either a positive or a negative form:

Negative: Closed Saturday at noon.

Positive: Open until noon on Saturday.

The positive expression is always more appealing. Focus on what can be done rather than on what can't be done. In general, avoid negative words, such as the following:

can't	bad	trouble
impossible	unfortunately	unable
unwilling	inferior	misfortune
failed	problem	misunderstand
claim	unlikely	loss

Also, avoid expressions that imply that you don't trust your reader:

You claim. . .

If what you say is true. . .

Your request came as a surprise. . .

Avoid expressions that imply that your report is inadequate and those that the reader will consider presumptuous.

I *hope* that this report answers your questions.

Why *not* give my suggestion a try?

If this report hasn't answered your questions, do not hesitate to call me.

You *must* act on this immediately.

You *should* follow my suggestions.

You *need* to consider the following alternatives.

Every now and then, however, you will need to make a forceful negative statement to avoid misleading your reader:

Product *Y* has performed so poorly in the test market that we should halt production immediately.

Confidence does not mean a Pollyanna, everything-is-perfect approach to writing or management. It is rather a determination to *solve* problems instead of complaining about them. Occasionally negative language will help achieve a positive solution.

CORRECTNESS

Naturally, a report must present correct facts and figures if it is to be useful to the reader. Double-check all figures and statements for accuracy. Identify for your reader which statements are fact and which are opinion.

Your report will also be more effective if you use correct spelling, grammar, and mechanics. Correctness in these areas is not only an aid to readability and clarity, but also an indicator of a writer's care and attention to detail. Be sure to look up any words you are unsure of, review any punctuation rules that give you difficulty, and proofread carefully to eliminate simple mechanical errors. See Appendix C for a brief review.

CONVERSATIONAL TONE

Your reader should be able to understand you quickly and easily. A natural, inconspicuous, conversational writing style will help your reader focus on the most important aspect of your report—its contents. While some reports may need to contain complex technical or legal information, the bulk of the information in even the most complex report can be presented simply and clearly. When possible, use conversational words.

Conversational, however, does not mean "chatty." Many letters and memos contain language that is too informal for use in most reports. The conversational style needs to be adapted to the audience for and purpose of the report. If your style is too informal, your reader will conclude that you don't take the problem (or your reader) seriously. If your tone is too formal, your reader will conclude that you are cold and mechanistic in your thinking. The best approach is a balance that results from using simple, conversational language while avoiding slang, legalese, and business clichés.

Not This	But This
beg to advise	tell
please find enclosed	the enclosed booklet
in the final analysis	finally
a viable alternative	a possibility
in regard to	of, about
in order to utilize	to use
parameters (nontechnical)	limits, aspects
it is my conclusion that	I conclude
impact (as a verb)	influence

In addition to the absence of legalese and business clichés, conversational tone requires the kind of variety and emphasis normally present in oral communication. In conversation, we use our voices, gestures, and the exchange of information provided by questions and answers to keep the conversation from becoming monotonous. In written communication, we can use variety of sentence length and type, paragraph length, and vocabulary to make writing interesting.

STYLE

Functional writing may be either formal and impersonal or informal and personal. Many companies prefer reports written in one style or the other. Formal, impersonal style avoids the use of personal pronouns, uses longer sentences, and uses abstract nouns and technical terms not often used in conversational English. Informal, personal style is conversational English. It uses technical terms when required by context and uses personal pronouns where they would naturally be used in conversation.

Some people believe that the formal, impersonal style is more objective than the informal, personal style. We disagree. Objectivity is a result of the quality of the research, fairness in analyzing data, and accuracy in presentation. Compare the following examples:

Formal: The experimenter divided the subjects into two equal groups.

Informal: I divided the subjects into two equal groups.

Formal: The decision was made to terminate employees in ascending order of seniority.

Informal: I decided to lay off people according to their seniority.

Formal: A study of the relative merits of the two computer systems in question has led to the conclusion that System *A* is the superior system. System *A* is therefore recommended.

Informal: I recommend computer System *A*. After studying System *A* and System *B*, I concluded that *A* would be better for our purposes.

Informal, personal English is more readable and clearer. Formal, impersonal style forces the reader to ask *who* and *what* questions. It implies, rather than stating explicitly, who is performing what action. With formal style, readers have to stop and ask themselves, *who* is the experimenter, *who* is recommending.

Should you work for an organization that requires the formal style of writing, try to make your reports as lively and as readable as possible by using active instead of passive voice and by using nouns in the place of pronouns so that the person performing the action will be clear.

Not this: It was concluded that . . .

But this: The writer concluded that . . .

SUMMARY

Functional writing communicates ideas quickly and accurately without drawing attention to itself. Functional writing is designed to save the reader's time and energy. The characteristics of functional writing are readability, clarity, courtesy, conciseness, confidence, correctness, and conversational tone.

Readability formulas developed by Rudolf Flesch and Robert Gunning use sentence length and word difficulty to test readability. The Gunning Fog Index provides an indication of the amount of education required to read a passage. Diction—or word usage—also influences readability. In general, short familiar words with limited connotations are easier to read and understand. Report writers need to develop a good vocabulary so that they can be sure they are using words correctly. Specific language, sentence length and variety, and paragraph order and length also contribute to readability. Active voice, appropriate verb tenses, and appropriate use of figures of speech improve readability by making writing more interesting.

Readable writing also emphasizes important points and subordinates less important material. Emphasis and subordination result from contrast and variety in placement, proportion, language, and mechanics.

Clarity is the report writer's first obligation. The report must transfer ideas from writer to reader without misunderstanding. In addition to being readable, a clear report uses explicit language and provides complete details. Report writers also need to take the reader's point of view into account. This is known as courtesy. The you-attitude and a problem-solving, cooperative approach will ensure courtesy.

Good reports are concise, focusing on the problem and on possible solutions. Good reports are also confident, expressing ideas in positive terms. Avoid negative language, terms that imply that you don't trust your reader, and expressions that imply that your report is inadequate. Reports must be correct in form and content if they are to be effective. Conversational tone and an informal, personal style will contribute to the readability and overall effectiveness of a report as well.

EXERCISES

Review Questions

1. In what way are reports functional writing?

2. What does the dictionary tell us about words?

3. What are the common ways words are misused?

4. What is the difference between a word's denotative meaning and its connotative meaning?

5. What are the main figures of speech, and what are their functions?

6. What is the difference between jargon and slang?

7. Why are specific words better than general words in most cases? When are general words preferred?

8. How does sentence structure contribute to readability?

9. How do paragraph length and development contribute to readability?

10. What are the differences between active and passive voice? When should each be used?

11. In what ways are similes and metaphors different?

12. When are analogies appropriate in business and technical reports?

13. What are the principal means of controlling emphasis and subordination in written material?

14. Why is explicit language better than implicit language in most situations? When is implicit language preferred?

15. What is the you-attitude?

16. How does a report writer achieve conciseness?

17. What kinds of negative expressions should report writers avoid?

18. Why should report writers avoid legalese and business clichés?

19. What are the differences between a formal, impersonal style and an informal, personal style?

20. Why is clarity a report writer's first obligation to the reader?

Problems

1. Select three sample short reports for analysis (or, if more convenient and your instructor permits, three articles from *Time, Newsweek, Forbes, Business Week, Fortune,* or another magazine or journal important for your career area).
    a. On one report, identify each sentence according to whether it is a topic sentence, sentence of clarification, sentence of limitation, or support sentence.
    b. On one report, identify all figures of speech, and describe how each functions within the sentence or paragraph.
    c. Apply the Gunning Fog Index to each of the three reports.
    d. Select the report that you consider the most readable of the three. Write a one- or two-page memo stating the reasons you believe that the report you selected is the best.

2. List all the words you can think of that mean "to move by the power of one's feet" and provide the denotations and connotations for each word.

3. Using one of your own short reports or papers,
    a. Apply the Gunning Fog Index.
    b. Identify topic sentences, sentences of clarification, sentences of limitations, and support sentences.
    c. Evaluate the variety in sentence length and type.
    d. Locate and explain any figures of speech.

   e.   Discuss the effectiveness of the language from the standpoint of clarity, courtesy, conciseness, confidence, correctness, and conversational tone.

4.   Write a three-page directive explaining the advantages of the informal, personal style and encouraging its use.

Notes

[1]Rudolf Flesch, *The Art of Plain Talk* (New York: Harper & Row, 1946); and Robert Gunning, *The Technique of Clear Writing* (New York: McGraw Hill, c. 1952, rev. ed., 1968).
[2]Gunning, 1968 ed., p. 39.

CHAPTER 14

Solving Common Writing Problems

While no two reports are identical, a report writer faces the same tasks repeatedly: beginning, defining terms, describing mechanisms or processes, classifying and interpreting data, concluding, and editing. Because every report will require most of these tasks, mastering the general principles involved will save you a great deal of time in report preparation.

Topics

Definitions
Descriptions and Classifications
Introductions
Summaries, Conclusions, and Recommendations
Abstracts
Editing
Committee Reports

In the previous chapter we looked at the ways in which language and writing style contribute to the effectiveness of reports. In this chapter we discuss the application of those principles to the most common writing tasks.

DEFINITIONS

Because definitions provide the basis for many discussions, they are an essential component of most reports. As a report writer, you'll need to be concerned not only about *what* to define but also about *how* to define it.

Definitions have two purposes: (1) they can clarify what something is for a reader not familiar with the subject, or (2) they can explain the subject in a way that goes beyond the needs of clarity. Both clarifying definitions and extended definitions provide meaning for unfamiliar terms and new meaning for familiar terms.

What to Define

Deciding what to define can present problems. A nontechnical audience will need definitions of technical terms but will be confused if the terms are defined with equally technical language. A technical audience, on the other hand, would be insulted if you defined common technical terms or sacrificed precision by expressing a technical concept in nontechnical language.

Determining what to define will require an understanding of your readers and their backgrounds and expectations. In general, however, you should define

1. *Familiar words used in an unfamiliar way.* When a common word has a technical or special meaning, let the reader know how the word is being used. (The word "apron," for example, has a variety of specialized meanings depending on the field. It can be part of a lathe, part of a runway, part of a stage, or part of a dock—all in addition to the common meaning familiar to chefs and backyard barbequers.)

2. *Technical terms for which there are no nontechnical equivalents.* (The word *modem* is an example. It stands for "modulator-demodulator" and refers to a device for converting a computer output signal into a form suitable for transmission over telephone lines and the telephone signal back into the proper form for a computer.)

3. *Words whose meanings you wish to restrict.* Occasionally, you will need to let your reader know how you intend for a word to be used because several interpretations are possible. If you were writing a report on office conflict, you would need to define *conflict* for your reader. *Conflict* can mean either a fruitful discussion of differences or a pitched battle.

How to Define

The basic rule for defining those terms that require it is to keep the definition brief. When possible, clarify the meaning of the word by using a synonym or phrase in apposition to the word you wish to define.

Before the furnace can be repaired, all *clinker* (residue) must be removed.

> The *moratory contract* **(term),** *which delays payment* **(definition)** un- til 2 January, **was necessary to prevent default on outstanding obli-** gations.

When a simple word or phrase is insufficient to define a term, you can clarify the meaning of the word in a sentence. Sentence definitions can be either informal or formal depending on context and the needs of the reader. Informal definitions are usually incomplete, providing only enough knowledge of the term for the reader to understand its use in the one context. Formal definitions designate the class to which the term belongs and then provide the features that make the term differ- ent from the other members of the class.

Informal: The new operation will require ultraviolet filters to prevent damage to the *retina*. The retina is the light-sensitive lining of the inner eye. Damage would result in blindness.

Formal:

Term	Class	Features
Stress is	any influence on a person	that tends to be mentally disruptive and results in physical or emotional distress.

Whether your sentence definition is informal or formal, be careful to avoid using the term to define itself, and avoid using *where* and *when* in defining a term.

Incorrect: Stress is any stressful situation.

Incorrect: Stress is when you feel physical or emotional distress.

When the meaning of a term is a major element of the report, you will need to provide an extended or amplified definition. In many ways, for example, this book is an extended definition of the term *report*. A report on insurance coverage might need an extended definition of bodily injury, or a report on management techniques might require an extended definition of quality circles. Possible topics for inclusion in an extended definition include the following.

Etymology   The history of the word may provide a better under- standing of its current meaning. The origin and development of the word, however, may not serve to clarify its current meaning. Even when the etymology does not clarify current meaning, it may help provide a starting point for a detailed analysis.

Background   What factors have influenced the development and cur- rent use of the term? The background may be related to the etymology of the term, but background also includes discovery, development, and application of the term being defined.

The etymology of the word *computer*, for example, would discuss its origins in the Latin word, *computare*, to reckon together. The background of the word would discuss the invention and development of electronic computers.

Illustrations   Examples and illustrations, whether verbal or graphic, are one of the best methods for clarifying the meaning of a term. Abstract terms, such as *liberal, conservative, morale,* and *efficiency,* can only be clarified by providing examples. Certain technical terms, too, can only be understood if the reader can *see* what the item looks like. What is a camshaft? How does one work? If you need to define a camshaft, you would need to provide an illustration similar to that in Exhibit 14.1.

Descriptions and analyses   When the item or concept consists of several parts, each part should be described and explained. What does the item do? How does it work? How does it relate to the other parts and to the whole? Descriptions of mechanisms and processes, classifica-

EXHIBIT 14.1
Illustration

tions, and interpretations are all important enough to merit separate discussion.

Comparison and Contrast How is the item or concept being defined similar to or different from other items or concepts with which the reader would already be familiar? When possible do both:

A is similar to B in that. . .

A, however, differs because. . .

Because comparison and contrast is a form of analogy, you'll need to focus on significant similarities and differences to convey an accurate impression.

Connotations When a word has a particular set of associations, you may need to clarify the meaning the word has within the context of the report. Patriotism, for example, can be the "last refuge for a scoundrel" or "courageous self-sacrifice in defense of one's country."

Where to Place Definitions

When you have only a few terms that require definitions and you can define them briefly and simply, it is best to include the definitions in the text immediately following the term. Definitions within the text, however, interfere with readability when they are either long or numerous. Unless you are presenting an extended definition central to your discussion, consider placing definitions in a special section in the introduction, in footnotes, or in a glossary.

Introduction When the terms are critical to understanding your report, include a list of technical terms requiring definitions in the introduction. Readers already familiar with the terms can skim the list to see whether you have attached special meaning to a term.

Footnotes When some of your readers will understand all the terms used but others will not, footnotes are the best solution. Readers who are familiar with the terms may ignore them; readers who are not familiar with them won't have to flip forward (to a glossary) or backward (to the introduction) to find the definitions.

Glossary Placement in the glossary is the least obtrusive method of providing definitions. It is also the method most likely to be ignored. When most of your readers will understand the terminology in the report and none of the terms are critical to understanding the purpose of the report, a glossary can be a useful aid to readers unsure of some meanings. Tell the reader early in the introduction that the glossary is available.

DESCRIPTIONS AND CLASSIFICATIONS

Descriptions play an important role in many reports. Many problems—and their solutions—in modern business center on mechanisms or processes with which the reader will be unfamiliar. The main challenges in writing descriptions are in providing information appropriate to the readers' needs and in using language that presents an accurate picture of the mechanism or process.

**Describing
Mechanisms**

In describing a mechanism, you have five things to consider: (1) what it is, (2) what it does, (3) how it does it, (4) what it looks like, and (5) why your reader needs to know.

Stating what a mechanism is, is primarily a matter of defining it. To what class does the mechanism belong, and what features differentiate it from other mechanisms in its class? A report on restaurant management, for example, might require descriptions of microwave ovens and food processors. How is a microwave different from other ovens? In what ways is a food processor different from other kitchen equipment?

The reader will also need to know the purpose of the mechanism. Obviously, the purpose and the definition are closely related. Saying what a microwave oven *is* requires a statement about what one *does*. The purpose can often be clarified by including the reporter's "serving men": *who* uses the mechanism, *when* it is used, *where* it is used, and *why*. Accuracy is critical. A microwave oven, for example, is not simply used to cook or heat food—it is used to cook or heat food *quickly*, which may be an important fact for restaurant management.

How does the mechanism work? When the mechanism is of critical importance to the report, you should provide a complete analysis of the mechanism, including a description of each of its parts. This is especially true when the mechanism is new, unusual, or complicated. Photographs, cut-away and exploded drawings (which reveal the relationships of the parts to each other and to the whole), and flow charts (which show how the action of one part influences another) may be necessary to clarify the way the mechanism works.

The description should also include information about the size of the mechanism. What are its size, weight, shape, color, material of composition, and finish? What is the physical relationship of the parts to the whole (as opposed to the mechanical relationships)? How does the mechanism fit into the surrounding environment?

Finally, all of the previous aspects must be considered in terms of how much the reader knows about the mechanism already and the use to which she or he will put the information. Is your reader going to build, use, or make a business decision about the mechanism? A reader who wanted to build a microwave oven would obviously need to know more about it than someone who was simply going to use one, and a reader who was making a decision about whether to install them in a restaurant would be less concerned with how microwaves work than with how they influence food preparation and delivery.

Describing Processes	A process involves action over time. You may need to describe the action of a mechanism or the actions of people engaged in a particular activity. How does a television set transform the signal it receives into pictures and sound? How does one use a food processor?

Describing processes requires chronological and spatial organizational patterns (see Chapter 12). To be able to understand the process, the reader will need to know

1. The purpose of the process
2. The nature of any equipment involved
3. The steps in the process
4. Any hazards or special precautions

The typical automobile owner's manual contains several descriptions of processes. After describing the features of the car and identifying all the important parts of the mechanism, the owner's manual describes the steps involved in starting the car, in changing a tire, in finding the problem when the car won't start, and perhaps other processes as well.

Descriptions of this sort require extensive graphic aids: flow charts, pictures of the mechanism or of a person performing the activity, and pictures featuring close-up details of important steps can contribute to reader understanding.

Again, a critical consideration is what your reader will do with the information. Is your reader going to perform the process, or does your reader simply need a basic understanding of the process to be able to make a decision about it? Suppose, for example, you are writing a report recommending that your company invest in an exercise room and equipment so that employees can maintain physical fitness before and after work and on their lunch breaks. You would need to describe the equipment required and the general ways in which it is used, but you would not give complete descriptions of how to use each piece of equipment.

**Classifying
Mechanisms and
Processes**

Classification is a system of defining a whole in terms of its parts. As we mentioned in Chapter 12, the division of a whole into parts needs to be logical and consistent. Functions, materials, locations, benefits, and disadvantages are common bases for classification in reports.

Classification is a useful form of presentation when you have several items to discuss and when these items have significant similarities and differences. Small computers, for example, could be classified according to size (micro or mini, amount of internal memory) or use (personal or business). Within each category, different computers would have features in common and differences that could lead to a basis for selecting one brand or model for a specific application.

INTRODUCTIONS

In most cases, the introduction of the report proper will follow an abstract of the complete report. Nevertheless, an introduction, as the formal beginning of the report, must accomplish at least three objectives. First, it must place the report in a communication context that makes sense to the reader. Second, it must create interest in the topic. And third, it must give the reader a good idea of what to expect in the rest of the report.

Context

You will recall from our previous discussion of emphasis that the beginning of any unit is a place of emphasis. Readers will pay close attention to an introduction and form opinions about the entire report based on the material you present first. This is true regardless of the length and formality of the report. Even in a short report of one or two pages, the introduction needs to orient the reader to the topic, be interesting, and provide a guide to the material that follows.

Longer reports require a fuller introduction. Certain topics are traditionally included in introductions to complete analytical reports. Most of them are intended to contribute to one of the three main objectives.

Origin and History of the Report Where did the idea of the report originate? Who authorized it, and what problem did he or she think that the report could help solve? Because answers to these questions are probably already known to the reader, they are usually presented in a letter of authorization, letter of transmittal, or both. Even though the reader for whom the report is written is familiar with this information, it should be included because it may have historical significance.

When the problem developed over time, it may prove useful to include a discussion of the history of the problem so that similar problems can be recognized more quickly in the future. Unless the history or development of the problem is of special significance, subordinate this information to something of more interest to the reader.

Subject and Purpose   Even if the origin and history are covered in the letters of authorization and transmittal, the first two or three sentences of the introduction should include a statement of what the report is about (subject) and the benefit to be gained (purpose—or objective, goal, or aim). The first sentence should give the reader a reason for reading the entire report.

The most common phrasing for the purpose statement is, "The purpose of this report is. . ." This phrasing is acceptable and will accomplish its objective, and many companies prefer such wording because it forces a writer to state a specific purpose. Through overuse, however, it has become both a little hackneyed and self-conscious. When possible, begin without drawing such obvious attention to your beginning. Below are some possibilities.

Hackneyed and
Self-Conscious: The purpose of this report is to recommend sending our sales staff to the three-day motivational seminar sponsored by the University of Illinois.

Better: Our sales staff could benefit by attending the three-day motivational seminar sponsored by the University of Illinois.

Better: The three-day motivational seminar sponsored by the University of Illinois would offer our sales staff the opportunity to improve their understanding of the relationship between motivation and sales.

Better: Sending our sales staff to the three-day motivational seminar sponsored by the University of Illinois would result in a 12–15 percent increase in sales over the next six months.

Each of the "better" purpose statements above implies the purpose while emphasizing the benefit. Even when the report does not offer a benefit, the purpose can be implied rather than stated explicitly.

Explicit: The purpose of this report is to explore the risks of asbestos poisoning in our Millview Plant.

Implicit: The risk of asbestos poisoning continues to be a problem in our Millview Plant.

Explicit: The objective of this study is to determine the advantages and disadvantages of subcontracting the thermoplastic skylights for our modular houses.

Implicit: Subcontracting the production of the thermoplastic skylights for our modular houses would save us approximately $4,500 a year but would cost us 14 jobs and reduce worker morale.

In each case, the opening emphasizing the *idea* of the purpose, rather than the purpose itself, is a stronger, more interesting opening.

Definition of the Problem   The introduction should include a clear statement of the problem, including its scope and limits. See Chapter 6.

Research Methodology The reader will also need to know how you went about gathering data. Include both secondary and primary sources. When many secondary sources are important enough to include, consider adding a section on the review of the literature. Being specific about research methodology is especially critical when you have used experimental methods to collect information. The reader will use your descriptions of the research methodology to evaluate your conclusions and recommendations. See Chapters 7 and 8.

Limitations Not every experiment turns out as expected. Lack of funds, lack of time, difficulties with sample size, or unexpected and unavoidable conditions might all contribute to a report's being not so complete or objective as you would like. Negative factors that influence the reliability of the report belong in the introduction.

Limitations, however, should not be used as an excuse for a poor report. Be specific about how the lack of funds hampered your investigation or about what you would do if you had more time. Make sure that the limitations really are limitations and not attempts to cover up a lack of preparation on your part.

Definitions When definitions are included in the introduction, they may be placed in paragraph form where they occur naturally. This is the least obtrusive way to define terms when only a few terms require definition. If your list of terms is long, it's best to set a section of the introduction aside for listing the terms in alphabetic order and providing their definitions.

Report Plan The report plan is the road map that tells readers where the report will take them. Because it gives them an overview of what they will encounter, the report plan helps readers concentrate on the content rather than on what the writer is going to include next.

As is true with the purpose statement, the report plan can be stated either explicitly or implicitly.

Explicit: This report is divided into five main sections: Possible Benefits, Potential Difficulties, Costs, Savings, and Adjustments.

Implicit: The five factors of most significance are the possible benefits, the potential difficulties, costs, savings, and the necessary adjustments to the new system.

Telling the reader what to expect in the rest of the report is a well-accepted formula. In fact, one of the clichés of effective communication is, "Tell 'em what you're going to tell 'em; tell 'em; and then tell 'em what you've told 'em." The trick is to stress the principal ideas or areas of concern by repeating them without giving your readers the idea that you don't trust their ability to remember the important points. As with the problem statement, the report plan is best stated implicitly because an explicit statement is too obvious in most cases.

Techniques

Not all reports will require each of these aspects. The length and content of the introduction should be relative to the length and content of the report as a whole. The following techniques apply regardless of the length or content of the introduction.

1. Do *not* use the word *Introduction* as a heading. The reader already knows that the beginning is the beginning.

2. A short introduction (no more than two paragraphs) may follow the title without a separate heading.

3. Longer introductions should begin directly after the title with a general statement emphasizing the benefits or significant ideas in the report. Place the first heading after the general statement. This heading should be general enough to include the rest of the items covered in the introduction. See Chapter 12 for more information about headings.

4. The length of the introduction should not exceed 5 percent of the report as a whole.

5. Subordinate the obvious to the significant. Do not say, "I developed a questionnaire to discover. . ." Instead, say "The questionnaire I developed concentrated on three main factors. . ."

SUMMARIES, CONCLUSIONS, AND RECOMMENDATIONS

Ending a report or section of a long report also presents particular problems. The ending section (or sections) needs to clarify the significance of the report and, when appropriate, tell the reader who should do what next. Also, the end of the report should imply that the report is finished and complete. The three ways to accomplish these objectives are summaries, conclusions, and recommendations.

Summaries

Informational reports, which present findings only, often end with a summary listing the important findings. A summary is simply a brief restatement of the main points already presented. A summary, therefore, should never present new information. In extremely long reports, it may prove useful to summarize each main section before proceeding to the next.

Conclusions

Like summaries, the conclusion section of a report never contains new material. The conclusion should be a logical and objective result of the material presented previously. In addition to the need for logic and objectivity in drawing conclusions, writers need to ensure that they present conclusions clearly and label them as such. The two most common errors in writing conclusions are the failure to state who is doing the concluding and the tendency to present conclusions as facts rather than as inferences based on fact.

Poor: Based on these findings, it is concluded that . . .

Better
(informal):   Based on these findings, I conclude that . . .

Better
(formal):   Based on these findings, the experimenter concludes that . . .

Poor: For our purposes, television advertising obviously provides the best exposure for the investment.

Better: For these reasons, I conclude that television represents the best investment for our advertising dollar.

Depending on the number and distinctness of the conclusions, you may wish to place them in a tabulated list, which may be either numbered or unnumbered. When you have only two or three conclusions, setting them off by tabulation (indentation) may seem pretentious. When you have several conclusions, however, your reader will remember them better if you set them off in a special way. A numbered list implies a hierarchy (in which 1 is the most important) or an order (chronological or spatial) not implied by an unnumbered list. Items in an unnumbered list may be set off with asterisks (*), bullets (•), or hyphens (--).

Recommendations

When recommendations are called for, they almost always appear as the last section in the report. As they depend on the conclusions, they often appear in a combined section that proceeds directly from the conclusions to the recommendations. When more than one solution to a problem is possible, the alternatives may be mentioned before the recommendation.

Conclusion: As a result of my study of staff and equipment needs, I conclude that we need an additional 4,500 square feet of plant space.

Alternative: Although we have the room to expand, the age of our current facility is such that the cost of maintenance may soon exceed the cost of new construction.

Recommendation: For this reason, I recommend that we begin the search for a suitable construction site and begin planning for a new facility.

Unless the recommendations are self-explanatory, provide some explanation for them so that they don't seem too arbitrary. Also, if you have several recommendations, you may wish to tabulate them.

Reports written in deductive structure will, of course, have at least a brief mention of the major conclusions and recommendations in the initial position. In most reports, this opening section is not as thorough as the final section. When the complete conclusions and recommendations are presented first, a summary of the most important points is sufficient for ending the report.

ABSTRACTS

An abstract, (also known as synopsis, epitome, or precis) is a condensed version of the entire report. For this reason, abstracts are written after the report is complete and follow the same basic outline in both order and proportion as the entire report. The abstract is a critical part of a report. It may, in fact, be the only part of a report to which the reader pays close attention. For this reason, abstracts should be prepared carefully. Because the results, conclusions, and recommendations are the most important part of the report, abstracts tend to emphasize them by affording them relatively more space proportionally than they have in the report proper.

Types of Abstracts

Abstracts are of two basic types: descriptive or summarizing. Summarizing abstracts are also referred to as "informational" because they include, rather than simply describe, the main points of the report. Descriptive abstracts are not used often because they provide little more than a listing of the topics covered in the report. Summarizing abstracts, on the other hand, present the major ideas presented in each section of the report.

Length

As a rule, an abstract is about 10 percent the length of the entire report, with two exceptions. First, a standard abstract must not exceed one typewritten page. The abstract, however, may be single-spaced even if the report is double-spaced. To save space, abstracts of this variety do not contain headings. In recent years, a longer variation of the abstract, known as the *executive summary*, has become increasingly popular.

The brief, one-page abstract is useful for duplicating and distributing to people who do not need to see the entire report but who have an interest in the problem or the proposed solutions. Abstracts of this sort may also appear in professional journals or company publications.

The executive summary, on the other hand, is designed to save the reader the effort of reading the entire report. In preparing an executive summary, the report writer attempts to cover all the important aspects of the report in three to five pages. The executive summary is considered a preliminary part of the report, just as is the traditional abstract, so it is numbered with lowercase Roman numerals instead of the arabic numbers used for the report proper. The executive summary uses headings for the major topics included in the report and provides sufficient details for an executive to make a decision in all but the most critical situations.

EDITING

Editing is the process of revising the report once it is written and preparing it for distribution.

Before you can edit, you must have a product to edit. Editing is a process of changing the first, or rough, draft of the report into the polished piece you intend to submit.

The First Draft

Few writers are able to produce fully satisfactory first drafts. In fact, most people find that they produce a better final product if they write quickly—almost haphazardly—the first time through to make sure they include all the important ideas.

The tentative outline and the results of your research will provide a guide for you to follow in writing the first draft. If you can't think of something to say about a particular topic, skip it. You can return to it later. Writer's block is much more likely to occur if you believe that the first draft must be "perfect." The function of the first draft is to provide an organized body of material suitable for revision.

The Revised Report

Once you have most of your ideas on paper (or stored in a word processor), you can begin the task of polishing the material into its final form. In many respects, this entire book is about the subject editing—what you should be looking for as you prepare your report for submission.

Your first concern should be for correctness and objectivity. Grammar, mechanics, spelling, facts, and figures should all be free from error. Appendix C provides a quick overview of the most common grammatical problems. Double-check your figures and facts. We will focus here only on those editing techniques that apply to improving an already well-thought-out report.

Ensuring Cost Effectiveness While you should naturally want your reports to be as good as they can be, you also have to recognize that no report is ever perfect. There is a point beyond which continued revising is an unnecessary expense. The time you spend revising and the improvements you can expect will produce an exponential curve, as illustrated in Exhibit 14.2.

EXHIBIT 14.2
Revision Time and Improvement

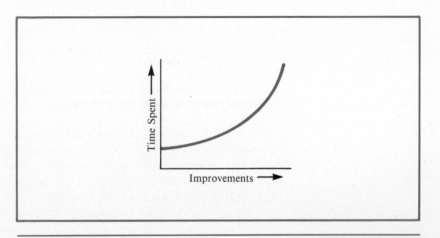

The exact curve would, of course, vary from person to person and from report to report, but the general shape would remain the same. The major improvements can be achieved quickly and easily. Once you have taken care of the major problems, subsequent improvements make less and less difference to the quality of the report while taking more and more time.

Cost effectiveness is also influenced by any deadline you may have. Many deadlines in business are absolutes. If a boss suggests that you have a report ready to go by the 12th, she or he may well mean that the report had better be ready, or else. While you may be able to obtain an extension in some cases (especially when you can show that the person requesting the report will benefit from the delay), don't count on one. Be prepared to do the best job you can in the time available.

Condensing   Reports place a premium on conciseness. While editing, look for and eliminate redundancies, deadwood, and unnecessary repetition.

Redundant: *The color* red
Square *in shape*
A *bad* disaster
Today's *modern* computer systems
Postponed *until later*
At *the* present *time*
Revert *back*
Only this solution *alone*

Deadwood: This report deals with *the matter of* employee morale.

There is only one solution *that* is possible.

The following statistics *serve to* support my conclusions.

It was during this time *that* the company was founded.

The site *located* in Missouri . . .

The illustration *which is shown* on p. 27 of Appendix A illustrates . . .

Unnecessary repetition: *The problem of* improving employee morale is one of our most serious *problems.*

Our *facility* is going to be the largest *facility* of its kind in the world.

The results, as *computed* by our DEC 10 *computer*, are as follows . . .

I will have to *repeat* the experiment *again*.

Verbiage of this variety obviously takes up space. You may discover however, that even when you have eliminated all wordiness, you still need to condense your report to meet certain space requirements. Many companies and foundations, for example, place specific limits on the length of proposals they will consider.

When you do need to condense beyond the usual requirements of eliminating wordy expressions and unnecessary repetitions, you face essentially the same problem as you do when writing an abstract or executive summary. The following procedure will help you produce meaningful condensations.

1.   Content
    a.   Find the topic sentence for each paragraph and make sure that it contains the most important idea (a general principle) in that paragraph.
    b.   Find the most significant support for each topic sentence.
    c.   Locate any other essential details in the report which were not included in a topic sentence or the main support sentence.
    d.   Evaluate items in a, b, and c against your length requirements. Add details in order of their significance from the reader's point of view.

2.   Style
    a.   Subordinate ideas of secondary importance to those that have greater significance.

        Change this: Site A is bounded on the North by Ellinger's Bog. The bog is a breeding ground for mosquitoes but does not support significant wildlife. If we were to drain the bog, Site A would be ideal for the construction of our new plant.

        To this: Site A, which is bounded on the North by Ellinger's Bog, would be ideal for the construction of our new plant if we drain the bog and eliminate the mosquitoes' breeding ground.

    b.   Combine sentences by making one subject serve for two verbs or one verb do for two objects. Embed one sentence within another.

        Change this: The Japanese system of management has resulted in continued high levels of productivity. It has also resulted in an unusually high level of employee morale.

To this: The Japanese system of management has resulted in continued high levels of productivity and an unusually high level of
employee morale.

Change this: Line four has mechanical difficulties at least once a
week. This has a detrimental effect on the morale of those who
work on the line or depend on it for parts.

To this: The continual difficulties on line four have a detrimental effect on the morale of those who work on the line or depend on
it for parts.

3.   Appearance
    a.   Single space instead of double-spacing. Paragraph more often
to increase white space.
    b.   Decrease side margins.
    c.   Eliminate one or two levels of headings.

Expanding   In most cases, editing problems are caused by the need
to condense. The need to expand is usually the result of a failure to be
complete in the first place. Because of the high value placed on conciseness in business and the professions, you will probably need to
expand under two circumstances only. First, you may need to add
details to provide further support for one of your conclusions. Second,
you may need to expand to increase readability or clarity.

As you examine the first draft of your report, check to see
whether you have supplied sufficient evidence to support all your conclusions. Are you making "mental leaps" from an item of evidence to
a conclusion that your reader may not follow? If so, expand by adding
the missing link. Provide all the details necessary to lead your reader
from your beginning point to your conclusion.

Writing that is too condensed is often difficult to read, not only
because it omits details that may be necessary for a full understanding,
but also because it packs a great deal of information into each sentence. Just as we can combine sentences to condense information, we
can break complicated (compound-complex and embedded) sentences
into several simple sentences. Simple sentences require more space to
express ideas, but they are easier to understand.

Rearranging   The first draft may reveal that the tentative outline will
not prove adequate for the final report. You may need to change your
order of presentation from deductive to inductive, or you may find
that factors you thought would be significant were not so important as
factors you had not anticipated. Do not be afraid to scrap your original
outline and to rearrange whole sections of your report. In fact, one of
the questions you ask yourself at the completion of each rough draft is
whether other arrangements of the material are possible and whether
any of the alternatives would improve your report.

You might also need to rearrange portions of some sections to control emphasis or to provide better transition from one part to the next. Recall that the beginning and ends of units (whether sentences, paragraphs, or sections) are the parts to which the reader will pay closest attention. Rearrange material when necessary to place the important words and ideas at the beginnings and ends of units.

If you are working from hand-written or typed copy, you may wish to cut and paste to achieve the new arrangement. Simply cut the material out of one section and use paste, staples, or tape to paste it into its new location. When only a sentence or two requires moving, you may wish to encircle the sentence and draw an arrow to show its new location. The proofreader's marks in Appendix F illustrate common marks for indicating changes in written material.

Using Word Processing Equipment

Word processing equipment can't do anything for you that you can't accomplish with pen and paper or with a typewriter. It will, however, perform many functions for you more quickly and easily. Word processing equipment has demonstrated its usefulness sufficiently that companies—and individuals—are buying units about as quickly as they can be produced. As someone working in business or a profession, you may already be using a word processor or text-editing computer or be using one in the near future.

Although we don't intend to provide a complete orientation to word processing equipment here, we would be remiss if we failed to give you some idea of how the equipment works and of what it can do for you.

Word processors are essentially computers that have been especially designed and programmed to handle written materials. Many mini- and microcomputers can also accept text-editing or word processing programs, but they are not so "user friendly" as the word processing equipment. In spite of the fact that the computers require a greater degree of user knowledge, they offer two advantages over the word processing equipment. They are generally less expensive, and they can perform a much wider range of applications.

With a relatively inexpensive computer and the correct programs for it, you would be able to prepare your text, automatically tabulate the results of your research, perform any necessary statistical computations, and turn figures into accurate and appropriate graphic aids.

Regardless of the kind of equipment you use, you will enter your material into the system's memory by using a standard typewriter keyboard. At present, many companies still follow the practice of having secretaries perform the tasks of document entry and production. The desire for increased efficiency, however, is leading to direct entry by the originator of the document. When writers enter their own material, they are able to change words, condense, expand, or rearrange material by proofreading what they have typed on the TV-like screen (known as a CRT—cathode ray tube). The document (memo, letter, or long report) does not need to be printed until the writer has made all changes and selected the best format.

Editing Others and Being Edited Different people have different ideas about how an idea should be expressed. When you begin working, you will find that your supervisors will edit your materials and request revisions before they will agree to "sign off" on them and send them forward. Once you have a few years of experience behind you, you will have the responsibility of ensuring that the work leaving your area of responsibility meets the standards it should.

Whether you are being edited or editing the work of others, you'll need to remember that writing is an intensely personal activity. Writing style is an extension of a person's personality and thought processes, and editorial suggestions are frequently perceived as threats. Learning to produce reports that satisfy your supervisors and helping others improve their writing are a normal part of business life. Accept the comments of others as the legitimate expression of their perceptions. In most cases you will be able to revise your reports to meet your boss's expectations without drastically altering your own writing style. When you are doing the editing, attempt to suggest improvements without implying that the material is poorly planned or poorly written. Positive suggestions for changes will work better than critical remarks. The proofreader's marks in Appendix F are an effective and convenient way of communicating about and commenting on written material.

In general, you should give your boss the kind of report she or he desires. Make sure, however, that any final report with your name on it is an objective and honest presentation of facts. Should your boss suggest that you make a change that would reduce the reliability of the report, you'll need to discuss that change with your boss and perhaps a higher ranking officer in the company as well. You can never tell how far or to whom a report will go, and if the report contains mistakes, it will reflect badly on you. Naturally, you should never ask someone working for you to falsify information in a report or letter.

COMMITTEE REPORTS

Because modern technology has resulted in a great many areas of specialization, it is increasingly common for organizations to assign groups of people to investigate and solve problems. Putting a new product on the market, for example, would require representatives from production, marketing, and finance to coordinate activities. This group of specialists may need to cooperate in writing one or more reports. Committees usually go about writing group reports in one of two ways. They may have each person write the section most appropriate for him or her. Or they may work as a group to produce the first draft. Each way has advantages and disadvantages.

Individual Responsibilities

When all members of the group are competent and willing to work efficiently, having each member be responsible for a specific area will produce a better report more quickly than group writing. One person (usually the best writer) will still need to edit the parts and assume responsibility for the report as a whole, but most of the first draft is produced by those people who fully understand what they are writing about. The entire committee would review and sign off on the edited copy before it would be sent forward.

The disadvantages of this kind of group writing are that in many cases not everyone can be relied on to produce high quality material on time and that the person responsible for editing may not understand the technical aspects presented in some sections. Either of these disadvantages may result in delays.

Group Efforts

Sometimes, the best way for a committee to produce a report is to set aside a block of time, sit down together, and piece the report together based on the evidence that each member brings to the meeting. Group writing of this variety is not always easy. Group members frequently spend too much time discussing matters of style during their meetings rather than leaving stylistic changes to editing the draft copy.

The group writing process does help ensure that each person will participate, but it may prove a time-consuming way of producing a first draft. Once the first draft is complete, the entire group would edit, and one person would be responsible for incorporating all changes. Individual committee members would need to sign off on the report before it was sent forward.

SUMMARY

Report writers repeatedly face many of the same writing tasks. Definitions are an important writing task because they clarify the unfamiliar and help explain a mechanism, process, or idea. Terms can be defined in a word, phrase, or sentence either in the text, footnote, glossary, or special section of the introduction. Occasionally, an extended definition will be necessary to explain the meaning of a term.

Writers also need to describe mechanisms and processes in many reports. Definitions may help describe. Descriptions of mechanisms should include both physical characteristics and functions. Descriptions of processes should include the purpose, equipment, steps, and hazards that may be involved.

Classification, another important writing task, is a system of defining a whole in terms of its parts. It focuses on similarities and differences and is fully discussed in Chapter 12.

Introductions need to accomplish three objectives: (1) place the report in an appropriate communication context, (2) create reader interest, and (3) give the reader a preview of the rest of the report. An introduction should be approximately 5 percent as long as the report proper. Formal introductions may contain the origin and history, subject and purpose, definition of the problem, research methodology, limitations, definitions, and a report plan. The word *Introduction* does not make a good heading.

Summaries, conclusions, and recommendations are also important writing tasks. Summaries reiterate in condensed form; they do not introduce new material. Conclusions are inferences based on facts presented. The report should make the distinction between the facts and conclusions clear and should identify who is doing the concluding. Recommendations are decisions or actions that the writer believes to be logical in light of the conclusions.

An abstract (synopsis, epitome, or precis) is a condensed version of a report and is prepared after the report is complete. It is a preliminary part of the report and gives the reader a quick overview of the contents. An executive summary is longer than an abstract and provides more information.

Editing is necessary because very few writers are able to produce satisfactory written material the first time around. Editing is the process of polishing the rough draft to produce a high-quality final product. In revising, writers will need to ensure cost effectiveness, to condense, expand, and rearrange. Using word processing equipment may simplify these tasks.

Writers may have their reports edited by others and may be responsible for editing others' reports. Accept and give criticism with a positive attitude. Use standard proofreader's marks to convey ideas on written material.

Committee reports may be necessary because of occupational specialization. Individual members may write separate sections for editing by the best writer, or the group as a whole may work on the entire report. Either way, the entire group will need to sign off on the report before it is sent forward.

EXERCISES

Review Questions

1. What are the differences between a dictionary definition and the kinds of definitions you would provide in a business or technical report?

2. What is an extended definition?

3. Where should definitions be placed in a report?

4. What are the differences between formal and informal definitions?

5. List and describe six possible types of information for inclusion in an extended definition.

6. List and describe the five elements that should be included in a description of a mechanism.

7. List and describe the four elements that should be included in a description of a process.

8. Under what circumstances is classification a useful form of presentation?

9. What are the three main objectives of an introduction?

10. How long should an introduction be?

11. What topics might be included in the introduction in a complete analytical report?

12. Give an example of an effective purpose statement.

13. What is the function of the report plan? Give an example of an effective report plan statement.

14. List and explain five general techniques that apply to writing introductions.

15. What objectives should the end of the report accomplish?

16. Explain the differences among summaries, conclusions, and recommendations.

17. What are the advantages for using a tabulated list for conclusions and recommendations?

18. Describe the differences between the two types of abstracts.

19. What are the differences between an abstract and an executive summary?

20. List and describe the main considerations of the editing process.

21. List and describe the principal techniques for condensing written material.

22. List and describe the principal techniques for expanding written material.

23. What is word processing equipment, and how can it help report writers?

24. What are the hazards involved in editing the writing of others and having your own writing edited by someone else?

25. What are the advantages and disadvantages of the two main techniques for writing committee reports?

Problems

1. Provide word, phrase, sentence, and extended definitions for three technical terms in your area of specialization.

2. Provide word, phrase, sentence, and extended definitions for the following terms: *modem, emulsifier, bobbin, encomium,* and *kata.*

3. Classify and describe one of the following: lawn mowers, sewing machines, bicycles, fishing rods and reels, food processors, small computers, synthetic fuels.

4. Describe the process of developing, building, or using the mechanism you described in problem 3.

5. For any of the longer reports you may have been assigned, submit your abstract, introduction, and appropriate summaries, conclusions, and recommendations.

6. Write an executive summary for the report used in problem 5.

7. In groups of three to five, work with others to write a five to seven page report on word processing equipment. Assume that a friend who writes technical manuals on a freelance basis has asked you to investigate word processing equipment for her and to make a recommendation. She can afford to spend about $8,000. Each person in the group should edit and submit a final version of the report.

8. Condense the report in problem 7 to three pages.

9. Expand the report in problem 7 to ten pages.

10. Your boss has asked you to prepare an executive summary of this report writing text. He wants to know whether this book will help with the reports he has to write.

CHAPTER 15
Presenting the Data Visually

"A picture is worth a thousand words."

Topics

Fundamentals
Identification and Mechanics
Classification
Tables
Figures
Computer Graphics

In previous chapters we have talked about presenting data clearly and concisely, quantitatively and qualitatively. Now we'll discuss techniques for presenting data graphically so that your reader can have a complete picture of what you want to say.

FUNDAMENTALS

Although some people refer to graphic aids as visual aids, most people make a distinction between the two terms. Graphic aids refer to tables and figures presented in written material to clarify a discussion, whereas visual aids refer to such materials as models, chalkboards, flipcharts, and slides used in oral presentations.

Graphic aids are used to clarify and help present complex information. We need the words first to explain, and then we use the graphic aids—the pictures—to assist the words. Words are the primary means of presentation; graphic aids are secondary supports. Graphic aids are just that—aids and supplements—not substitutes; they do not take precedence over or substitute for words. Graphic aids are placed *after*—not *before*—the prose that mentions them. In other words, we first describe or explain, and then we present the material graphically.

Never include a table or figure in the report without a reference to it. As we will discuss later in the chapter, just as the prose must be independent of the graphic aid, so, too, the graphic aid must tell the entire story without the prose. If the table or figure were extracted from the prose, the prose should be complete without it, and the graphic aid should be complete without the prose.

Because of the increase in the number of reports—possibly as a result of computers and word processors—busy executives don't have the time to read through long reports. They want facts and figures that can be read quickly and easily. And so, report writers are providing a second report—a summary report supported by graphic aids. This trend makes the self-sufficiency of graphic aids even more important.

Graphic aids are used only when they are needed to clarify a discussion and not just for adornment. When the information is clear and the reader will not have difficulty interpreting it, a graphic aid would be superfluous.

Purposes

The primary purpose of graphic aids is to present a picture of what the prose says. The "picture" can be in the form of a table or figure. Graphic aids convert and condense complex information into a pictorial form, helping the reader "see" relationships. Graphic aids also emphasize material which needs extra attention or coverage. Because they present a vivid image, graphic aids are easy to read, remember, follow, and interpret. And finally, graphic aids enhance the appearance and readability of the report, making it more attractive to readers.

Placement

Ideally, graphic aids are placed as close as possible to the prose they illustrate. Do not, however, insert one within a paragraph. When a graphic aid is small, it can go on the same page as the prose, following the paragraph that refers to it. Do not divide an illustration that can be placed on one page—place it on the following page. When a graphic aid takes a full page, place it on a page facing the explanation or on the next page available following the explanation. When the explanation itself occupies several pages, however, place the graphic aid on the first full page that follows the first mention of it. Illustrations too wide for regular placement may be placed sideways on a single page or on continuing pages, with the top of the page at the left.

Avoid long tables. When it is necessary to continue a table onto a second page, write "continued" at the bottom of the page and begin the second page with the number and title of the table plus the word "continued." Also, repeat column headings on the second and following pages of the table.

When graphic aids are not essential but can be useful to the reader, place them in an appendix along with other long and complex graphic aids.

Subordination

When it is necessary to refer the reader to a table or figure, the emphasis should be on the statements or comments made about the illustration and not on the table number or location. The significant fact is that you want the reader to see a relationship or make a comparison in a particular table, so you would refer to the table or figure number subordinately by placing it in a dependent clause (see Chapter 12). Here are a few examples:

As shown in Exhibit 4, . . . (main clause)
As Table 3 indicates, . . .
As Chart 1 illustrates, . . .
. . ., while Figure 5 shows . . .
. . ., as is shown in Exhibit 4.
. . . (see Map 2).

IDENTIFICATION AND MECHANICS

Identify tables and figures by their numbers rather than by saying "the table above," "the figure below," "the following table," or the "preceding map."

All graphic aids should be self-explanatory. This means that they need complete identification—title, number, key or legend, and documentation of sources. In addition, graphic aids need to be presented so that they are attractive and inviting to the reader. The following paragraphs will help you present graphic aids attractively.

Size

How large should your graphic aid be? It depends. How complex is the information it presents? How important is the information? How much data does it contain? What size graphic aid will look best with the other material you must present? What size is necessary for readability? The size of a graphic aid is best determined by the importance, the amount, and the nature of data contained in it. Does the aid need to be enlarged? Can the print be reduced? Could a photograph, for example, be reduced from 8 1/2″ × 11″ to a 5″ × 7″ without losing important detail?

When the illustration is simple, a quarter or a third of the page might be sufficient. When the illustration is complex or important, use a half or full page. Sometimes, when an illustration is much larger than the page size, (1) you can have it photographically reduced or (2) you can fold the wider paper into thirds, quarters, or whatever is best to fit the size of the other pages. To make it easy for your reader to open and read folded pages, fold from the outside in and from the bottom up. Also, illustrations that cannot be folded, stapled, or punched, can be inserted into a "pocket" on a page. See Exhibit 15.1.

EXHIBIT 15.1
Folded Sheets

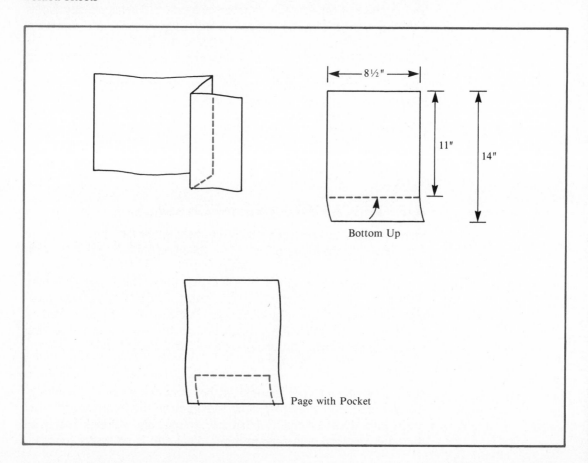

Bottom Up

Page with Pocket

**Ruled and
Border Lines**

To help display information attractively, use ruled lines and borders. Vertical and horizontal lines within a complex table separate columns and rows neatly and make data easier for the reader to grasp. Omit vertical and horizontal lines when tables are simple and the columns are far enough apart. Finally, separate the table or figure from the report text by placing a horizontal line above and below the graphic aid or enclose the entire table or figure with a border to enhance and emphasize it. Lines which cannot be made on the typewriter should be made with a ruler and pen using India ink. When rulings are used, leave three blank spaces above and below the graphic aid. Leave at least one inch of space above and below the graphic aids when no rulings are used.

Color

The use of color can add sparkle. Color attracts attention and produces a positive image. It is especially useful when you want to emphasize differences. For example, in a pie chart sectioned in thirds, you might want to use a different color for each third. In a line chart using three plot lines, you could use a separate color for each line. Bars and columns can also be made attractive with the use of color, especially when crosshatching or shading is desirable. If you use color, remember that it will not photocopy. Design your report so that it will reproduce attractively in black and white.

Check with local office supply or art stores for materials and advice. Clerks at these stores can recommend products that will help you prepare professional graphic aids.

**Labels and
Numbers**

All graphic aids in the report are labeled (Table, Figure, Chart) and numbered so that they can be identified and located. The table of contents usually contains a list of illustrations. Generally tables are assigned arabic numerals and are numbered consecutively and separately from other graphic aids. Tables can also be numbered in capital Roman numerals (I, II, III, an so on), but this practice is declining.

When a report contains several different types of graphic aids, such as 1 chart, 2 diagrams, 3 maps, and 1 model, you can group them into tables and figures. For example, you might have Table 1, Table 2, Figure 1, Figure 2, Figure 3, and so on.

When a report, however, contains numerous examples of different types, each type could be numbered consecutively. For example, you might have Table 1, Table 2, . . . Table 15; Model 1, Model 2, . . . Model 10; Diagram 1, Diagram 2, . . . Diagram 8; Chart 1, Chart 2, . . . Chart 20; and so on. When the list of graphic aids is long, it is usually presented in a table immediately following the table of contents with the caption, "List of Illustrations."

Titles

Each graphic aid is titled (or captioned) appropriately for its contents. The title should be not only concise but also descriptive. Whenever possible, include the Five *Ws* of information—who, what, when, where, and why.

In traditional practice, table titles, typed in all capitals, began on the second line *after* the table number and above the tabular illustration. Figure titles, typed in capital and lowercase letters or all capitals, begin on the second line *below* the illustration, preceded by the figure number. Increasing in popularity, however, is the practice of placing titles above the illustrations, preceded by their numbers and labels and using capital and lowercase letters for both tables and figures. For example:

Table 1. Job Qualifications for a Secretary

Figure 1. Map of Will County

The title may be centered, or as is more common now, typed at the left margin of the illustration. When a title requires more than one line, single space the additional lines. If a title is a complete sentence, it ends with a period (or question mark); otherwise, no end punctuation is used.

Footnotes

The information gathered from primary research and presented in tables and other graphic aids by the report writer is considered primary data and does not need to be footnoted. If documentation is necessary, you would write in the footnote position, "Source: Primary." See Exhibit 15.3 on page 306.

Footnotes for graphic aids are required when

1. A secondary source is used.
2. A reference is needed to explain or clarify an item.
3. Directions, keys, legends, or scales are necessary for reading or interpreting. Generally, keys and legends are typed on the graphic aid itself rather than at the bottom of the graphic aid.

It is possible that a table or figure may require all three references. The footnote for a secondary source is always the first one, and does not begin with an arabic number as do other footnotes in the report. It begins at the left margin with the word *Source* followed by a colon, two spaces, and then the documentation (see Chapter 8).

For a footnote referring to any part of the graphic aid, you may use lowercase letters (a, b, c, etc.), asterisks (*, **, ***), degree symbol (°), or daggers and double daggers (†, ††) followed by the notation. When using symbols, be sure that the symbol also appears at the end of the word (or item) to which reference is being made. Sometimes you may wish just to type the word *Note* followed by a colon, 2 spaces, and then the notation.

Footnotes are typed on the second line below the graphic aid. They are single-spaced with double-spacing between footnotes. The lowercase letters or symbols used to designate footnotes may be placed either as a superior or on-line. Follow the same format throughout the report.

CLASSIFICATION

Graphic aids can be broadly classified as tables and figures. Tables can be further classified as informal or formal and general or special.

Tables

A table consists of data—qualitative, quantitative, geographic, time series—arranged systematically in rows and columns: what is called tabular form. Tables may also consist entirely of words as shown in Exhibit 15.2. Technically, tables are not truly graphic, but because they do provide information in a nonnarrative manner, they are appropriately classified as graphic aids.

When data are presented in paragraph form, it is difficult for the reader to see details and relationships. Tables, therefore, are used to present data so that the reader can readily see relationships and make comparisons.

Compare, for example, the information in the following paragraph and the information in Exhibit 15.3.

> In 1975 there were 3,205 work stoppages, 1,410,000 workers involved, and 32,300,000 idle worker days. In 1976 there were 3,105 work stoppages, 1,300,000 workers involved, and 30,146,000 idle worker days. In 1977 there were 3,010 work stoppages, 1,004,385 workers involved, and 29,430,976 idle worker days. In 1978 there were 4,581 work stoppages, 1,989,786 workers involved, and 38,000,456 idle worker days.

EXHIBIT 15.2
Table of Words Only

Table 2. Principal Parts of Verbs		
Present	**Past**	**Past Participle**
am	was	been
begin	began	begun
break	broke	broken
choose	chose	chosen
do	did	done
eat	ate	eaten

EXHIBIT 15.3
A Table

Table 5 Work Stoppage: 1975–1978			
Year	Number of Stoppages	Number of Workers Involved	Number of Idle Worker Days
1975	3,205	1,410,000	32,300,000
1976	3,105	1,300,000	30,146,000
1977	3,010	1,004,385	29,430,976
1978	4,581	1,989,786	38,000,456
Source: Primary			

Although both contain the same information, it is easier to read and interpret the data in the table than in the narrative. Also, the table is more physically attractive than the solid block of figures and prose.

Types of Tables

Tables can be classified as informal and formal, or general and special.

Informal Tables Informal tables present a single group of data, usually in columns with white space around them to emphasize the data—numerical or verbal. Informal tables

1. Are short and simple
2. Are not numbered or titled
3. Are not included in the List of Illustrations in the Table of Contents
4. Are not framed
5. Do not use vertical or horizontal lines within them
6. Break up a page of prose

Here's an example of an informal table:

The five candidates for the school board are

Name	Age
Donald Fordyce	41
Mary Litten	32
Lyndon Medema	46
Shirley Stryker	52
Justine Vicol	44

Formal Tables   Formal tables present complex data in rows and columns that interact with each other to show comparisons and relationships. Formal tables

1.   Contain several columns and rows of data
2.   Use vertical and horizontal rulings
3.   Are numbered and titled
4.   Are framed
5.   Are included in the List of Illustrations in the Table of Contents

General Tables   General tables present detailed and descriptive data collected by the researcher for general information but not used for analytical purposes. An example of a general table would be a copy of a questionnaire with the total number (percentages or averages) of responses recorded for each item. Also, most Federal government tables (e.g., census) are general tables containing original information for the public's use. General tables are also called *repository* tables because they store information. General tables usually appear in the appendix.

Special Tables   Special tables (also called analytical tables) provide information that resulted from an analysis of the raw data collected by the researchers. An example of a special table would be specific questions taken from the questionnaire and presented in table form for an analysis in the report. Only desired data, then, will be presented for emphasis and for comparison. These tables appear in the report near the section where they are discussed.

Parts of a Table

A table consists of several parts. Different names may be applied to these parts, but generally they are referred to by the names that follow. The layout and identification of parts of a formal table are illustrated in Exhibit 15.4.

I.   Heading
    A.   Table Number
    B.   Table Title
        1.   Subtitle, if any
        2.   Headnote
II.   Body
    A.   Stub
        1.   Stub Head
        2.   Stub Item
            a.   Substub I
            b.   Substub II
    B.   Spanner Head
        1.   Column Head
        2.   Subhead
    C.   Field
        1.   Rows
        2.   Columns
III.   Notations
    A.   Source
    B.   Footnotes

EXHIBIT 15.4
Typical Formal Table

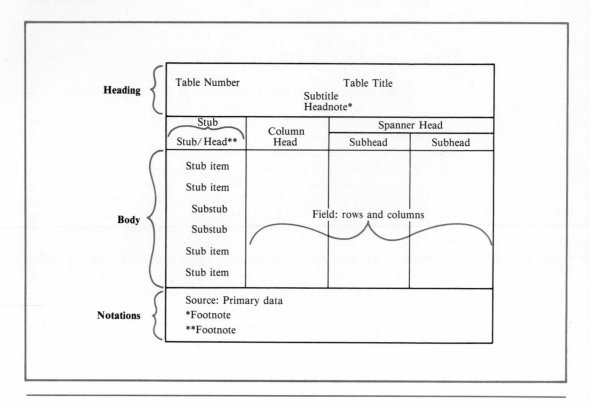

Every column and every row must have a heading that identifies the data, and these headings must be parallel. Table number, title, source, and footnotes have already been discussed.

The first column on the left is the stub column. When it is a title, the title is referred to as the stub head. A stub is a title to the horizontal row of data. To show categories within the stub column, indent two or three spaces to show the subordination. A spanner head extends over several column heads. Column heads are titles of vertical columns, and the field or body is the actual data found in the rows and columns.

Construction Guidelines

Although the construction of tables will vary according to the data they present and the creativity of the report writer, here are some general construction guidelines for all tables.

1. Number and title each table.

2. Tables should be self-explanatory. When taken out of context, they must be clear to the reader.

3. Mention the table in the text before presenting it.

4. Give page number and table number when referring to earlier or later tables.

5. Identify every column and row. Use subtitles when necessary.

6. Align digits from the right. Use decimals rather than fractions and align decimal points. For example,

3	.002
15	3.1
232	2.25
1,691	43.170
15,284	162.1498

7. Use footnotes for clarification. Source footnotes appear immediately below the table and are usually placed within the border.

8. Do not use ditto marks; they can be confusing.

9. Use three hyphens (---), alternating periods and spaces (. . .), or "N.A." for a blank space or to indicate that information is not available.

10. Symbols, such as #, %, °, may be used in column headings to conserve space.

11. Place dollar signs and other symbols before the first entry at the top of the column and with the totals.

12. Indent total and mean lines (and other lines) that summarize preceding data. Total lines appearing at the beginning of the table for emphasis are not indented.

13. Make tables attractive, inviting, readable, and clear.
    a. Use plenty of white spaces within and around them.
    b. Use horizontal and vertical lines sparingly and carefully.
    c. Avoid heavy use of lines which can give a cluttered appearance.
    d. Frame the table with rulings above and below or surrounding it.
    e. Do not extend the table beyond the margins of the page.

14. Round off figures when appropriate. Do not round off numbers that require exact calculations.

15. Arrange data in a logical order—chronologically, alphabetically, geographically, descending, ascending, or by cost, quantity, or other important facts. Exhibits 15.5, 15.6, 15.7, and 15.8 illustrate various kinds of tables.

EXHIBIT 15.5

Table

Table 5.	Head Coaching Salaries				
Name	Sport	Years	Salary	Ranking in District	Ave. Salary in District
Lester Salisbury	Football	*	$ 37,950	5th	$ 35,282
Edward Roberts	Basketball	*	37,500	3rd	32,197
Mark Goodwin	Golf	13	33,017	1st	20,858
David Perry	Hockey	*	32,500		
Lynn Maltzan	Basketball & Softball	19 7	31,752	1st	16,533
Karl Koltoff	Cross Country & Track	12	30,779	1st	22,039
John Svircek	Men's Gymnastics	16	29,478	1st	18,956
Chris Powers	Baseball	7	29,022	2nd	22,956
Mike Murphy	Men's Tennis	9	27,169	2nd	16,038
John Arnold	Men's Swimming	3	21,980	4th	16,798
Tom Ovibowetz	Cross Country & Track	2	20,900	3rd	17,181
Charles Pelligrimi	Soccer	5	18,200	2nd	14,306
Sue Kathleen	Women's Gymnastics	3	18,200	2nd	14,249
Margaret Kraft	Volleyball	4	18,200	4th	15,358
Irene Karens	Women's Tennis	4	18,200	4th	12,595
	TOTALS		$404,847		$274,925
	AVERAGES		$26,990		$19,638

NOTE: This chart is based on the 1981-82 academic year and does not include part-time coaches.
* denotes first year coach.

[a]Horizontal tables should be placed so that they are readable when the material is turned clockwise. The heading should always appear on the left-hand side, whether the report is bound or unbound, printed on one side or on two sides.

EXHIBIT 15.6

Table

Table 10.	Third Quarter Highlights for Ace Company		

(in millions except per share)	1981	1980	% Change
Sales and Revenues	$5,418	$5,542	- 2.2
Net Income	$ 163	$ 166	-11.7
per Common Equivalent Share	$ 1.10	$ 1.13	-12.0
Average Common Equivalent Shares	147	147	+ .3
Dividends Declared per Common Share	$ .67	$ .65	+ 3.1
Stockholders' Equity	$5,936	$6,236	- 4.8
per Common Share	$37.78	$39.28	- 3.8

EXHIBIT 15.8
Table

Estimated Expenditure on "Entitlement" Programs Fiscal Year 1981
Billions of Dollars

Social security	138.0
Federal civilian retirement	17.5
Military retirement	13.7
Other retirement & disability[1]	7.0
Veterans' compensation, medical care, pensions, other benefits	23.0
Medicare & medicaid	60.4
Unemployment compensation	19.7
Food stamps & other nutrition aid	16.2
Other aid for the needy[2]	19.7
	315.2

[1] Mainly railroad retirement and coal miners' disability.
[2] Mainly Aid to Families with Dependent Children, Supplemental Security Income and the Earned Income Credit on income taxes.

EXHIBIT 15.7
Table

Expenditure on Major Programs that are Currently Indexed
Billions of Dollars

	1969	1973	1981
Federal civilian retirement	1.8	4.5	17.5
Military retirement	2.4	4.4	13.7
Coal miners' disability	—	1.0	1.1
Food stamps & other nutrition aid	0.6	3.6	16.2
Social security	26.8	48.3	138.0
Railroad retirement	1.5	2.4	5.3
Supplemental security income	—	—	7.2
Veterans' pensions	2.1	2.6	3.8
Indexed total	4.2	13.5	202.8

Source: The Conference Board, Economic Road Maps, Nos. 1922–1923, March 1982.

FIGURES

Figures refer to all graphic aids except tables. They are not substitutes for tables; tables give exact values, and figures give approximate values. Data presented in pictorial form are easier to comprehend than that presented in tables.

Three main types of graphs (also called charts) are the line, bar, and pie.

Line Graphs   Line graphs (or curve charts) are best used to depict trends or changes over time, such as price changes, or relationships between two or more variables.

These variables are shown along two axes, commonly referred to as the Y axis (vertical) and the X axis (horizontal). These axes divide data into four quadrants, as shown in Exhibit 15.9.

EXHIBIT 15.9
Grid Showing Four Quadrants

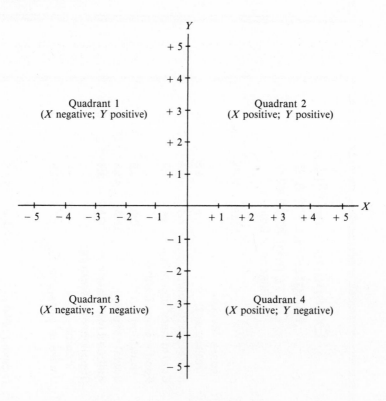

Most business applications involve positive values in both axes. For this reason, most business graphs show only the second quadrant of the grid in Exhibit 15.9.

The line graph has

1. Two scales with specified values.
    a. A vertical scale for the amount (dollars, sales)
    b. A horizontal scale for time (years, months)

2. Two axes, one for each scale
    a. A vertical axis (or Y axis) called the ordinate which represents the dependent variable
    b. A horizontal axis (or X axis) called the abscissa, which represents the independent variable.

3. A plot line or curve, which represents the data.
    a. Keep plot lines to a minimum.
    b. When more than one plot line is used, make the lines clearly distinguishable from each other by the use of color or by variations in the lines—solid lines (_____), dots (....), dashes (----), or the like.
    c. Remember that the greater the number of lines, the more difficult the graph will be to read. (See Exhibit 15.10).
    d. To identify for your reader the different lines used, include a legend within the line chart.

4. A complete grid when accuracy is essential to construction and interpretation.
    a. A grid is the pattern of horizontal and vertical lines that form squares when the scale marks are extended horizontally and vertically across the graph.
    b. In most graphs, the grid can be omitted. (See Exhibit 15.11).

EXHIBIT 15.10

Line Graph with Six Plot Lines

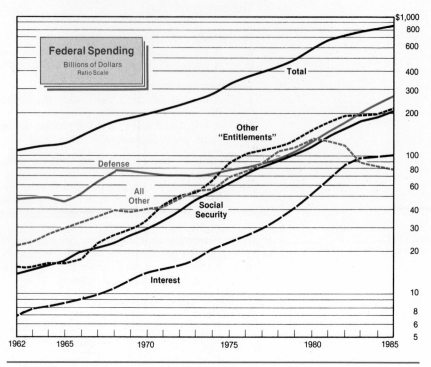

Federal Spending
Billions of Dollars
Ratio Scale

Total

Other "Entitlements"

Defense

All Other

Social Security

Interest

Source: The Conference Board, Economic Road Maps, Nos. 1922–1923, March 1982.

EXHIBIT 15.11
Line Graph Showing Grid

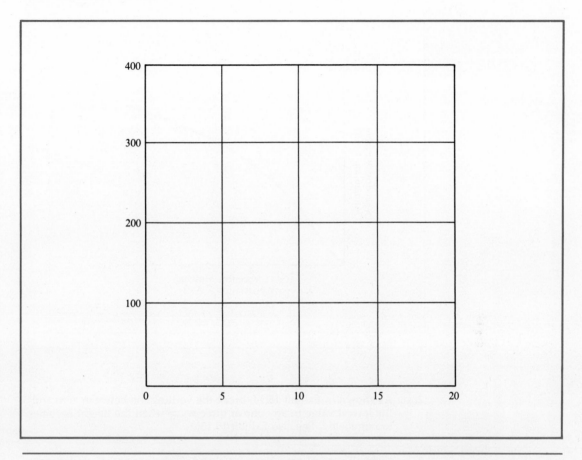

Exhibit 15.12 illustrates a simple line graph with one plot line.

Follow these guidelines when designing line charts.

1.   Begin the vertical line (Y axis) at zero to show the entire graph in
      proportion and to avoid misrepresentation, as shown in Exhibit
      15.13.

      The horizontal line (X axis) does not have to begin with zero because
      it represents time, an independent variable.

EXHIBIT 15.12
Simple Line Graph with One Plot Line

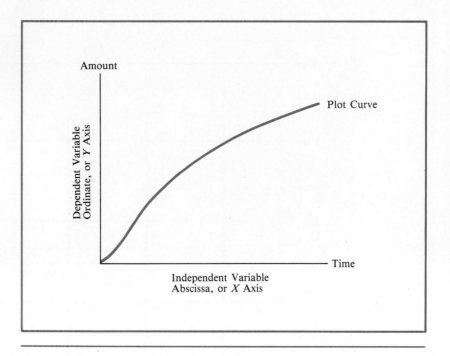

2.   As shown in Exhibit 15.14, break the vertical line between zero and
      the lowest value in any one of three ways when the height becomes
      too unwieldy. See also Exhibit 15.13.

3.   Keep all vertical gradations equal and all the horizontal gradations
      equal; otherwise, you can distort the graph and deceive the reader.
      In other words, use equal spaces for equal amounts. See Exhibit
      15.15.

4.   Select appropriate values for use on the X axis and the Y axis. The
      values you select will alter the appearance of your graph and influ-
      ence the reader's impression of your data. See Exhibit 15.16.

      In Exhibit 15.16 either graph could be valid and accurate under cer-
      tain circumstances. They do, however, give decidedly different visual
      impressions.

EXHIBIT 15.13

Comparing Two Versions of a Line Graph Showing Lowest Usage Value

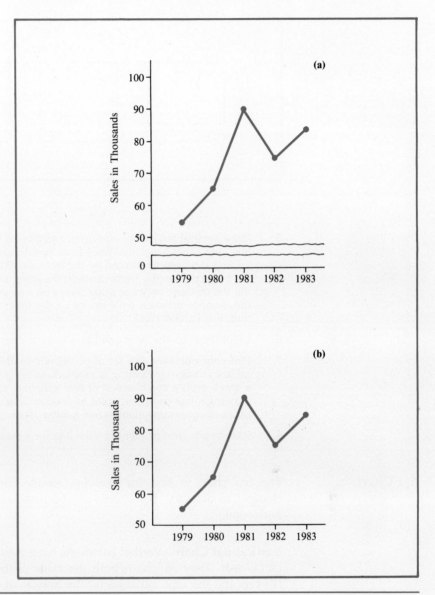

EXHIBIT 15.14
Ways to Break Vertical Scale of Line Graph

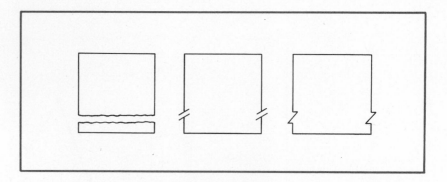

5. Draw vertical lines from equidistant points on the horizontal base line, and draw horizontal lines from equidistant points on the vertical axis. The spaces formed by the lines should be square or nearly so. Make the height approximately the same as the width. Expanding the distance between scale marks on one axis while contracting the distance between scale marks on the other axis creates a distortion. See Exhibit 15.17.

6. Label items on the horizontal and vertical lines.

7. Plot your numbers as a set of points where the horizontal and vertical lines intersect. Plotting is easily done on graph paper. A point on a graph plots a combination of two variables. Connect points by drawing a line from one point to another. The line of the graph is a series of connecting points. See Exhibit 15.18.

8. Include a legend to identify each line for a multiple line graph.

Bar Charts

The bar chart is best for showing simple comparisons, especially changes in quantity. Bar charts can be presented either vertically or horizontally.

Vertical Bar Chart   Vertical bar charts have their bases at the horizontal (X) axis. They are charts with the value of the bars on the vertical (Y) axis and the time variables on the horizontal (X) axis because time is an independent variable and independent variables are always on the X axis. See Exhibit 15.19 for an illustration of a vertical bar chart.

Use vertical bars (1) for comparing data over a certain time so that the time scale would be on the X axis, and (2) for representing height.

EXHIBIT 15.15
Comparing Two Line Graphs Showing Even and Uneven Gradation

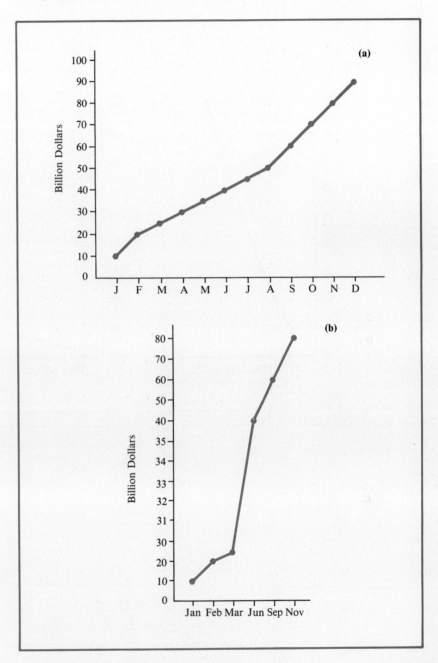

EXHIBIT 15.16

Different Graphs Presenting the Same Information

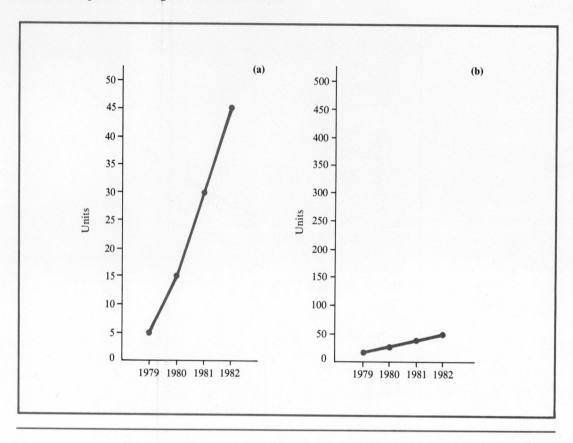

EXHIBIT 15.17

Three Comparable Line Graphs with Different Vertical Scales

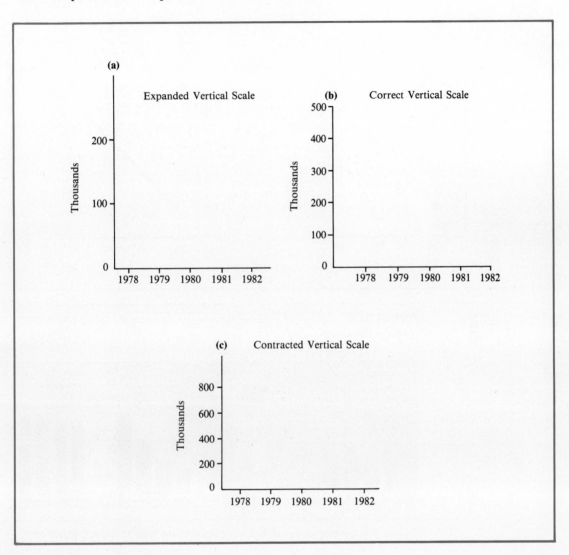

EXHIBIT 15.18
Plotting and Connecting Points

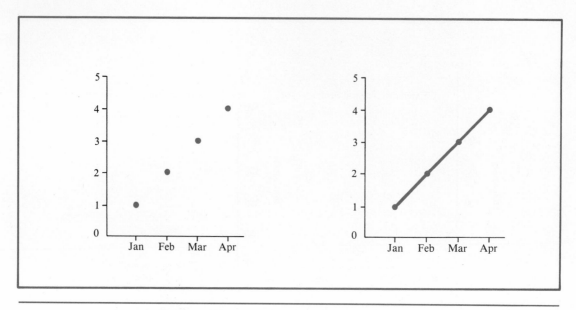

EXHIBIT 15.19
Vertical Bar Chart

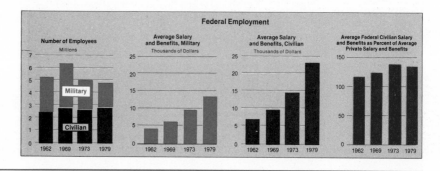

Source: The Conference Board, Economic Road Maps, Nos. 1922–1923, March 1982.

Histogram   A vertical bar chart illustrating a frequency distribution is a histogram, as shown in Exhibit 15.20.

Because a histogram has no spaces between columns, leave a space of at least one half the width of the bar at each end of the X axis. In the histogram, columns are adjacent or contiguous to each other because the intervals of distribution are continuous, as might be the case with income, age, height, or weight. See Chapter 11 for a description of continuous data.

EXHIBIT 15.20
Histogram

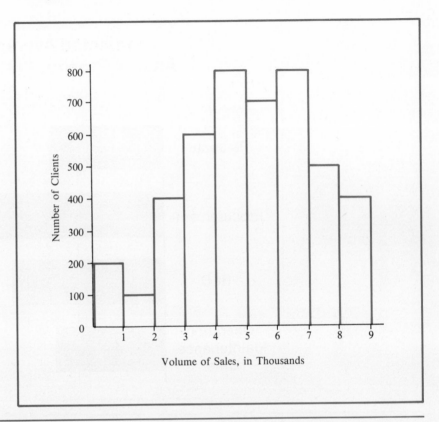

Volume of Sales, in Thousands

Horizontal Bar Chart   A horizontal bar chart has its base at the vertical *(Y)* axis. Use horizontal bar charts (1) for comparing data for a particular point in time, and (2) for representing distance. Exhibits 15.21 and 15.22 illustrates horizontal bar charts.

Variations of the simple bar chart are the multiple bar chart, the bilateral bar chart, and the segmented bar chart.

Multiple Bar Chart   When you want to compare two or three variables within a single bar chart, use a multiple bar chart, as shown in Exhibit 15.23.

The multiple bars are distinguished one from the other by color, shading, or crosshatching. Avoid comparing more than three variables for a single item on one chart. For example, you could compare five

EXHIBIT 15.21
Horizontal Bar Chart

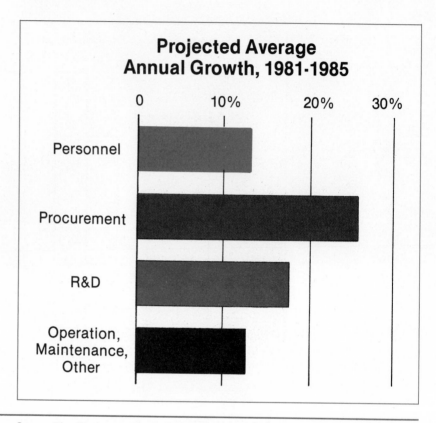

Source: The Conference Board, Economic Road Maps, Nos. 1922–1923, March 1982.

sections of the United States but only three or fewer variables for each of the five sections.

Bilateral Bar Chart A bilateral bar chart (also called the plus and minus or positive and negative chart) shows increases on one side of a zero line and decreases on the other side of the zero line, as illustrated in Exhibits 15.24 and 15.25.

The zero line is at or near the middle of the graph so that space is provided for both the positive and negative bars. Bilateral charts use either vertical or horizontal bars and are used for showing percentage change and whenever data to be presented have both positive and negative values.

EXHIBIT 15.22
Horizontal Bar Chart

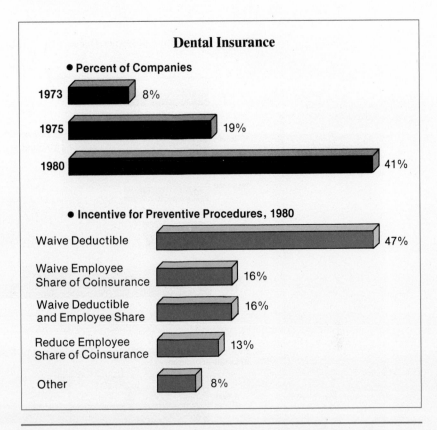

Source: The Conference Board, Economic Road Maps, Nos. 1920–1921, February 1982.

Segmented Bar Chart   The segmented bar chart (also called compo-
nent-part or subdivided bar chart) is used to show the composition of
the variables being compared, as shown in Exhibits 15.26 and 15.27.

Bars can be both horizontal and vertical. When crosshatching,
shadings, or colors are used to distinguish each segment, a legend
should be included on the chart. When using color, start with the dark
colors at the base and move up to lighter colors.

When a segmented bar chart is used to indicate percentages, each
bar in the chart equals 100 percent. Because each bar represents 100

EXHIBIT 15.23
Multiple Bar Charts

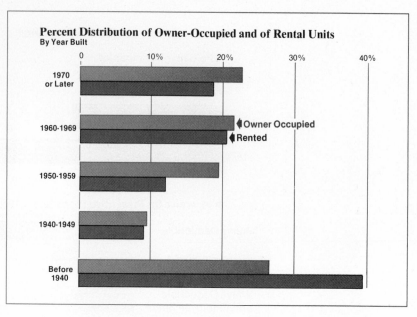

Percent Distribution of Owner-Occupied and of Rental Units
By Year Built

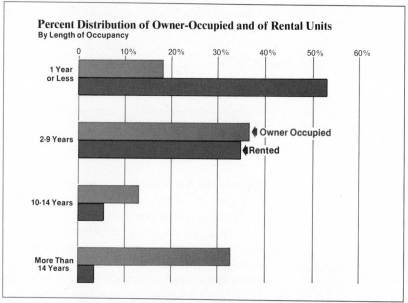

Percent Distribution of Owner-Occupied and of Rental Units
By Length of Occupancy

Source: The Conference Board, Economic Road Maps, Nos. 1918–1919, January 1982.

EXHIBIT 15.24
Bilateral Bar Chart

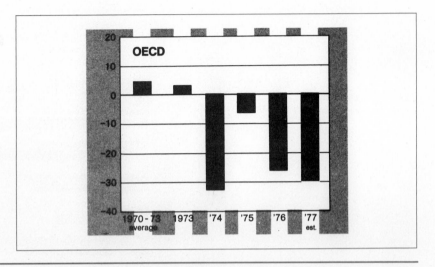

Source: The Conference Board, Road Maps of Industry, No. 1819, November 1977.

percent, each is the same length or height, but the size of the segments vary according to their percentages. For example:

50%	50%

= 100 percent

25%	25%	25%	25%

= 100 percent

A single segmented bar may be used to show percentages of a whole, as shown in Exhibit 15.28. It is a variation of a pie chart, or a bar chart used horizontally or vertically, or it can be in the shape of a company's product.

Guidelines The following guidelines will help you prepare bar charts.

1. Begin the vertical (Y) axis at zero.

2. Break the vertical line with a wavy line or slash marks between zero and the lowest value when the height becomes too great.

3. Use grid lines only when necessary to help the reader compare lengths. If bars are horizontal, then the grid lines are vertical and vice versa.

EXHIBIT 15.25
Bilateral Bar Chart

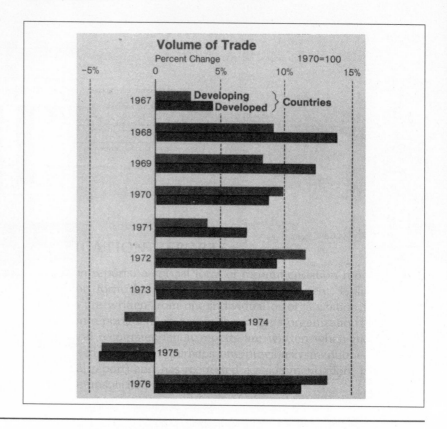

Source: The Conference Board, Road Maps of Industry, No. 1819, November 1977.

4. Keep all the vertical gradations equal and all the horizontal gradations equal.

5. Keep the width of all bars equal to avoid distortion of the data. Keep the width of the space between bars equal. For emphasis, make the bars wider than the space between the bars.

6. Arrange bars alphabetically, chronologically, numerically, or in descending (generally preferred) or ascending order. See Chapter 11 for various ways to present data.

7. Use color, shading, or crosshatching for emphasizing, contrasting, and distinguishing bars from each other.

8. Include a legend to identify various bars on a multiple-bar chart.

9. Label items on the horizontal and vertical lines and the bars. Place figures within bars or at the top of each bar to give the exact amount. Additional bar charts are presented in Exhibits 15.29 and 15.30.

EXHIBIT 15.26
Segmented Bar Chart

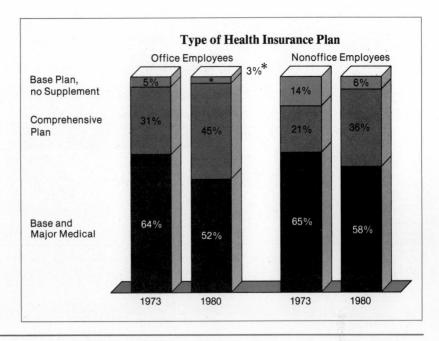

Source: The Conference Board, Road Maps of Industry, No. 1819, November 1977.

EXHIBIT 15.27
Segmented Bar Chart

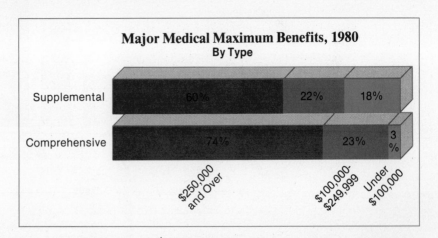

Source: The Conference Board, Road Maps of Industry, No. 1819, November 1977.

EXHIBIT 15.28
Single Segmented Bar Chart

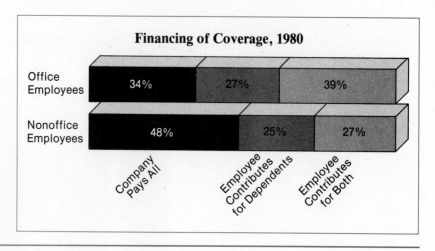

Source: The Conference Board, Economic Road Maps, Nos. 1920–1921, February 1982.

EXHIBIT 15.29
Bar Chart

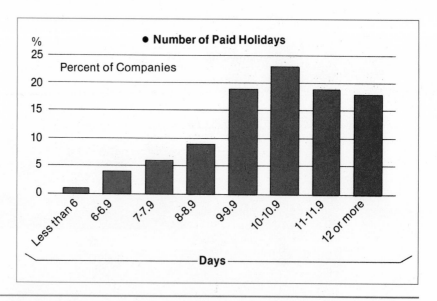

Source: The Conference Board, Economic Road Maps, Nos. 1920–1921, February 1982.

EXHIBIT 15.30
Bar Chart

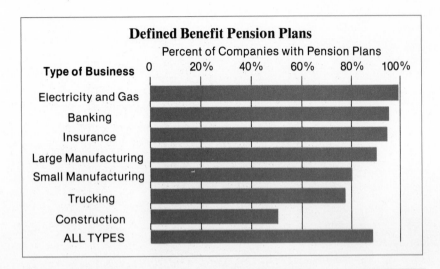

Source: The Conference Board, Economic Road Maps, Nos. 1920–1921, February
1982.

Pie Charts

Pie charts (also called circle graphs) are used to depict parts of a whole. The pie or circle is the whole; the slices or segments are the parts. These parts must add up to 100 percent, as shown in Exhibit 15.31.

To avoid misrepresentation in a pie chart, include not only the description of each segment, but also the percentage figures which are the most important information for making quick and easy comparisons.

The following guidelines will help you prepare pie charts.

1. Convert raw figures into percentages whenever possible.

Raw Data	Percentage
115 ÷ 1,000 = 0.115 × 100 = 11.5	
202	20.2
294	29.4
389	38.9
1,000 total number	100 percent

2. Start segmenting your pie chart by making the first radial line at the 12 o'clock position, continuing clockwise in descending order, from the largest to the smallest percentage.

38.9, 29.4, 20.2, 11.5

EXHIBIT 15.31
Pie Chart

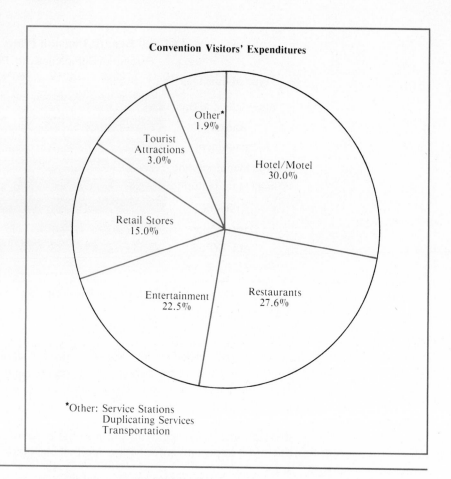

Convention Visitors' Expenditures

Other*
1.9%

Tourist
Attractions
3.0%

Hotel/Motel
30.0%

Retail Stores
15.0%

Entertainment
22.5%

Restaurants
27.6%

*Other: Service Stations
Duplicating Services
Transportation

3. Convert percentages to degrees.

Percentage			Degrees
11.5	× 360 (degrees in a circle) =	41.40 rounded off to	41
20.2	=	72.7	73
29.4	=	105.84	106
38.9	=	140.04	140
100	percent		360 degrees

4. Use a compass to draw a circle and locate its center.

5. Use a protractor for exact segmentation.

6. Have at least three parts; otherwise the chart is not necessary. Avoid having more than seven segments. Combine several small categories in a single segment labeled "Miscellaneous" or "Other," which is al-

ways the last segment, even though it may be larger than the preceding segment. When appropriate, include a description of "Other." For example:

$$\text{Other}\begin{cases}\text{Paper}\\\text{Pens}\\\text{Pencils}\end{cases}$$

7. Identify each segment (description and figure) horizontally within the circle if room permits; otherwise, use guide lines with the identification placed outside.

8. Coloring, shading, or crosshatching can be used for emphasis.

9. Make the size of the pie chart appropriate for the page.

Pictograms

A pictogram (pictograph or pictorial chart), a variation of the bar chart, uses pictures or symbols rather than lines or bars to represent data. For example, coins, books, houses, ships, people, animals, or barrels can be used to depict appropriate data. See Exhibit 15.32.

Pictograms should

1. Present simple information
2. Use representative pictures and symbols that are easily recognized by the reader
3. Show quantities by number of units rather than by differences in sizes
4. Present units that are identical and of equal size

Although pictograms attract attention because of their novelty and eye appeal, they can easily mislead readers and distort data. Consider the following example.

Let's say you want to compare the average monthly oil production of Company A (10,000 barrels) and Company B (20,000 barrels). You could use a vertical bar chart as follows:

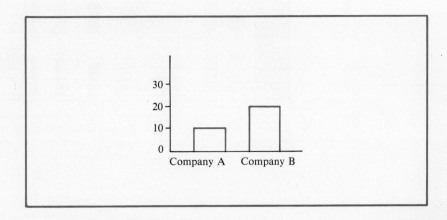

EXHIBIT 15.32
Pictogram

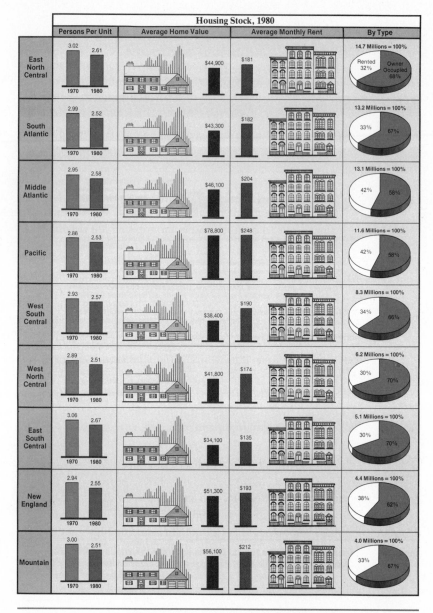

Source: The Conference Board, Economic Road Maps, Nos. 1918–1919, January 1982.

The chart is clear. Company B produces twice as much as Company A. But because you want to attract the reader's attention with a more appealing and pertinent picture, you decide to use a pictogram. A common approach is to use one barrel to show the production capacity of Company A and a barrel twice as big to indicate the production capacity of Company B.

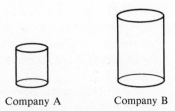

Company A   Company B

The problem with this is that the visual representation misleads the reader because barrel B is twice as high as barrel A. It is also twice as wide, which gives it the appearance of having four times the volume. Worse, because readers tend to supply the implied third dimension, barrel B may appear to have eight times the volume of barrel A. To prevent misrepresentation and distortion, keep the barrels uniform in size, adding barrels to show increased production.

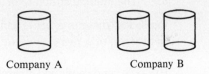

Company A   Company B

Photographs

Photographs can be very useful in business reports. Photographs are important because they

1. Have visual appeal
2. Provide accurate representations
3. Are persuasive as evidence or proof
4. Can clearly identify elements of complex layouts, machinery, etc.
5. Can provide aerial views of large geographic areas

6.   Can show comparisons with before and after pictures
7.   Can give good overall views or focus in on one detail

Companies use photographs in their annual reports to show new buildings, plants, or products. Insurance companies especially use photographs to show the extent of damages. One example of the persuasive power of a photograph was offered by an irate motorist who submitted a photograph of the chuck hole in the road that damaged his radial tire and rim with his claim to the road commissioner. As a result of the photographic proof, he was reimbursed for repairs.

Photographs not only can be taken quickly and easily but also can be reproduced in seconds, especially with the latest models of cameras. Builders, contractors, and designers can take photographs and pencil in notations rather than laboriously prepare sketches or diagrams.

Photographs, however, provide only a surface print and cannot give a dimensional picture. A good photograph is well focused and concentrates on one aspect; it does not look cluttered.

Diagrams

A diagram is a sketch or drawing designed to demonstrate or explain the relationship of parts. It has an advantage over a photograph because it can include as much detail as is needed for the reader. Diagrams are used for illustrating

1.   How to assemble a product
2.   How to repair an item
3.   How to operate a piece of equipment
4.   How one item interacts with another
5.   How to get from one point to another
6.   The internal structure of an item

Exploded diagrams are excellent for showing the reader the component parts of a piece of equipment, as shown in Exhibit 15.33.

Cutaway and exploded diagrams are drawn by artists who can provide the precision needed to prepare them.

Organizational Charts

An organizational chart indicates the flow of authority, responsibility, and chain of command within an organization and the relationship among positions.

Because organizational charts show graphically who reports to whom, new employees especially appreciate them for viewing the various levels and divisions within a company.

Organizational charts will vary from one organization to another. They can be vertical—starting at the top and branching downward; or horizontal—starting at the left and branching to the right. Some organ-

EXHIBIT 15.33
Diagram

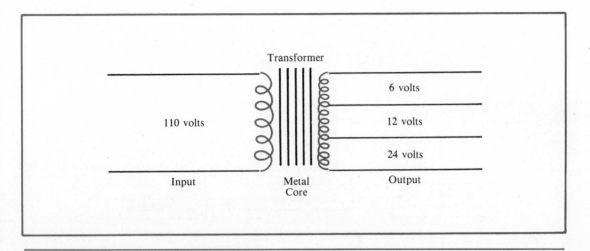

izational charts may be circular, showing authority coming from the center and branching outward. Exhibit 15.34 illustrates an organizational chart.

Flow Charts

A flow chart is a schematic representation of a sequence of steps; it traces the movement of a product, process, or procedure from beginning to end. Steps in the procedure are stated in boxes with arrows indicating the flow of direction.

Because flow charts outline specific steps, they are valuable for visualizing the sequence of activities involved in a particular process. Flow charts are frequently used in production; sales; accounting; and for various office systems, such as work flow, mail handling, and filing. Exhibit 15.35 illustrates a flow chart.

Maps

When you wish to show representation that is dependent on geographical or spatial relationships, maps (or cartograms) are your best choice. They can be specific geographic areas, such as counties, cities, states, regions or countries. Color, shading, crosshatching, charts, pictures, numeric figures, dots, and other symbols are used to indicate the characteristics in each of the various geographic segments. When using dots, each dot must be the same size and represent a given quantity.

Maps are useful for comparing quantitative data by geographic locations. Companies use maps in annual reports to show distribution

EXHIBIT 15.34
Organization Chart

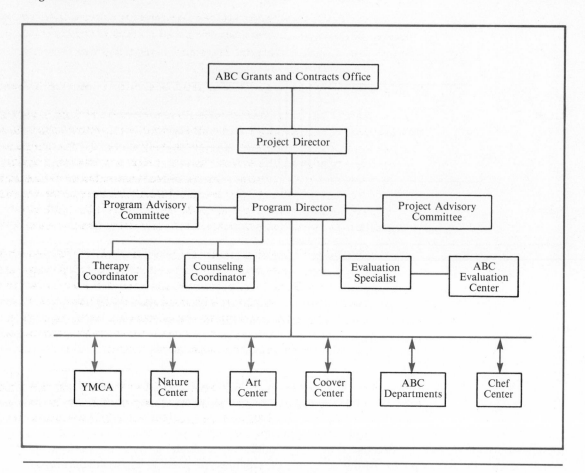

of dealers, stockholders, products, sales, resources, and so forth. Exhibits 15.36 and 15.37 illustrate maps.

Other Graphic Aids

Although we have discussed several of the frequently used graphic aids, you may select still other designs that would best present your data graphically. For example, blueprints, scattergrams (See Chapter 1), and samples of fabrics or other materials (paper, paints) all can help you communicate your data. Your imagination will help you present the best picture for your audience—use it!

EXHIBIT 15.35
Flow Chart

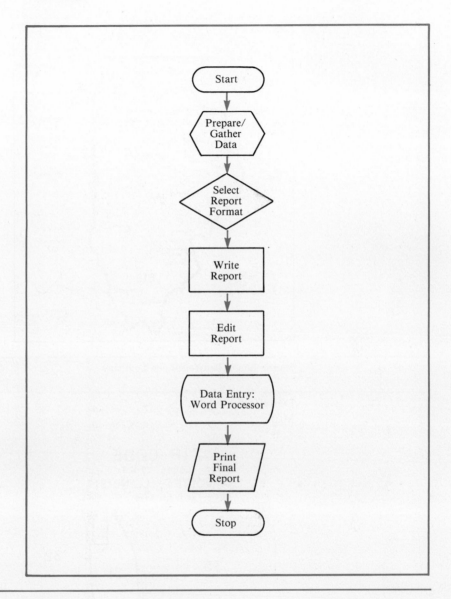

COMPUTER GRAPHICS

Computers have revolutionized report writing by their capabilities for presenting complicated data in dramatic forms. What was done traditionally by pen, pencil, compasses, and protractors can be done quickly, easily, and accurately by the computer. Instead of having art-

EXHIBIT 15.36
Map

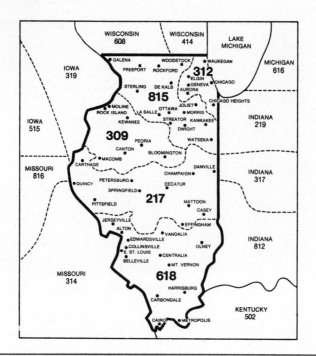

Source: Illinois Bell Telephone Company

EXHIBIT 15.37
Map

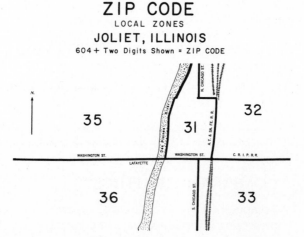

Source: United States Postal Service

ists or skilled technicians laboriously design graphic aids, the report writer can employ the computer to prepare easy-to-comprehend charts and graphs: line graphs, bar charts, pie charts, diagrams, flow charts, organizational charts, and maps. The report writer selects the design that will best display the data, and then has the computer create the appropriate business graphic.

Business graphics, as computer graphics are being called, convert endless columns of data into charts and figures. They can

1. Schedule projects and production
2. Project worker hours and costs
3. Estimate costs
4. Record sales and stock activities
5. Keep schedules of costs current

Business graphics, in fact, can take any numerical information and convert it into easy-to-comprehend charts and graphs.

Application

Business graphics can be used to

1. Monitor performance in such areas as marketing, production, and finance
2. Compare expenditures against the budget
3. Market products by convincing prospects or clients that a purchase should be made
4. Compare sales and earnings with past performances and company projections
5. Serve as a presentation tool in the boardroom
6. Alert personnel to potential problems
7. Help in the decision-making process
8. Analyze and test designs

Advantages and Disadvantages

Business graphics have many advantages and few disadvantages.

Advantages The major advantages of business graphics are that they

1. Make information more visible
2. Combine and plot information stored in the computer without having to re-enter data
3. Create charts from data not already in the computer when computer production costs would be lower than manual production costs
4. Achieve a high degree of accuracy
5. Create designs on short notice and thereby present up-to-date data, rather than waiting for weeks for artists to draw designs that could then be obsolete

6. Create, modify, and print charts and graphs easily

7. Can be produced in a variety of colors

8. Allow you to load, plot, and analyze data

9. Draw almost any kind of design, which can then be changed repeatedly

10. Speed production

Disadvantages   Computer graphics have two disadvantages:

1. The high cost of computers to produce them
2. The need for qualified personnel to operate the computers

SUMMARY

Graphic aids refer to tables and figures presented in written material to clarify a discussion. Graphic aids are not substitutes for words, and are placed after the prose that explains them. The primary purpose of graphic aids is to present a picture of what the prose says. The picture can be in the form of tables or figures. Graphic aids also emphasize material which needs extra attention or coverage, convert and condense complex information into a pictorial form, and enhance the appearance of the report.

All graphic aids should be self-explanatory, and their sizes should be determined by the importance and the amount of data they contain. Ruled lines help to separate data, and border lines attractively display the graphic aid. Color is used to emphasize differences and to create an inviting picture.

All graphic aids in the report are labeled and numbered so that they can be identified and located in a report that has a list of illustrations included in the Table of Contents. When necessary, give documentation.

A table consists of data arranged systematically in rows and columns. Tables can be classified as informal and formal, special and general. Figures refer to all other graphic aids except tables. The three main types of graphs are the line, bar, and pie. Line graphs are best used to depict trends over a time period; the bar chart is best for showing simple comparisons; and pie charts are used to depict parts of a whole.

Other graphic aids include pictograms, photographs, diagrams, organizational charts, flow charts, maps, scattergrams, and samples.

Computer graphics, made by a computer, convert endless columns of data into charts and figures.

EXERCISES

Review Questions

1. What are graphic aids? Give five examples.

2. What are the purposes of graphic aids?

3. Where are graphic aids placed in the report?

4. How should you refer to graphic aids in the report? Why?

5. What does it mean to say that graphic aids should be self-explanatory?

6. How large should a graphic aid be?

7. When do you use ruled lines in graphic aids?

8. When do you use color in graphic aids?

9. Why are graphic aids labeled and numbered?

10. When are footnotes for graphic aids required?

11. How can tables be classified? Explain each.

12. Define the three main types of graphs, and tell when you would use each of them.

13. What is the difference between a vertical bar chart and a horizontal bar chart?

14. What is a histogram? multiple bar chart? bilateral bar chart? segmented bar chart?

15. What is a pie chart?

16. What are computer graphics?

17. Why is it important to begin the vertical axis at zero?

18. In a pictogram, why is it important to keep symbols a uniform size?

19. Illustrate three ways to show a break in the vertical line.

20. Why are photographs important in business reports?

Problems

1. Select the most effective graphic aid for illustrating each of the following.
   a. A breakdown of your time for a typical week.
   b. A comparison of three brands of typewriter according to price, weight, and special features.
   c. How Company X spent its revenue.
   d. The number of units of Product Y produced during four quarters.
   e. A comparison of the percentage of decrease or increase in sales for September as compared with August sales.
   f. Net profits over a five-year span.
   g. Number of tasks completed for each month for one year by three employees.
   h. Gross sales for a 10-year period.

i. Population of the United States by geographic divisions.
j. System for handling mail in Company Y.
k. Position of authority and responsibility and the relationship of each position to the others for Company A.
l. Components of a bicycle.
m. Changing prices of Product A and Product B over the past year.
n. An illustration of a broken carton.
o. An illustration of a damaged ship.
p. A comparison of five fruits on the basis of calories, nutritional value, and cost.
q. Census information from the government.
r. Profits and losses for five stores of one chain for five years.
s. Net income for five organizations.
t. Percentage changes (negative and positive) in sales.
u. How a company's income dollar was earned.
v. How dollars were spent for five items over a five-year span.
w. Percentage breakdown of company's product.
x. Allocation of time spent on a project.
y. Daily high and low temperatures for one week.

2. Illustrate a flow chart for a process or procedure with which you are familiar. Include a full title and provide a prose discussion.

3. Prepare a poster that illustrates five different kinds of graphic aids that you found in magazines, current newspapers, or brochures. Include a line graph, a bar chart, and a pie chart. You may photocopy graphic aids that appear in books or other library materials.

4. Prepare an organizational chart for an organization where you work or go to school.

5. Construct a pie chart to illustrate your monthly expenditures. Include a full title and provide a prose discussion.

6. Draw a diagram showing the layout of
   a. An office
   b. Your home or apartment
   c. Library
   d. Store
   e. A recreational center

7. Gather statistics—age, height, weight—on the members of your class, family, or club and arrange the information in a table.

8. Gather statistics of your choice from a group of ten people and present the data in a table.

9. For each of the following graphic aids, give a specific example of data it could illustrate effectively.
   a. Formal table
   b. Line chart—one item
   c. Line chart—two items
   d. Vertical bar chart
   e. Histogram
   f. Horizontal bar chart
   g. Multiple bar chart
   h. Bilateral bar chart

     i.   Segmented bar chart
     j.   Pie chart
     k.   Pictogram
     l.   Photograph
     m.   Diagram
     n.   Organizational chart
     o.   Flow chart
     p.   Map
     q.   Samples

10.   Using reference books, such as

Business Statistics

Demographic Yearbook

Federal Reserve Bulletin

Information Please Almanac

Statistical Abstract of the United States

Statistical Yearbook

Statistical Yearbook of the United Nations

World Almanac and Book of Facts

select data to construct
     a.   A formal table
     b.   A line chart—one item
     c.   A line chart—two items
     d.   A vertical bar chart
     e.   A horizontal bar chart
     f.   A multiple bar chart
     g.   A bilateral bar chart
     h.   A segmented bar chart
     i.   A pie chart with at least five divisions
     j.   A pictogram
Number graphic aids consecutively, and give each a title. Label all parts and provide a legend when necessary. Use a separate sheet of paper for each graphic aid. Use at least five different sources and provide documentation. Use a ruler and India ink for drawing lines. Type all information. Provide a prose discussion for each.

11.   Prepare and submit all the necessary graphic aids which you will use in the major report(s) you are writing this semester or term.

PART V
Applications

CHAPTER 16
Common Types of Reports

Although no two reports will be identical, some types of reports have become common because they have demonstrated their usefulness in solving certain kinds of recurring problems. These reports have more in common than they have differences. Regardless of type, a report should convey information quickly and clearly to a reader who needs the information to make a decision.

Topics

Progress Reports
Proposals
Justification Reports
Staff Reports
Feasibility Reports
Short Informational and Analytical Reports
Evaluations
Accident Reports
Annual Reports
Library Research Reports
Reports of Experimental Results
Audit Reports
Special Applications

It would be virtually impossible to include a complete listing of all the types of reports used on a regular basis in business, industry, and the professions. In this chapter, we present a wide variety of the most common types. You will quickly see that these types are the logical result of applying the general considerations we've been discussing in the previous 15 chapters to specific situations.

When you begin working and writing reports for an organization, you will need to discover exactly what your supervisor and others in the organization expect to be included in specific reports. Even when your boss uses the same descriptive word that we use here, she or he may expect a report that either includes additional components or excludes some of those we suggest. The only way to be sure that you are providing the right type of report is to ask. Nevertheless, you will undoubtedly encounter the report types we present here, and in most cases they will include the components we suggest.

PROGRESS REPORTS

A progress report is an informational report designed to inform the reader of the progress on a particular project over a particular time. Some projects may require only one or two progress reports. Others may call for a series of reports, the final one to be submitted upon completion of the project. Many periodic reports are essentially progress reports as they include information about the status of a project or activity. In some organizations, progress reports are referred to as status reports.

A progress report usually includes the following components:

1. Identification of the project and the time period covered
2. A summary of previous progress
3. A description of the progress during the time covered by this report, including
   a. problems encountered and solved,
   b. problems not solved, and
   c. explanations for any delays
4. A summary of the plans for completing the project, including significant dates

Progress reports vary in length from one-page summaries to book-length studies with many pages of statistical or technical information. The physical presentation of progress reports will naturally be influenced by the length, formality, and content of the report. See Exhibits 4.5, and 16.1 for sample progress reports.

PROPOSALS

Proposals are an increasingly common report form. In a proposal, the writer offers to solve a problem for the reader in exchange for something. Because the writer will benefit if the reader accepts the proposal, proposals—or more appropriately, cover letters accompanying them—usually contain a persuasive element not found in other reports. Proposals, however, are legitimate reports; the information they contain must be accurate, impartial, and complete.

Proposals may be requested by an organization with a problem, or the writer may assume that an organization has a problem which he or she is uniquely qualified to solve. A proposal and subsequent letter of acceptance constitute a contract to perform certain work in a specified way.

EXHIBIT 16.1
Progress Report

Time Period Covered[a]

Brown and Bacon Construction
1591 Duxbury Boulevard
Charleston, WV 25306

June 23, 19xx

TO: Arnold Eisenberg, Project Manager

FROM: Anne Houck, Supervisor

SUBJECT: Restoration of Heritage Hall

This report covers the period from June 7, when the restoration of Heritage Hall began, to June 21.

Crew Hired

Hideyoshi Musashi, Robert Wallechinsky, and I arrived in Richmond, VA, on June 6. We spent June 7, 8, and 9 hiring the carpenters, plumbers, and electricians needed to begin the process of restoration.

Work Completed

Exterior work is proceeding on schedule. The eaves have all been replaced, and the carpenters have begun replacing the rotten wood on the north side. Three (of 27) windows have been replaced with double-glazed replicas.

All of the plumbing will need to be replaced. New fixtures have been installed in the upstairs bath, and the main drainage pipes are in place.

The electricians have installed the new panel and have completed rewiring the kitchen.

Problems Encountered

I have not been able to hire someone qualified to restore the marble stairway. Your original suggestion to use Leonardo Di Salvo from Milan, Italy, may prove the most economical solution.

As usual with restorations of buildings as old as Heritage Hall, most walls are out of plumb. We are restoring plumb where possible and custom fitting when necessary.

Work Scheduled

The plumbers are working on installing the supply lines and water heater. Tomorrow they will install the new fixtures in the downstairs bath.

---

[a]If the subject line or a special "period covered" line does not specify the time covered by the report, the first sentence should do so.

Solicited Proposals

Solicited proposals, those requested by an organization, are usually widespread invitations to bid. In some cases, the organization will expect the proposal to contain complete and accurate specifications on the work to be done. In others, the organization wishes to receive a possible solution or solutions to a problem and will wish to discuss specifics later. The request for proposals (RFP) may appear in business

EXHIBIT 16.1
Progress Report *(continued)*

Directive for Further Action[b]

Arnold Eisenberg   June 23, 19xx   2

None of the old wiring (installed between 1927 and 1934) is reusable. In
most cases, we will be able to pull the new wire through the existing conduit.
Several rooms will require additional wiring.

Except for the construction required for the new marble stairway, we expect
to be through with the rough work by August 1, two weeks ahead of schedule.
If we encounter no additional difficulties, I will begin hiring painters the
first week in August. We should begin the process of stripping and refin-
ishing by the tenth.

Please check once more on the availability of craftsmen qualified to restore
the stairway. If we are to remain on schedule, we will need to begin work
on the stairway by August 20.

---

[b]In addition to reporting on what was accomplished, problems encountered, and
plans for completing the project, a progress report should let the reader know if he/
she needs to take any action.

journals or, for government work, in government publications. An organization might also request proposals from specific companies or individuals by mail. Typically, organizations or individuals wishing to
submit a proposal in response to an ad in a journal will need to write
for a specific RFP. Many companies, especially those offering grant

money, and foundations have developed specific formats and procedures for proposals, which you will need to follow exactly.

Occasionally, you may be asked to submit a proposal as a result of a conversation you've had with an officer or agent of an organization. More often, however, you will need to compete with others—perhaps a great many others—who will also be submitting proposals. When you receive a request to submit a proposal, you'll need to study the invitation carefully to determine whether you can solve the problem or meet the specifications as required. You'll also need to determine whether you or your organization are better qualified to solve the problem than others who will probably be submitting proposals.

Solicited proposals often provide specific guidelines for completion, including requests for details about methodology, techniques, funding, and personnel. When an invitation to bid does not contain specific guidelines, use the pattern presented for unsolicited proposals.

Unsolicited Proposals

When you perceive a problem in an organization or industry that you are qualified to solve, you may send a letter of inquiry to determine interest or send your proposal and a letter of transmittal. When you do not have specific guidelines for preparing the proposal, include the following components:

A Summarizing Introduction   The initial section may be the only part of your proposal your audience reads. For this reason it will need to demonstrate that you understand the problem, have a method to solve it, and have the ability to complete the necessary work. Give the reader an overview of the entire proposal, focusing on your objective and approach, your proposed solution, the benefit the audience would receive if you do the work, and the main reason you or your organization should do the work. Unless the problem and proposed solution are specifically technical, omit technical details from this section.

A Detailed Problem Statement   What is the problem? Both solicited and unsolicited proposals need to demonstrate that the writer understands the reader's problem. Your problem statement should include an accurate description of the problem itself and a description of the problems associated with solving that difficulty. What will you and the reader have to do to solve the problem, and what difficulties will you encounter as you work to solve the problem?

A Statement of Methodology   What will you do to solve the problem? How do you know it will work? Your reader will want to see proof that you know how to solve the problem. Have you conducted a preliminary investigation? Have you solved a similar problem previously? Place the results of research and descriptions of techniques in this section, and place documentation (questionnaires, computer print-outs, calculations, or other statistical evidence) and other supporting details in an appendix.

A Project Management Statement What will you do, when will you do it, how will you go about it, and how much will it cost? The reader will want you to be as specific as possible. If you and the reader are simply exploring possibilities, be specific about how you will conduct the preliminary investigation. Remember that your proposal is an offer to perform work, and once accepted, it will be legally binding. Give the reader specific dates and lists of materials and other resources. Clarify who will report to whom, and let the reader know how you will measure your progress and at what intervals you will report on your progress to your reader.

A Statement of Your Qualifications What makes you or your organization uniquely qualified to solve the reader's problem? When your qualifications are not already well known to your audience, you will need to prove your credibility. What training and experience do you and the others involved have? What are your resources? What proof can you offer that you can perform the necessary work? Your reader will probably want to see the resumes of key personnel, so consider placing them in an appendix. Exhibit 16.2 illustrates a typical proposal.

EXHIBIT 16.2
Proposal

Cover Sheet Form[a]

THE BIG BYTE EDUCATION FOUNDATION

20525 MaryAnn Avenue, Cupertino, CA 95014

GRANT PROPOSAL RECORD

Organization: Midwestern Business College
     Address: Chicago, IL

Responsible Officer for Contact: Principal Investigator: Robert Farentino, Ph.D.
     Dr. Albert Smith   Address: Department of Management
                                                         Information Systems.
Address: Division of Sponsored Research   MBC, Chicago, IL
     Midwestern Business College

Phone: Value of Hardware Requests   Estimated Project Time (months):
517-383-1907 $5,900   12 months

Programs and/or materials that would result from this project:

1. A unique set of algorithms for evaluating student writing, initially applied
    to business communication course content.

2. A workbook and series of diskettes comprising a CAI package for college-
    level instruction in business communication.

Project Abstract:

   This project will create CAI materials to help teach concepts of business
   communication to undergraduate college and university students. The
   materials will benefit students by allowing them to develop required skills
   at their own rate in a nonthreatening atmosphere. They will benefit teachers
   by reducing the time required to evaluate student writing and by providing a
   logical, uniform basis for evaluating business letters and reports. The
   materials should also prove beneficial to those in business who wish to
   improve written communication skills.

   Within each unit, the materials will proceed from simple (quizzes requiring
   recall only) to complex (message assembly from given components and message
   creation). A student may need to repeat material or may be rewarded for
   superior performance. Tutorials will be incorporated in a game structure
   to enhance motivation.

   A unique set of algorithms for evaluating student writing will be developed
   and applied to business communication course content. The product will
   consist of (1) a student workbook containing instructions and problems, (2)
   a set of diskettes containing simulations and evaluative programming, (3) a
   user orientation and record keeping diskette, (4) an instructor's manual
   orienting teachers to the material, and (5) an instructor's diskette for
   profiling the class and evaluating student performance.

   Dissemination of the materials will be through a commercial publishing
   house. The approximate market size is 500,000 business communication
   students a year.

---

[a]Many proposals must be completed on forms designed by the company requesting
them. Note that the cover sheet for this proposal requests specific information and
provides space for only an extremely brief summary. The letters used with the
headings throughout the proposal refer to questions in the original request for proposal (RFP).

EXHIBIT 16.2
Proposal *(continued)*

HARDWARE BUDGET REQUEST

Qty.	Manufacturer's Name and Product Number	Product Name/Description	Item Cost	Total Cost
	All items manufactured by Apple			
2	A2S1048	Apple II Plus with 48 K RAM	$1,530	$3,060
2	A3M0039	Apple Monitor III with Green Screen	250	500
2	A2M0044	Apple II Disk Drives with Interface	645	1,290
2	A2M0003	Apple II Disk Drives only	525	1,050

Total Cost _____$5,900_____

Transfer Total Cost to Cover Sheet

EXHIBIT 16.2
Proposal *(continued)*

GRANT PROPOSAL

COMPUTER ASSISTED INSTRUCTION IN BUSINESS COMMUNICATION

B. Project Objectives

1. College courses in business communication currently require instructors to spend excessive amounts of time grading papers, but also suffer from
a lack of uniformity in grading standards from instructor to instructor. A
CAI program in business communication would benefit students by allowing them
to develop required skills at their own rate in a nonthreatening atmosphere
and by providing consistent and predictable objectives. The program would be
adaptable to freshman composition, report writing, and technical writing
courses as well as to education and training programs in business and industry. The materials would also benefit teachers by allowing them to spend
less time evaluating written work and more time developing creative teaching
strategies and by helping establish uniform grading standards for written
business messages. We anticipate improving student performance and reducing
teacher-evaluated papers by 50% at the same time.

Current CAI materials in business communication and related areas are of
two types: simple drill and practice/tutorial programs (Atari) or sophisti-
cated writing analysis programs (GMI's "star"). The first type is not well
suited to teaching the complex concepts of college-level writing. The second
does not include an instructional component and is not well suited to the
hardware available at most colleges and universities.

Our project will be the first to provide both instruction and evaluation
for written material in a form suitable for use on microcomputers.

The CAI package will use computer assisted testing, tutorials, and simulations (with the emphasis on simulations) to teach the concepts. The major
simulation used throughout the seven-unit package will be the student's
development from an entry-level employee to one of the senior officers of
a company. At each stage, the "employee" will be asked to write certain
types of business communication (e.g., positive, neutral, and negative
messages). Depending on how well the student does, the student could be
dropped back to a previous unit, given a PERK (e.g., car, salary increase),
or moved to a high level position (the next unit). Point totals will be
kept so that some elements of a game are introduced into the package.

The tutorials will be written as simulations. For example, in preparing
a negative response letter, the student will be asked to assemble a message
from a numbered set of sentences. The computer will then evaluate content
and structure of the letter based on variance from an optimal letter.

A special algorithm will evaluate letters composed by students in response
to problems posed in the manual. This algorithm will evaluate for writing
style, correctness, and message structure. It will offer many of the features
included in more complex programs without requiring an extensive internal
memory.

EXHIBIT 16.2
Proposal *(continued)*

  2. The product will consist of a workbook (containing instructions, information needed to understand the simulations, and problems) and a set of diskettes (containing quiz materials, PERK information, and evaluations). The
package will also contain a diskette for user-orientation and record keeping
and a teacher's diskette, which will provide a profile of class progress.

  The initial program will be designed especially for the nearly 500,000
college students who take a business communication course each year. Subsequent programs will address the needs of education and training programs in
business, report writing, and English composition.

  3. The workbook and diskettes will be published and marketed by a commercial publisher of college textbooks.

C. The Development Plan

  1. The development of this package will follow a standard systems approach
as espoused by W. J. Dick (see Bibliography). A set of goals and objectives
has been written and mockups of standards are being constructed to enable the
content experts to visualize a completed unit. When a microcomputer becomes
available, a prototype unit (or prototype sections of units) will be developed.
This prototype will be evaluated for its ability to teach, for its ease of use,
and for its ability to motivate students. Results of this evaluation will be
incorporated into a fully developed pilot version of the package. Again, a
formative evaluation will be performed on this version, measuring the same
characteristics as for the prototype. Additional evaluation will compare the
CAI exercises with "standard" exercises used in classes at MBC. Finally, a
production version of this package will be developed incorporating the results
of the pilot version evaluation and a final evaluation will be performed.

  2. Robert Farentine, Ph.D.   10 hours a week
      Caroline Phillipsm, Ed.D.   10 hours a week
      Melanie Schlosser, Ph.D.   10 hours a week
      Scott Steele, Ph.D.   10 hours a week
      Brenda Winter (Ph.D. candidate)   10 hours a week

  3. Assuming we receive equipment in time, we anticipate presenting a complete pilot version at the International Convention of the American Business
Communication Association in October 19xx in New York City. Our time table
is as follows:

  Times (in months)

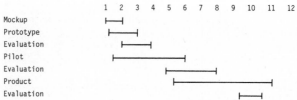

EXHIBIT 16.2
Proposal *(continued)*

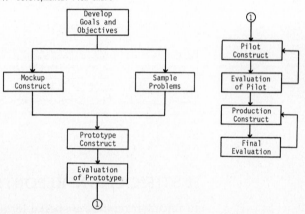

4. Developmental Flow Chart

D. Equipment Justification

The equipment listed in A2 is the minimum necessary for creating and evaluating the materials. Because evaluation at prototype and pilot stages is essential to the software development, two systems are necessary to permit a sufficient number of students to complete testing procedures. Two disk drives are necessary because the program will be designed to minimize the number of disk changes. One disk will contain the program; the other will contain the files.

E. Available Facilities

The Department of Business Education and Administrative Services, Midwestern Business College, Chicago, IL 60055, will make office space available for the equipment.

The Department will provide access to appropriate utilities for operation of the equipment, and maintenance is available locally through The Computer Room, 455 N. Michigan, Chicago, IL 60657.

F. Evaluation Procedures

As stated in C1, the development plan includes several evaluative components. In addition, The Dryden Press will conduct a market survey and arrange

EXHIBIT 16.2
Proposal *(continued)*

```
        for outside agencies to test and evaluate the program at prototype and pilot
        stages.

    G.  Background Information

        1.  Resumes of key personnel are attached.
        2.  A bibliography of key articles is attached.
        3.  A description of Midwestern Business College is attached.
        4.  The required letter of approval is attached.

    Attachments omitted to save space.
```

JUSTIFICATION REPORTS

Justification reports, a special form of recommendation report, are another report form that contains a persuasive element. Unlike proposals, which are written from one individual or organization to another, justification reports remain within the writer's organization.

Typical recommendation reports are written when management has observed a problem (perhaps one previously mentioned in an informational report) and has requested a recommendation. Justification reports are unsolicited recommendation reports.

The writer initiates a justification report when she or he observes a problem and wishes to recommend a solution. Many companies have established specific formats and guidelines for unsolicited recommendation reports. In the absence of such guidelines, be sure to cover the following topics:

Purpose   What are you recommending? What problem will your recommendation solve?

Advantages   What will your organization gain if your recommendation is accepted? Be specific about costs (initial and continuing) and savings.

Method   How will you implement your recommendation? What procedures will you use?

Conclusions   How do you know that your recommendation will result in the anticipated savings? The conclusions should *justify* the recommendation.

Discussion Amplify the preceding sections by including information about the history of the problem, previous attempts to solve it, alternative solutions, and secondary benefits that might result.

EXHIBIT 16.3
Justification Report

PC Form 30-30
Rev 4-80

Parker Corporation
Interoffice Correspondence

TO: Alice Ferrick   Copies To:

FROM: Donald Persing

DATE: October 14, 1982

SUBJECT: Purchase of a Comp 600 Phototypesetter

Recommendation[a]

I recommend that we purchase a Comp 600 phototypesetter for use in the Communications Department. A Comp 600 will save Parker approximately $2,500 a month in fees to outside suppliers. The initial investment of $32,500 would be recovered in less than 15 months.

Cost and Savings

The purchase cost of a Comp 600 is $32,500. The annual service contract is $1,200, and typical costs for supplies will amount to $2,300 a month. The Comp 600 will allow us to do in-house all the art work currently being sent to outside suppliers. Appendix A* lists the art projects completed over the last quarter showing fees paid and estimated labor and supplies costs for the Comp 600. The mean figures are as follows:

		Comp 600	
Supplier Fee (Paid)	Labor		Supplies
	1 1/2 hours ($32)		$145
$630	$177		

As we have between four and seven projects each month requiring art, the Comp 600 should easily be able to save us $2,500 a month. That saving, plus the investment tax credit and standard depreciation, should make the Comp 600 a good investment.

Procedure

Because the Comp 600 does represent a substantial investment, I recommend that we initially lease with the option of buying. A three-month lease will cost $2,700, all of which will be applicable to the purchase price if we decide to purchase before 90 days expire.

The lease period would allow us to obtain a more accurate fix on costs and would also permit us to evaluate the versatility and quality of work of the Comp 600.

_____
*Appendices omitted to save space.

[a]Whenever your recommendation is the most important part of your report, consider putting it in the first sentence. Delay making your recommendation only when the reader would react negatively to it unless you provide good reasons to support it first.

EXHIBIT 16.3
Justification Report *(continued)*

Alice Ferrick   October 14, 1982   2

<u>Conclusions</u>

Should the Comp 600 perform as expected, Parker could save $30,000 a year and
have better control over the production of art work.

<u>Discussion</u>

The Comp 600 phototypesetter is a quality piece of equipment manufactured by
Redkey Printing and Electronics. Appendix B contains Redkey's descriptive
brochure, and Appendix C is a letter I received about the Comp 600 from Terry
McDonald, Vice-President of Corporate Communications, Beta-Naught, Inc.

Installation of the equipment could take place three weeks after we sign the
lease-to-buy agreement. Redkey will provide 15 hours of instruction covering
operation and routine maintenance for three employees. I suggested that David
Winesoup be placed in charge of the Comp 600, with Sally Meyers and Roger
Bently also being trained to use it.

STAFF REPORTS

Although the term *staff report* may be applied to almost any report a
supervisor's staff produces for him or her, it is most often used to
indicate a recommendation report requested by a supervisor or manager. Length, format, and components of staff reports will vary widely
depending on the situation. Exhibit 16.4 illustrates one possibility.

EXHIBIT 16.4
Staff Report

Specialized Format[a]

DATE: August 2, 1979

SUBJECT: P.C. #12-79-22, Park-Emerson Rezoning

APPLICANT: Stanley G. Hagarty

OWNERS: James S. Gilley, Jr. & Hoyt L. Pitrim

LOCATION: Eastside of South Park Street, generally between Emerson
                   and Maple Streets

CURRENT ZONING: Zone 6 (Apartment-Hotel District) and
                   Zone 7 (Dwelling-Apartment District)

PETITIONED
ZONING: Zone 5A (Professional Office District)

ACREAGE: 1.9±acres

SURROUNDING
ZONING: North--Zone 6
                   South--Zone 6 and 7
                   East --Zone 7
                   West --Zone 4

SURROUNDING
LAND USE: North--Single-Family Homes & Vacant Land
                   South--Vacant Land
                   East --Single-Family Homes & Vacant Land
                   West --Commercial Uses

CURRENT LAND
USE OF SUBJECT
PARCEL: Vacant Land

LAND USE PLAN
RECOMMENDATION: Residential Low Density

ZONING HISTORY: The Subject Parcels have been Zone 6 and 7 since 1954.

INTENT OF
APPLICANT: To construct offices on the subject site.

STAFF RECOM-
MENDATIONS: The Planning Division recommends approval of the request from
                   Zone 6 to Zone 5A, excepting the parcel located in Zone 7
                   fronting Park Street for the following reasons:

                   1. Low Density Residential Land Use as recommended in the
                      Land Use Plan would not be reasonable for this site in
                      terms of traffic noise generated by South Park Street.
                      It is not likely that single-family or low density resi-
                      dential development would locate on this particular site
                      due to the size of the site.

[a]Note the specialized format. The readers of this report would be familiar with the format and would appreciate being able to find essential information quickly and easily. Note also that the discussion follows the recommendations so that only those readers who are concerned about the rationale for the recommendations need to read the supporting reasons.

EXHIBIT 16.4
Staff Report *(continued)*

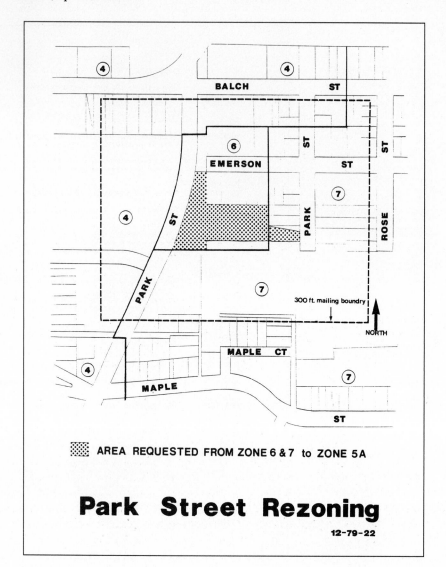

AREA REQUESTED FROM ZONE 6 & 7 to ZONE 5A

Park Street Rezoning

12-79-22

EXHIBIT 16.4
Staff Report *(continued)*

2. Conditions have changed in the area since 1954 when Zones 6 and 7 were designated as the appropriate zoning districts. In terms of change, Park Street was widened from 2 to 4 lanes and the Jewel-Osco shopping center was constructed directly west of the subject parcel. Little or no residential housing has developed in this area since 1954.

3. The uses permitted in Zone 5A would be reasonable for this particular site and would not adversely affect the area or existing neighborhood. Zone 5A uses are low intensity type uses and would not have an impact on the adjacent area.

4. Zone 5A would provide a transition between Park Street and the neighborhood to the East and North.

5. The City of Randolph currently has a very low vacancy rate for existing office space. The Randolph Gazette reported in an article on July 15, 1979, that the current vacancy rate is between 1 and 2 percent.

6. The subject site is adjacent to the Crosstown Commercial node. The Comprehensive Plan indicates that this node should be maintained as a community shopping center-office park area; however, Limited Commercial (office use) is the most reasonable use for this particular site.

7. We further recommend that the existing Zone 7 parcel fronting on Park Street remain in Zone 7.

FEASIBILITY REPORTS

A feasibility report is designed to answer questions about the possibility and desirability of understanding a particular course of action. It may be simply interpretive (presenting and explaining the data) or analytical (including conclusions and recommendations).

Feasibility reports are usually preliminary investigations designed to answer questions about *whether* an action would be possible or desirable rather than about *how* an objective should be accomplished. A feasibility report will provide the direction for continued exploration of the problem or experimentation with possible solutions. Exhibit 16.5 shows an example of a feasibility report.

EXHIBIT 16.5
Feasibility Report in Personalized Letter Format

Pro-Ease Communications

19 Kalona Avenue
Des Moines, IA 50312
344–5555

January 27, 1983

Mr. Scott Perrin, President
Perrin and Associates
2020 Johnston Road
Des Moines, IA 50324

Yes, Mr. Perrin,

it would be possible to install a satellite antenna system on top of the Perrin Bank Building.

The installation, however, would not be easy. Because both installation and maintenance of any of our satellite antenna systems require easy access, the current stairwell would need to be remodeled, and the 8' vertical ladder should be eliminated and replaced with conventional stairs. Further, access to the stairway should not be through the vice-presidents' office complex.

I believe these alterations are necessary if you are to obtain full use of and satisfaction from your own satellite antenna.

Should you decide to pursue intallation, I will be glad to work with the contractor of your choice in preparing your building for the antenna.

Give me a call.

Howard Severson, Jr.
Howard Severson, Jr.
President

Personalized Opening Phrase[a]

Personalized Closing[b]

[a]Personalized letter format omits the salutation but uses the reader's name in a brief opening phrase that simulates the appearance of the salutation. Some people consider this style friendlier than the traditional, ''Dear Mr. Perrin.''

[b]The personalized format also omits the complimentary close, substituting a brief, appropriate phrase.

SHORT INFORMATIONAL AND ANALYTICAL REPORTS

Short reports are far more common in business than long reports. In general, the length of a report is directly related to the complexity of the problem. As the problem becomes more complex, the coverage of it necessarily becomes more complex and detailed. Short reports, whether informational or analytical, are usually (though not always) less formal than long reports.

Because they are shorter and less formal, they often omit many of the preliminary and supplemental parts included in formal reports. They will also require fewer levels of headings and may eliminate introductions and summaries. While each short report will have different requirements depending on the situation and context, consider making the following changes in presentation form as the report becomes shorter and less formal.

Step 1:
    a.   Omit the title fly
    b.   Omit the letter of authorization
    c.   Include the synopsis within the letter of transmittal

Step 2:
    a.   Omit the table of contents
    b.   Omit the letter of transmittal, and provide the synopsis in the introductory paragraph

Step 3:
    Use letter or memo format (which eliminates the title page)

Exhibits 16.6 and 16.7 illustrate short informational and analytical reports.

EXHIBIT 16.6
Short Informational Report in Caption-Style Format

Computer Date Form[a]

Harwick Word Processing Consultants Ltd.
12302A Jasper Avenue, Edmonton, Alberta T5N 3K5
(403) 488—0752

harwick
Word Processing

1981 11 18

Joel P. Bowman
College of Business
Dept. of Bus. Ed. and Admin. Svcs.
Western Michigan University
Kalamazoo, Michigan 49008

Subject: Caption-style Report Format

PURPOSE

This is in response to the queries in your 3 November 1981 letter concerning the "report format" used in my letter to the committee.

NOT AN ORIGINAL IDEA

My first task at Syncrude was to develop the standards for technical manuals.

One of our owners, Esso--the Canadian Exxon affiliate--used a layout similar to this for its manuals.

After researching readability and legibility-- boy! can Journal of Applied Psychology articles be boring--I modified the format somewhat and adopted it for use in Syncrude.

GOOD POINTS

For manuals--and reports--captions allow for creation of an index and table of contents. The writing of captions is much more rigorous when they have to be used in this manner.

We teach people that the captions function like headlines in a newspaper. As such, they must be descriptive of the material which follows.

Captions really help when you're trying to find specific information--especially when you're referring to a previously read document. (One accounting firm using the style cites the biggest advantage as being able to find infor- mation fast--like the "note to file" on the conversation with a given client on a given topic.)

[a]Note the computer date form. Many companies use this date form for internal messages and on company forms. It is not used much in correspondence or in business reports.
Source: Report courtesy of Raymond W. Beswick, Partner, Harwick Word Processing Consultants.

EXHIBIT 16.6

Short Informational Report in Caption-Style Format *(continued)*

GOOD POINTS
(continued)

We teach people to read the subject titles and then the captions. This gives them a good idea of what is being covered and in what order. (Reading speed is increased if these are known.) It also allows readers to pick-and-choose what to read--for example, why would a subject matter expert want to read something captioned "basic technical descrip-tion"?

The layout allows the text to be in about 4 inch lines. This is an ideal length for speed reading. (Look at the line length of a pocket book sometime.) The layout is psychologically good because the page is not intimidating to look at--compare it with a page of "wall-to-wall" words.

BAD POINTS

Using the layout does take more paper--but we consider this to be more than offset by the benefits.

Also, "conservatives" rebel at the sight of this unconventional page layout. (One of our clients used it for a very conservative client of theirs and received a call stating that the report was unacceptable in this format!)

MEMOS AND REPORT, TOO

As I was charged with developing spoken and written communication courses as well as the manuals program at Syncrude, it was "a natural" to consider using the layout for letters, memos, and reports.

Letters can use it but you really have to know your audience. Often, we'll use a conven-tionally set-up covering letter and attach a "report" in caption style.

The format is not universally used in Syncrude memos and reports. However, anything which is typeset automatically goes into the format.

OTHER USES

I've alluded to several other users. We've installed caption style in several government departments, accounting firms, oil companies, and a firm of insurance adjusters.

EXHIBIT 16.6
Short Informational Report in Caption-Style Format *(continued)*

OTHER USES   (There's an interesting anecdote associated
(continued)   with the insurance adjusters. We asked them
          if we could use them as a reference. They
          said, basically, "hell, no. We've got a com-
          petitive edge using this writing style and
          layout and we don't want to lose it!")

If you want any more information, just let me know.

Ray

Raymond W. Beswick
Partner

P.S. How do you like the new letterhead?

EXHIBIT 16.7
Short Analytical Report

ADDING LIGHT GAUGE
PREFINISHED FRAMES
TO CURRENT LINE

Prepared for
Norman R. Menning, President
Sanders Steel Company
Fairview, New Jersey

Prepared by
Andrea Brody
Central Marketing Group
Detroit, Michigan

12 September 1982

EXHIBIT 16.7
Short Analytical Report *(continued)*

12 September 1982

Mr. Norman R. Menning, President
Sanders Steel Company
Fairview, NJ 08606

Dear Mr. Menning:

Here is the report you requested on 22 June assessing the potential of a light gauge (18-22) prefinished steel door frame to
supplement your current line of heavy duty frames.

I recommend that Sanders either begin producing the light gauge
steel frames or acquire a manufacturing facility currently producing them.

Our study reveals that light gauge prefinished frames are gaining
market share, especially on the West Coast and in Florida and
Georgia. The market for the lighter frames is already extensive,
and it seems to be growing as well, as prefinished steel frames
are replacing conventional door frames in many construction markets.

The light gauge prefinished steel door frames are as functional
and long lasting as conventional frames; plus they offer lower
price, ease of installation, a variety of colors, and years of
maintenance-free operation.

I have enjoyed preparing this report, Mr. Menning. Please let
me know when I can help again.

Sincerely,

Andrea Brody

Andrea Brody
Market Researcher

EXHIBIT 16.7

Short Analytical Report *(continued)*

ADDING LIGHT GAUGE PREFINISHED
FRAMES TO CURRENT LINE

I recommend that the Sanders Steel Company either begin manufacturing light gauge (18-22) prefinished steel door frames or
acquire a manufacturing facility currently producing them.

This report is the result of a study authorized on 22 June
1982 by Mr. Norman R. Menning, President of Sanders Steel Company.

Purpose and Scope

As a result of loss of market share, especially on the West
Coast, Sanders Steel Company hired Central Marketing Group to
study the current and future impact of light gauge prefinished
steel door frames on several construction markets. The objectives of the study were to identify and define:

- Market size.
- Product features desired.
- Principal producers.
- Major end-use markets.
- Representative prices.
- Future trends in product use.

The scope of the study did not include a detailed explanation
of market size and trends for conventional, heavy gauge (14, 16,
and 18) unfinished steel door frames.

Methodology

A sample of 600 door frame distributors was selected to
include an equal number of dealers handling Sanders conventional
frames and those handling the light gauge prefinished frames only.
State populations and predicted growth rates were used to determine the number of dealers selected from each state. Table 1,
Appendix A,* shows the breakdown by geographic area.

I mailed questionnaires to the dealers on 15 July and began
phoning those who had not responded on 15 August. By 1 September,
I had received complete information from 372 dealers, an ample
number on which to base predictions.

_____
*Appendix material omitted to save space.

EXHIBIT 16.7
Short Analytical Report *(continued)*

2

I tabulated each question by geographic region, distributor status, frame types handled, and dollar volume of sales of pre-finished light gauge and conventional frames. The questionnaire and tabulations are presented in Appendix B.

Findings

The questionnaire revealed the following facts about the dealers and the market for light gauge steel prefinished door frames:

1. The survey revealed that 87.2 percent of the dealers stock both conventional and light gauge steel door frames. Only those dealers who do not stock wood doors carry the conventional frames only.

2. The average dealer has a sales volume of $182,000 a year, with approximately 17 percent accounted for by steel door frames of all types.

3. Those dealers handling both types of door frames reported that the light frames accounted for 23 percent of their door frame sales.

4. A majority (67 percent) of the dealers prefer handling the light gauge prefinished steel frames. The features most often cited were price, ease of installation, absence of maintenance, colors, and availability.

5. The average cost of a prefinished frame to a dealer is $23.47. The selling price to contractors is $33.39, which provides a mark-up of 42 percent. The cost to dealers for prefinished steel with a high quality door is 5 percent less than the cost of a prehung wood unit.

6. Office buildings and high-rise apartment buildings are the most common end-use application.

7. Residential use has increased by 12 percent each year since 1979 in spite of the housing slump caused by the recession.

8. Increased urbanization and the continual increasing costs of wood and the labor associated with wood products will ensure a growth market for light gauge steel prefinished doors.

Producers

The two largest producers of light gauge prefinished steel doors are Barnes (Sunnyvale, CA) and Advance (Dallas, TX), with 38.6 percent and 29.5 percent of the market, respectively.

EXHIBIT 16.7
Short Analytical Report *(continued)*

```
                                                                    3

                           Conclusions

         Based on the sample, I conclude that total sales of conven-
    tional and prefinished frames will amount to $5.6 million.  Of
    this, prefinished frames will account for close to $2 million.

         Dealers uniformly predicted that increased urban construc-
    tion consisting of high density housing and office complexes
    would increase the demand for light gauge prefinished steel
    door frames.  Statistics compiled by the Federal Government
    and such publications as Predicasts support dealer predictions
    (see Appendix C).

         Dealers currently carrying Sanders conventional steel frames
    indicated that they would prefer stocking prefinished frames
    manufactured by Sanders rather than the brand they now carry.


                          Recommendations

         Sanders should begin producing light gauge prefinished steel
    frames or acquire a facility currently manufacturing such frames.
```

EVALUATIONS

Procedures, products, projects, and people are all required to undergo occasional evaluations. Someone with expertise in a given area will be asked to report on the adequacy of something or somebody to perform a given job.

Procedures, Products, and Projects

Evaluations of procedures, products, and projects are almost always analytical reports in which the writer, because of her or his experience in an area, examines the procedure or item in question and renders an opinion about its adequacy. Recommendations for changes or improvements are usually included as well.

A company might, for example, hire a consultant to evaluate its computer system to determine whether a new system would be a good investment. Or an organization might hire a time-and-motion specialist to evaluate work flow within a plant. The length and formality of evaluation reports will vary according to the situation and people involved. Exhibit 16.8 is an example of an evaluation of a product.

EXHIBIT 16.8
Evaluation of a Product

February 11, 1982

TO: Mort Wetherspoon
           Bill Warren
           Lee Rauch
           Duane Kohr

FROM: Mark Schadlein

SUBJECT: ARTIC BONE REMOVER/GRINDER EVALUATION

On February 6, 1980, testing of the Artic bone remover/grinder was concluded. The decision was made to return the unit to Artic. Its bone removing capabilities were inferior to the Weiler system currently in use.

Testing included evaluation of product quality, grinding rates, and bone removing capabilities. Tests were conducted at Toledo on January 22, 23, and February 6.

Results

On January 22, approximately 500 pounds of meat were ground through the Artic. Grinding rate and finished product were determined acceptable by Toledo Quality Control personnel and me.

On January 23 and February 6, comparisons were made between the Artic bone remover/grinder and the Weiler bone remover/ grinder. On each testing date 6,000 pounds of meat were ground through both the Artic and Weiler grinders. "Like" preblends were used in each test situation. On January 23, ejected material flow rates were set at 8#/1000# on each system. This was done in an effort to minimize processing variables and obtain a comparison strictly on bone removing capabilities. Results from this testing showed that the Weiler system removed more bone than the Artic.

On February 6, a similar test was conducted. For this test, however, the Weiler ejected material flow rate was set at 8#/1000# and the Artic flow rate was set at 2#/1000#, the recommended setting for the Artic. Again, the Weiler system proved superior in bone removal. The following table summarizes the Artic evaluation.

EXHIBIT 16.8
Evaluation of a Product *(continued)*

```
ARTIC BONE REMOVER/GRINDER EVALUATION
Page 2
February 11, 1982
```

Date	Grinder	Preblends	Grinding Rate (lbs./minute)	Ejected Material Flow Chart	Avg. Bone Removed (grams/1000# ground)
1/23	Weiler	3YL 0018 03 3XF 0021 04	350*	8#/1000#	4.8
	Artic	3YL 0018 03 3XF 0021 04	480	8#/1000#	0.5
2/6	Weiler	3YL 0032 07 3XF 0032 05	350*	8#/1000#	9.4
	Artic	3YL 0032 07 3XF 0032 05	495	2#/1000#	0.5

*Typical grinding rate for Weiler grinders at Toledo.

<u>Conclusions</u>

The Artic bone remover/grinder is an impressive piece of machinery. It can produce a quality product (from an appearance standpoint) at a high grinding rate. Within Eckrich processing parameters, however, its bone removing capabilities are inferior to those of the Weiler system.

Further testing in bone and gristle reduction will concentrate on the 1/2-inch grind size of the 3YL lean preblend.

If you have any questions, please let me know.

MS/bme

Personnel

Nearly everyone who works in an organization is evaluated on a regular basis. Most organizations provide forms to help managers be complete and objective. While the topics covered by the form will vary from organization to organization and from occupation to occupation, most cover the following areas:

Knowledge of job duties/responsibilities

Quality of work

Quantity of work

Reliability

Ability to follow instructions

Initiative

Attitude toward work, others, and the organization
Promotability

If you ever need to evaluate a subordinate without a form, use the categories above as headings and provide objective and specific comments for each area. Examples showing strengths and weaknesses in each area are helpful. Memo format would be appropriate in most organizations. Exhibit 16.9 illustrates a report evaluating an employee.

EXHIBIT 16.9
Report Evaluating an Employee

BORROUGHS
A DIVISION OF LEAR SIEGLER, INC.
3002 N. BURDICK STREET · KALAMAZOO, MICHIGAN 49007

PERFORMANCE
APPRAISAL
INTERVIEW

MANAGEMENT
PERSONNEL

Employee Name:_____

Position:_____

Date:_____ Review Period:_____

Date of Interview:_____

Appraiser:_____

Employee Signature:_____

Source: Form courtesy of Burroughs Division/Lear Siegler, Inc.

EXHIBIT 16.9
Report Evaluating an Employee *(continued)*

INSTRUCTIONS TO APPRAISOR
AND APPRAISEE:

The appraisal you are about to record and discuss is intended to be a summarization of supervisory judgments about performance - that is, about how work is achieved rather than about quantitative results as such. The appraisal process is intended to result in: (1) a clear understanding of how performance is judged, and (2) mutually understood goals and plans about any changes in future work performance and/or change in duties.

The appraisal is a result of judgments, not of measurements. Therefore, the appraisal judgments should be viewed as approximations rather than as precise numbers even though numbers are used in the scales for convenience in locating or representing judgments made.

RATING LEVELS

OUTSTANDING (9 - 10):   Exceptional, superior, near perfect.

EXCELLENT (7 - 8):   Considerably above average.

SATISFACTORY (5 - 6):   Meeting acceptable standards.

LESS THAN SATISFACTORY (3 - 4):   Not quite meeting acceptable standards.

NOT ACCEPTABLE (1 - 2):   Serious deficiency.

N. A.:   Not applicable.

EXHIBIT 16.9
Report Evaluating an Employee *(continued)*

PERFORMANCE FACTORS

COMMUNICATION:
Expressing points of view and information
clearly and concisely in written and   RATING LEVELS
oral forms.

0 .. / .. / .. / .. / .. / .. / . . / . . / . . / . . 10

CONTROL:
Effective use of assigned people, equipment
and staff while meeting cost and quality
standards.

0 .. / .. / .. / .. / .. / .. / . . / . . / . . / . . 10

DECISION-MAKING:
Screening facts and making sound,
timely decisions.

0 .. / .. / .. / .. / .. / .. / . . / . . / . . / . . 10

DELEGATION:
Assigning work and authority appropriately
to others with appropriate follow-up.

0 .. / .. / .. / .. / .. / .. / . . / . . / . . / . . 10

DEVELOPMENT OF PERSONNEL:
Effectively selecting, counseling and training
subordinates, collaborating in plans for their
professional and personal growth.

0 .. / .. / .. / .. / .. / .. / . . / . . / . . / . . 10

PLANNING:
Arranging work systematically and in
practical ways, establishing priorities
for efficiency.

0 .. / .. / .. / .. / .. / .. / . . / . . / . . / . . 10

PROBLEM ANALYSIS:
Breaking problem tasks or situations into
essential components logically and systematically, gathering facts and evaluating
them accurately.

0 .. / .. / .. / .. / .. / .. / . . / . . / . . / . . 10

QUALITY OF WORK:
Thoroughness, accuracy and overall caliber
of completed work.

0 .. / .. / .. / .. / .. / .. / . . / . . / . . / . . 10

QUANTITY OF WORK:
Accomplishments in relation to requirements;
results in relation to objectives and timeliness.

0 .. / .. / .. / .. / .. / .. / . . / . . / . . / . . 10

EXHIBIT 16.9
Report Evaluating an Employee *(continued)*

PERSONAL FACTORS

ABILITY TO WORK WITH OTHERS:
Establishing and maintaining productive
working relationships with others.

RATING LEVELS

0 .. / .. / . / .. / .. / .. / . . / . . / . / . . / . .. 10

ADAPTABILITY:
Reaction to change while working
towards desired results.

0 .. / .. / . ./ .. / .. / .. / . . / . . / . / . . / . .. 10

ATTITUDE:
Commitment to and concern about
company doing well.

0 .. / .. / .. / .. / .. / .. / . . / . . / . / . . / . .. 10

CREATIVITY:
Ability to devise improved or new
procedures or applications in pursuit
of new results.

0 .. / .. / .. / .. / .. / .. / . . / . . / . / . . / . .. 10

INITIATIVE:
Self-starting in dealing with work tasks
or problems.

0 .. / .. / .. / .. / .. / .. / . . / . . / . / . . / . .. 10

JUDGMENT:
Identification and evaluation of alternative courses of action towards desired
results.

0 .. / .. / .. / .. / .. / .. / . . / . . / . / . . / . .. 10

LEADERSHIP:
Influencing subordinates and associates
toward accomplishment of desired results.

0 .. / .. / .. / .. / .. / .. / . . / . . / . / . . / . .. 10

PERSISTENCE:
Pursuit of progress towards results even when
encountering lack of interest and/or
opposition.

0 .. / .. / .. / .. / .. / .. / . . / . . / . / . . / . .. 10

PERSUASIVENESS:
Influencing behavior changes on the part
of other people.

0 .. / .. / .. / .. / .. / .. / . . / . . / . / . . / . .. 10

SELF-CONFIDENCE:
Self-assuredness, including under pressure;
sense of personal competence.

0 .. / .. / .. / .. / .. / .. / . . / . . / . / . . / . .. 10

SELF-DEVELOPMENT:
Accomplishing self-improvement with goals.

0 .. / .. / .. / .. / .. / .. / . . / . . / . / . . / . .. 10

EXHIBIT 16.9
Report Evaluating an Employee *(continued)*

CONCLUSIONS: This section is intended as a vehicle for summarizing the results of the appraisal process overall.

SIGNIFICANT MAJOR ACCOMPLISHMENTS is intended as an opportunity for the supervisor to highlight particular accomplishments by the employee which may not be visible on the Factor ratings. Here there might be elaboration of the accomplishments referred to in any given Factor rating so as to amplify the meaning of the rating given.

DEVELOPMENTS OR IMPROVEMENTS SINCE LAST REVIEW should be used to call attention to Factor ratings which reflect particularly noteworthy changes in performance since the last review. Comments about the extent to which the individual may have (or has not) achieved developmental goals and objectives set previously may also be included here.

DEVELOPMENT GOALS AND PLANS is where statements of what the employee is going to try to do more or less of, in some particular behavior, as referred to in any of the Factor ratings. Please try to be specific about what behavior is being focused on for change.

CAREER ADVANCEMENT POTENTIAL should include any comments about this aspect of the employee's future career as viewed by either employee and/or supervisor. This is a very sensitive topic and should be addressed with appropriate care to be realistic yet try to avoid encouraging or discouring an employee to excess.

LIKELY REPLACEMENTS is intended to contain a list of other specific positions within the company from which the employee's position could realistically be filled, as viewed by both supervisor and employee.

OVERALL PERFORMANCE RATING should contain reference to the employee's performance as generally being classified as Outstanding, Excellent, Satisfactory, Less Than Satisfactory, or Not Acceptable, along with any appropriate elaborative remarks deemed relevant by the supervisor.

EXHIBIT 16.9
Report Evaluating an Employee *(continued)*

<u>CONCLUSIONS</u>

SIGNIFICANT MAJOR ACCOMPLISHMENTS:

_____
_____
_____
_____

DEVELOPMENTS OR IMPROVEMENTS SINCE LAST REVIEW:

_____
_____
_____
_____

DEVELOPMENT GOALS AND PLANS:

_____
_____
_____
_____

CAREER ADVANCEMENT POTENTIAL:

Employee Views: _____
_____
_____

Supervisor Views: _____
_____
_____

EXHIBIT 16.9
Report Evaluating an Employee *(continued)*

LIKELY REPLACEMENTS:

_____

_____

OVERALL PERFORMANCE RATING:

_____

_____

OVERALL COMMENTS:

    Supervisor:_____

    _____

    Employee:_____

    _____

ACCIDENT REPORTS

Most organizations have specific forms for use in reporting accidents. Because accidents, especially those involving serious injury, are traumatic, the forms can be an important aid to objectivity. Accuracy and objectivity are the two critical requirements for accident reports.

When you must report an accident and you do not have a form, be sure to cover the reporter's six "serving men":

Who: Who was involved? Who else might have observed the accident? Who might have had difficulties with any equipment involved previously? Who was notified first?

What: What actually happened? What equipment was involved? What events immediately preceded the accident?

Where: Where did the accident happen? Where were the people involved immediately before the accident occurred? Where were they afterward?

When: At what time did the accident occur? In what order did events take place? How long did it take for help to arrive?

Why: Why did the accident happen? What seemed to be the cause of the accident?

How: How did one thing lead to another? How could similar accidents be avoided?

EXHIBIT 16.10
Accident Report

SANDERS STEEL COMPANY
Fairview, New Jersey 08606

ACCIDENT REPORT

1. Type of Accident: Personal injury. Hand caught in metal press.

2. Data and Time Accident Occured: December 15, 19xx, at 2:00 p.m.

3. Personnel Involved: Charles Marczynski

4. Witnesses: None

5. Details: Marczynski was cleaning the press when the brake slipped, and his hand was caught between the ram and the table.

6. Cause of Accident: Human error caused the accident even if the brake is defective. The operation manual specified that the press must be turned off for cleaning.

7. Medical Disposition: Marczynski is in the hospital. He will lose at least three fingers and will be unable to work for at least six months.

8. Recommendations: New warning labels should be installed on all presses to remind operators to turn presses off before cleaning.

ANNUAL REPORTS

Individuals, departments (and other divisions), and organizations are usually required to prepare annual reports. Annual reports are essentially informational progress reports that provide a record of activities over a given time. They may include budget or other financial statements, and they may include plans for the next reporting period.

Individuals and departments usually report according to objectives set and met, including explanations for those objectives not met and statements of progress on long-term objectives. Both individuals and departments may need to account for expenditures, and departments would need to account for changes in personnel, equipment, or operating procedures.

Most organizations also prepare annual reports that present information about the status of the organization to interested parties. Personnel, equipment, procedures, financial data (assets, liabilities, income, expenditures, projected income, and projected expenditures), and other details influencing the organization should all be included. Length and format vary greatly from organization to organization. Churches, for example, might provide parishioners with an inexpensively reproduced report only a few pages long containing news of members, donations to charities, work on the church, and the like. A Fortune 500 company, on the other hand, would prepare an impressive package of accomplishments, plans, and financial status.

LIBRARY RESEARCH REPORTS

All complete analytical reports begin with a review of secondary sources. If the procedure required to gather primary data is either expensive or time consuming, the results of library research may be presented first. Management can then base its decision on whether to proceed with primary research on the materials gathered from secondary sources.

Library research reports may be informational (presenting only that information gathered from secondary sources), interpretive (explaining the relevance of the information to the writer's organization), or analytical (drawing conclusions and making recommendations). The format may vary from informal (memo) to formal depending on the length and importance of the topic. Because documentation plays such an important role in these reports, make sure that you use the most reliable sources available, that you report on them accurately, and that you cite them correctly.

REPORTS OF EXPERIMENTAL RESULTS

Different subjects will have different requirements for reporting experimental results, and if you are involved in experimental research, you will need to have copies of appropriate laboratory, publication, and style manuals. We will focus here on those factors common to reports of experimental results.

The objective of these reports is to convey enough information to enable a reader to replicate (duplicate) the experiment and obtain the results. For this reason, absolute accuracy in reporting the following topics is essential:

Method: *What* did you do, and *how* did you do it? Who were your subjects? How many were there? How did you select them? What were their demographic characteristics?
What materials did you use? Be specific about even seemingly ordinary details (not *a chair*, but *a typical classroom chair with attached right hand table*). For special equipment, state the manufacturer's name and the model number. What procedure did you follow? What were your variables? What changes did you introduce? What measurements did you apply?

Results: What were the results of the experiment? Present the data without interpretation. Include appropriate tests for significance.

Discussion: Do the results support your original hypothesis? Interpret and evaluate the results, clarify any limitations in the study, and explain the significance of the results.

Documentation: Provide complete citations for all references. Use the method of citation common in your field of research.

AUDIT REPORTS

Short- and long-form audit reports are an accountant's method of verifying an inspection of a firm's financial records. The short-form report appears as a standard part in the financial section of corporate annual reports, and over the years accountants have agreed to the language illustrated in Exhibit 4.10. The long-form audit report contains more information about the audit, including tests performed and exceptions to standard accounting principles.

SPECIAL APPLICATIONS

In addition to reports, people working in business, industry, and the professions may be responsible for a wide variety of writing that calls for many of the same skills required for writing reports. Some of the more common writing tasks are journal publications, procedure manuals, job descriptions, employee publications, public relations brochures, and corporate annual reports.

Journal
Publications

Each journal has its own requirements for submitting articles for review. These requirements are usually specified on one of the first pages of each issue of the journal. Most journals will specify a style sheet for use as a guide in manuscript preparation.

In writing for publication in a journal, your purpose and audience remain the most important considerations. The editors of the journal will have a good idea of what their audience will want and expect in an article, so pay particular attention to what the editors have to say about appropriate material. If you are uncertain about the suitability of an article for a particular journal, send a letter of inquiry to the editor. If you want the journal to return your manuscript, include a postage-paid reply envelope large enough to accommodate the materials.

Procedure Manuals

Procedure manuals are a description of the process to be followed in performing a particular act. The writer needs to remember that the reader will not be familiar with the process and will need to explain each step in its proper order. Do not give in to the natural tendency to make assumptions. A new computer operator, for example, needs to be told how to turn the machine on.

Job Descriptions

Job descriptions delineate areas of responsibility. They are necessary for two reasons: first, they clarify who is to be responsible for what work; and second, they indicate what qualifications a person must have to perform the work. Job descriptions usually include the following information:

1. Job title

2. Description of primary duties

3. Description of secondary duties

4. List of required equipment and materials

5. Descriptions of special requirements

6. Job functions
   a. Supervisor
   b. Subordinates
   c. Work flow
   d. Promotional route

7. Qualifications
   a. Education
   b. Experience
   c. Required exams or licenses
   d. Special (when appropriate)
      (1) Height
      (2) Weight
      (3) Sex
      (4) Vision (color and/or acuity)
      (5) Hearing
      (6) Strength
      (7) Reflexes

**Employee
Publications**

Large organizations almost always have at least one employee publication to help communicate matters of importance to employees. Company newsletters; special brochures about insurance, new products, retirement benefits, and other items of interest; and a wide variety of announcements all help keep the organizational members working together to meet common objectives.

Most of this material is informational. It conveys accurate and reliable information to an audience that will base decisions on the information. Suppose your company provided several options for health insurance—a group program with different coverages and rates, and membership in two different health maintenance organizations. You would need to explain all the options, including their advantages and disadvantages, to the employees so that each could make a logical selection of health insurance.

**Public Relations
Materials**

Nearly every decision made in a modern organization is subject to public scrutiny. For this reason, organizations must work constantly to provide the public with accurate information about personnel, policies, procedures, projects, and plans. Large organizations usually hire public relations specialists to manage the PR function. Nevertheless, every employee will have an impact on the public's perception of the organization.

Managers especially need to ensure that the public hears about the good as well as the bad, about the achievements as well as the accidents. When a report contains information about an accomplishment or deals with an issue of importance to the community, cooperate with the PR staff in making the information available to the appropriate media.

The corporate annual report is probably the best known use of a report to convey a public relations message. Corporate annual reports are designed to provide stockholders, potential investors, employees, and interested others with an understanding of (and a favorable view of) the organization's activities and financial status.

One of the most difficult communication skills to master is the art of maintaining accuracy and reliability while presenting things in a favorable light. This can usually be accomplished by emphasizing positive factors while subordinating the negative. The use of positive language (describing a cup as half full rather than half empty) also helps. When you are tempted to omit negative information from a public report, remember that nothing is more important than your credibility. The public will never forgive being lied to. Your reports to the public should follow the same standards for accuracy and reliability that you follow in reporting to management.

SUMMARY

No two reports are identical, but some types of reports have become common because they have demonstrated their usefulness in solving certain kinds of recurring problems. Each of these types is a logical result of applying the general techniques of report writing to a specific situation.

Each organization and individual has different expectations about what a report should include. The only way to be sure that you are providing the right information is to ask.

Progress reports provide information about the progress on a project over a particular time. They vary in length from one-page summaries to book-length studies.

Proposals, whether solicited or unsolicited, are offers to solve a problem, usually in exchange for a fee. A proposal and letter of acceptance constitute a contract.

Justification reports, also known as recommendation reports, are writer-initiated efforts to convince management to solve a problem in a specific way.

A feasibility report answers questions about the possibility and desirability of undertaking a particular course of action. It may be interpretive or analytical.

Short informational and analytical reports follow all of the rules for longer reports except that as the length decreases, they omit some of the parts included in longer reports. They also tend to be less formal.

Evaluation reports discuss the adequacy of something or someone to perform a given job. Procedures, products, projects, and personnel require evaluation from time to time to see whether improvements are necessary or possible.

Accident reports are another common type. Most organizations use a form to help report accidents accurately. When no form is available, be sure to clarify who, what, when, where, why, and how.

Annual reports are prepared by individuals, departments, and organizations. They include a record of progress as measured against objectives, financial data, and plans for the future.

Library research reports are reports on secondary resources. They may be informational, interpretive, or analytical. They are useful to determine whether the time and experience of primary research would be a good investment.

Reports of experimental results may be necessary to justify a decision. Absolute accuracy is essential in reporting the method, results, and implications of the study.

Audit reports are an accountant's method for verifying an inspection of a firm's financial records. The short-form report is a standardized statement that appears in most corporate annual reports. The long-form report varies according to tests performed and to exceptions in standard accounting principles.

Those responsible for writing reports may also be responsible for journal publications, procedure manuals, job descriptions, employee publications, and public relations materials. In each of these special applications, the writer should be accurate, reliable, and complete.

EXERCISES

Review Questions

1. Why do you need to ask your supervisor for specific information about the kind of report you are to write?

2. What is a progress report, and what should it include?

3. What are the differences between solicited and unsolicited proposals?

4. What is the basic organizational pattern for a proposal?

5. Why does a writer need to be especially accurate when writing proposals?

6. In what way are justification reports recommendation reports? What makes them different?

7. What should a justification report contain?

8. What is a staff report?

9. What is a feasibility study?

10. Aside from length, what are the differences between short and long informational and analytical reports?

11. What is the function of an evaluation?

12. What are the differences in report content between evaluations of products and those of personnel?

13. What should an accident report contain?

14. What are the differences among individual, departmental, and corporate annual reports?

15. What is the main use for library research reports in business, industry, and the professions?

16. What should be included in reports of experimental results?

17. What is the function of an audit report?

18. In what way does the other writing you will be required to do on the job resemble report writing?

19. What should be included in a job description?

20. Describe and explain the public relations function of corporate annual reports and other business publications.

Problems

Many of the problems appropriate for this section are included in Appendix B, Report Problems. In addition to those problems presented explicitly, other problems are implied. In writing one of the complete analytical reports, for example, you might be required to prepare

1. A proposal

2. An outline

3. One or more progress reports

4. A library research report

5. A report of experimental results

6. A paper prepared for publication in a professional journal

7. The complete analytical report itself

Progress Reports

1. Select a project you are currently working on, and prepare a progress report on your efforts and plans for completing it. Use memo format.

2. You are in charge of one of the projects listed below. Prepare a progress report for the appropriate person. In each case, assume that the project is about half complete.
   a. Installing a new main frame computer for your company
   b. Conducting the annual United Way campaign for your community
   c. Preparing a Boy/Girl Scout Camp for summer occupancy
   d. Remodeling a bank
   e. Preparing a weekend managerial seminar on report writing
   f. Preparing the marketing strategy for a new product
   g. Preparing the prototype of a new, fuel efficient car
   h. Conducting an audit of a multinational corporation
   i. Investigating a case of embezzlement in your company
   j. Preparing an advertising campaign for the product of your choice
   k. Converting an apartment complex into condominiums
   l. Making a multi-million dollar movie
   m. Conducting a tour of the United States for a popular performer or group

Proposals

1. Select a problem with which you are familiar and propose a solution. Use an appropriate format based on length, content, and audience.

2. National Discounts, a major retailer, is interested in hiring your management consulting firm to solve its morale problem. Nick Yamana, Vice-President of Personnel, has asked you to submit a proposal.

3. You believe that the hospital in your community should allow your catering service to assume the responsibility for all hospital meals.

You believe that you can provide meals, including those for patients with dietary restrictions, at a lower cost than the hospital currently charges.

4.   You've been invited to bid on the design and construction of a new building (be specific about size, function, and other details). Submit a proposal, preliminary drawings, and estimates of costs.

5.   National Computer Brokers, a national chain of computer outlets specializing in micro- and minicomputers for personal and business use, is looking for a new advertising agency. You've been asked to submit a proposal.

6.   As governor, you'd like to attract more firms to your state. Select a business you believe would make a good contribution to your state's economy, and send a proposal.

7.   You believe that a new "super train" running at high speed on a special track (that eliminates grade crossings) between New York City and Washington, DC could be profitable. Propose that the government finance the construction of the train and the preparation of the railbed for the new train.

8.   Propose that your company institute a Quality Circle program.

Justification Reports

1.   Your company has had a hiring freeze for over a year now, and your department is currently three people short. The work is beginning to pile up. Justify hiring a new person, being specific about job duties, benefits to the company, costs, and savings.

2.   Your department handles a lot of repetitive typing. Justify the purchase of a new word processor.

3.   You do a lot of traveling for your company. The company's current practice is to give you a travel advance (in cash) for air fare and hotel expenses. Other expenses must be charged to your own credit card, and you apply for reimbursement after you return from your trip. Write a justification report demonstrating your need for a company credit card.

4.   Justify the installation of a cafeteria offering subsidized meals to the members of your organization.

5.   Justify the elimination of your company's cafeteria, which offers subsidized meals to company employees.

6.   As Vice-President of Public Relations for a large chemical company, justify an increased public relations program, including media training for all high-ranking company officers (in addition to traditional PR functions).

7.   Your company is considering dropping sponsorship of a series of high-quality TV dramas because the ratings have been low (be specific about GRPs). You believe that even if the audience is small, it represents the population you wish to reach. Justify continuing to sponsor the show.

8. Justify the adoption or elimination of a policy or procedure with which you are familiar. Provide specific information about the organization.

Evaluation Reports

1. Evaluate a product with which you are familiar.

2. Evaluate a procedure with which you are familiar.

3. Using the form presented in this chapter as a sample, evaluate hypothetical individuals who have been working for you for one year.

Accident Reports

Locate newspapers accounts of accidents that occurred in your community. Assume that you were the investigator for a concerned organization (company involved, insurance agency) and write the accident reports. Change the names of the people and organizations involved, and make up any additional details required for completeness.

CHAPTER 17

Oral Reports and Presentations

Your ability to express yourself orally can be an asset that will help make you a success in life no matter what career you choose. Every managerial position requires regular oral reports, and the better your skills at presenting material orally, the more knowledgeable you will appear. A successful oral presentation to the right audience can make a significant contribution to your career.

Topics

Preparation
Visual Aids
Delivery
Audience Participation
Feedback
Video Tape Presentations
Team Presentations

Most important business reports are written, but many of these written reports will have to be prepared orally as well. In addition, routine business life will require many less formal oral reports. The short, informal talks are those given when a supervisor calls you in the office and asks for the sales figures for the week or when the manager stops by your desk and asks for your recommendation on a particular policy or procedure. Longer, more formal speeches include those given to groups at sales conventions, Board of Directors' meetings, dinner meetings, conventions, seminars, and civic gatherings, such as the Chamber of Commerce or City Commission meeting.

Oral reports have one advantage over written reports: message transmission and feedback are immediate. Oral communication provides speaker and listener with the opportunity to discuss and exchange information until the message is clearly understood.

Oral communication is important, too, because it provides you with an opportunity to express your convictions and beliefs as well as your ideas. If you're a dynamic speaker, you can impress others not only with your knowledge but also with your personality. For this reason, oral reports can be more persuasive than their written counterparts.

Your ability to communicate orally is especially important when you apply for a job. When you can express yourself well, you have an edge. Also, once you have the job, an ability to communicate orally will separate you from those who are ineffective communicators. Your oral skills can be the reason for your advancement on the job and your success in life.

Effective oral communication calls for all of the same skills that contribute to effective written communication. See especially those techniques outlined in Chapter 12. In addition, oral reports call for special skills of preparation, delivery, use of visual aids, audience participation, and feedback. This chapter will emphasize those techniques required for formal oral reports. If you master those, the shorter, informal presentations will be easy.

PREPARATION

Two general aspects of oral reporting are preparation and delivery. Preparation includes determination of the purpose, audience analysis, and organization.

Purpose

The three purposes of oral presentations are (1) to inform, (2) to persuade, and (3) to entertain. Technically, oral reports fall into the first category, even though they also perform the other report functions of interpreting and analyzing data, drawing conclusions, and making recommendations.

Inform When you are asked to report on a study you conducted, conduct a training seminar, explain a procedure or policy, describe a new product or service, or convey information to an audience, your general purpose is to inform.

Informational talks present objective data, such as facts and figures, explanations, or descriptions. So that your audience will understand the information you present, concentrate on clarity. A clear and well-organized message helps your audience remember the content. Select words that convey your exact meaning, and when you're describing an item that is unfamiliar to your audience, use analogies. Analogies compare the known with the unknown (see Chapter 10).

The organizational pattern of an informational presentation is similar to the pattern used for written messages. When your audience will accept your message, use the immediate presentation, beginning with your main point first and then concluding with supporting details.

When your audience may reject your message, use the delayed presentation by beginning with supporting details and summarizing with conclusions and recommendations.

Persuade When you want your audience to accept or reject a proposal, buy or sell a product or service, change a behavior or attitude, vote on an amendment, or support a cause, your general purpose is to persuade.

Persuasive talks require logical and psychological appeals in addition to facts and figures. As in written communication, persuasive presentations use the following pattern of organization.

Attract Attention Begin by asking rhetorical questions, giving startling statistics, telling amusing anecdotes, or showing how the audience will benefit from the presentation, product, or proposal.

Arouse and Maintain Interest Provide explanations and definitions. Provide physical and psychological descriptions. How will the audience benefit?

Convince and Prove Deliver the facts. Demonstrate the product. Supply samples. Tell how others have benefited (give names). Provide testimonials. Give the results of performance tests.

Ask for Action Having described the product, service, or concept, and convinced your audience, you end your persuasive presentation by encouraging them to act as you requested.

Entertain Oral presentations meant to be entertaining include humorous speeches, drama, suspense stories, and dramatic readings. Entertaining an audience requires enthusiasm, colorful and descriptive language, body movement, vitality, creativity, and genuine love for people and attention.

Although the purpose of some oral presentations is pure entertainment, most business presentations use entertainment within an informative or persuasive context to provide a release from tension, stress, boredom, or fatigue. Humor can be effective in changing the pace, proving a point, relating to an audience, and attracting and holding an audience's attention.

Here are a few guidelines for including some entertainment in your presentations.

1.   Know your audience. Will they appreciate humor?

2. Avoid ethnic, religious, and other jokes that belittle, ridicule, insult, offend, or embarrass others.

3. Make your humorous material relevant to your topic.

4. Practice telling jokes to your friends first. If they laugh, use the jokes on your audience.

5. Keep humorous stories short and to the point.

Audience Analysis

The most important step in developing an oral presentation is to analyze your audience. In addition to those questions applicable to all reports you should also consider:

1. What is the size of your audience? 5? 25? 50? 500? 5,000?

2. What is their educational background? high school? college? Do they hold degrees? bachelor's? master's? doctorate? In what areas? educational? technical? medical?

3. What are their occupations? educators? government employees? business people? technical people? medical personnel?

4. What is the background of your audience? age? income? social? cultural? religious? political?

5. Are the members of your audience male? female? mixed?

6. What is the audience's relationship to you? personal? professional?

7. What does the audience know about your subject? What don't they know about it?

8. Why does the audience want to hear you?

9. What is your purpose in addressing the audience?

10. What is the attitude of the audience toward you? your topic? What are your audience's biases?

11. Does the audience expect a speech that will inform? convince? persuade? entertain?

Other questions you should consider when preparing your oral presentation are

1. How much time do you have or need? 20 minutes? 45 minutes? one hour?

2. Will you allow for questions and answers? If so, how much time?

3. Are you the keynoter? luncheon or banquet speaker?

4. Where will your presentation be held? classroom? conference room? meeting room? auditorium?

5. Which visual aids will best communicate your message? boards? charts or graphs? projectors? video tapes?

You may not be able to obtain answers to all your questions. But the more answers you have, the better the relationship will be between you and your audience and the more appropriate your presentation. Many presenters make the mistake of assuming that their audience has the same background, interests, and attitudes as they do. A speaker with a technical background in a subject addressing a nontechnical audience faces the same difficulties as a writer attempting to explain a technical subject in a report to a reader without technical expertise.

How do you analyze an audience? The best way, of course, is to talk directly with the people who will compose your audience. Obviously, this method is impractical, and in most cases, impossible. So, your next step is to ask the person who invites you to give the presentation. That person is usually familiar with the group members and the group's goals and objectives.

Once you have the information about your audience, how does it influence you? When you know, for example, that the size of your audience will be large, you would select visual aids appropriate for that size group. You would want to be sure that everyone could hear and see you. Also, you know that with a large audience, the greater the chance for having a heterogeneous group—a group that will have variation in attitudes, education, and knowledge about the subject.

A large, diverse group presents a difficult challenge; if you attempt to meet everyone's needs, your presentation will lose focus and you'll please no one as a result. Attempt instead to meet the needs of a representative member of the audience. You won't please everyone equally, but at least you'll be addressing the needs of most members of the audience.

Regardless of its size, you should attempt to discover the attitude your audience has toward you and your topics. When you know, for example, that your audience has a positive attitude toward you and your topic, you can begin immediately with your subject matter. On the other hand, if you know that your audience has a negative attitude toward you, you may wish to have someone else give the presentation. If that is impossible, try to find out why the audience has those negative thoughts. If you know the audience has a positive attitude toward you but a negative attitude toward your subject, you can plan your presentation to allay those negative feelings. Begin your presentation with something positive and try to explain why you have taken your particular position.

When you know, for example, the educational level of your audience and how much they know about the subject, you can adapt your vocabulary for your audience, explain terms you know they won't understand, and use visual aids that will clarify and emphasize major points.

Remember that, unless you are reporting to one person only, no audience is uniform or completely homogeneous. You analyze the audience as best you can so that you know what to emphasize and what to avoid. Understanding the audience's makeup enables you to select your topic, to tailor your presentation, and to adapt your material to their needs and interests. The more you know about your audience in advance, the better you can predict how they will respond to you and your message, and the more effective you will be as a speaker.

Organization

After you have determined the general and specific purposes of your oral presentation and have analyzed your audience, your next step is to collect all the information, materials, examples, statistics, and visual aids that you'll be using and arrange them in an orderly manner.

The order of arrangement will depend on the purpose of your presentation, the audience, the setting (physical environment), and the circumstances (psychological environment). Several methods of arrangement are available—deductive, inductive, chronological—and are discussed in Chapter 11.

But no matter what arrangement you select, all oral presentations will have three main parts—opening, body, and closing.

Opening

The purpose of the opening (or introduction) is to (1) establish rapport with the audience, (2) attract the audience's attention, (3) create interest in your subject, and (4) orient the audience to the purpose and plan of your presentation.

Your opening is critical because the way you begin will usually determine the audience's attitude toward you and your message. The following techniques have been used effectively by professionals.

1. Unusual, suspenseful, or startling statement; arresting fact
2. Reference to the audience or to familiar event
3. Rhetorical question
4. Quote
5. Joke
6. Humorous story
7. Anecdote
8. Background information
9. Preview or plan of your presentation
10. Benefit or promise to solve a problem
11. Goodwill statement

Techniques that you should avoid are

1. Apologizing to your audience
2. Criticizing the circumstances, setting, competitor, or opponent
3. Condemning or complaining
4. Using profanity

These techniques could alienate you from your audience. No matter what technique you select to begin your oral presentation, it must be relevant to your topic; otherwise, you are wasting not only your time but also your audience's. A successful opening is one that has the audience anticipating the heart of your presentation.

Before you actually begin your presentation, mingle and talk with members of your audience whenever possible. Doing so will help you establish rapport. Also, be alert for any information that you could use within your talk. Information gleaned from the audience beforehand will help you identify with the group.

After you have been introduced, be sure to thank the person who introduced you and the person who invited you to speak. Also, it is a good idea to get the audience involved at the beginning of the presentation. With large groups, you can do this by having them applaud someone in the group, perhaps the chairperson who organized a successful program. Another way to involve a large audience is to have them raise their hands in response to questions about their interests. Small groups may answer questions directly, or introductions may be used to relax the group.

Body

Just as the body of the written report is its heart, so, too, is it the heart of the oral report. The opening is the introduction that tells your audience what you're going to say, the body is where you tell them, and the closing is the conclusion that summarizes what you have told them.

Like the written report, the oral report contains a central thesis (theme) with main ideas and supporting details. The central theme, which gives the purpose of the presentation and summarizes the main idea, is usually stated immediately after the introduction.

Following the central theme are the main ideas with their supporting details, which in turn support the central theme. A good oral presentation will not have more than five main ideas because it is difficult for an audience to retain more than that.

Supporting statements include definitions, descriptions, examples, illustrations, visual aids, statistics, testimonials, and quotations. They all help convince and prove that what you're saying has credibility. In outline form, you would have

                    Central Theme
  I.   Main Idea 1
       A.   Supporting Details
       B.   Supporting Details
 II.   Main Idea 2
       A.   Supporting Details
       B.   Supporting Details
III.   Main Idea 3
       A.   Supporting Details
       B.   Supporting Details
            1.   Subsupporting Material
            2.   Subsupporting Material

See Chapter 12 for a discussion of the various ways to arrange the content of the body of the oral report.

Closing

The closing or conclusion is the clincher of the oral presentation and, some authorities say, the most important part because it is the last impression the audience will have of you.

The conclusion recaps, restates, or summarizes the central theme—it tells the audience what you've told them. The conclusion is the action ending. It can propose a solution, quote an authority, challenge the audience, recommend a course of action, or visualize the main ideas of your presentation.

The *worst* way to conclude is by saying, "That's it," or "That's all," as if you didn't know how to end or what else to say. You should also avoid saying, "Thank you," as though you are grateful they haven't left yet. When you indeed are thankful for an audience's participation or attention, be specific about what you are thanking them for: "Thank you for your warm response."

VISUAL AIDS

In written reports, graphic aids clarify complex information. In oral reports, visual aids are effective in helping the audience understand the oral message.

Visual aids are used in oral presentations to

1. Clarify concepts
2. Attract attention
3. Add interest
4. Support statements
5. Convince the audience
6. Emphasize facts
7. Simplify ideas
8. Increase retention
9. Prove points
10. Enliven presentations
11. Reinforce verbal messages
12. Supplement speech
13. Minimize misunderstandings
14. Explain statistics or relationships
15. Add variety
16. Help the speaker remember the material

Like graphic aids, visual aids supplement the text; they are not substitutes for it. They are planned and prepared to aid the speaker get the message across to the audience. Visual aids are important because they help the audience remember. Studies have shown that we remember only about 25 percent of what we hear, but we remember approximately 40 percent of what we see, and nearly 60 percent of what we hear *and* see.

Although the most important visual aid is the speaker (see nonverbal communication, at the end of this chapter), the frequently used visual aids are boards, charts and graphs, handouts, samples, models, projectors, and video tapes.

Boards

Chalkboards, display boards, poster boards, and flip charts are the main types of boards used to present visual material. Boards may be used to present outlines, key terms, formulas, flow charts, or graphs.

Line graphs, bar charts, pie charts (see Chapter 15), and other miscellaneous charts, such as diagrams and layouts, can be prepared ahead of time and displayed on just about every medium—boards, flip charts, transparencies, and slides. Charts and graphs are used effectively when statistical data need to be presented to show percentages, trends, and relationships. The main advantages of using charts and graphs as visual aids are that they are portable, easy to prepare, easy to handle, recalled easily, and can be prepared ahead of time. Their disadvantages are that they are difficult to prepare in sizes appropriate for large groups and generally require professionals to prepare them attractively.

Chalkboards Chalkboards are familiar to all of us. Most conference rooms and meeting rooms have them installed permanently. Portable chalkboards are also readily available. The main advantage of chalkboards is that they are one of the easiest and least expensive visual aids. Their main disadvantage is that space is limited, and messages must be continually written and erased, which is an inconvenience to the speaker and sometimes a distraction to the audience.

Boards can be prepared ahead of time. For example, you can place an outline of your speech on the board before the talk, and then refer to it during the presentation. When you decide to use a chalkboard, remember the following guidelines.

Write Legibly Make characters (words and symbols) large enough so that everyone can see and read what you have written on the board. Stand to the left and write toward the right until you get to the middle of the board. When you get to the middle of the board, switch sides. Stand to the right and start writing at the middle working toward the right.

Keep Messages Simple Use key words or phrases rather than complete sentences.

Stand to the Side of the Board After you have written your message on the board, stand to one side to make your comments.

Use a Pointer When it is necessary to single out a fact, use a pointer rather than your finger.

Keep the Board Clean After you have made comments on what you have written on the board, erase the board and go on to another topic. Boards filled with writing can distract the audience.

Display Boards Felt, flannel, peg, and magnetic display boards are used when the information will be displayed throughout the presentation or when the speaker wishes to add on to the display as the speech progresses. The felt or flannel board has a rectangular surface and is covered with flannel or felt. Display items are backed with material that adheres to the flannel or feltboards. The speaker can add on to the display or rearrange items already displayed. Peg boards have small holes to receive hooks for holding items. Peg boards are especially useful for displaying three-dimensional objects. Magnetic boards require magnetized letters, figures, and objects that adhere to the surface of the board. The main advantage of using felt, flannel, peg, and magnetic display boards is that the speaker can relocate items and create new messages without too much difficulty. Their disadvantage is that they are not flexible and not always available. Display boards can be mounted on the wall, placed on an easel or tripod, or stand by themselves.

Poster Boards Many speakers prefer poster boards for presentations for several reasons:

1. They are readily available.
2. They can be prepared ahead of time.
3. They are portable.
4. They are inexpensive.
5. They can be used on both sides.
6. They can be mounted most anywhere—wall, easel, tripod, table, podium.
7. They come in a variety of colors and textures.
8. They come in standard sizes of 20″ × 24″.

The main disadvantage of poster boards is that they are inappropriate for large groups. Posters are most effective when they are prepared professionally, which can be expensive. Remember these guidelines when preparing posters:

1. Use a separate poster for each idea.

2.   Keep the message simple. Use as few words as possible. Avoid clutter.
3.   Use broad, bold lettering so all can see the message.
4.   Use color for emphasis.
5.   Make the posters attractive by providing plenty of white space.

Flip Charts   Flip charts consist of a pad of paper—usually 28″ × 34″—mounted on an easel or tripod. They, too, are easy to prepare and inexpensive. Sheets can be prepared ahead of time or during the presentation. When the speaker is finished with one sheet, he or she merely flips it over and goes on to the next sheet. Should the sheet be needed later, the speaker can flip the sheets back. Although black markers are best for flip charts because they show up the best, color markers are good for highlighting points. The main disadvantage of flip charts is that they are small and not effective for large audiences.

Handouts

Handouts are written materials distributed to the audience either before or after the oral presentation. If handouts serve as worksheets, for example, they should be distributed ahead of time; otherwise, distribute them at the end to avoid having people looking at them during your presentation. Handouts can be color coded for easy reference. They can be single sheets of information; packets or folders of many sheets; or copies of pamphlets, brochures, books, or magazines. Handouts are useful for

1.   Providing statistical or complex data
2.   Providing material you don't have time to cover
3.   Serving as an agenda
4.   Evaluating your presentation

The main advantage of handouts is that each person has an individual copy of the material that may be kept. People like handouts. The disadvantage of handouts is that they can be expensive to distribute to large groups, especially if they consist of several pages.

Samples

Samples are used to show audiences the actual object. The main advantage of using samples in an oral presentation is that they are authentic; they are not models or replicas. When objects are small, they can actually be passed around in small groups. When objects are large, they can be displayed on a table or platform for all to examine. The disadvantage of using samples is that they may be too small or too large to display conveniently, in which case models would have to be used.

Models

When an object cannot be displayed for one reason or another (too small, too large, or unavailable), a model, usually built to scale, represents the object. Models may be used by architects to show the plans or design for a new building, by sales people to demonstrate a new product, or by engineers to illustrate a particular system. The advantage of using models is that sometimes they can be more effective than the actual sample. A model of an engine, for example, can be disassembled so that the audience can see the internal workings. Also, an enlarged model of a small object can be viewed by the audience better than the actual sample. In some cases models may be a good deal less expensive than a sample; in other cases a model may be costly or unavailable for showing.

Projectors

The four main projectors are overhead, opaque, slide, and movie.

Overhead Projectors The overhead projector projects images on a screen. Material to be projected is placed on a transparency, a thin sheet of thermoplastic especially designed to accept images, usually by a process of heat transfer.

The speaker, facing the audience, can stand next to the overhead projector and point out important facts on the transparency using a pointer or pencil. The speaker can also highlight material on or add material to a transparency by using a special felt-tip marker.

Transparencies are available in several colors. Material may also be added to a transparency by means of overlays. An overlay begins with a single transparency. Additional transparencies are attached and exposed one at a time. Place the second transparency over the first one, the third over the second, and so on until you achieve your composite picture.

Overhead projectors are probably the most popular and most widely used visual aids in oral presentations because of their many advantages over other visual aids. The overhead projector

1. Is easy and simple to use
2. Can be used in a fully lighted room
3. Can be used for any size group—large or small
4. Lets you face the audience and maintain eye contact
5. Permits you to cover material point by point
6. Puts you in control. By turning off the projector, you direct the audience's attention to you and away from the screen.
7. Can be operated by the speaker or another person
8. Permits the speaker to mark on a transparency as it is being shown on the screen

9. Is portable

10. Is silent and does not distract the audience

11. Permits the speaker to point directly on a transparency rather than on the screen

Another advantage is that transparencies can be easily, quickly, and inexpensively made on many copy machines. One disadvantage of the overhead projector is the initial expense, although overhead projectors can be rented for nominal fees at most convention sites. Another disadvantage of the overhead projector is that it is subject to breakdowns. Lamps burn out frequently, so it is a good idea to have a spare one on hand.

Although a separate screen is best for showing images, a wall would suffice. Practice your presentation before you deliver it to an audience. You will need to find the best place for stacking the transparencies you're about to use and those you've used already. You'll also need to coordinate transparencies with the relevant material in your presentation so that you use each transparency at the proper time.

The following guidelines will help you prepare transparencies.

1. Write large and legibly.

2. Title and label all information on a transparency.

3. Use colored markers (available at office supply stores) on clear transparencies for emphasis.

4. Use colored transparencies for eye appeal.

5. Limit each transparency to a key idea. Avoid solid blocks of material.

6. Provide plenty of white space.

7. Prepare neat, well-planned, and well-balanced transparencies.

8. Frame transparencies you plan to reuse for ease in handling and storage.

Opaque Projectors Like the overhead projector, the opaque projector also projects images on a screen. Unlike the overhead projector, though, it projects images from materials typed or printed on opaque paper. And that is the main advantage of the opaque projector. You don't need to prepare transparencies. You can use any available printed material appropriate for your presentation—pages from a book or magazine, pictures and photographs, business forms, and other similar items.

The major disadvantage is that an opaque projector requires a dark room, which puts the speaker at a disadvantage. The speaker in effect loses control of the audience. Other disadvantages are that opaque projectors are expensive, awkward, generally unavailable, and noisy.

Slide Projectors Slide projectors are popular for showing photographs or pictures of people, places, and things. The main advantages of a slide projector are the realism of the color and the accuracy of the photographs. In other words, slide projectors provide for true and accurate reproductions. Slide projectors also have remote controls which allow the speaker to operate the projector from the front of the room. The disadvantage of slide projectors is that the room must be dark, which again puts speakers at a disadvantage because they no longer have eye contact with the audience.

Audiotapes When a special message must be delivered with word-for-word accuracy, a tape recorder may be used in conjunction with a slide presentation to present material in a prearranged order. When using audiotapes, be sure that they are clear and audible. When the tape is garbled and the audience must strain to make out the words, everyone becomes frustrated.

Movie Because movies provide both motion and sound, they give a more realistic, and, hence, believable presentation of information. Movies, however, are substitutes for the oral presentation and not supplements. They replace the speaker. The main advantage is that they provide the movement and sound needed in certain situations. When the same information must be delivered in the same way to different audiences in different locations or at different times, a movie may be the most economical means of conveying the message. Salespeople, for example, use movies to show their products or services; engineers use them to show how their mechanisms or systems operate. The disadvantages of movies are that they are expensive and require a projector, screen, and a dark room.

Television and Video Tapes

Closed-circuit television, video tape recorders, and monitors have been effective instructional devices and are being used increasingly in oral presentations for many reasons.

1. They allow for filming interviews, demonstrations, events, working operations, on-the-spot activities, and other scenes and situations that lend themselves to being taped.

2. They provide for immediate feedback. After rewinding, the tape can be played again for a complete critique.

3. They provide an opportunity for the speaker to rehearse the presentation on tape, play it back so it can be analyzed or critiqued by another person, and rehearse it again.

4. Video tapes can be used repeatedly. When you no longer wish to use a particular tape, erase it and use it again.

5. Because video tapes do not require film processing and developing, you don't have to wait to see the recorder message.

6. They eliminate handling of all other visual aids that are to be used in the oral presentation and free the speaker to concentrate on other elements of the presentation. By video taping charts, graphs, diagrams, and other visuals ahead of time the speaker doesn't have to worry about working with them during the actual presentation. The speaker merely plays the video tape and can observe the audience's reactions.

7. Video tapes can be edited. Sections of unwanted or unnecessary tape can be removed. Once the desired segments have been joined, the viewers will be unable to detect the splice. Tapes can also be shortened or lengthened to fit a specific time requirement.

The disadvantage of using television and video tapes are that, although the camera and recorder are portable, the equipment necessary for play back—television or monitors, carts and stands, and electrical cords and outlets—can be bulky and cumbersome. Also, monitors are inappropriate for large audiences unless several can be placed throughout the room or large wall-sized screens are available so that everyone can see.

Guidelines

People expect visual aids in oral presentations, and effective speakers use them. Visual aids not only help the speaker control the meeting but also keep the audience alert and attentive to what the speaker is saying. Your success as an oral presenter will depend to some extent on the visual aids you select and how skillfully you use them. The following guidelines apply to the various aids in general.

1. Prepare visual aids in advance.
2. Keep them organized.
3. Keep them clear, uncluttered, and brief.
4. Keep them simple and understandable.
5. Make them legible. Print. Use bold, black lettering or bright colors. Use only large capital letters.
6. Make them realistic.
7. Keep them manageable.
8. Check them for accuracy.
9. Use only relevant information.
10. Place them where everyone can see them.
11. Use only visual aids appropriate for your presentation.
12. Stand to the left or right of the visual aid; don't block the audience's view.
13. Remove visual aids after they have served their purposes.
14. Adjust the projected images by focusing, raising, or lowering them.
15. Use the projector's on/off switch to control the audience's attention.
16. Use a pointer for directing the audience's attention to particular points.
17. Have them prepared by a professional.

18. Check to see that you have all the necessary equipment, such as extension cords, spare lamp, empty reel, pointer, markers, chalk, eraser, pen and pencils, hooks and pins, stands and charts. Also check for electrical outlets in the room when you'll be using electrical equipment.

19. Check visual aids before the audience arrives. Sit in a far corner to test visibility. Focus a transparency (or film) ahead of time.

20. Face the audience at all times, and maintain eye contact. Avoid talking to visual aids or turning your back to the audience.

21. Test all equipment and make sure everything is in operating order.

22. Be creative when preparing visual aids.

DELIVERY

Once you have done your homework—selected and researched your topic, determined your purpose, analyzed your audience, and organized your material for presentation—you are ready for the delivery of your message.

You've seen and heard good speakers—in the classroom, on stage, or on television. You know a good speaker when you hear one. Just what are the physical characteristics of good speakers? In addition to preparing quality materials, good speakers know how to overcome stage fright and how to make a good appearance. They also know how to use their body movements and how to use their voices.

Stage Fright

For many people, giving a speech can be a traumatic experience. Before they go on stage, their pulse rate increases, perspiration drips, hands tremble, and the body quivers. Butterflies are in the stomach, and breathing is difficult.

According to *The Book of Lists*,[1] speaking before a group is first on the list of the 14 most common human fears.

Feelings of nervousness and tension are normal even for professional speakers and generally are more noticeable to the individual than they are to the audience. Some of the world's greatest orators—Demosthenes, Lincoln, Churchill—had speech impediments, which they were able to overcome with practice and persistence. And so can you.

The following guides can help you reduce your anxieties about giving an oral presentation.

1. Select a familiar topic, one in which you are sincerely interested and about which you have strong convictions.

2. Prepare for your presentation. Research your topic and know it thoroughly. Prepare more material than time will permit to present.

3. Practice your speech repeatedly until you're confident in what you say and how you say it. Do not, however, memorize your speech.

4. Use gestures and movements to help channel your nervous energy.

5. Have a positive mental attitude toward yourself and your audience. Tell yourself that you're competent and confident, and that's what you'll be.

6. Remember that some nervousness is normal and can actually work for you rather than against you. Your audience probably won't notice that you're nervous unless you tell them. Use the extra energy to gain enthusiasm.

7. Be enthusiastic and excited about what you have to say. Be lively, and so will your audience.

Appearance

To create a successful image, speakers should consider carefully their overall appearance. Remember the sayings: (1) You do not have a second chance to make a first impression, and (2) You give two speeches at the same time—the one heard and the one seen.

Your audience will form its first impression of you by your appearance. And speakers show an interest in their audience by dressing neatly and appropriately. Inappropriate dress detracts from your message. In a formal setting, formal attire is a must—in cooler months, a three piece suit for men and a suit or dress with jacket for women. In less formal situations, men may wear a sports jacket and slacks, and women wear dresses. Wear comfortable clothing and choose colors that complement you. Avoid extremes in dress, flashy colors, and trendy fashions. Be conservative rather than flamboyant.

Speakers should also concentrate on other factors that contribute to their total grooming—hair, fingernails, shoes, jewelry, and cologne. Neatness counts: hair should be trim and clean, clothes pressed, shoes polished and well maintained, jewelry and cologne used sparingly, and fingernails manicured. Men may wish to shave right before a presentation to avoid "five o'clock shadow." Women may wish to touch up their makeup before stepping on stage.

Avoid chewing gum and smoking. Nothing is more distasteful than to see a speaker chewing gum and trying to speak at the same time. Words come out garbled, and, of course, the sight of the jaws going up and down and the sound of cracking gum are offensive to an audience. Smoking is another nervous habit that speakers should avoid when giving a presentation. In addition to being distracting and distasteful, smoking can actually be a health hazard for some people in the audience.

When you're on the platform giving an oral presentation, keep in mind that you're on display. All eyes are on you, and you want to look your best and be your best.

Body Movements

Body movements are significant and speak more loudly than words. As a speaker, you should know what they are and how to use them effectively. The three main body movements are posture, facial expressions, and gestures.

Posture Your posture communicates a powerful message to your audience whether you're sitting, standing, or moving. A slovenly or slouching posture portrays disrespect, laziness, indifferent attitude, a lack of interest, and careless physical habits. And when you display careless physical habits, your audience will assume you also have careless mental habits.

Standing or sitting erect, on the other hand, shows vitality, respect, interest, alertness, and a positive mental attitude. Strong, definite movements—especially when walking—project confidence; weak, hesitating movements reflect insecurity.

To present the perfect posture, speakers should stand firmly on both feet. Shifting weight from one foot to another indicates a speaker who is uncomfortable, ill at ease, or nervous. The speaker who has good posture—head erect, shoulders back, and stomach in—commands the audience's attention. Poor posture—head down, shoulders rounded, and stomach out—portrays a lack of confidence, enthusiasm, and forcefulness.

Facial Expressions The face is a potent source of information; it can form over twenty thousand facial expressions. Facial expressions, including smiles, frowns, scowls, and grimaces, reveal emotions such as happiness, sadness, anger, delight, love, and hate. When you're feeling good about yourself, your facial expressions will show your confidence. When you're uncomfortable and nervous, your facial expressions will reveal your anxiety. Develop a positive mental attitude so that you can face an audience with a smile, an expression that shows interest, warmth, and goodwill.

Eye contact can also reveal your feelings. People who avoid direct eye contact seem to say, "I feel inferior," "I'm guilty," "I'm unprepared," "I'm not interested," or "I'm afraid." When you avoid eye contact with your audience, you can't see how they are reacting to your message.

A good speaker, one who has control and confidence, looks the audience in the eyes and not over their heads. The speaker is saying "I'm interested in you," "I respect you," or "I'm attentive to your needs." A good speaker doesn't stare at one person but scans the entire audience looking directly into their eyes, observing their behavior, and nonverbally asking for their approval. When a speaker observes that the audience is bored or lost, he or she can change the pace, ask questions, or call for a stretch break.

Gestures Gestures are motions made by our bodies to help express our thoughts. Gestures are normal reactions in communication with others. For example, we nod our heads in agreement, and we shake our heads when we disagree. Some people use gestures more than others. Some seasoned speakers use gestures intuitively; some beginning speakers are inhibited and are unable to move, let alone gesture.

Gesturing can be very effective in speaking. Gestures can contradict, complement, or substitute for words. A clenched fist, for example, can signify conviction, a bang on the lectern can call attention to the audience, and a frown can indicate anger.

Speakers also use gestures to emphasize and enumerate. For example, a speaker points the index finger for emphasizing a fact, or raises the fingers one at a time to enumerate 1, 2, 3 . . .

Too much gesturing, however, can be distracting. Learn to use gestures spontaneously and sparingly. As a speaker, observe also the gestures of your audience. When you see their heads nodding and their bodies fidgeting and twisting in the chairs, adjust your presentation—announce a ten-minute break.

Voice

Vocal qualities and elements, such as volume, rate, pitch, diction, and paralanguage, are other primary sources of information in communication. They communicate our attitudes and emotions to the audience.

Volume   Volume—or loudness of sound—is a quality that all speakers need to develop to get their messages across to an audience. Obviously, if your message is to be heard, you need to project your voice; that is, increase its volume and power so that everyone can hear you. Speakers also need to adjust the volume of their voices to the size of the audience, the size of the room, and to other noises surrounding them while they are giving an oral presentation.

Variations in volume—loud to soft—are effective in controlling an audience's attention. For example, speakers who do not vary the volume of their voices lack interest and expressiveness. Variation in volume is needed to alert the audience to what's important and to emphasize key ideas. Speaking loudly for the entire presentation not only wears out the speaker but also the audience.

Rate   The rate (or pace) of speaking—fast or slow—will depend to some extent on the material being presented. When material is uncomplicated or less important, you can increase your pace; when material is complex, essential, and important, decrease your pace so that the audience has time to digest the information.

Beginning speakers usually speak too fast because they are nervous. And when speakers are nervous, they can't breathe properly; they're gasping for breath, which makes them uncomfortable and the audience uncomfortable, as well. Also, audiences find it difficult and tiring to follow a speech that is delivered rapidly.

Experienced and professional speakers possess the art of increasing or decreasing their rate of delivery at appropriate times to achieve their desired effect. They adjust their rate according to their audiences and their material.

Pauses help to slow a speaker's rate of delivery and are effective in gaining the audience's attention. When you practice your oral presentation, deliberately plan pauses to emphasize particular points.

Pitch   Pitch refers to the highs and lows in our voices. When speakers do not vary their pitch the result is a monotone. Speakers who speak in a monotone lull their audiences to sleep and come across as being lazy and lifeless. Being enthusiastic and excited about your message, however, can eliminate sameness of pitch. When you're excited, your voice automatically changes pitch, which dispels monotone.

Because everyone is capable of achieving a variety of ranges in pitch, you can improve your pitch by practicing. Record your presentation on a tape recorder, listen to yourself, and have someone else listen and evaluate your voice. Where do you need to improve? Practice repeatedly, and your voice will improve.

Diction   Speakers who do not enunciate their words, who garble or mumble, who swallow or mispronounce their words, are violators of good diction—speaking clearly and distinctly. Pronounce every syllable in a word. For example,

Say: *interest*, rather than *intrest*
       going to, rather than *gonna*

and pronounce words correctly:

Say: *get*, rather than *git*
       for, rather than *fir*
       want to, rather than *wanna*
       yes, rather than *yeah*

When you're not sure of the correct pronunciation of a word, check the dictionary. To improve poor diction, open your mouth wide and pronounce words correctly, clearly, and distinctly.

Paralanguage   Paralanguage refers to the nonverbal voice qualities (pitch, volume, rate) and to vocalizations (throat clearing, coughing, laughing, crying). Similar to paralanguage are meaningless words, habitual expressions, and mindless repetitions, a few of which are *um, uh, okay, you know, and what not, you see,* and *see what I mean.*

Paralanguage communicates our attitudes and emotions. By paralanguage, we tell our audience whether we are nervous or relaxed or comfortable or uncomfortable. The audience, for example, can detect variations in our pitch and sense our nervousness.

Effective speakers learn to control nervous mannerisms by practicing their presentation on audio and video recorders.

AUDIENCE PARTICIPATION

Because people learn by doing and because people learn from each other, have the audience participate in your oral presentation. You can do this in several ways.

Introduction You can get the audience involved by having them introduce themselves to each other when the group size permits such an activity. Participants enjoy exchanging demographic information—name, company name, occupation, and reason for attending the session. As mentioned earlier, have the audience applaud someone for something (chairperson for organizing) early in your presentation. Getting the audience involved from the beginning helps you establish rapport with them.

Body You can involve the audience by having them respond to a question by a show of hands or by calling out their responses. Another effective technique is brainstorming. You give the audience about five or ten minutes to write down their ideas, suggestions, or solutions to a problem that you've posed, and then record their responses on a chalkboard, flipchart, or transparency. You can also involve the audience by having them engage in games, role playing, and written exercises. When the group size permits it, break the audience into groups or teams of four to six people to discuss a problem or situation. After an audience has been sitting for about an hour, give them the opportunity to stand and stretch.

Conclusion Questions and answers always provide an excellent opportunity for the audience to express themselves.

Audience participation is especially helpful when your presentation is for an hour or more. Shorter talks require less participation.

FEEDBACK

Feedback is an important ingredient in oral presentations. When you want to know whether the audience has heard and understood your message, you need some kind of feedback. Feedback also helps you to improve your future presentations.

Nonverbal

One form of feedback is the audience's nonverbal behavior: puzzled looks, shaking and nodding heads, smiles, frowns, looks of approval or disapproval. When you observe this nonverbal behavior in an audience, you can adapt your speech in several ways: ask questions, restate the information, give illustrations, use visual aids, draw diagrams, or give a stretch break.

Verbal

Verbal feedback includes oral commentaries and written evaluations. Oral feedback is obtained through questions and answers. In informal presentations, the speaker may invite questions at any time during the presentation; in more formal situations, the speaker may call for questions only at the end of the presentation.

Observe the following suggestions when conducting the question-and-answer period after a presentation.

1. Repeat the question for the entire audience when it is necessary.
2. Keep your answers and explanations brief.
3. Give your undivided attention to the questioner when the question is being asked, but observe the entire audience as you give your response.
4. Do not spend too much time with one questioner. Acknowledge another questioner in another section of the room.
5. Answer one question at a time even if two are asked at the same time.
6. Admit it when you don't know the answer to a question. The audience will appreciate your honesty.
7. Give everyone an opportunity to ask questions. Take questions from all sections of the room—front and back, sides, and middle.
8. Invite people for a further discussion after the time period has elapsed. Or, when the room will not be used by another group, allow the audience to leave and continue to discuss an issue with those most interested.
9. Do not argue with a heckler. Answer the questions and be friendly.
10. Do not spend too much time with a hostile questioner. Answer the person courteously and quickly and move on to someone else.

So that you can improve your future presentations and identify your strengths and weaknesses, obtain feedback from your audience. Your audience will make comments informally to you and to others, and formally on an evaluation sheet, when one is provided. Because people can remain anonymous, written evaluations are more reliable than oral evaluations.

When evaluation sheets are not provided by the organization or individuals who invited you to give the presentation, prepare your own. Exhibit 17.1 illustrates an evaluation sheet.

EXHIBIT 17.1

Sample Evaluation Sheet of an Oral Presentation

Speaker _____

Topic _____

	Good	Acceptable	Poor
I. Organization			
A. Introduction			
1. Attracts attention	___	___	___
2. Creates interest	___	___	___
3. States purpose	___	___	___
B. Body			
1. Clarifies central theme	___	___	___
2. Emphasizes main ideas	___	___	___
3. Provides examples, explanations, descriptions, and definitions	___	___	___
C. Conclusion			
1. Summarizes	___	___	___
2. Restates theme	___	___	___
3. Has action ending	___	___	___
II. Content			
A. Clear	___	___	___
B. Easy to follow; logical	___	___	___
C. Well organized	___	___	___
III. A. Delivery			
1. Appearance	___	___	___
2. Audience involvement	___	___	___
3. Creative	___	___	___
4. Enthusiasm	___	___	___
5. Eye contact	___	___	___
6. Facial expression	___	___	___
7. Gestures	___	___	___
8. Mannerisms	___	___	___
9. Poised and relaxed	___	___	___
10. Posture	___	___	___
11. Preparation	___	___	___
12. Timing	___	___	___

EXHIBIT 17.1
Sample Evaluation Sheet of an Oral Presentation *(continued)*

	Good	Acceptable	Poor
IV. Voice			
A. Volume (loud-soft)	___	___	___
B. Rate (fast-slow)	___	___	___
C. Pitch (high-low)	___	___	___
D. Diction			
1. Clear and distinct	___	___	___
2. Correct pronunciation	___	___	___
3. Correct grammar	___	___	___
E. Paralanguage			
1. Throat clearing, coughing, nervous laughter	___	___	___
2. Meaningless words ("um," "ah," "you know," "okay," "and whatnot," "you see"	___	___	___
V. Visual Aids			
A. Accurate and attractive	___	___	___
B. Readable	___	___	___
C. Simple and clear	___	___	___
D. Relevant	___	___	___

Additional Comments:

_____

_____

_____

_____

TELEVISION AND VIDEO TAPE PRESENTATIONS

The chances are that someday you'll be asked to give an oral report on television or on video tape. What will you do? How can you prepare? Here are some pointers that may help.

1. You are the visual aid so your image is important. Even though a makeup artist may do touch-ups on you, you should pay particular attention to your total grooming.

2. Most of what has been said about preparation and delivery of oral presentations also applies to television and video taped presentations. Note especially what has been said about nonverbal communication—posture, gestures, voice.

3. Timing is most important; be sure to practice your speech so it can be given in the allotted time.

4.   Limit your topic to one central idea. Select only those words that will best convey your message. Use concrete and specific words rather than abstract and general words.

5.   Watch the television show you'll be appearing on at least three times to see how the host interviews the guests and how the questions are handled.

6.   Ask whether the show will be video taped or aired live. When the show is taped, editing can distort your message.

7.   When possible, have the film crew avoid the "talking head" presentation. Film from a variety of distances and angles. Obtain professional help with filming and editing.

TEAM PRESENTATIONS

Sometimes individuals who have expertise in various areas are asked to give a presentation as a group. For example, group presentations have been effective in persuading businesspeople to invest in a certain project, in informing a company how a system will operate, or in explaining why a company should build a plant at a particular location.

When planning a group presentation, observe the following guidelines.

1.   Divide the time more or less equally for each speaker.

2.   Plan the presentation so that continuity prevails. You want a unified presentation and not a series of isolated individual speakers. Each speaker should tie in with what the preceding speaker has said and should make reference to the succeeding speaker.

3.   Avoid repetition and overlap. Speakers should have a specific topic not covered by any of the other speakers.

4.   Direct the presentation to the audience and not to the other team members.

5.   Have one member of the team serve as moderator or coordinator for the group. The moderator would be responsible for
      a.   Introducing each member of the team.
      b.   Making sure that each speaker observes the time limit.
      c.   Handling the question-and-answer period.

SUMMARY

Oral reports are spoken messages given to two or more people. They are used every day in business at all levels of management. Oral communication is important because message transmission and feedback are immediate. Oral communication is important, too, because it provides you with the opportunity to express your ideas and beliefs, and to impress others with your knowledge and your personality. Your oral skills are important when you go to apply for a job or when you want to be promoted.

Two general aspects of oral reporting are presentation and delivery. Preparation includes determination of your purpose, audience analysis, and organization. The three purposes of oral presentations are to inform, to persuade, and to entertain. The most important step in developing and planning an oral presentation is to analyze your audience. Understanding the audience's makeup enables you to select your topic, tailor your presentation, and adapt your materials to their needs and interests. All oral presentations are organized into three main parts—opening, body, and closing.

Visual aids are effective in helping the audience understand the oral message. The most frequently used visual aids are boards, charts and graphs, handouts, samples, models, projectors, and television and video tapes.

Delivering the oral presentation involves overcoming stage fright, knowing how to dress, knowing how to use body movements effectively, and using the voice to its best advantage.

Because people learn by doing and because people learn from each other, have the audience participate in your oral presentation. Feedback is important. When you want to know whether the audience has heard and understood your message, you need feedback—oral and written.

When asked to give a television or video tape presentation, practice your speech so that it can be delivered in the allotted time. Also, limit your topic to one central idea and select only those words that will best convey your message.

When planning a group presentation, divide the time equally for each speaker, plan the presentation so that continuity prevails, avoid repetition and overlap, and have one member of the team serve as a moderator.

EXERCISES

Review Questions

1. Define oral reports. Give two examples of oral reports.

2. Why is oral communication important?

3. What are the three purposes of oral presentations?

4. What is the organizational pattern when your purpose is to inform? persuade?

5. How do you analyze an audience?

6. What are the three main parts of an oral presentation?

7. What is the purpose of the opening of an oral presentation?

8. What is the purpose of the conclusion of an oral presentation?

9. What are the three main body movements?

10. What are gestures?

11. Define volume, rate, and pitch.

12. Define paralanguage. Give three examples.

13. Name three ways an audience can participate in your oral presentation.

14. Why is feedback important?

15. Give five reasons for using visual aids in oral presentations.

Presentation Problems

1. You've been asked to give a 15-minute after-dinner speech to 500 accountants, who have had a "taxing" day attending meetings. Select a topic that would be interesting and entertaining to accountants.

2. One of your responsibilities as president of an organization (club, fraternity, sorority, professional group), is to give the welcome at the organization's annual conference. Prepare and present a five-minute welcoming speech to about 200 members of your organization.

3. Prepare and present a five-minute oral presentation that illustrates how to do something (repair a leaky faucet, install a garage door opener, change a spark plug, landscape the lawn, change a tire). Specify your audience.

Oral Report Problems

1. Prepare a five-minute oral report for any written report you have been working on during the term. Specify your audience.

2. Make a three-minute persuasive oral presentation to your wealthy aunt and uncle. Ask them to lend you $5,000 to complete your college education.

3. As chairperson for a site selection committee (city and hotel) for the National Association of (your choice)'s annual convention, present the committee's recommendations to the Association's Board of Directors.

4. As public relations director for a company of your choice, you have been asked to present a five-minute oral report to your Board of Directors on how to improve company morale among the employees.

5. You are a representative from the Southern Power Company. Prepare a five-minute oral presentation to the Home Owners' Association's monthly meeting of approximately 100 members on how to conserve energy in the home.

6. Prepare and present a five-minute oral presentation on a topic of your choice. Use appropriate visual aids.

7. You're the spokesperson for a team of engineers (carpenters, technicians, analysts) who have perfected a new process (procedure, system, mechanism). Persuade the president and vice-president of the company to accept and adapt your process.

8. As a student or employee, select a problem that your school or office is trying to solve. Present your solution in a five-minute oral report to the office manager and supervisors or to the Student Government Association.

9. Prepare and present a five-minute oral presentation to incoming freshmen during orientation week about your college's professional and social organizations which they may wish to join.

10. Prepare and present a five-minute oral presentation to parents who will be attending Parent Orientation Day. You'll want to tell the parents something about housing and food services, financial aid and scholarships, health care services, and extracurricular activities.

11. As a student, prepare and present a ten-minute oral presentation to the dean of your college on why the college should offer a particular course in your area of interest.

12. Interview a top executive in a local business on the importance of oral presentations. Present your findings in a five-minute oral report to the class.

13. You would like to see a change in parking regulations (registration procedures, vacation scheduling, or promotion policies). Prepare and present a five-minute oral presentation to supervisors, managers, faculty, Board of Directors, or any group that will accept or reject your suggestion.

Note

[1]David Wallechinsky, Irving Wallace, and Amy Wallace, *The Book of Lists* (New York: Bantam Books, 1977), p. 469.

APPENDIX A
Statistical Tables

TABLE 1:

Standard Normal Curve

Value in Table is $P(0 \le z \le z_0)$

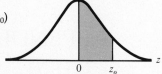

z_0	.00	.01	.02	.03	.04	.05	.06	.07	.08	.09
0.0	.0000	.0040	.0080	.0120	.0160	.0199	.0239	.0279	.0319	.0359
0.1	.0398	.0438	.0478	.0517	.0557	.0596	.0636	.0675	.0714	.0753
0.2	.0793	.0832	.0871	.0910	.0948	.0987	.1026	.1064	.1103	.1141
0.3	.1179	.1217	.1255	.1293	.1331	.1368	.1406	.1443	.1480	.1517
0.4	.1554	.1591	.1628	.1664	.1700	.1736	.1772	.1808	.1844	.1879
0.5	.1915	.1950	.1985	.2019	.2054	.2088	.2123	.2157	.2190	.2224
0.6	.2257	.2291	.2324	.2357	.2389	.2422	.2454	.2486	.2517	.2549
0.7	.2580	.2611	.2642	.2673	.2704	.2734	.2764	.2794	.2823	.2852
0.8	.2881	.2910	.2939	.2967	.2995	.3023	.3051	.3078	.3106	.3133
0.9	.3159	.3186	.3212	.3238	.3264	.3289	.3315	.3340	.3365	.3389
1.0	.3413	.3438	.3461	.3485	.3508	.3531	.3554	.3577	.3599	.3621
1.1	.3643	.3665	.3686	.3708	.3729	.3749	.3770	.3790	.3810	.3830
1.2	.3849	.3869	.3888	.3907	.3925	.3944	.3962	.3980	.3997	.4015
1.3	.4032	.4049	.4066	.4082	.4099	.4115	.4131	.4147	.4162	.4177
1.4	.4192	.4207	.4222	.4236	.4251	.4265	.4279	.4292	.4306	.4319
1.5	.4332	.4345	.4357	.4370	.4382	.4394	.4406	.4418	.4429	.4441
1.6	.4452	.4463	.4474	.4484	.4495	.4505	.4515	.4525	.4535	.4545
1.7	.4554	.4564	.4573	.4582	.4591	.4599	.4608	.4616	.4625	.4633
1.8	.4641	.4649	.4656	.4664	.4671	.4678	.4686	.4693	.4699	.4706
1.9	.4713	.4719	.4726	.4732	.4738	.4744	.4750	.4756	.4761	.4767
2.0	.4772	.4778	.4783	.4788	.4793	.4798	.4803	.4808	.4812	.4817
2.1	.4821	.4826	.4830	.4834	.4838	.4842	.4846	.4850	.4854	.4857
2.2	.4861	.4864	.4868	.4871	.4875	.4878	.4881	.4884	.4887	.4890
2.3	.4893	.4896	.4898	.4901	.4904	.4906	.4909	.4911	.4913	.4916
2.4	.4918	.4920	.4922	.4925	.4927	.4929	.4931	.4932	.4934	.4936
2.5	.4938	.4940	.4941	.4943	.4945	.4946	.4948	.4949	.4951	.4952
2.6	.4953	.4955	.4956	.4957	.4959	.4960	.4961	.4962	.4963	.4964
2.7	.4965	.4966	.4967	.4968	.4969	.4970	.4971	.4972	.4973	.4974
2.8	.4974	.4975	.4976	.4977	.4977	.4978	.4979	.4979	.4980	.4981
2.9	.4981	.4982	.4982	.4983	.4984	.4984	.4985	.4985	.4986	.4986
3.0	.4987	.4987	.4987	.4988	.4988	.4989	.4989	.4989	.4990	.4990

From ELEMENTS OF BUSINESS STATISTICS by R. C. Gulezian. Copyright © 1979 by W. B. Saunders Company. Reprinted by permission of Holt, Rinehart and Winston.

TABLE 2:
Student-t Distribution

Table gives t_0 such that $P(t \geq t_0) = \alpha$

df	$\alpha = .10$	.05	.025	.01	.005
1	3.078	6.314	12.706	31.821	63.657
2	1.886	2.920	4.303	6.965	9.925
3	1.638	2.353	3.182	4.541	5.841
4	1.533	2.132	2.776	3.747	4.604
5	1.476	2.015	2.571	3.365	4.032
6	1.440	1.943	2.447	3.143	3.707
7	1.415	1.895	2.365	2.998	3.499
8	1.397	1.860	2.306	2.896	3.355
9	1.383	1.833	2.262	2.821	3.250
10	1.372	1.812	2.228	2.764	3.169
11	1.363	1.796	2.201	2.718	3.106
12	1.356	1.782	2.179	2.681	3.055
13	1.350	1.771	2.160	2.650	3.012
14	1.345	1.761	2.145	2.624	2.977
15	1.341	1.753	2.131	2.602	2.947
16	1.337	1.746	2.120	2.583	2.921
17	1.333	1.740	2.110	2.567	2.898
18	1.330	1.734	2.101	2.552	2.878
19	1.328	1.729	2.093	2.539	2.861
20	1.325	1.725	2.086	2.528	2.845
21	1.323	1.721	2.080	2.518	2.831
22	1.321	1.717	2.074	2.508	2.819
23	1.319	1.714	2.069	2.500	2.807
24	1.318	1.711	2.064	2.492	2.797
25	1.316	1.708	2.060	2.485	2.787
26	1.315	1.706	2.056	2.479	2.779
27	1.314	1.703	2.052	2.473	2.771
28	1.313	1.701	2.048	2.467	2.763
29	1.311	1.699	2.045	2.462	2.756
∞	1.282	1.645	1.960	2.326	2.576

From "Table of Percentage Points of the t-Distribution." Computed by Maxine Merrington, *Biometrika*, Vol. 32 (1941), p. 300. Reproduced by permission of Biometrika Trustees.

TABLE 3:

Chi-Square Distribution

Table gives k such that $P(\chi^2 \geq k) = \alpha$

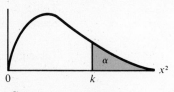

df			α		
	.0995	0.990	0.975	0.950	0.900
1	0.0000393	0.0001571	0.0009821	0.0039321	0.0157908
2	0.0100251	0.0201007	0.0506356	0.102587	0.210720
3	0.0717212	0.114832	0.215795	0.351846	0.584375
4	0.206990	0.297110	0.484419	0.710721	1.063623
5	0.411740	0.554300	0.831211	1.145476	1.61031
6	0.675727	0.872085	1.237347	1.63539	2.20413
7	0.989265	1.239043	1.68987	2.16735	2.83311
8	1.344419	1.646482	2.17973	2.73264	3.48954
9	1.734926	2.087912	2.70039	3.32511	4.16816
10	2.15585	2.55821	3.24697	3.94030	4.86518
11	2.60321	3.05347	3.81575	4.57481	5.57779
12	3.07382	3.57056	4.40379	5.22603	6.30380
13	3.56503	4.10691	5.00874	5.89186	7.04150
14	4.07468	4.66043	5.62872	6.57063	7.78953
15	4.60094	5.22935	6.26214	7.26094	8.54675
16	5.14224	5.81221	6.90766	7.96164	9.31223
17	5.69724	6.40776	7.56418	8.67176	10.0852
18	6.26481	7.01491	8.23075	9.39046	10.8649
19	6.84398	7.63273	8.90655	10.1170	11.6509
20	7.43386	8.26040	9.59083	10.8508	12.4426
21	8.03366	8.89720	10.28293	11.5913	13.2396
22	8.64272	9.54249	10.9823	12.3380	14.0415
23	9.26042	10.19567	11.6885	13.0905	14.8479
24	9.88623	10.8564	12.4011	13.8484	15.6587
25	10.5197	11.5240	13.1197	14.6114	16.4734
26	11.1603	12.1981	13.8439	15.3791	17.2919
27	11.8076	12.8786	14.5733	16.1513	18.1138
28	12.4613	13.5648	15.3079	16.9279	18.9392
29	13.1211	14.2565	16.0471	17.7083	19.7677
30	13.7867	14.9535	16.7908	18.4926	20.5992
40	20.7065	22.1643	24.4331	26.5093	29.0505
50	27.9907	29.7067	32.3574	34.7642	37.6886
60	35.5346	37.4848	40.4817	43.1879	46.4589
70	43.2752	45.4418	48.7576	51.7393	55.3290
80	51.1720	53.5400	57.1532	60.3915	64.2778
90	59.1963	61.7541	65.6466	69.1260	73.2912
100	67.3276	70.0648	74.2219	77.9295	82.3581

TABLE 3:

Chi-Square Distribution (continued)

α

0.100	0.050	0.025	0.010	0.005	df
2.70554	3.84146	5.02389	6.63490	7.87944	1
4.60517	5.99147	7.37776	9.21034	10.5966	2
6.25139	7.81473	9.34840	11.3449	12.8381	3
7.77944	9.48773	11.1433	13.2767	14.8602	4
9.23635	11.0705	12.8325	15.0863	16.7496	5
10.6446	12.5916	14.4494	16.8119	18.5476	6
12.0170	14.0671	16.0128	18.4753	20.2777	7
13.3616	15.5073	17.5346	20.0902	21.9550	8
14.6837	16.9190	19.0228	21.6660	23.5893	9
15.9871	18.3070	20.4831	23.2093	25.1882	10
17.2750	19.6751	21.9200	24.7250	26.7569	11
18.5494	21.0261	23.3367	26.2170	28.2995	12
19.8119	22.3621	24.7356	27.6883	29.8194	13
21.0642	23.6848	26.1190	29.1413	31.3193	14
22.3072	24.9958	27.4884	30.5779	32.8013	15
23.5418	26.2962	28.8454	31.9999	34.2672	16
24.7690	27.5871	30.1910	33.4087	35.7185	17
25.9894	28.8693	31.5264	34.8053	37.1564	18
27.2036	30.1435	32.8523	36.1908	38.5822	19
28.4120	31.4104	34.1696	37.5662	39.9968	20
29.6151	32.6705	35.4789	38.9321	41.4010	21
30.8133	33.9244	36.7807	40.2894	42.7956	22
32.0069	35.1725	38.0757	41.6384	44.1813	23
33.1963	36.4151	39.3641	42.9798	45.5585	24
34.3816	37.6525	40.6465	44.3141	46.9278	25
35.5631	38.8852	41.9232	45.6417	48.2899	26
36.7412	40.1133	43.1944	46.9630	49.6449	27
37.9159	41.3372	44.4607	48.2782	50.9933	28
39.0875	42.5569	45.7222	49.5879	52.3356	29
40.2560	43.7729	46.9792	50.8922	53.6720	30
51.8050	55.7585	59.3417	63.6907	66.7659	40
63.1671	67.5048	71.4202	76.1539	79.4900	50
74.3970	79.0819	83.2976	88.3794	91.9517	60
85.5271	90.5312	95.0231	100.425	104.215	70
96.5782	101.879	106.629	112.329	116.321	80
107.565	113.145	118.136	124.116	128.299	90
118.498	124.342	129.561	135.807	140.169	100

APPENDIX B
Report Problems

The reports you write as part of your report writing education should be closely related to the kinds of reports you will actually write on the job. Further, you should attempt to write several types of reports that will be common to the kind of work you expect to do after graduation.

The problems in this section are designed to give you the opportunity to prepare more than one report dealing with the same area of concern. For each of the problems, you might prepare any of the following in addition to a complete analytical report:

1. A feasibility study
2. A proposal
3. A progress report (or series of reports)
4. A report of library research
5. A report of experimental results
6. A synopsis
7. An executive summary
8. A journal publication based on the report
9. Evaluations of personnel, procedures, or products involved in your project
10. Appropriate inserts for employee publications or for individual, departmental, or corporate annual reports
11. One or more oral reports

Each of the cases presented here requires additional information. For some cases, you can assume the data and provide details based on your imagination. In other cases, you'll need to conduct at least secondary and perhaps primary research to collect the necessary data. When a case involves a fictional company for which or in which you are to conduct research, you may use a similar local company as a source of information, or you may ask other students to complete appropriate questionnaires. The use of local companies should be coordinated by your instructor so that no one company has too many students requesting permission to conduct research.

For each of the following problems, perform any statistical analyses necessary to validate the reliability of your conclusions.

1. What kinds of reports are written by those working in your area of specialization? Do the kinds of reports differ at entry level, middle management levels, and upper-level management positions?

2. Several of the doctors on the staff at the hospital you manage have asked you to purchase a CAT-Scan device. Should the hospital invest in one? Prepare your report for the hospital's board of directors.

3. Your company is a major manufacturer of main-frame computer systems. Should your company attempt to enter the micro-and mini-computer business?

4. Evaluate computer scanning devices recently installed in many grocery stores. How well do they work? What do customers think of them? You work for a local grocery store chain, and the president of the company is considering installing them in all your stores.

5. Your company is about to introduce a new product (your choice). As a member of the Marketing Division, you've been asked to plan a marketing strategy for the product. Prepare your recommendations for the Vice-President of Marketing.

6. The Dean of the College of Business has asked you, Chairperson of the Department of Accountancy, to prepare a report on the demand for accountants over the next ten years. Be sure to consider the impact of computers and computerized accounting systems.

7. As a member of a management consulting team, you have been assigned the responsibility of evaluating and making suggestions for improvements in the following areas:

   a. Inventory control
   b. Profit planning
   c. Return on equity
   d. Capital investments and depreciations
   e. Bad-debts policy and collection procedures

   Select a company with which you're familiar, and prepare your report.

8. Should your company invest in regular motivational seminars? As Director of Education and Training, you've been asked to evaluate the effectiveness of motivational seminars.

9. What form of instruction is most effective for orienting new employees to your company? New employees have to know company objectives; the way departments relate to each other; a wide variety of policies, fringe benefits, and other items of information that will clarify how their jobs fit into the organization as a whole.

10. A contractor has asked you to explain the advantages and disadvantages of buying and leasing capital equipment.

11. The president of your company recently read a report claiming that smokers are less productive than nonsmokers. She has asked you to verify or disprove that report. She also wants to know whether it would be advisable to prohibit smoking except during regularly scheduled break periods. Would smokers feel so resentful about a no-smoking rule that their productivity would be lower still? Should the company hire only nonsmokers in the future?

12. As an investment counselor, you've been asked to advise a client who has $430,000 to invest. What do you recommend and why? How can your client evaluate the trade-off between risk and return?

13. Your state senator has asked you—as a person knowledgeable about business—to evaluate the business climate in your state. What can the state do to encourage business and industry to locate new plants in the state? Should the state work to recruit any particular business or industry?

14. What changes will take place in labor-management relations over the next ten years? How will those changes affect your company? Prepare a formal report for the president of your company, who will be sharing your report with the board of directors.

15. Explain the expression, "Business doesn't pay taxes; it only collects them" to the U.S. Representative from your district.

16. Your supervisor, the Assistant Vice-President of Marketing, will be visiting a number of foreign countries to explore the possibility of establishing markets for your products (select a product or products with international potential). Before he leaves, he wants to know more about business customs and the business climate in the following countries: England, France, Germany, Mexico, Japan, and South Korea.

17. Your company has developed a new instant coffee. To produce it, you use a new evaporation process that reduces the caffeine content by 60 percent and enhances flavor. The result is a better tasting coffee with a low caffeine content. Will people buy the coffee? Which people might buy the coffee? How should the coffee be packaged and presented?

18. Should your company install cassette tape players in company cars so that employees can listen to educational and motivational tapes while driving? Should the company also provide the tapes? The Training Manager has asked for your recommendation.

19. Should your school—or community—install a central parking garage? How should the garage be financed?

20. The department of which you are manager maintains an honor-system coffee pot for the 43 members on your staff. If each person puts in 10 cents for each cup of coffee, the fund should be large enough to pay for the coffee and to save enough to buy a new pot when the current one burns out. Unfortunately, you have been coming up several dollars short each week. What, if anything, should you do about it? Rather than make a decision and force it on your staff, you decide to investigate the problem and share your findings in report form with your staff.

21. As a member of Rotary (substitute any comparable organization), you've been placed in charge of planning the association's national convention, to be held in your town in two years. The president of your local chapter wants to know who should do what and when to make the conference a success. What will the costs of the conference be? How will those costs be financed? How many people will attend? Where will they stay? How long will they stay?

22. Your company is about to repair its offices and conference rooms. What colors should be used? Should all the rooms be painted the same color, or should your company attempt to use color to control the moods of the people in them? Should the employees have a choice? Prepare a report for the Director of Personnel, who is in charge of selecting the paint.

23. Should your company invest in a company gym and jogging track? Would employees use the facilities? If so, when? Also, would the company receive any return for its investment? If so, what?

24. Select three or four similar products appropriate for use in your area of specialization (drafting tables, typewriters, computers, pieces of lab equipment) and evaluate their advantages and disadvantages. Assume that you've been invited to present your findings and recommendation to the president of a company that would use the kind of equipment you've examined.

25. A church group in your community purchased a satellite antenna for the purpose of taping broadcast movies and reshowing them for a fee. Lately, some of the members have begun to worry about the legality of the taping and reshowing. They've asked you to investigate and to recommend possible alternative methods of raising funds.

26. Your company, Faultless Fabrics, produces three brands of jeans— Sylvia Lannon, expensive designer jeans for women; Brad Barker, expensive designer jeans for men; and jean-o's, inexpensive but durable jeans for men, women, and children. You've been asked to determine how these products should be marketed in your area. The Vice-President of Marketing wants to know whether Faultless Fabrics should open its own store (which could stock additional merchandise) or market through existing outlets.

27. One of the by-products of your manufacturing process is phosphate, which you have been discharging into the local water system. Several of the lakes in the area have recently begun to show signs of eutrophication. Environmentalists in the area are blaming your plant. The president of your company has asked you to prepare a report outlining both a course of action and the best method of communicating that action to the public. She also wants to know how much it will cost to implement your recommendations. Your effluent contains 127–196 ppm of phosphate, 47 ppm of nitrogen, and trace amounts of 12 common minerals.

28. Your company is a major manufacturer of defense-related electronic equipment. You've been asked to investigate and report on state-of-the-art industrial security systems. Prepare an informative report for the president and board of directors.

29. Evaluate the food being served in your company (or school) cafeteria. What changes should the catering company make in the food, the way it is prepared and served, and costs?

30. How can your organization best identify potential leaders? Prepare a report for the Vice-President of Personnel.

31. Alvin Toffler's *The Third Wave* suggests that word and data processing equipment will make the present role of secretary obsolete. The Vice-President of Corporate Planning has asked you to prepare a study of the electronic office at your organization. How many executives are likely to master the keyboarding skills necessary to make the electronic office function? When is the impact likely to be felt? Who will be affected? What will happen to productivity? How will morale be influenced?

32. As a research assistant for your state governor, prepare a report on the effects of alcohol abuse in the state. How much does it cost? How many people are affected? Can the state take any steps to control it?

33. Your large, multinational corporation has asked you to investigate the problems caused by two-career families. Is there any way your company can avoid the problems caused by the conflicting needs of the corporation and husbands and wives whose careers are leading in different directions?

34. Over the past ten years, your company has grown tremendously, and your number of stockholders has grown as well. Your earnings have been high, and your company president thinks that it's time to produce a first-rate annual report. He has asked you to recommend style, format, and content. Give examples of what to include and what to avoid in annual reports.

35. The Vice-President of Personnel has asked you to report on what the recent studies of behavior modification have to say about decreasing absenteeism. Are any of the new techniques applicable to your company?

36. How is your company perceived by the community? Use a specific local company and investigate. Does the company need to take any action to improve its image? Prepare the report for the company president or plant manager.

37. What legislation currently pending (local, state, or federal) will influence your company (be specific in selecting a company)? The president of your company wants a concise summary of the legislation and your opinion of the impact it might have on your company.

38. You work for a major American automobile manufacturer, and you have been asked to find out what owners of foreign cars like about them. What can your company do to prevent further erosion of market share to imports?

39. What skills does a person need to be successful in your area of specialization? Your professional association has asked you to research and report on the necessary skills. Your report will be published in

an upcoming issue of the professional journal in your discipline. Companies will use the information to help make hiring decisions, so include a section on what recruiters should look for when interviewing.

40. What responsibility should your company assume for staff development? The Director of Personnel has asked you to discover whether the money the company might spend on staff development—including job training, training for new jobs as old jobs become obsolete, and advice about and help with qualifying for promotions—will be worth it.

41. You are a Site Selector for a fast-food chain known for its high quality beef, chicken, cheese, and fish sandwiches for lunch and dinner. You also offer a breakfast menu of pancakes, waffles, French toast, eggs, and all the toast a person can eat. Your prices are a little higher than other better known fast-food restaurants, but your quality is worth it. Should your chain, Sandwich Earl's, open a restaurant in your town? If so, where should it be located?

42. Should your company institute an incentive program for its sales staff? Your sales representatives currently work for a commission, which ought to encourage them to sell as much as possible without additional incentives. Would some form of recognition prove a better incentive than additional money? Be specific in selecting a company and product line.

43. The local Chamber of Commerce has asked you to evaluate your community from the perspective of business climate. What do local businesses like about it? What do they dislike? What can the Chamber do to improve the business climate?

44. Should your company institute a Quality Circle program? Where did the idea of Quality Circles come from, and do the Circles work?

45. What is likely to happen to interest rates in the next ten years? Should your company borrow the money to build a new facility now, or do a little remodeling now and wait several years before building? Be specific about the company, its current facility, and the costs of new construction.

46. You work for the owner-builder of a luxury apartment complex in your area. You will have 88 two-and three-bedroom units, each with its own laundry facilities. What kind of washer and dryer should be installed in the apartments?

47. You work for a large manufacturing company. Recently, one of your employees fell off scaffolding four stories high and was killed. It was discovered that he was drunk. Now the company president wants to know whether alcoholism is a problem in your company. Should your company attempt to do anything about it? What do other companies do?

48. Your company needs a specific policy on sexual harassment. What is it? What should a woman—or man—do who believes that she or he is the victim of sexual harassment? What evidence is necessary? What kinds of protection should be offered to victims? How do you prevent false accusations?

49. Your boss is in the process of building the world's largest us
    lot. She's asked you to determine what kind of lighting syste
    should install.

50. Many companies in your industry have recently unionized. Y
    company does not yet have a union, though some of the em
    have been discussing the possibilities. Should your company
    avoid unionization, and what will it need to do to prevent th
    from organizing? Prepare your report for the president.

51. Your supervisor, Beth Marks, Manager of Corporate Commu
    wants to know which forms of communication are most effec
    with which employees. You have the following kinds of emp
    office workers, maintenance workers, management personne
    technicians, and scientists. You have the following forms of c
    nication: supervisor to subordinate, bulletin boards, PA syste
    memos to office mailbox, letters to home, company newslette
    company bulletins. How should important announcements b
    municated? Do the different forms of communication serve d
    functions?

52. A multinational corporation has decided to form a new subsi
    You have been hired to run the department or laboratory in
    area of specialization. (You'll need to be specific about the pr
    service the new company will produce/market.) Submit a rep
    lining and justifying your needs, including space, equipment
    plies, and personnel.

APPENDIX C
A Brief Guide to Correct English Usage

Ignorance of the ways in which the English language should be used is one of the main impediments to writing quickly and easily. Regardless of your occupation, writing—reports, letters, documentations, procedures—will play an important role in your career. To be comfortable submitting copies of your materials for the review of others, you will need to feel confident in your ability to use English correctly.

The guide we present here is not meant to serve as a substitute for a complete handbook of English use. It is designed to be a quick and handy reference to the common problems of usage you encounter while using this text as a source of information about report writing. People who write regularly on the job should invest in one of the many English handbooks. In addition to a handbook, those who wish to have their writing reflect the full extent of their abilities should invest in copies of the following books:

Bernstein, Theodore M. *The Careful Writer: A Modern Guide to English Usage.* New York: Atheneum, 1980.

A thorough, entertaining, and authoritative guide to English usage arranged in alphabetical order for quick reference.

Brusaw, Charles T. Gerald J. Alred, and Walter E. Oliu, *The Business Writer's Handbook,* 2d ed. New York: St. Martin's Press, 1982.

An alphabetic guide to problems of English usage. Covers all problems report writers are likely to encounter.

Strunk, William Jr. and E. B. White. *The Elements of Style.* New York: Macmillan, 1959.

A classic guide to writing style and correctness. Every one should own a copy of this short paperback.

Williams, Joseph M. *Style: Ten Lessons in Clarity and Grace.* Glenview, IL: Scott, Foresman, 1981.

Deals with larger, more difficult issues than Bernstein or Strunk and White. Concentrates on sentence and paragraph construction.

Zinsser, William. *On Writing Well,* 2d ed. New York: Harper & Row, 1980.

    Good coverage of techniques for solving common writing problems; contains useful hints for controlling emphasis and subordination.

USING WORDS CORRECTLY

Adjective/Adverb Confusion

Adjectives modify nouns and pronouns. Adverbs modify verbs, adjectives, and other verbs. They cannot be used interchangeably.

Wrong: He always writes *concise.* (Adjective in place of an adverb.)

Right: He always writes *concisely.* (Adverb used correctly.)

Right: He always writes *concise* memos. (Adjective used correctly.)

Some sentences change meaning depending on whether an adjective or adverb is used:

I feel *bad.* (Adjective meaning, "I do not feel well.")

I feel *badly.* (Adverb meaning, "My sense of touch is impaired.")

Many adjectives become adverbs by the addition of *ly,* and many others have the same form whether serving as an adjective or an adverb. When in doubt, check a dictionary.

Among/Between

Use *among* for groups larger than two.

Wrong: *Between* the three of us . . .

Right: *Between* you and me . . .

Right: *Among* the three of us . . .

Amount/Number

Use *amount* for quantities that cannot be counted. Use *number* to refer to items that can be counted.

Right: The *amount* of gasoline purchased . . .

Right: The *number* of gallons of gasoline . . .

As to

As to is an indefinite way of saying *about, of,* or *whether.* Avoid it when possible.

Indefinite: The instructions were not clear *as to* assembly procedures.

Better: The instructions were not clear *about* assembly procedures.

Center on

Because the verb *center* means "to gather to a point," it should be followed by *in, on,* or *at* and not by *about* or *around.*

Wrong: The problems *center about* managerial communication style.

Right: The problems *center on* managerial communication style.

Compose/Comprise

Both compose and comprise refer to the relationship between a whole and its parts. *Compose* is used to refer to the parts that make up the whole. *Comprise* is used to refer to the whole that includes the parts. *Comprise* is not used with the preposition *of.*

Right: The new soft drink was *composed* of secret ingredients.

Right: The organization *comprises* six divisions.

Contact

Contact is best used as a noun meaning the act or state of touching. As a verb, *contact* should usually be replaced by a more exact substitute, such as *write, call,* or *visit.*

Imprecise: Please *contact* me when I can help again.

Better: Please *call* me when I can help again.

Divided into/Composed of

Something can be *divided into* parts, and it can be *composed of* parts, but meanings are not interchangeable.

Right: I *divided* the orange *into* sections

Right: The orange is *composed of* skin, juice, pulp, and seeds.

Different from

Although some authorities accept *different than* in comparative constructions, *different from* is usually preferred. (For a full discussion, see Bernstein, pp. 139–141.)

Poor: This is *different than* that.

Better: This is *different from* that.

Done

Done is not an acceptable substitute for *finished* or *complete*. *Done* can be used to mean "sufficiently cooked."

Wrong: The project is *done*.

Right: The project is *complete*.

Right: The hamburgers are *done*.

Enthuse

Enthuse is not an acceptable substitute for *enthusiasm* or *enthusiastic*.

Wrong: Alicia was *enthused* about her promotion.

Right: Alicia was *enthusiastic* about her promotion.

Etc.

Et cetera, abbreviated etc., means "and other things of the same kind." Use *etc.* only when the items included will be clear to your reader.

Wrong: Remove the shop equipment: the drill press, the lathe, *etc.*

Right: Count by even numbers: 2, 4, 6, 8, *etc.*

Foreseeable Future

How much of the future can be foreseen? If something is a prediction, say so.

Wrong: We will have no difficulties in the *foreseeable future*.

Right: I predict no future difficulties.

Have Got

Have got is a particularly inelegant redundancy.

Wrong: *Have* you *got* a new model on the market yet?

Right: *Do* you *have* a new model on the market yet?

Hopefully

Do not use *hopefully* as a substitute for *I hope*.

Wrong: *Hopefully*, it won't rain.

Right: *I hope* (or she hopes or they hope) it won't rain.

Impact

Do not use *impact* as a verb.

Wrong: Will that *impact* on this department?

Right: What *impact* (noun) will that have on this department?

Right: Will that *influence* this department?

-ize

The suffix *-ize* is suitable for use with some words: *burglarize, hospitalize, computerize*. When used to form words for which adequate substitutes already exist, however, the new *ize* word reveals a poor vocabulary. If in doubt, consult a dictionary.

Not this	But this
Finalize	Complete
Prioritize	Rank
Solidize	Solidify

Less/Fewer

Use *less* for quantities than cannot be counted. Use *fewer* to refer to items that can be counted.

Right: We've had *less* success than they have had.

Right: We had *fewer* sales this month than they had.

Needless to Say

If it is needless to say something, don't say it. If you do need to say it but it may be obvious to your reader, find a less obtrusive way of subordinating it.

That/Who

Although *that* can be either a demonstrative pronoun or a relative pronoun in referring to people, it is usually better to use *who* as a relative pronoun when referring to people.

Right: *That* man sold me the car. (Demonstrative pronoun.)

Right: He is the man *who* sold me the car. (Relative pronoun.)

Right: Here is the house *that* she told me about. (Relative pronoun.)

Thanking in Advance

To thank someone in advance is presumptuous because it implies that the person has no choice but to do as you have asked. It also suggests that you are too lazy to write a second note to thank the person after he or she has helped.

Wrong: *I thank you in advance* for your cooperation.

Right: I would appreciate your cooperation. (Thank the reader *after* she or he has cooperated.)

-wise

As a suffix, *wise* means "to be knowledgeable about" (pennywise, worldlywise) or "in the manner of" (clockwise, otherwise). Do not use *-wise* to mean "about the matter of."

Wrong: *Qualitywise,* this procedure is superior.

Right: This procedure results in superior quality.

Wrong: The new company will add a lot to the community *jobwise.*

Right: The new company will provide a number of new jobs in the community.

USING SENTENCES CORRECTLY

Sentences are the basic building blocks of thought. Words themselves convey an image or a concept, but until we know the context in which a word will be used, we cannot assign it specific meaning. The word *effect,* for example, can be either a noun or a verb, depending on how it is used.

Kinds of Sentences

Sentences are simple, complex, compound, or compound-complex. A *simple sentence* contains one subject and one verb.

The bridge collapsed.

A *complex sentence* contains one independent clause (can stand alone as a sentence) and one dependent (subordinate) clause.

Because it was poorly designed (dependent clause),

the bridge collapsed (independent clause).

The bridge collapsed because it was poorly designed.

Complex sentences are useful to control emphasis in a sentence because readers pay more attention to information presented in the independent clause than they do to information in the dependent clause.

After reviewing the data, *I concluded that the bridge was poorly designed* (main point).

Because the bridge collapsed, *we reviewed our procedures for conducting stress tests* (main point).

A *compound sentence* contains two independent clauses (simple sentences) joined by a coordinating conjunction. Compound sentences are useful for linking or contrasting ideas of equal importance.

The bridge collapsed, and we had no insurance.

The bridge collapsed, but no one was injured.

Compound-complex sentences contain two independent clauses and one or more dependent clauses. Compound-complex sentences are useful for showing the relationships among ideas.

When the bridge collapsed (dependent clause),

we had no insurance (independent clause), but no one was

injured (independent clause).

Purposes of Sentences

In addition to being classified according to type, sentences are classified according to their purpose: declarative, interrogative, imperative, or exclamatory. By far, most sentences are *declarative*—they make an assertion or statement about something.

Our third quarter profits are up 39 percent.

Interrogative sentences ask questions.

What was our sales volume this quarter?

Imperative sentences give orders.

Bring me the file on Ehrle.

Exclamatory sentences express strong feelings.

Think of the college graduate who can't make an oral presentation!

Control of Sentences

An effective writer combines sentence kind and purpose to achieve a particular effect. The parts of the sentence should combine into a unified, logical whole so that each part has a specific job to do and makes a specific contribution to the complete thought. The ideas in a sentence should be related, and that relationship should be clear to the reader.

Unrelated: Qualified forecasters anticipate a substantial increase in business investment by fall, and the market value of gold is at an all-time high.

Related: Qualified forecasters anticipate a substantial increase in business investment by fall, and productivity should increase as a result of the new capital investment.

Transition Elements in sentences are either joined by conjunctions, conjunctive adverbs, subordinating adverbial conjunctions, or simple adverbs. These elements serve to control sentences by showing the relationships between the parts of the sentence.

Simple Adverbs	Conjunctions	Conjunctive Adverbs	Subordinating Adverbs
better	and	also	after
beyond	but	anyway	although
here	or	besides	as
suddenly	for	consequently	because
then	nor	finally	before
worse	so	furthermore	if
	yet	hence	once
		however	since
		incidentally	that
		indeed	though
		instead	till
		likewise	unless
		meanwhile	until
		moreover	when
		nevertheless	whenever
		next	where
		otherwise	wherever
		still	while
		then	
		therefore	
		thus	

These words, and many other words and phrases, show relationships between parts:

Addition: and, also

Comparison: similarly, likewise

Contrast: but, however

Cause and effect: hence, therefore

Summary: in brief, for example

Exemplification: in brief, for example

Time or place: first, second, now, later, here, there

Variety In addition to controlling the relationships between sentences and sentence parts, writers need to control the kinds of sentences used to achieve variety. Variation in sentence pattern helps make writing interesting. Just as a report composed of all simple sentences would obviously make for dull reading, a report with too many complex or compound sentences would be uninteresting, though the reason would not be so obvious.

The two most common problems writers have are beginning too many sentences with subordinate clauses and joining too many simple sentences with conjunctions to form long series of compound sentences.

Change this: *Because annual sales figures indicate a need for improved market strategy,* Morgan Corporation should hire an outside consultant to review current practices and to recommend changes. *Although outside consultants have been used in the past with little success,* the right consultant could make a significant contribution to our market strategy. *After reviewing the proposals submitted by three leading consulting companies,* I have concluded that Lissakers, Inc. has the most to offer.
(Three complex sentences beginning with subordinate clauses.)

To this: Because annual sales figures indicate a need for improved market strategy, Morgan Corporation should hire an outside consultant to review current practices and to recommend changes. The right consultant could make a significant contribution to our market strategy, and the problems we've experienced in the past with outside consultants can be overcome. I recommend that we accept the proposal submitted by Lissakers, Inc.
(One complex, one compound, and one simple sentence.)

Change this: Word processing equipment is proliferating, *and* the office of the future has already arrived. The cost of computing power has been dropping rapidly, *and* now almost any company can afford one or more desktop minicomputers capable of processing, storing, and retrieving documents. The new equipment promises to reduce costs and increase productivity, *but* many executives resist using it because they feel that the terminal's keyboard is more suitable for their secretaries than for them.
(Three compound sentences.)

To this: Word processing equipment is proliferating. As a result of the rapid drop in the cost of computing power, the office of the future has already arrived. Now almost any company can afford one or more desktop minicomputers capable of processing, storing, and retrieving documents. Although the new equipment promises to reduce costs and increase productivity, many executives resist using it. They feel that the terminal's keyboard is more suitable for their secretaries than for them.
(Three simple sentences, two complex sentences.)

AVOIDING COMMON SENTENCE ERRORS

The most common errors in written reports occur within sentences. While grammarians don't always agree on the correct use of language, a few rules are universally accepted and should be considered absolutes. The most important grammatical rules have been established because they contribute to clarity and the logical communication of ideas.

Subject-Verb Agreement (Agr)

A verb must agree with its subject in person and number. Because irregular verbs are the only ones that change forms with changes in person, they usually present little difficulty.

	Singular	**Plural**
1st person:	I go	We go
2d person:	You go	You go
3d person:	He, she, it *goes*	They go

	Singular	**Plural**
1st person:	I run	We run
2d person:	You run	You run
3d person:	He, she, it *runs*	They run

	Singular	**Plural**
1st person:	I am	We are
2d person:	You are	You are
3d person:	He, she, it *is*	They are

Irregular verbs present few problems because they are the verbs used most frequently. Agreement in number causes problems when writers are uncertain whether a subject is singular or plural and when subjects and verbs are separated by an intervening phrase or clause.

Singular: *Bill has* written the report. *It is* now being typed. *He thinks* it will please the Director.

Plural: *Bill and John have* written their reports. *They are* now being typed. *They think* that the reports will please the Director.

Sometimes agreement is influenced by the connective element used. When two elements are connected by *and*, the verb is usually plural. When the elements are connected by *with, or, together with*, or *as well as*, the verb is often singular.

Singular: This report, *along with* the four others submitted, *is* necessary to understand the problem.

Plural: This report *and* the four others submitted *are* necessary to understand the problem.

Collective nouns can also cause problems. Collective nouns are words that name a group of objects, persons, or acts. They require singular verbs and pronouns when the entire group is intended and plural verbs and pronouns when individual units of the group are meant. Typical collective nouns are

army	gang
athletics	group
audience	herd
class	jury
committee	majority
company	mankind
contents	number
couple	offspring
crowd	politics
dozen	public
faculty	remainder
family	team

The *committee* (singular) *has* (singular) decided to table the motion.

The *company* (singular) *is* (singular) moving to Hastings.

Some collective nouns always take plural verbs.

The *police were* helpful in pointing out our need for increased security.

The *people need* to know.

The *cattle were* sold at auction

But: The entire *herd was* sold at auction.

Intervening phrases or clauses can also cause problems.

The marble *statue,* having stood in Florence for 600 years, *was* moved to Dallas to grace the entry of Canoil, Inc.

After undergoing 32 hours of training, the new *managers*—each of whom must successfully complete the business presentation course—*are* required to write summaries of the management training program.

Pronoun-Antecedent Agreement (Ref)

A pronoun must have a clear and logical antecedent with which it agrees in person, number, and gender. Because pronouns derive their meaning from the nouns—or previous pronouns—to which they refer, accurate pronoun references are essential to clear writing.

Margaret thought that everyone would approve of *her* report.
(*Margaret* is the antecedent of *her*.)

The *company* will succeed if all *its* employees work together.
(*Company* is the antecedent of *its*.)

The Board *members* voted "No" on the proposal because *they* felt that the project would be too expensive.
(Board *members* is the antecedent of *they*.)

The rules governing pronoun-antecedent agreement are essentially the same as those governing subject-verb agreement: (1) plural antecedents require plural pronouns, and (2) singular antecedents require singular pronouns. In addition, masculine antecedents require masculine pronouns, while feminine and neuter antecedents require feminine and neuter pronouns respectively.

Fred forgot *his* notes.
Alice forgot *her* notes.
The *notebook* was not in *its* proper place.

Indefinite pronouns, which almost always require singular pronouns, take their gender from the antecedent. When the gender is unknown, writers should be careful to avoid sexist language.

> *Everyone* **in the Women's Division won** *her* **game.**
> *Everyone* **in the Men's Division won** *his* **game.**
> *Each* **of the engineers completed** *his* **or** *her* **report on time.**
> **A** *manager* **needs to make** *her* **or** *his* **decisions quickly.**

When possible, use plural constructions to avoid the awkwardness of repeating he/she constructions.

> *All* **the engineers completed** *their* **reports on time.**
> *Managers* **need to make** *their* **decisions quickly.**

For more information on techniques for avoiding sexist language, see Judy E. Perkins, ed., *Without Bias: A Guide for Nondiscriminatory Communication,* 2d ed. (New York: John Wiley & Sons, 1982).

Collective nouns may be either singular or plural, and require either singular or plural pronouns, depending on meaning.

> **The** *committee* **accepted** *its* **new responsibility graciously.**

> **The** *audience* **left** *their* **seats before the presentation was complete.**

Pronoun Case (Case)

The form of the pronoun varies according to the function it performs in the sentence. Pronouns that function as subjects are in the nominative case; pronouns that function as objects are in the objective case; and pronouns that refer to a previous noun or pronoun are in the reflexive case. Pronouns showing ownership are in the possessive case.

Nominative	Objective	Reflexive	Possessive
I	me	myself	mine
you	you	yourself	yours
he	him	himself	his
she	her	herself	hers
it	it	itself	its
we	us	ourselves	ours
you	you	yourselves	yours
they	them	themselves	theirs

Common pronoun errors include the following:

Wrong: *Me* and Allen computed the data.

Right: Allen and *I* computed the data. (Pronoun serves as a subject.)

Wrong: The agreement between *he* and *I* is complete.

Right: The agreement between *him* and *me* is complete. (The pronouns serve as objects of the preposition *between.*)

Wrong: A man like *yourself* should know better.

Right: A man like *you* should know better. (The pronoun is the object of the preposition *like*.)

Right: *You* should complete this project by *yourself*. (The reflexive pronoun intensifies the subject of the sentence.)

Sentence Fragments (Frag)

Most written English requires complete sentences. A complete sentence consists of at least one subject and one verb and expresses a complete thought. A complete sentence makes sense when standing alone. A sentence fragment, on the other hand, is an incomplete part of a sentence, which may be missing a subject or a verb or may depend on some other element to complete its thought.

Fragments may result from punctuating subordinate clauses, verbal phrases, prepositional phrases, or appositives as sentences.

Fragment: Because they had missed the meeting.

Sentence: Because they had missed the meeting, they failed to note the changes in specifications on the working drawings.

Fragment: During rush hour traffic.

Sentence: During rush hour traffic, the traffic signal follows a predetermined two-minute sequence.

Fragment: After complete reconstruction

Sentence: The building will be ready for occupancy only after complete reconstruction.

Fragment: Who reports directly to the Vice-President of Finance.

Sentence: All expenditures must be approved by the Operations Manager, who reports directly to the Vice-President of Finance.

Failure to write in complete sentences is usually considered a serious error. Unless used carefully for special effect (primarily in fiction and direct mail advertising), fragments suggest carelessness or a lack of knowledge about sentence structure. Because a complete sentence is necessary to express a complete thought, ideas expressed in fragments are unclear and difficult to follow.

Run-on Sentences (R-O)

Run-on sentences are two or more sentences connected with insufficient separation. Sentences may be separated by a period, a semicolon, or a comma and a conjunction.

Run-on: Profits increased by 47 percent in the fourth quarter the press was very quick to report the gain.

Corrected: Profits increased by 47 percent in the fourth quarter. The press was very quick to report the gain.

Or: Profits increased by 47 percent in the fourth quarter; the press was very quick to report the gain.

Or: Profits increased by 47 percent in the fourth quarter, and the press was very
      quick to report the gain.

While not so serious a detractor from clarity as is a fragment, a run-on
sentence also suggests carelessness or failure to understand sentence
structure.

Run-on sentences often result from a writer's failure to use a
comma in addition to a conjunction.

Run-on: The press overlooked the 44 percent increase in capital investment and
          only one side of the story appeared in print.

Corrected: The press overlooked the 44 percent increase in capital investment, and
            only one side of the story appeared in print.

Another common cause of run-on sentences is punctuating for a conjunctive adverb (however, besides, therefore, consequently, etc.) as
though it were a conjunction.

Run-on: The press doesn't deliberately distort the facts, however a built-in bias
          against business may influence the selective perception of some reporters.

Corrected: The press doesn't deliberately distort the facts; however, a built-in bias
            against business may influence the selective perception of some reporters.

Or
(even better): The press doesn't deliberately distort the facts; a built-in bias against
                business, however, may influence the selective perception of some reporters.

Comma Splice (C/S)

A comma splice results when two sentences are joined by a comma
only.

Comma Splice: Raw material substitutions are not permitted, impurities must be
                below the 0.04 percent level specified.

Corrected: Raw material substitutions are not permitted. Impurities must be below
            the 0.04 percent level specified.

Misplaced and Dangling Modifiers (Mod)

Prepositional phrases, subordinate clauses, participial phrases, infinitive phrases, adverbs, and adjectives all add meaning and precision to
sentences by modifying the more general meaning provided by the
subject and verb. A modifier (word or phrase) is misplaced when it
seems to modify something it logically can't, or when the reader can't
be certain what the writer meant.

A dangling modifier is one that cannot logically modify any word
in the sentence. In general, modifiers should be placed directly before
or after the word or words they modify.

Misplaced modifier: No one I know would eat a steak in a restaurant that was not
                      cooked the way she or he wanted it.

Correct: No one I know would eat a steak that was not cooked the way he or she
          wanted it in a restaurant.

Better: No one I know would eat an improperly cooked steak in a restaurant.

Dangling Modifier: Driving over the bridge, the structural defects were clearly visible.

Correct: Driving over the bridge, I could clearly see the structural defects.

Shifts (Shift) and Parallel Construction (// cst)

To be clear, a sentence must be consistent. Shifts in person, number, verb tense or mood, or voice detract from clarity.

Shift: One (3d person) should never forget your (2d person) reader's needs. (shift in person)

Correct: Never forget your reader's needs.

Correct: One should never forget the reader's needs.

Shift: A person (singular) should prepare their (plural) reports carefully. (shift in number)

Correct: A person should prepare his/her reports carefully.

Shift: I would go. Will you? (shift in mood)

Correct: I would go. Would you?

Correct: I will go. Will you?

Shift: I have considered your proposal, and it has been decided to postpone any action until the end of the month. (shift in voice)

Correct: I have considered your proposal, and I have decided (or simply "and decided") to postpone any action until the end of the month.

Just as shifts tend to confuse readers by altering perspectives in midsentence, an absence of parallelism confuses readers by presenting similar concepts in uncoordinated grammatical form. Parallel grammatical structure is required for clarity whenever similar elements are joined by coordinating conjunctions or correlative conjunctions, arranged in a list, compared, or contrasted.

Faulty: We met our production quota and also affirmative action.

Parallel: We met our production quota and also satisfied affirmative action guidelines.

Faulty: New employees need to learn how to write reports and oral presentations as well.

Parallel: New employees need to learn how to write reports and to make oral presentations as well.

Faulty: Not only was I interested in his ideas but also his manner of presenting them.

Parallel: I was interested in not only his ideas but also his manner of presenting them.

Faulty: The new word processing center will alleviate the problems we've been having with the shortage of secretaries, the backlog of correspondence, and losing documents.

Parallel: The new word processing center will alleviate the problems we've been having with the shortage of secretaries, the backlog of correspondence, and the loss of documents.

Faulty: It is better to rely on market research than making wild guesses.

Parallel: It is better to rely on market research than to make wild guesses.

PARAGRAPHING

Writing clear, grammatically correct sentences is the single greatest obstacle for most writers, and most problems with writing occur at the sentence level. Effective writing, however, requires not only that sentences be clear, correct, and effective, but also that sentences be connected into larger units that are also clear and effective.

In connecting sentences to form paragraphs and paragraphs to form complete reports, the writer needs to provide clear and distinct statements about the topic being discussed and to organize material so that related ideas are close together.

Topic Sentences

In general, each paragraph should focus on one central idea, which should be expressed in a topic sentence. The remaining sentences in the paragraph should clarify, limit, or support the topic sentence.

Topic Sentence: Running a business is not easy.

Sentence of Limitation: As any business owner knows, money, employees, and customers are all sources of difficulty.

Sentence of Clarification: Because a business must make a profit, a businessperson constantly worries about the costs of staying in business.

Support Sentence: Equipment, raw materials, advertising, rent, insurance, and employees are all costs that must be considered in determining the cost of a product. (Rest of paragraph—or paragraphs—would describe the kinds of problems caused by employees and customers.)

Paragraph Organization

It is easier for the reader to follow a paragraph when the topic sentence is first. Placing the topic sentence in the initial position provides the reader with a road sign indicating the direction the paragraph will take. Such a paragraph is organized as follows.

Topic Sentence: Generalization

Sentence 2: Support

Sentence 3: Support

Sentence 4: Support

Or, when the paragraph is longer and more complex:

Topic Sentence: Generalization

Sentence 2: Clarification

Sentence 3: Limitation

Sentence 4: Support

Sentence 5: Support

Sentence 6: Limitation

Sentence 7: Support

Sentence 8: Support

Sentence 9: Limitation

Sentence 10: Support

This is the most effective form of paragraph organization when the reader is willing to accept the generalization expressed or implied in the topic sentence.

When the reader is likely to reject the generalization in the topic sentence, however, the supporting sentences should precede the topic sentence.

Sentence 1: Specific fact (support)

Sentence 2: Specific fact

Sentence 3: Minor conclusion (limitation)

Sentence 4: Specific fact

Sentence 5: Specific fact

Sentence 6: Minor conclusion

Topic Sentence: General conclusion

Coherence and Transition

A paragraph or complete report is coherent when all the parts add up to a unified whole and the relationships among the thoughts are clear and easily discerned. While the relationship between sentences—and between paragraphs—may be either explicit or implied, it must be sufficiently clear for the reader to follow without rereading. The principal ways of indicating relationships and providing transition are the following.

Repetition   The repetition of key words and ideas, or the use of pronouns to stand for key words and ideas, provides continuity. Repetition shows the reader that the same idea is still being discussed.

Cause and Effect   When a writer can show that one event has caused another, such words as *because, thus, therefore, then,* and *as a result,* indicate a cause-effect relationship.

Comparison/Contrast   Pointing out similarities *(like, similar to)* and differences *(although, however, on the other hand)* clarifies the relationship between two items or ideas. This is an effective way of providing transition.

Time and Place   References to movement in time *(yesterday, today, tomorrow),* or movement in space *(here, there, above, below),* or a combination of the two *(meanwhile, in Detroit . . .)* are the most common transitional devices.

AVOIDING OTHER COMMON DIFFICULTIES

Awkward Expressions (Awk)

Occasionally a phrase, clause, or sentence will be awkward without having anything specifically wrong with it. Awkward phrasing, unnatural word order, or constructions that force the reader to read more than once to be sure of your meaning need revising.

Check placement of modifiers and recast to achieve a more direct word order (subject-verb-object).

Capitalization (Cap)

Capitalize

1.   The first word in a sentence.
2.   The first word in a quoted sentence.
3.   Proper nouns and adjectives, including names of places (cities, counties, countries), races, languages, days of the week, months, companies, and historical events.
4.   The first word in each item of a vertical list.
5.   Words in titles, except short prepositions. Capitalize the first word of the title even if it is a short preposition.
6.   Abstract nouns when they are personified, refer to ideals, or stand for institutions (Good, Evil, the Church, the Company, our Department).

Do not capitalize

1.   Seasons of the year (summer, fall, winter, spring).
2.   Directions (east, west, north, south). But capitalize regions (the East, the South) because they are places.

3.   The first word of items in a list contained within a paragraph.

4.   Subjects or fields of study (chemistry, accountancy, marketing), except for languages (Chinese, Russian, German, English).

Numbers

Use figures for

1.   Numbers above ten.
2.   Dates and time (with a.m. and p.m.).
3.   Dimensions.
4.   Monetary sums. (For even amounts, omit the decimal and ciphers.)
5.   Statistics and numbers with decimals.
6.   Series of more than two numbers.
7.   References to pages and chapters.

Do not use figures (use words)

1.   To begin a sentence. Recast the sentence if the number is large.
2.   When use of a figure would confuse the reader, as with two numbers in sequence (two 2 × 4s).

Use figures or words for numbers between one and ten, depending on company style. Except in dates, phone numbers, and street addresses, use a comma to separate each group of three digits.

1983 (date)   **62081 (street address)**
1,983 (number)   **62,081 (number)**

Use cardinal figures (1, 3, 8,) when the day follows the month.

February 8   August 12

Use ordinal numbers (1st, 2d, 3d, 4th) when the day precedes the month.

We should have the contracts by the 15th of May.

Express dates in month-day-year sequence or day-month-year sequence.

April 14, 1983   14 April 1983

APPENDIX D
Punctuation

Ampersand &

Use the ampersand, a symbol for the word *and*, when it is used as part of the official name of an organization. Spell out the word *and* in other contexts; do not use an ampersand.

Peat, Marwick, Mitchell & Co. audits the books for us each year.

Apostrophe '

Use the apostrophe to show possession.

**boss's office   Pomaz' report   men's club
Dee and Bee's Shop**

Use the apostrophe to form contractions.

don't   she'll   he'd   can't   it's

Do not use the apostrophe with personal pronouns.

yours   hers   his   its

Note: Be especially careful to avoid confusing *it's* (it is) with the personal pronoun *its*.

***Its* cost was too high.**

***It's* time to order supplies.**

Asterisk *

Use the asterisk to refer the reader to a footnote.

The increased cost would be $1,500 before taxes.*
***See Table 4.1**

Brackets [ ]

Use brackets to insert parenthetical expressions, remarks, or corrections into existing text. Brackets (as opposed to commas, dashes, or parentheses) indicate editorial insertions rather than textual commentary.

> **After the officers [Jack Hammon and Art Bellow] presented their report, the president proposed that it be approved.**

Colon :

Use the colon before lists, enumerations, and such expressions as *the following, as follows,* and *these.*

> **The supervisor asked for the following three reports: Bell's report on telephone techniques, Schully's report on taxes, and Mostel's report on graphic aids.**

Use a colon after a salutation when using mixed punctuation.

> **Dear Ms. Anderson: Ladies and Gentlemen:**

Use the colon to separate hours and minutes

> **3:15 p.m.   9:15 a.m.**

Use the colon to indicate that the following statement amplifies a preceding clause.

> **Our new microcomputer has been successful: so successful that we are more than six months behind in deliveries.**

Comma ,

Use a comma before a coordinating conjunction (*and, or, but,* or *for*) that connects two complete sentences.

> **Our supervisor announced the new procedure, and the workers implemented it immediately.**

Use a comma after introductory words, phrases, and clauses.

Words: Of course, we'll need to have the manuals before we can make the changes.

Phrases: To make the necessary repairs, we had to hire a technician.

Clauses: Whenever we hire new employees, we always explain their insurance benefits carefully.

Use a comma to set off nonrestrictive clauses.

> **After the meeting, which lasted two hours, we went to lunch.**

Use a comma to separate items in a series.

> **Business reports are used to inform, to convince, and to entertain.**

Use a comma to set off parenthetical expressions.

> **The newsletter, however, printed only half the story.**

Use a comma to set off words that explain or identify preceding nouns.

> **Sue Meyers, our office manager, announced the new procedures for filing documents.**

Use a comma to separate two or more words that modify the same noun.

> **The tall, distinguished looking gentleman gave the invocation.**

Use a comma to separate items in an address or a date.

> **The meeting will be on Saturday, July 12, 1983, at 9 a.m.**

> **She worked for five years for Blaine Brothers, 265 N. Hampton Road, Canton, OH, and then for four years for Stewart & Clark, 630 East Monroe Street, Cincinnati, OH.**

Use a comma to set off nouns of direct address.

> **Barb, will you please answer the telephone?**

Dash —

Use a dash when a comma is not sufficient emphasis.

> **We strongly recommend that all employees—especially those hired in the last two months—seriously consider signing up for liability insurance.**

Use a dash to show hesitation.

> **She had one thing on her mind—getting promoted.**

Diagonal /

Use a diagonal between letters in some abbreviations and expressions and between numerals in fractions.

> **c/o Donaldson Brothers**

> **and/or**

> **3/4   1 5/8**

Ellipsis . . .

Use ellipsis marks (three spaced periods with one space before and after each period) to show the omission of words from a quotation. When omission occurs at the end of a sentence, use the ellipsis, leave a space, and then use the closing punctuation mark for the sentence.

> **The warranty says: "This warranty will remain in effect for all parts and labor . . . for one year from date of purchase."**

Use ellipses in advertising material for emphasis.

> **The handy XL–140 will**
> **. . . act as a sorter . . . an organizer . . . a work saver.**

Exclamation Point !

Use the exclamation point to express strong feelings.

> **That's beautiful!   I don't believe a word of it!   No!**

The exclamation point is rarely used in business writing.

Parentheses ()

Use parentheses to set off nonessential expressions.

> **Please call me (556–1389) when you have questions.**

Use parentheses to set off references.

> **Construction should begin April 1 (see contract for details).**

Use parentheses for enumerated items.

> **The three major divisions are (1) introduction, (2) body, and (3) conclusion.**

Period .

Use a period at the end of a declarative sentence, an imperative statement, or a polite request.

> **The reports should arrive by June 1.**
> **Let me know when you plan to leave.**
> **May we have your reply before 15 April.**

Use a period after abbreviations and initials.

> **a.m.   p.m.   B.A.   M.S.   Ph.D.   Tues.   Oct.   E. T. Brown**

Use a period to indicate decimals.

> **1.5 percent   2.5 inches**

Use periods after letters and numbers in outlines and in enumerated lists.

> **1. a.   I.**
>
> **2. b.   A.**
>
> **3. c.   B.**
>
>   **II.**

Question Mark ?

Use a question mark after a direct question.

Have you been able to reach Mr. Jorgenson?

Use a question mark with statements with questions.

You did receive the material, didn't you?
We'll sign the contract in June? (meant as a question)
He'll receive $4,000 (?) a month. (expresses doubt)

Use a question mark after a series of questions. The question mark is followed by two spaces at the end of a sentence, but by one space within a sentence.

Do they have offices in Detroit? Los Angeles? Boston?

Quotation Marks " "

Use quotation marks for direct quotations.

Helen said, "The prices are effective immediately."

Use quotation marks for titles of articles, chapters of books, songs, and poems.

Before you complete the assignment, check the article, "Working Together," by R. J. Rodosky.

Chapter 2, "Elements of Effective Communication," is well written.

In American usage, periods and commas go *inside* the quotation marks. All other punctuation goes *outside* unless it is part of the original quotation.

He told us to read the article, "Marketing Strategies."

Who wants to read "Marketing Strategies"?

He asked, "Have you read the article, 'Marketing Strategies'?"

Semicolon ;

Use a semicolon to connect two complete sentences when a conjunction is omitted.

They wrote the first book in three months; they wrote their second book in eight months.

Use a semicolon to separate items in a series containing commas.

They visited offices in Syracuse, NY; Stillwater, OK; and Glendale, CA.

Underscore _____

Use the underscore for words italicized in print.

> It is not <u>what</u> you say, but <u>how</u> you say it.

Use the underscore for titles of literary and artistic works, such as books, long poems, magazines, newspapers, movies, television shows, plays, musicals, and operas.

> Our president regularly reads <u>The Wall Street Journal</u>.

> They enjoyed the film, <u>Star Trek I</u>, which grossed a record $14.3 million in its first weekend.

APPENDIX E
Job Application Materials

The material in this Appendix is designed to help you prepare the materials you will need to use when you apply for a job. These consist of a resume, letter of application, and follow-up correspondence.

Resume

Every professional person should maintain an up-to-date resume, or record of achievements, at all times. The resume lets a reader review a candidate's qualifications for employment quickly and easily. To accomplish this purpose, it must be highly organized and structured to emphasize the person's main qualifications.

Formats for resumes may vary, but regardless of the format used, the resume should arrange main entries and dates so that they may be read quickly and easily. Printed resumes are generally more successful than typewritten resumes.

A resume should be either one full page or two full pages long. One and a half typewritten pages may be condensed to one printed page, and three typewritten pages may be condensed to two printed pages. Although many personnel directors express a preference for one-page resumes, two-page resumes have proved generally more successful.

Your resume *should* include the following information:

1. Your *name*.

2. Your complete *address* and *phone number*. You may include two addresses (school and mailing) if you will be moving soon after your resume is prepared. Be sure to include area codes (phone numbers) and zip code (addresses).

3. *Job objective* or "Qualified by" line. Let your reader see in the first few lines either what you think you can do (job objective) or provide a quick overview of what you have done.

4. *Education.* When and where did you go to school? What degree(s) will you earn by what date? List the schools you have attended in reverse chronological order (most recent first). The degree-granting institution is the school that confers honors and your major and minor. If you are a new college graduate, your education will be an important qualification, so amplify your educational achievements by listing courses or by describing main projects. If you list courses, do so by *title* and not by course number. *Management 404* does not tell a reader what the course was about. *Organizational Behavior* specifies the topic of the class and says something about what you should have learned.

5. *Experience.* What is your work history? List jobs in reverse chronological order. Consider placing career related experience in a separate category. For each entry, give the dates of employment, your job title, name and complete address of your employer, and your duties and responsibilities. Use language that emphasizes your initiative and special achievements.

6. *Academic and employment references.* Give the titles, names, complete business addresses, and phone numbers for at least three instructors or work supervisors who have agreed to serve as references for you.

7. *The date prepared.* Placing the date of preparation at the end of the resume assures the reader that the resume is current.

Your resume *may* include the following additional entries:

1. *Military experience.* If you have served in any branch of the Armed Forces, you should include the record of your military achievements. Include dates of service, highest rank, date and type of discharge. Also, include your duties and responsibilities (number of personnel supervised) as with other job entries.

2. *Publications.* If you have published articles, short stories, or poems, provide a list of publications. Use a standard bibliographic entry form.

3. *Extracurricular activities,* hobbies and interests. If these activities show initiative, leadership, or aptitude for the kind of work you plan to do, they may be worth including.

4. *Memberships.* Include memberships in professional associations. Memberships in social and service organizations may be worth including, especially if you have had leadership positions.

Do *not* include

1. *Personal details,* such as height, weight, age, sex, or marital status *unless* the job for which you are applying specifically requires it.

2. A *photograph,* unless the job for which you are applying specifically requires it.

3.   *Personal references.* Relatives, neighbors, doctors, dentists, rabbis, ministers, and priests should not be used as references on your resume. Employment application forms sometimes ask for names of people who know you well. List personal references there. Use only academic and employment references on the resume.

Exhibit E.1 illustrates the application of these principles.

EXHIBIT E.1
Resume

DENICE D. TROPP

Present Address	**Permanent Address**
530 Locust St., Apt. #1	R#1 Box 911
Kalamazoo, MI 49007	Buchanan, MI 49107
(616) 344-2296	(616) 695-5325

QUALIFIED BY

A thorough education in all aspects of **management**, including **feasibility studies**, combined with an excellent background in **business communication** and **general business** and more than five years of full- and part-time work experience.

EDUCATION

Sep 1980 to
Aug 1982
Bachelor of Business Administration, cum laude (3.77 GPA), August 1982, Department of Management, College of Business, Western Michigan University, Kalamazoo, MI 49008.

Major
MANAGEMENT. 8 courses, 24 credit hours. Advanced courses include Management Analysis and Behavior I, II; Management Analysis and Organizational Design I, II; Personnel Management; Administrative Behavior; and Organizational Behavior.

Double
Minor
BUSINESS COMMUNICATION. Department of Business Education and Administrative Services. 7 courses, 21 credit hours. Advanced courses include Organizational Communication, Report Writing, and Publicity and Public Relations.

GENERAL BUSINESS. Department of General Business. 7 courses, 21 credit hours. Courses include Statistics, Finance, Accounting, Economics, Business Law, Marketing, and Management.

Sep 1978 to
Apr 1980
Associate of Arts Degree, April 1980, College of Arts and Sciences, Southwestern Michigan College, Dowagiac, MI 49047.

Education financed 100% by scholarships, loans, and part- and full-time employment.

SPECIAL PROJECTS

Sep 1981 to
Dec 1981
PUBLIC RELATIONS, Department of Business Education and Administrative Services, Western Michigan University. Designed and implemented a promotional campaign for Alpha Beta Chi.

Jan 1982 to
Apr 1982
FEASIBILITY STUDIES, Department of Management, Western Michigan University. Managed a task group of 8 people, supervised activities, and conducted a feasibility study integrating relevant variables, analyses, and data into an operating subsidiary company.

WORK EXPERIENCE

Sep 1981 to
Present
Retail Sales Person, Steketee's Department Store, Kalamazoo, MI 49001. Assist customers, open and close department, and handle routine paperwork. Work 15-22 hours a week during the school year.

Source: Courtesy of Denice D. Tropp

EXHIBIT E.1
Resume *(continued)*

DENICE D. TROPP
Continued

Sep 1980 to Apr 1981	**Receptionist**, Britton Hadley Hall, Western Michigan University, Kalamazoo, MI 49008. Greeted guests, helped students with problems, sorted and distributed mail, and handled routine paperwork. Worked 12-20 hours a week during the school year.
Jun to Sep 1979 & 1980	**Card Puncher**, Radewald Farms, Niles, MI 49120. Dealt with a group of field workers and was in charge of keeping count of the amount of produce each picked a day; checked the quality of produce picked. Worked 40-60 hours a week during the summers.
Sep 1979 to May 1980	**Secretary**, English Department, Southwestern Michigan College, Dowagiac, MI 49047. Worked independently and gained proficiency in typing and editing. Worked 20 hours a week during the school year.
Sep 1977 to Sep 1978	**Secretary**, Food Specialities, Buchanan, MI 49107. Calculated daily orders, entered accounts receivable and payable invoices, and typed and edited business letters. In charge of entire office for three weeks while full-time secretary was away. Worked 20 hours a week during the school year and 30-40 hours a week during the summer.

SCHOLARSHIPS, AWARDS, AND MEMBERSHIPS

Sep 1978 to Aug 1982	National Standard Competitive Scholarship, Board of Trustees Scholarship at Southwestern Michigan College, Western Michigan University Academic Scholarship, Bowman and Branchaw Business Communication Scholarship, President's List at Southwestern Michigan College, Dean's List at Western Michigan University, Nominee for 1982 Presidential Scholars Convocation, Beta Gamma Sigma membership, Corresponding Secretary for Alpha Beta Chi.

CREDENTIALS

Official transcript and University Placement Service's data sheet are available from Western Michigan University Placement Services, Kalamazoo, MI 49008. (616) 383-1710.

REFERENCES

Dr. Henry Beam, Department of Management, Western Michigan University, Kalamazoo, MI 49008. (616) 383-4081.

Dr. Joel P. Bowman, Department of Business Education and Administrative Services, Western Michigan University, Kalamazoo, MI 49008. (616) 383-1703.

Dr. Bernadine P. Branchaw, Department of Business Education and Administrative Services, Western Michigan University, Kalamazoo, MI 49008. (616) 383-1908.

Mr. John Prothro, Store Manager, Steketee's Department Store, Kalamazoo, MI 49001. (616) 382-5900. Extension 31.

Prepared March 1982

Letter of Application

The letter of application is essentially a letter of transmittal which accompanies the resume. It is prepared *after* the resume is complete and is designed to interpret the resume in the light of a specific reader's needs.

The letter should begin by applying for a specific job (*not* a "position," "opening," or "anything available"). It should amplify and interpret information on the resume, rather than merely repeat it. The letter should prove to the reader that you are ready and qualified to perform useful work. Use your education and previous experience to provide evidence of your ability to meet objectives. Mention personal qualities (initiative, perseverance, ability to communicate) that will be an asset on the job. *Show* that you have these qualities by giving illustrations; do not simply *tell* the reader that you have them.

Close the letter by asking for an interview. Do *not* ask for a job

EXHIBIT E.2
Letter of Application

530 Locust Street, Apt. #1
Kalamazoo, MI 49007

March 3, 1982

Ms. Mona Erickson, Personnel Officer
First National Bank and Trust Company of Michigan
108 East Michigan Avenue
Kalamazoo, MI 49007

Dear Ms. Erickson:

Please consider me for the management trainee job you advertised in the Kalamazoo Gazette on March 2, 1982.

With my education in management and business communication, I could contribute to First National Bank's excellent management program. In one of my management courses, I managed a group of eight people and gained experience in both problem solving and dealing effectively with others.

My education in business communication and management also gives me the ability to express my ideas clearly and effectively, both orally and in writing; and, through my various jobs over the last five years, I gained much experience in dealing with the public. In my advanced courses, I established the skills required to develop, edit, and present various business reports, which would be especially helpful in organizing statements and information for your organization.

I am a person who accepts challenges and responsibilities with the enthusiasm and dedication of a professional. As a manager, I would have the opportunity to develop this professional attitude to its fullest and at the same time make a valuable contribution to your company.

After you read my resume and talk with the people listed as references, I would welcome the opportunity to discuss my qualifications with you. I would be available for an interview on short notice.

Sincerely,

Denice D. Tropp

Denice D. Tropp

enc

Source: Courtesy of Denice D. Tropp

in the letter; discuss the job in the interview. The letter of application should not be longer than one page. Exhibit E.2 illustrates a letter of application.

Follow-up Correspondence

If you do not receive a response to your initial application within four weeks, send a second application consisting of your letter and resume. Keep accurate records of to whom you wrote at which company and on which dates you sent your materials.

When your letter and resume have secured an interview, you will need to send a thank-you letter to the interviewer after you have met with her or him. Use this letter to tell the reader either that you are still interested in the job or that you are no longer interested.

If you are still interested in the job, you may use the letter to supply additional information that will show your qualifications for the job. If the interviewer voiced objections to hiring you (lack of experience, too young or too old, education not ideally suited to the type of work), use the follow-up letter to overcome those objections.

Exhibit E.3 shows an example of a follow-up letter.

EXHIBIT E.3
Follow-up Correspondence

---

530 Locust Street, Apt. #1
Kalamazoo, MI 49007

April 2, 1982

Ms. Mona Erickson, Personnel Officer
First National Bank and Trust Company of Michigan
108 East Michigan Avenue
Kalamazoo, MI 49007

Dear Ms. Erickson:

Thank you for discussing First American Bank Corporation's trainee program with me on March 26, 1982.

As we discussed, I am not graduating until August, and you are looking for two trainees to hire in April. After I graduate, however, I would be interested in learning more about your company.

Your programs and your organization impress me very much, and I believe that I can make valuable contributions to your company. Should you decide to hire another trainee at the end of the summer, please consider me for that job. I will be available to work at the beginning of September.

Sincerely,

Denice D. Tropp
Denice D. Tropp

Source: Courtesy of Denice D. Tropp

APPENDIX F

Correction Symbols and Proofreaders' Marks

Ab: Abbreviation. Avoid abbreviations in formal communication. With the exception of commonly used abbreviations (U.S., AFL), spell out the term the first time it is used and place the abbreviation in parentheses.

Ac: Accuracy. Be sure that names, addresses, and other information are correct.

Adapt: Adaptation. Adapt your message to your reader. Use individual names.

Agr: Agreement. Subjects and verbs must agree in number and in person. Pronouns and antecedents must agree in number, person, and in case.

Amb: Ambiguity. Statement is unclear.

Ap: Appearance.

Apos: Apostrophe.

Awk: Awkward.

Cap: Capitalize.

Case: Grammatical case. Use subject, object, and reflexive cases correctly.

Chop: Choppy. Use a variety of sentence structures. Avoid using all simple and short sentences.

Cl: Clarity. Message is unclear.

CM: Confidence in your message.

Coh: Coherence. Writing should flow smoothly from one sentence to another. Watch transitions between sentences and between paragraphs.

Con: Conciseness. Eliminate all unnecessary words and phrases.

Coop: Cooperation of equals. Avoid projecting either feelings of superiority or inferiority.

CR: Confidence in your reader.

CS: Comma splice. Separate two or more independent clauses with a period, a comma and a coordinating conjunction, or a semicolon.

CT: Conversational tone. Use natural language. Avoid jargon, clichés, and trite expressions.

D: Diction. Check dictionary for correct use of word.

Emp: Emphasis. Stress the point or idea.

Enc: Enclosure. See Exhibit 3.3.

Exp: Expletive. Omit wordy and weak expressions, such as *it is, there are, there is.*

F: Format. Check margins, letter or report parts, and placement.

Fig: Figure. Use figure.

Fl: Flattery. Don't exaggerate.

Frag: Fragment. Sentence must express a complete thought and contain a subject and a verb.

Gob: Gobbledygook. Garbled expressions or excessive use of legalese.

Gr: Grammar fault.

Imp: Imply. Imply negative and obvious ideas rather than state them explicitly.

Jar: Jargon. Avoid words used to impress the reader.

K: Awkward.

lc: Lower case. Do not capitalize.

Log: Logic. Check the relationships between ideas.

MM: Misplaced modifiers. Place modifiers close to the words they modify.

Neg: Negative. Use positive language.

Obv: Obvious. Omit or subordinate statements that the reader already knows.

OC: Overconfidence. Avoid assuming that your reader will behave a certain way because you desire it.

Org: Organization. Use the best organizational pattern for achieving your objectives.

P: Punctuation. Punctuate correctly.

PD: Psychological description. Interpret facts and features in terms of reader benefits.

// cst: Parallel construction. Use the same kind of grammatical structure for related ideas.

Pas: Passive voice. Use active voice. Passive voice is weak and wordy. Use passive voice to de-emphasize a reader's mistake.

PV: Point of view. State in terms of reader's viewpoint.

RB: Reader benefit. Emphasize what the reader will gain.

Red: Redundant. Unnecessary repetition.

Ref: Reference. Incorrect or indefinite reference of pronoun.

Rep: Repetition. Wordy.

RO: Run-on sentence. Running two sentences together without a mark of punctuation.

SB: Should be. Change wording as indicated.

Sp: Spelling error.

Spe: Specificity. Be specific. Use concrete and specific words rather than abstract and general words.

Stet: Let it stand.

Sub: Subordinate. Place emphasis on important, positive ideas.

Syl: Syllabication. Divide words between syllables.

T: Tense. Use correct tense.

TR: Transition. Show relationship from one idea to another.

V: Variety. Vary sentence length and type. Vary paragraph length.

W: Wordy. Omit redundancies and other dead wood.

WC: Word choice. Poor choice. Use another word.

X: Obvious error. Proofread.

YA: You-attitude. Keep the reader in the picture. Use *you* and *your* rather than *I* and *we*.

=   Align horizontally.

|| Align vertically.

≡   Capitalize (or cap).

‿   Close up.

⟆   Delete.

∧   Insert.

⋏   Insert comma.

⊙   Insert period.

/   Lower case (or lc).

[Move left.

]   Move right.

⌐   Move up.

⌣   Move down.

][Center.

⁋   Paragraph.

Space.

ⓢⓟ   Spell out.

∼   Transpose.

INDEX